PRAISE for
Pince-Nez Press School Guidebooks

"Finally someone is asking the right questions."
—Admission Director of a San Francisco independent school

"No other resource provides as much information on private schools."
—Parent

"Ninety percent of the questions we are asked in the admission process are answered in your book."
—Admission Director, Bay Area independent school

"A big thank you for creating these very helpful books for parents."
—Parent, San Francisco

"As an Admissions Director, I use this as my go-to guide."
—Admissions Director of a Marin independent school

"I found this book to be a very vital tool in my search for just the right school for my child,"
—Parent, Palo Alto

"Parents rely heavily on the information in your books."
—Admission Director of a San Francisco independent school

"Pince Nez Press of San Francisco publishes several books that are outstanding for parents looking for schools for their children. All of these meticulously researched, independent guides, written by parents and educational consultants, contain no advertising, and schools do not pay to be in them. Rather, they are based upon visits to the schools, extensive questionnaires, and interviews with the school heads and admission directors."
— *Bay Area Parent* magazine

Private K-8 Schools of San Francisco & Marin (6th Edition)
by Betsy Little, MBA, MA, and Paula Molligan, MBA, MA

ISBN: 978-1-930074-23-1
Library of Congress Control Number: 2010932393
Copyright © 2010 Susan Vogel

Pince-Nez Press, LLC
San Francisco/Salt Lake City
www.pince-nez.com
pincenezpress@gmail.com
(415) 267-5978

Printed in the United States

Private K-8 Schools

of

San Francisco & Marin

• Sixth Edition •

by

Betsy Little, MBA, MA

and

Paula Molligan, MBA, MA

PINCE-NEZ PRESS

To our grandchildren

Contents

SCHOOLS BY COUNTY

SAN FRANCISCO

Adda Clevenger Junior Preparatory and Theater School for Children
Brandeis Hillel Day School
Cathedral School for Boys
Children's Day School
Chinese American International School
Convent of the Sacred Heart Elementary School
Corpus Christi Elementary School
Discovery Center School
Ecôle Notre Dame des Victoires
French-American International School
The Hamlin School
Hillwood Academic Day School*
Holy Name of Jesus School
Katherine Delmar Burke School
Kittredge School
Krouzian-Zekarian-Vasbouragan Armenian School
The Laurel School
Lisa Kampner Hebrew Academy
Live Oak School
Lycée Français La Pérouse, The French School
Marin Preparatory School
Megan Furth Catholic Academy

Mission Dolores Catholic School
Our Lady of the Visitacion School
Presidio Hill School
St. Anne School
St. Anthony Immaculate Conception School*
St. Brendan School*
Saint Brigid School
St. Cecilia Elementary
Saint Charles Borromeo School*
St. Finn Barr School*
St. Gabriel School
St. James School
St. John's School*
St. Mary's Chinese Day School*
Saint Monica School
St. Paul's Elementary School
St. Peter's School*
St. Philip School
St. Stephen School
St. Thomas More School*
St. Thomas the Apostle School*
Saint Vincent de Paul School
Sts. Peter and Paul Salesian School
San Francisco Adventist School*
San Francisco Day School
San Francisco Friends School
The San Francisco School
San Francisco Waldorf School
School of the Epiphany*
Star of the Sea School*
Stuart Hall for Boys
Synergy School
Town School for Boys
Voice of Pentecost Academy*
West Portal Lutheran School
Zion Lutheran Day School

MARIN
Brandeis Hillel Day School
Cascade Canyon School
Good Shepherd Lutheran School*
Greenwood School

Lycée Français La Pérouse, The French School
Marin Christian Academy
Marin Country Day School
Marin Horizon School
Marin Montessori School
Marin Primary & Middle School
Marin Waldorf School
Montessori de Terra Linda
Mount Tamalpais School
The New Village School
North Bay Christian Academy*
Our Lady of Loretto School*
Ring Mountain Day School
St. Anselm School*
Saint Hilary School
St. Isabella School*
Saint Mark's School
St. Patrick School*
St. Raphael School*
St. Rita School*
San Domenico School
* Indicates short entry at back of book

SCHOOLS BY TYPE

INDEPENDENT SCHOOLS (Nonprofit, members CAIS)

Brandeis Hillel Day School, Marin
Brandeis Hillel Day School, San Francisco
Cathedral School for Boys
Children's Day School
Chinese American International School
Convent of the Sacred Heart Elementary School
French-American International School
The Hamlin School
Katherine Delmar Burke School
Live Oak School
Lycée Français La Pérouse, The French School
Marin Country Day School
Marin Horizon School
Marin Primary & Middle School
Mount Tamalpais School
Presidio Hill School

Saint Mark's School
San Domenico School
San Francisco Day School
San Francisco Friends Schools
The San Francisco School
Stuart Hall for Boys
Town School for Boys

OTHER NONPROFIT SCHOOLS
Cascade Canyon School
Greenwood School
The Laurel School
Marin Montessori School
Marin Preparatory School
Marin Waldorf School
Montessori de Terra Linda
The New Village School
Ring Mountain Day School
Synergy School
San Francisco Waldorf School

PROPRIETARY SCHOOLS
Adda Clevenger Junior Preparatory and Theater School for Children
Discovery Center School
Hillwood Academic Day School*
Kittredge School

CATHOLIC SCHOOLS
Convent of the Sacred Heart Elementary School
Corpus Christi School
Ecôle Notre Dame des Victoires
Holy Name of Jesus School
Megan Furth Catholic Academy
Mission Dolores Catholic School
Our Lady of Loretto School*
Our Lady of the Visitacion School
St. Anne School
St. Anselm School*
St. Anthony Immaculate Conception School*
St. Brendan School*
Saint Brigid School

St. Cecilia Elementary
Saint Charles Borromeo School*
St. Finn Barr School*
St. Gabriel School
Saint Hilary School
St. Isabella School*
St. James School
St. John's School*
St. Mary's Chinese Day School*
Saint Monica School
St. Patrick School*
St. Paul's Elementary School
St. Peter's School*
St. Philip School
St. Raphael School*
St. Rita School*
St. Stephen School
St. Thomas More School*
St. Thomas the Apostle School*
Saint Vincent de Paul School
Sts. Peter and Paul Salesian School
San Domenico School
School of the Epiphany*
Star of the Sea School*
Stuart Hall for Boys

JEWISH SCHOOLS
Brandeis-Hillel Day School, Marin
Brandeis-Hillel Day School, San Francisco
Lisa Kampner Hebrew Academy

OTHER RELIGIOUS SCHOOLS
Cathedral School for Boys
Good Shepherd Lutheran School*
Krouzian-Zekarian-Vasbouragan Armenian School
Marin Christian Academy
North Bay Christian Academy*
San Francisco Adventist School*
Voice of Pentecost Academy*
West Portal Lutheran School
Zion Lutheran Day School

Girls
Convent of the Sacred Heart Elementary School
The Hamlin School
Katherine Delmar Burke School

Boys
Cathedral School for Boys
Stuart Hall for Boys
Town School for Boys

Elementary Schools with Preschools
Children's Day School
Chinese American International School
French-American International School
Good Shepherd Lutheran School*
Greenwood School
Krouzian-Zekarian-Vasbouragan Armenian School
The Laurel School
Lisa Kampner Hebrew Academy
Lycée Français La Pérouse, The French School, San Francisco & Marin
Marin Christian Academy
Marin Horizon School
Marin Montessori School
Marin Primary & Middle School
Marin Preparatory School
Marin Waldorf School
Montessori de Terra Linda
Presidio Hill School
Ring Mountain Day School
Saint Hilary School
St. Paul's Elementary School
St. Philip School
St. Raphael School*
St. Rita School*
Sts. Peter and Paul Salesian School
San Domenico School
The San Francisco School
San Francisco Waldorf School
Voice of Pentecost Academy*

ELEMENTARY SCHOOLS WITH HIGH SCHOOLS

Convent of the Sacred Heart Elementary School
French-American International School
Lisa Kampner Hebrew Academy
Lycée Français La Pérouse, The French School, San Francisco
San Domenico (girls day/boarding high school)
San Francisco Waldorf School
Stuart Hall for Boys
Voice of Pentecost Academy*
* Indicates short entry at back of book

INTRODUCTION

The information contained in this Guide is based upon (1) information provided by the schools in response to a questionnaire sent to the schools; (2) interviews with admission directors and principals; (3) visits to most of the schools (usually up to a two-hour visit per school including classroom visits); and, in some cases, (4) publicly available information on the schools. The additional schools listed in the back of the Guide, as well as any new schools between the revisions, are invited to provide full information in the next edition. Schools do not pay to be included in this Guide—it is not advertising. Quotations are used to note qualitative information provided by the schools. Should a school choose not to answer any part of the questionnaire it is noted as N/P (not provided), and if the information requested is not applicable it is noted as N/A. Quotations from schools may be altered by use of abbreviations or by editing or use of punctuation to shorten length of quote to meet space restrictions.

This Guide is intended to provide a starting point for parents in the private school search. No one school is best for all students; consequently, no attempt is made to rank or rate schools. Moreover, what families are looking for in a school will vary considerably. Some may be looking for a school that sends a good number of graduates to particular high schools while others may be interested in a spiritual environment or a particular educational philosophy. It is important for families to consider the fit between their student and family needs and a school's offerings.

Some parents seek advice from educational consultants who specialize in narrowing school choices that fit a family's individual needs. Consultants specialize in knowing the ethos and culture of a school and can save a great deal of time and money in recommending the best school placement.

PRIVATE SCHOOLS

In the lexicon of this Guide, "private schools" mean schools established and controlled by a non-governmental agency or individual and are supported by tuition and endowment. Within this very broad category are schools that are set up as non-profit, tax-exempt corporations with boards of trustees known as independent schools; privately owned tax-paying schools known as proprietary schools; and religiously affiliated schools. Tuition dollars are the main source of income for private schools. This allows many private schools to spend two to three times more dollars per student than many public schools. These extra tuition dollars along with endowment funds and money from restricted and unrestricted donations underwrite salaries, professional development, financial aid, enrichment programs, and facility improvements. Most schools strive for 100% parent participation in their annual appeals as the percentage makes a statement in attracting outside funding for grants and foundation support. These organizations look to the financial contributions of the school's current parents, faculty and alumni as a reflection of satisfaction with the school.

Approximately 9% of students in California attend private schools; and in San Francisco about 30% of students attend private schools. Marin County has the second highest enrollment of students in private schools at 19% followed by San Mateo County at 15% and Napa County at 13% (Source:www.sfgate.com).

REGULATION OF PRIVATE SCHOOLS

Although California private schools are not regulated by the California Department of Education, most private schools are members of national education associations which require adherence to strict guidelines for membership. In addition, many schools participate with outside agencies for accreditation. Private schools are not held to the public school minimum of instructional days per academic year, nor to a minimum number of instructional minutes in the school day. Private schools must comply with all state and local regulations relating to health, fire safety, earthquake safety, business licenses, and other matters. All school employees must also have a criminal check and be fingerprinted. They are not required to hire credentialed teachers. Private schools need only follow very general curriculum guidelines promulgated by the State Department of Education.

California law requires private elementary and secondary schools to file an affidavit with the California Department of Education. Any school with an enrollment of six or more students must be registered and a full list of these schools is available at www.cde.ca.gov/privateschools/data. html. The only effect of the filing is to deem students enrolled in the school non-truant. A filing is not accreditation.

TYPES OF PRIVATE SCHOOL

Private schools fall within three broad categories: independent, proprietary and religiously affiliated.

NON-PROFIT INDEPENDENT SCHOOLS

Although any school may call itself an "independent school," members of associations such as the California Association of Independent

Schools (CAIS) and the National Association of Independent Schools (NAIS), are non-profit organizations governed by their own boards of trustees as opposed to being governed by a central diocese, church's board of trustees, or some other off-site entity. The NAIS requires that its members be "primarily supported by tuition, charitable contributions, and endowment income rather than by tax or church funds." To be eligible for NAIS membership, schools must be independently governed by a board of trustees, practice nondiscriminatory policies, be accredited by an approved state or regional association, and hold not-for-profit 501(c) (3) tax-exempt status. (For more information, see the NAIS web site at www.nais.org and the CAIS web site at www.caisca.org.)

Generally, a board of trustees provides oversight of the school's administration. The trustees are composed of parents, community leaders, and others dedicated to the school's mission. Trustees are normally invited to serve as volunteers for terms of two to four years, and board meetings are typically closed to non-members.

CAIS describes independent schools as "pre-collegiate, non-profit institutions governed by boards of trustees and supported by tuition revenue, charitable contributions, and endowment income. Through the accreditation process, schools hold themselves publicly accountable to all who seek assurance that they meet high standards of educational quality, operation, and staff competence" (www.caisca.org). Schools cannot apply for membership until they have been in operation for five years, are incorporated as a non-profit, and meet CAIS standards and those of visiting committee of the CAIS Board.

Independent schools distinguish themselves by offering small class size and a wide range of co-curricular and extra curricular programs and by providing individual attention to students. Independent schools may have religious affiliations. Each independent school is responsible for its own curriculum. As tax-exempt organizations, they may be eligible for grant and/or foundation monies. Most independent schools expect that parents will make tax-deductible contributions to the school and/or be involved in fundraising activities.

Elementary schools in the Bay Area that are members of the Bay Area Directors of Admissions (BADA) have established "Principles of Good Practice" surrounding admissions. They share admission forms, deadlines, and notification dates. BADA member schools do not solicit donations for their schools from applicant families during the application period. Current members included in this Guide are: Brandeis Hillel Day School (San Francisco and Marin), Katherine Delmar Burke School, Cathedral School for Boys, Children's Day School, Chinese American International School, Convent of the Sacred Heart Elementary School,

French American International School, The Hamlin School, Kittredge School, Laurel School, Live Oak School, Lycée Français La Pérouse (San Francisco and Marin), Marin Country Day School, Marin Horizon School, Marin Montessori School, Marin Preparatory School, Marin Primary & Middle School, Mount Tamalpais School, Montessori de Terra Linda, Presidio Hill School, Ring Mountain Day School, Saint Mark's School, San Domenico School, San Francisco Day School, San Francisco Friends School, The San Francisco School, Stuart Hall for Boys, Synergy School, and Town School for Boys.

PROPRIETARY SCHOOLS

Proprietary schools operate on a profit basis and may be corporations, partnerships, or sole proprietorships. These schools pay taxes like any other business. Donations to them are not tax-deductible though some schools set up foundations to receive contributions. Generally, they do not have boards of trustees, but they may have parent committees to advise owners on a broad range of topics. A number of proprietary schools are owned and run by one individual with a distinct vision. In such a school, parents should be absolutely certain that they agree and can fully support the vision of the director. Parents should also get assurances that the school would be able to continue to function if the director became ill or otherwise unable to direct the day-to-day activities.

RELIGIOUSLY AFFILIATED SCHOOLS

Few generalities can be made about religious schools except that they seek to instill moral values. Religiously affiliated schools, both Christian and non-Christian, vary in degree as to the level of sectarian integration of the curriculum. In addition, the percentage of the prevailing religious affiliation varies from one school to another with some schools requiring membership of a particular religion as an admission requirement and others welcoming students without regard to religion. Families choose religiously affiliated schools for a variety of reasons including: family or cultural tradition; appreciation for the concurrent teaching of values alongside academics; and a perception of higher academic standards, higher standards of behavior, and a better peer group.

Catholic: All the Catholic schools in this Guide fall within the Archdiocese of San Francisco. There are three types of Catholic schools: parochial schools, which are attached to a parish; independent Catholic schools, which are non-profit organizations with their own boards of trustees; and Archdiocesan schools, which were parochial schools until their parishes closed.

Catholic parochial schools do not necessarily have a high percentage of Catholic students. Some schools that once primarily served the needs of parish families are now serving neighborhood populations that may or may not be Christian. Nevertheless, all students are required to take religion classes and attend mass.

Catholic schools establish their own curricula following Guidelines published by the San Francisco Archdiocese. Although each school is afforded limited autonomy, the Archdiocese dictates most procedural and legal matters. Some parochial schools have an advisory school board on which parents may serve, and most have parent-teacher committees. Schools within the Archdiocese normally share admissions deadlines and dates on which they send out notification letters. A few Catholic schools choose an independent association with CAIS and NAIS, and therefore share admission deadlines with BADA schools. Catholic schools may also be members of the Western Catholic Educational Association (WCEA) or the National Catholic Educational Association (NCEA). These associations advance the recognition and support of Catholic education.

Christian: The term "Christian school" is used in this Guide to refer to schools that are independent and are governed by a self-perpetuating board. Some may be a ministry of a particular congregation. The Association of Christian Schools International (ACSI) provides educational assistance to Christian schools.

Jewish: Jewish day schools are designed to provide students an academic program that includes Judaic studies within a Jewish cultural environment. Students learn to appreciate and celebrate Jewish practices and philosophies. The Partnership for Excellence in Jewish Education (PEJE) is comprised of philanthropic partners whose mission is to increase Jewish day school enrollment in North America. PEJE assists schools in developing internal capacities focusing on grant making, conferences, advocating for excellence in Jewish education, and providing expertise in strengthening Jewish day schools.

PUBLIC SCHOOLS

The Bay Area has many excellent public grade schools. Public schools are funded by local, state, and federal dollars. They are controlled by the local board of education and owned by the public. Information on public schools can be obtained from each school district or from the Department of Education in Sacramento. Numerous websites provide information on Bay Area public grade schools.

Charter schools are publicly funded schools that are granted a high degree of autonomy. In California there are over 800 charter schools.

They are unique in that they can control their own budgets, staffing, and curriculum (Source:http://www.myschool.org/association/). The charters may be granted by a local school board or the California State Board of Education. These schools must adhere to the terms of their charter involving their students and their achievement or their charter can be revoked. Lotteries are used to determine admission with priority for enrollment based on factors such as district residency, participation in establishing the school, employee status, etc. The lottery establishes a waitlist for any openings that may develop.

ACCREDITATION AND ASSOCIATIONS

The accrediting organizations seek to foster excellence in education. Accreditation is based on criteria such as student assessment and support, curriculum review, promotion of student learning, academic standards, financial stability, and physical and human resources. Accreditation is optional; schools are not required to be accredited, however, certain exceptions apply to schools receiving public funds. Public schools have the option of refusing to accept credits from schools that are not accredited. The main accrediting agency for schools below the college level in California is the Accrediting Commission for Schools, which is an arm of the Western Association of Schools and Colleges (ACS/WASC).

The accreditation process requires extensive documentation of a school's goals and objectives, a self-evaluation performed by the school staff and community, and an on-site visit to the school by a team of educational professionals. The evaluating team validates the internal study and recommends a term of accreditation to the Commission. Schools that seek accreditation may apply for candidate or interim status with ACS/WASC. All schools are subject to a full review every six years. If a school has not met all ACS/WASC criteria, it may receive a shorter term of accreditation requiring additional reports and visits. If parents have questions about accreditation, they may contact the Accrediting Commission for Schools at (650) 696-1060.

Another accrediting organization in California is the California Association of Independent Schools known as CAIS. To be a voting member of CAIS a school must be accredited by CAIS. It is an association of over 190 schools in California wherein each school's accountability is open for public review to assure the school meets high standards in their quality, operations, and staff. Schools complete a self-study which is evaluated by an on-site visit of education professionals. Schools are accredited for a maximum of six years, and must complete an interim report between accreditation visits to track the school's adherence to any

CAIS recommendations. CAIS is a collaborative partner with WASC and NAIS. CAIS can be reached at (310) 393-5161.

The Association of Christian Schools International (ACSI) accredits Christian schools, although Christian schools may also apply for joint ACSI/WASC accreditation or be only ACSI accredited. Any questions regarding accreditation may be directed to (719) 528-6906.

The National Lutheran School Accreditation (NLSA) organization offers Lutheran schools the opportunity to go though a voluntary self-study and evaluation accreditation process. It evaluates Lutheran schools on the quality of a school's academics and programs and the spiritual dimension of the school. NLSA is governed by the National Accrediting Commission that is comprised of representatives from various participating Lutheran districts. Over 500 schools are currently accredited by this organization. Their contact information is (414) 529-6701.

Some schools, both non-profit and proprietary, choose not to go through the accreditation process because of the cost and the time involved. Each school must pay the expenses—including airfare, hotel, and meals—for a team of three to four evaluators to study the school for two to three days. Schools must involve parents, students, faculty, administration, and board members in their self-evaluation documentation. Schools that do not seek accreditation often consider their "stamp of approval" to be satisfied parents and successful high school placement, as well as the school's longevity.

The National Association of Independent School (NAIS) includes 1,300 independent schools and associations in both the United States and overseas. NAIS provides Principles of Good Practice for ethical behavior and advocates broad access in affirming principles of justice and equity. It is a membership organization, not an accrediting organization, with a national voice on behalf of member schools and it acts as a center for collective action. The voting membership comes from non-profit schools that have been established for over five years, are accredited by an independent organization recognized by NAIS, and demonstrate financially sound operations and non-discriminatory practices. For further information call (202) 973-9700.

Waldorf schools often choose to be members of The Association of Waldorf Schools, North America (AWSNA). This organization is designed to strengthen and support independent Waldorf schools as well as Waldorf teacher education institutes.

Similarly, the Association of Montessori Internationale (AMI) is a professional organization that adheres to traditional Montessori programs. The American Montessori Society (AMS) has incorporated more recent methods and materials into its programs. Parents should be aware that the word "Montessori" is not trademarked, thus anyone can use it.

The National Catholic Educational Association (NCEA) is a membership organization that provides individual, affiliate, and institutional memberships to Catholic educators. It is a voluntary association of institutions and educators affiliated with religious education programs, elementary and secondary schools, colleges and universities. It represents over 200,000 Catholic educators serving almost eight million students. The NCEA promotes the educational and religious mission of the Catholic Church, advocates Catholic education, and fosters collaboration within its membership.

The Western Catholic Education Association (WCEA) works collaboratively with WASC for school improvement and accreditation of Catholic school members. Their number is (714) 447-9824. Jointly they review the teaching, learning, and spiritual goals of member schools.

The National Association of Episcopal Schools (NAES) is independently incorporated and is a voluntary membership organization. It provides professional support and advocates for those who serve "Episcopal schools, Early Childhood Education programs and school exploration/establishment/expansion efforts throughout the Episcopal Church U.S.A. As a voluntary membership services organization, NAES does not accredit Episcopal schools, nor does it establish or have statutory oversight of the academic and religious programs or governance of any Episcopal school" (Source: http://www.naes.org/about/).

The Friends Council on Education (FCE) founded in 1931 promotes Quaker education and supports Friends education in maintaining their values-based learning. It also provides a professional educational development network for Friends schools. The Jewish Education Service of North America (JESNA) is an organization devoted to advancing Jewish learning. It works "to recruit talented educators, identify and disseminate models of excellence in education, and develop creative new approaches to expand the impact of Jewish education."

The Torah Umesorah is a national society for Hebrew day schools founded in 1945. This Orthodox organization of over 675 schools and yeshivos serves more than 190,000 students.

Many schools in the San Francisco area belong to the Bay Area People of Color in Independent Schools (POCIS). POCIS is a committee of NAIS and is organized to support national and regional goals for the betterment of people of color in independent schools (Source: www. ba-pocis.org). Summerbridge and Making Waves serve middle school students who face limited opportunities for academic success. Both programs provide a curriculum that is interactive and implemented by high school and college student mentors.

Schools also may be members of the Educational Records Bureau (ERB) or the Secondary School Admission Test Board (SSATB). The ERB is a non-profit organization that has 1,700 members from public and private schools in 46 states and 47 countries. The ERB publishes the following tests: the Comprehensive Testing Program (CTP 4), the Independent School Entrance Examination (ISEE), the Writing Assessment Program (WrAP), the Early Childhood Admissions Assessment (ECAA), the Writing Practice Program (WPP), and the Children's Progress Achievement Assessments (CPAA). To be a member of ERB, a school must be accredited.

The Secondary School Admission Test Board (SSATB) is a non-profit organization that not only provides the Secondary School Admission Test (SSAT), but also supports professional development of its members with publications and meetings. Likewise, the Independent School Management organization (ISM) is dedicated to the advancement of school management and is responsive to the needs of independent schools.

The International Boys School Coalition (IBSC) provides a means for educators to talk about the importance and relevance of educating boys. The National Coalition of Girls Schools (NCGS) is an association of girls independent, private and public day and boarding schools in the United States and abroad. The NCGS promotes the value and benefit of all-girl schools.

The Council of International Schools (CIS) members are accredited schools. CIS is a non-profit corporation registered in the United States but is administered in the United Kingdom.

The French Ministry of Education requires education standards to be followed in U.S. schools teaching French nationals. The Ministry sends a representative to make sure the teaching conforms to teaching programs, pedagogies, and examinations applicable in French schools. The schools must conform to the French criteria.

The schools in this Guide were asked to list membership organizations. Most of these organization acronyms are listed at the end of this Introduction. For the most part, these are all collaborative associations that enhance the respective educational goals of each interest.

FUNDAMENTALS OF ADMISSION
KEEPING A PERSPECTIVE
Parents and guardians (referred to in this Guide collectively as "parents") always worry whether they are doing the right thing for their child. It is easy for parents to get caught up in the whirlwind of private school admissions and lose perspective. The best advice for parents is to relax about the process as well as the outcome. Try not to become overly focused on any one school. A child's future success is not guaranteed because of admission to any given school. Admission decisions can be based on uncontrollable factors. Although admission to a particular school may appear tantamount in importance at the time, in reality there are always viable alternatives in both public and private sectors. Parents are encouraged to keep a healthy perspective throughout the admission process.

BEGINNING THE ADMISSION PROCESS
Parents should begin selecting potential schools through the information in this Guide and then reading the schools' websites for the specifics of each school's admission procedure. Some schools have their applications available online early in the summer while others might not have the information available until October. This information will include all pertinent steps and dates. The private school admission process usually begins with school tours as early as October and ends the following March when notification letters are sent. A few schools have begun to offer early tours in the spring preceding the Kindergarten fall application. Application deadlines are generally in December-January. Most schools adhere to a very strict policy regarding application deadlines and notification dates. Late applications are reviewed on a space-available basis.

Parents may also choose to attend a "Kindergarten Information Night" which is usually held in May each year in San Francisco for parents interested in learning more about private schools. This event is hosted by the Jewish Community Center. For further information, call (415) 292-1200. The Marin County Information Evening is hosted on a rotating basis and is oftentimes in May as well. Parents are encouraged to contact any one of the independent schools in Marin for specific information. Schools set up booths with their information and admission directors meet with parents/guardians and answer their questions.

For parents who apply to numerous schools, the admission process can be very stressful and the time commitment tantamount to a part-time job. It is especially difficult for parents with demanding or inflexible work schedules because of the amount of time needed for required appointments. Most schools mandate that parents/guardians attend a one to three hour tour that is usually held on a weekday when classes are in session. Evening open houses are available at some schools. If parents choose to apply, schools generally require both parents have a personal interview with the admission director. In addition, parents/guardians generally have to: bring their child to the school for an interview or a screening/observation and/or class visit/playdate during a weekday or Saturday which will last from one to three hours; complete an application; provide references and narrative evaluations from their child's current teacher(s); and pay a non-refundable application fee of up to $150 for each child per school.

TRANSFER STUDENTS
Transfer students share the same application, financial aid deadlines and notification dates as Kindergarten applicants. Some schools may accept applications year-round depending on space availability. For the most part, school year openings are rare and many schools do not enroll a new student mid-year. Schools do not usually know the number of openings available for grades one through eight until a few weeks before they make admission decisions.

Most schools will require a class visit for transfer students. The class visit is a very important determinant in the admission decision. Schools want to make sure the applicant is a good fit for their program academically and behaviorally. The school visit provides an opportunity for interaction in a classroom setting. It is also an opportunity for the applicant to get a feel for the school and meet potential classmates.

ADMISSION STANDARDS
Schools were asked if they have minimum admission requirements. This information should help families focus on realistic school possibilities based on their child's individual profile.

Admission committees attribute a great deal of importance in evaluating an application. They consider the parent interview, the student interview/visit, teacher recommendation(s), screening/test scores, academic records from any prior school, extra and co-curricular activities, and interests. Schools are looking to complement their current populations.

A helpful site to review is the Independent Schools of the San Francisco Bay Area: http://www.issfba.com. Please note the section entitled "First Choice Letters and Letters of Recommendation" as the

Admissions Directors have made a collaborative effort in stating their positions on these two issues.

STUDENT PROFILES

On paper, it can appear that all schools cater to the "best and the brightest" and offer a rigorous curriculum. Some parents have commented that it seems there is no place for "average" students. The category question of **"What sort of student do you best serve?"** is designed to give a sense of the "breadth" of students, in terms of abilities and varied talents and potential that the school serves.

TOURS

It is essential to begin the process early. At some schools, parents are expected to submit the application and fee prior to the interview and tour. School tours are time-consuming and often inconveniently scheduled but essential because they provide an opportunity to see the school in action. Schools that seem a perfect match on paper can become out-of-the-question after an on-site visit. Differences in school missions and philosophies are evident in classroom instruction. Seeing a variety of grade levels allows parents to get a better picture of a school's program. Parents should be observant of such things as: the level of participation and active engagement of the students both in and out of the classroom; student-teacher and student-student rapport; general sense of order; and the variety of work displayed.

APPLICATION

Many application forms request student and parent input as well as teacher recommendations. Parents may be asked to write short commentaries addressing topics such as why the school is a match for the child, the student's strengths and challenges, and special circumstances or other pertinent information. Some schools ask older applicants to describe their interests or hobbies, challenges and strengths, and co-curricular activities. Parents and students are encouraged to start early as this process can be time-consuming.

If a school is a member of the BADA group, the member schools will share recommendation forms required from the applicant's current preschool or elementary school teacher(s). The forms ask teachers to evaluate various aspects of a student's academic and personal qualities.

Catholic schools may require an Annual Parishioner/Church/Temple Certification Form. Even if a school does not require this certification form it advisable to submit one if applicable. Most certification forms ask a pastor, minister, or rabbi to certify that a family is registered, involved, and/or contributes to the parish/church/temple. Some forms ask parents to describe the family's spirituality in the event the family is not of any particular faith and does not attend a church.

Although being a member of the Catholic Church is not mandatory for admission consideration, most parish schools give preference to Catholic students within parish boundaries, and then to Catholic students outside the parish.

Jewish day school students are generally members of congregations or Jewish community centers. Jewish schools use different requirements of Judaic backgrounds and practices in identifying potential candidates for admission. Not all Jewish schools require that a student be Jewish. Applicants may be required to provide a Jewish professional recommendation provided by a rabbi, Jewish Studies teacher, cantor, or Jewish youth group leader.

Other religiously affiliated schools may have specific religious membership requirements. Generally schools include any such requirements in their admission information.

Some schools seek additional letters of recommendation. However, families should be very selective about the kind and type of additional information they submit. One admission director said, "The thicker the file, the thicker the student." Another admission director gave this rule of thumb, "If you are tempted to send extras, ask this: 'Does it demonstrate specific talents or abilities that won't come through in the application packet or process, and are those talents or abilities pertinent to the school's programs?'"

ADMISSION SCREENING AND TESTING

Most schools have cut-off dates for Kindergarten admission. Although the State of California mandates that a child turns five by December 2, many private schools encourage applicants with summer/fall birth dates to wait a year. Birthday "cut-off" dates vary by school. "K age requirement" in this Guide refers to the age the child must be for the first day of Kindergarten—not the age at the time of application. If applicants are "not yet ready for Kindergarten," schools will encourage the parent to give the child "the gift of time" by waiting a year. The median entry age for the many competitive independent schools approximates five years, seven months on the first day of Kindergarten. Parents should give serious consideration to this issue as a child who starts school too early may develop academic and/or social issues in middle school.

Admission screenings for young applicants range from one-on-one interviews to group play, and from general observations to standardized developmental assessments. Many schools look for "developmental readiness," to determine if a child's chronological age is in sync with a child's developmental age. This may include an assessment of a child's language, listening, motor, and social skills. In order to reduce multiple assessments of an individual child, some schools share screening results. This information will be included in a school's admission literature.

Parents worry about how their child will perform. Coaching or formally preparing for these screenings is not recommended. It is however, important a child be well-rested and healthy for the screening.

Generally, older applicants are required to spend a half/full day visiting the school, take a standardized test and have an individual or group interview. Sometimes schools interview candidates and administer an assessment on the same date the student visits the school. Other times, schools will have a separate date for the assessment or the interview. Individual schools require different admission tests. School records, including grades and standardized test scores, are automatically submitted for the Admission Committee's review after the parents sign a transcript release form contained in the admission information.

ADMISSION DEADLINES AND NOTIFICATION LETTERS

The application deadline normally is in either December or January. Interviews and student visits may be held as late as February, and the majority of schools mail acceptance notification letters in mid-March. The Bay Area Directors of Admissions (BADA) schools share the same mailing date in mid March; Catholic schools also share a mailing date which is usually February-March. Oftentimes, Catholic school notification letters are mailed before the BADA school letters. Parents are asked to make a commitment within a week of the notification date and the timing of the notification letters can be problematic. Schools will ask for a non-refundable deposit to secure a student's space for the fall. Deposits generally range from $300-$4,700 and are required to guarantee a student's place until the next payment, which is generally due in June or July.

ADMISSION DIRECTORS' ADVICE TO PARENTS

"Parents may have unrealistically high expectations of their children. We urge parents to set aside their own desires—such as those based upon social status, family expectations, or legacies—and to focus on what is best for their student. We recommend families talk first about realistic choices in terms of finances, geography, type of school (coed or single sex, religiously affiliated, etc.) and begin the search with these parameters in mind. Parents need to know that competition is keen for admissions to Bay Area schools as we clearly do not have enough spaces for all the qualified students who apply."

"Start early! The biggest mistake parents make is not being organized: call in time to schedule a school visit and request an application packet. Adhere to all application deadlines. Never suggest anything that could be interpreted as a bribe. Schools are looking to work in partnership with families and want to accept students who will be successful within their school environment."

Schools seek a "balanced class," considering many factors such as gender, birthdate, and academic achievement, etc. Admission decisions can be the result of many uncontrollable factors such as sibling applicants, legacies, gender balance, and more. Schools cannot possibly take all the qualified candidates who apply and must make very difficult decisions. Be respectful of the process and of a school's decision.

Parents and students do not have to attend every open house and every event the school offers. Attending school events, however, gives parents and students an excellent opportunity to learn more about a school and its student body. This research aids in making informed decisions.

INTERVIEWS
Through the interview process, parents and students have an opportunity to meet one-on-one with a school representative who is usually the Director of Admission. If possible, each parent should attend the interview. This meeting provides a chance for the school representative to personalize the process and help determine if there is a match between a family's needs/expectations and a school's offerings. Similarly, a family has an opportunity to get an impression of the school.

PREFERENCES
Schools with preschools give preference to current students for Kindergarten spaces. In addition, schools oftentimes give preference to siblings of current enrollees, legacies, and/or faculty children. Even if the numbers seem discouraging, it is advisable to apply as admission directors do not truly know the number of openings available until after the application deadline.

ADMISSION ETIQUETTE AND TIPS
Parents should relax, be on time for the interview, and meet all deadlines. It is advisable to call the school a few weeks before the deadline to make sure all required documentation is in order. Avoid excessive or solicitous

contact which might be perceived as overkill by the school. Avoid submitting more information than requested by the school.

Parents need to trust their intuition. All the research in the world is often not as reliable in choosing a school as a parent's intuition. Once parents have visited all prospective schools, and if one school is clearly a family's first choice, parents are encouraged to communicate this preference to the respective admission director by telling them "why" they think the school is a fit and "why" they would like to be there. It is not a guarantee of admission but it will be noted.

WHAT TO LOOK FOR IN A GRADE SCHOOL

There are many factors to consider when choosing a grade school. School size is one consideration. Local private elementary schools can range in size from fewer than 100 to more than 600 students. Large schools offer a larger pool of peers from which to choose friends, and often offer more choices of co-curricular activities and sports. A large school may appeal to more independent, self-directed students. Small schools often offer more individualized attention.

Additional considerations include class size and teaching styles. Some schools have mostly large classes with teacher-directed instruction, while other schools emphasize more experiential and individualized learning. Parents and students need to take learning styles and instruction preferences into consideration when evaluating schools.

Educational consultants, school advisors and teachers can be very helpful in recommending grade schools that would be a good match for students considering their individual interests, abilities, learning styles, and motivation.

SINGLE SEX OR COED

There are advocates for both single sex and coed school environments. Both groups have research to support their positions. The pros and cons of single sex or coed schools should be investigated and considered by families and students. It is important to be aware of the choices available and remain open to exploring both options.

RELIGIOUS AFFILIATION

Religiously affiliated schools require varying levels of religious participation. Parents should inquire as to the extent and content of the religion programs. Some school programs are designed to embrace a specific religion and mandate that the student be affiliated with it.

STANDARDIZED TEST SCORES

With an increased emphasis over the last decade on standards and accountability in education, standardized testing is included in many school programs. Standardized test scores are primarily used by private independent schools as internal mechanisms for the assessment of their programs and students. Most private schools do not publish standardized test scores, but suggest prospective parents gauge a school's merits by the success of their students, i.e., Johns Hopkins Talented Youth designees, high school placement, science fair winners, mathletes, etc. During the admission process, schools choose to select students with strong aptitude and achievement, and as a result, comparative norms among private schools are skewed.

ENDOWMENT

Endowments enhance a school's financial security. The interest on an endowment can be used for capital improvements, financial aid, faculty salaries and the like. Most schools solicit donations for building their endowments. If a school has a 501(c)(3) nonprofit designation, donations are tax deductible to the extent provided by law.

ENROLLMENT

Smaller schools may offer a more intimate setting with more individual attention and parental involvement while larger schools may provide more extensive facilities and programs as well as larger peer groups.

AVERAGE CLASS SIZE

Average class size in this Guide varies from 8 to 36 students. It is important to ask a school about the number of students, teachers, and teacher aides in the classroom. This statistic is different than the ratio of teacher to students found in the Faculty section of this Guide which is calculated by dividing the total students by total faculty.

SCHOOL YEAR

Most schools are open from late August to early or mid-June. There are many schools that have an extended school year or offer academic or recreational summer programs.

STUDENT BODY ETHNICITY

Each school in this Guide was asked to provide the ethnic makeup of its student body. This information may be important to parents who are looking for a school with ethnic diversity.

Cost

The schools included in this Guide charge tuition ranging from $3,000 to more than $26,715 annually. Parents should expect tuition increases from 1% - 10% annually regardless of the overall state of the economy. In addition to tuition, there can be additional fees for: field trips, uniforms, outdoor education, books, etc. Schools in this Guide were asked to identify approximate projected costs for family budgeting purposes. Most schools require parents to make an initial non-refundable deposit applicable to tuition upon acceptance to the school. Payment options for the remainder of tuition vary from school to school. Some schools allow parents to pay monthly while other schools have one or multiple installment payment plans. In addition, some schools offer sibling discounts. Many schools offer tuition refund plans which provide insurance for tuition payments should a student need to leave during the school year.

Parents need to consider the cost of extended daycare programs, after-school enrichment classes, and/or the expense of vacation coverage in cost forecasts. When parents choose a school, they are usually making a nine-year financial commitment. The schools included in this Guide were asked to provide the approximate annual tuition increase that parents can anticipate. Most schools try to provide timely notification of tuition and fee increases.

Indexed Tuition/Flexible Tuition/Financial Aid

Paying for private school tuition presents a challenge to many families. Schools are concerned about being able to serve an economic cross section of students. In order to broaden economic diversity, more and more schools are offering indexed, flexible tuitions, or financial aid. Most aid awarded is need-based. Indexed tuition, flexible tuition and financial aid decisions are based on a family's assets, family size, discretionary expenses, current and other educational expenses, as well as any extraordinary circumstances. This money is NOT a loan; consequently, it is not expected to be repaid.

Unless a school is using its own criteria, most schools participate in the School Scholarship Service (SSS). Aid using this service is based on a family's ability to pay as demonstrated by the information provided by parents on the SSS Personal Financial Statement (PFS) form. Both custodial as well as non-custodial parents need to provide the necessary financial information. Should one parent not be able to comply, an explanation will be required. All parents will be asked to include their most recent tax return and applicable attachments. This information is necessary whether parents are separated, divorced or not married.

While each family is expected to contribute to tuition to the maximum extent that is economically feasible, the schools do not expect tuition levels to be the same for all. Financial aid, indexed or flexible tuition funding is distributed from a school's operating budget, unrestricted endowment income, or specifically targeted funds. Schools encourage families to apply for financial aid if they have any concerns regarding their ability to pay full tuition. A financial aid administrator notes: "You know what the answer is if you do not apply for aid."

Aid forms are available with admission applications or online and are expected to be submitted by a deadline date. Schools do not guarantee funding as the number of requests usually exceeds the available funds. Consequently, they cannot fund all the deserving families and students who apply for aid. The schools try to be as equitable as possible giving first priority to their current families. Most of the time parents receive the aid offer with the acceptance notification letters. Usually the school will continue the financial aid award for the term of the student's enrollment assuming family circumstances remain unchanged. Generally, annual tax returns and relevant attachments, as well as the SSS form for divorced or separated parents, are required each year. Because of limited funding, schools want to make sure that need is demonstrated annually.

The Catholic school financial aid applications are processed by the Archdiocese, which offers limited financial aid grants.

Private scholarship funds are also available for students. Parents must show evidence of qualifying income status for funding eligibility. One of these sources is The BASIC Fund (Bay Area Scholarships for Inner-City Children) which grants up to a maximum of $1,600 per child wishing to attend a registered K-8 private school (415-986-5650, www. basicfund.org). Grants are based on household size and income, and the child must meet all academic and admission requirements of a registered private school. Currently, The BASIC Fund supports over 5,000 students in 300 different schools in Alameda, Contra Costa, Napa, Santa Clara, Solano, Sonoma, Marin, San Francisco and San Mateo Counties. The program is referred to as "Helping Hand" and promotes a partnership with parents and their involvement with their child's school. If a grant is awarded, the BASIC Fund will pay the school directly on the family's behalf. In addition, families may still apply for financial aid through an individual school's financial aid program. The family will be responsible to the school for any tuition costs and fees in excess of the BASIC Fund scholarship.

The Guardsmen Scholarship Program (415-856-0939, www. guardsmen.org) grants a maximum of $2,000 for students entering K-6 private schools in nine counties throughout the Bay Area. Presently

The Guardsmen supports 259 students. Students who are currently in the program will be supported through Grade 12 subject to an annual application, funding availability, a minimum 2.0 GPA, and family income eligibility. The application deadline is April 30 and the tuition assistance payment is made directly to the school.

If a family receives funding from either The BASIC Fund or The Guardsmen, they are not eligible to receive scholarship funding from the other.

SMART (Schools, Mentoring and Resource Team) "provides advocacy and support to motivated, financially-disadvantaged students in San Francisco." Founded in 1997, SMART is grounded by "the premise that the road to college must begin at a threshold transition for youth." SMART "targets middle school students and provides them with a unique opportunity to develop their academic and social skills in a rigorous setting. SMART works closely with independent middle school partners to secure placement and financial aid for our Scholars for sixth through eighth grades. While attending these schools, SMART provides supplementary skill-building through a comprehensive tutoring and mentoring program, an after-school program, six-week academic summer program, as well as a web of additional support services that help SMART Scholars succeed in what are new and often challenging surroundings." Scholars are also followed through 12th grade to ensure a successful placement into a four-year college. "Candidates must be in public school and demonstrate a strong academic potential, sincere motivation, and a commitment to participate in a year-round program." Deadline for applications are typically due mid-March during the student's 4th grade year (415-865-5400, www.theSMARTprogram.org).

Conventional loans and awards that DO need to be repaid for students who are thirteen years old and younger can be researched on the following site: http://www.finaid.org/scholarships/age13.phtml. Other sources might include home equity loans, 401(k) borrowings, personal loans, low interest credit card loans, and gifts. Parents can explore other funding sources such as gifts from grandparents and other family members, as currently, monetary gifts for tuition and other school expenses are not subject to gift tax if the tuition is paid directly to the school based on a school invoice. Always check with tax professionals for current regulations.

MISSION STATEMENT/ACADEMIC PROGRAM

Private schools in California are required to follow only general guidelines promulgated by the State in establishing their curricula. Under these guidelines, they are required to "offer instruction in the several branches of study required to be taught in the public schools of the state" (Education Code, Section 48222). The branches of education are broadly defined, leaving schools more latitude than guidance. For example, private schools are required to teach mathematics, including concepts, operational skills, and problem solving in grades one through six. Beyond these general mandates, each school makes its own curriculum decisions or implements the curriculum requirements or guidelines of its governing organization.

For this Guide schools were asked for their mission statement or educational philosophy and for a description of their academic program. It is important that parents understand and support the mission, philosophy and academic program of any school their children attend. The mission statement or philosophy describes the school's overall approach to education. Often such statements are very general. The language should, however, give an indication of the relative importance in the program of academics, spiritual education, character development, physical education, and other aspects of education. Parents should ask questions of the school to make sure they agree with and can support the curriculum. This is especially true if parents send a child to a religious school. Parents should consider how religion affects academic content in terms of faith-based topics and discussions, religious themes, and family life perspectives.

Teaching philosophies and methods evolve based on research and societal norms and expectations. Some parents may be surprised to find a plethora of pedagogical innovations that may include such practices as cooperative, experiential and differentiated learning, peer tutoring, inventive spelling, use of calculators and laptops, and project based learning.

Schools were asked about subject offerings including music, drama, art, PE, and foreign languages and the hours per week of instruction. Many schools are devoting considerable resources offering up-to-date technology and computer training such as information literacy, spreadsheets, multimedia presentations, computer graphics, word processing, video editing and keyboarding. Conversely, some schools choose to exclude computers from their classrooms based on philosophical reasons.

Parents who have strong feelings about what and how they expect their child to learn—whether in math, reading, writing, science, art, or other subjects—should make sure they select a school that will meet their expectations.

HOMEWORK

In this Guide, the schools have provided average homework time. Parents should take into consideration that this is just an average and homework time varies considerably from child to child. An increasing number of schools are posting homework assignments online.

HIGH SCHOOLS

Parents should consider a grade school's high school placement in gauging the effectiveness of a K-8 program. High school admissions reflect numerous factors such as students' academic, athletic, artistic qualifications; curricular and co-curricular high school offerings; economic, geographic considerations; and college placement. High schools may prefer students from one particular school more than another, or they may seek students from a variety of K-8 schools to create a more diversified student body.

A useful source to help evaluate high schools is *Private High Schools of the San Francisco Bay Area (4th Ed.)*, by Betsy Little and Paula Molligan. The book profiles 69 private high schools throughout the entire Bay Area with information on SAT scores, college placement, costs, and other factors. See the back of this Guide for more information.

FACULTY

Schools were asked for teachers' ethnicity, educational qualifications, and the teacher/student ratio. Private schools are required by law to have a criminal check of all employees. Teachers are not required to hold a California teaching credential. Many private school teachers are credentialed for the State of California while others hold credentials from other states. Private schools may use their discretion about teacher qualifications. For instance, schools may choose to hire a Ph.D. in biology to teach science without regard to a specific credential. Most private schools require teachers to have earned at least a bachelor's degree. Faculty qualifications are often described in school literature.

Private schools set their own policies concerning continuing teacher education/training. Teachers may be required to attend teacher in-service days and participate in various professional activities such as conferences and graduate level college courses.

The teacher/student ratio is sometimes deceiving. Parents are advised to get further explanations from the school for the teacher/student ratio. Check whether schools use full-time faculty or include aides in their statistic. Also ask if a portion of the class is separated or grouped together for certain subjects to accurately judge the effective teacher/student ratio. Find out if and how frequently full- or part-time aides are used in the classroom.

SPECIAL SUBJECT TEACHERS
This category refers to teachers whose area of expertise is in a given subject. These teachers are trained professionals for specific disciplines such as drama, art, foreign language, music, and computer technology.

MIDDLE SCHOOL
Many schools separate older students in a middle school section which may begin as early as fifth grade. Typically, these programs feature a curriculum specific to early adolescents. This may include departmentalization, accelerated classes, advisory groups, special elective course offerings, and interscholastic sports. Accelerated classes may be offered in a variety of subjects, and more often than not, schools are providing tracking in mathematics.

It is important for parents of all applicants to view classes in upper grades in order to observe what a school is building towards. Parents need to keep in mind that high schools use academic records primarily from sixth through eighth grade in determining admission eligibility.

Middle school programs usually sponsor a variety of social activities which can include hiking, bowling, pizza socials, school dances, ice skating, and the like. These activities are typically chaperoned by teachers and/or parent volunteers and are designed to promote positive social adolescent interactions.

SUPPORT SERVICES
Schools were asked about student support services that include licensed counselors, counselor/student ratio, and the number of learning specialists on staff. In addition, schools were asked to describe their support for learning differences and their high school placement program. As with the faculty/student ratio, these statistics can be misleading. Parents should inquire if the counselor's duties are primarily as advisors to faculty or if they work directly with students individually or in small group settings.

Similarly, parents should investigate available support for children with learning differences. Learning differences are often masked and not always apparent in young children, but become evident in middle school. Thus, parents of early grade applicants might not know if their child will need these services.

A learning difference or disability affects the way children of average to above average intelligence process, receive or express information.

With intervention and support a child can learn compensatory strategies. If a child has learning differences, it is important to choose a school that makes accommodations and provides the necessary support. The extent of services offered varies among the schools. Each school in this Guide was asked what special programs or resources it has for children with learning disabilities or differences. Some schools give students additional support such as: study guides, extra time on tests, an accommodated curriculum and/or tutorial assistance. If no programs or resources are provided by the school, students may be referred to outside tutors. Additional charges for many of these programs may be assessed and parents should inquire about the costs.

If parents are aware of any specific learning issues, it is advisable to discuss them with the respective admission director in order to ascertain if the school is an appropriate fit. Some of the schools in this Guide do an excellent job accommodating a broad range of student abilities.

High school placement services can range from no services to a full-time counselor. Admission to Bay Area high schools is extremely competitive and a daunting task for adolescents and parents. As a result, many families appreciate the assistance of school placement professionals.

STUDENT CONDUCT AND HEALTH

Schools were asked to describe their discipline/behavior policy as well as their preventative education and awareness programs. Schools described programs and/or policies such as: character development, diversity, and harassment. Parents should be comfortable with the behavior standards of an individual school so they can support the school's policies.

Private schools do not face the constraints that public schools do in removing students whose behavior is harmful to themselves or to other students. Private school reactions to discipline issues can be swift when necessary because they are not required to undergo a lengthy appeal process.

Schools were also asked about their preventive education programs such as drug/alcohol awareness, sex education classes, health issues and the like. This education is sometimes integrated within a specific discipline such as science and other times it is taught as a separate course.

ATHLETICS

Most schools in this Guide offer students physical education classes two to five times a week taught by a PE specialist. Many offer competitive sports beginning as early as third grade through intramural teams, private school leagues, or the Catholic Youth Organization (CYO).

Campus Life

Many Marin County schools offer campuses with park-like settings. Most San Francisco schools have limited outdoor facilities often using rooftops, paved playgrounds, or nearby parks for outdoor sports. Most schools in both locations offer lovely buildings, spacious well-equipped classrooms, libraries, computer labs, a gymnasium, and an auditorium or gathering space that accommodate the student body.

School libraries vary considerably in number of volumes, use of technology, square footage and ambience. Many educators view a library as a focal point of an elementary school and consider it an integral part of a school's academic life. Parents should take note of how welcoming a library appears to children. In addition, parents should inquire about library accessibility, library staffing and scheduled library time for students.

Many schools have designated state-of-the-art computer labs staffed by technology specialists. In addition, some schools offer wireless laptops for individual and/or general classroom use.

Extended Day Programs

Extended care programs should be evaluated for age-appropriate programs and age-appropriate security. Parents are encouraged to ask about fenced play yards, locked doors or gates leading to the play yards, and sign-in/sign-out procedures.

Parents should examine extended care facilities with the same care they give to the classroom. The extended day programs sometimes use common school areas such as classrooms and gymnasiums or they are housed in a separate designated facility. It is advisable to learn about the facilities, the staffing qualifications, programs offered, age groupings, space availability, the cost and vacation/holiday coverage. Some extended day programs offer relaxed free play in a home-like environment, and others can offer sports, language classes, and individual tutoring. Costs of extended care range from free to more than $18 per hour but drop-in care can cost more. The cost of after-school enrichment classes are usually in addition to extended day fees.

Extended care programs also vary in terms of flexibility. They may be limited to children who sign up for the entire semester or year, or they may allow occasional or drop-in use. Some schools automatically send children who are not picked up by dismissal time to the extended care program and charge the parents for "drop-in" care. Others send the children to the school office to wait for parents. At some schools, parents pay in advance for extended care and unused hours are not refunded; other schools allow parents to pay for hourly use.

Summer Programs

Nearly all of the schools in this Guide operate on a nine and one-half-month calendar from late August or early September to early or mid-June. Many schools have summer programs, but only a few offer summer programs that last the entire summer. If schools offer summer programs they are generally open to the public as well as to their current students.

Parent Involvement

All schools would like parents to participate in their fundraising efforts. Indeed, for schools to be attractive for grant and foundation support the schools must show a high level of parent, faculty, and alumni participation. Pledges or donations are encouraged because schools often depend on these funds to bridge the difference between tuition and actual educational costs. Schools count on families donating funds at giving levels appropriate to their financial situation. Many schools allow parents to make monthly payments toward their pledges or donations.

One of the signs of a good school is parent involvement. Schools often require parents to give a certain amount of time volunteering for activities such as fundraising, auctions, school maintenance, newsletters, and field trips. Sometimes schools offer weekend or evening opportunities or permit parents to pay a fee in lieu of volunteer hours.

What Sets the School Apart from Others

This category provides each school the opportunity to characterize its uniqueness. Parents should take special note of this category as an indicator of how a school differentiates itself from its colleague schools.

Editor's Notes

1. This Guide does not include schools primarily serving children with special needs. Parents should seek recommendations from school placement specialists as to these schools.
2. The information set forth in this Guide was gathered in Spring-Summer, 2010. Information was requested only from K-8 schools or schools that are in the process of expanding to K-8.
3. Schools that would like to be included in future editions of this book may contact Pince-Nez Press at (415) 267-5978 or pincenezpress@gmail.com.
4. Unless otherwise indicated, financial aid information relates to financial aid provided by or through the school, not aid from other sources.
5. Much of the information in this Guide reflects a compilation and summarization of the information provided by the schools. Quotations represent qualitative information provided by the school. These quotations might be altered by editing including the use of abbreviations, and punctuation to shorten the length of quotes to meet space restrictions.
6. San Francisco geographical districts noted by the editor after each school's address are based upon areas of the city recognized by the City Planning Department. If a second designation is given it is because the school is close to another district or because the second designation is a commonly used term for the area.
7. We have worked hard to make sure the information in this Guide is accurate as of the date of printing. Schools change their programs and costs regularly so parents should rely on a school's most up-to-date information. School's inclusion in this Guide is at the editor's discretion and invitation. Schools that did not respond to the survey in a timely fashion, or chose not to participate are listed in the back of the Guide.
8. Schools are secular unless otherwise noted.

Acronyms and Abbreviations

ABADO	Association of Bay Area Development Officers
ACS	Accrediting Commission for Schools
ALA	American Library Association
AEFE	L'Agence pour l'Enseignement Français à l'Etranger
AMI	Association Montessori Internationale
AMS	American Montessori Society
ASCD	Association for Supervision and Curriculum Development
ASCI	Associated Christian Schools International
AWSNA	Association of Waldorf Schools, North America
BAAD	Bay Area Admissions Directors (High Schools)
BADA	Bay Area Directors of Admissions (Grade Schools)
BADH	Bay Area Division Heads
BAIHS	Bay Area Independent High Schools
BAISHA	Bay Area Independent School Head Association
BAISL	Bay Area Independent School Librarians
BAMA	Bay Area Montessori Association
BASIC Fund	Bay Area Scholarships for Inner-city Children
BJE	Bureau of Jewish Education
CAIS	California Association of Independent Schools
CASE	Council for Advancement and Support of Education
CAT	California Achievement Test
CBSA	California Boarding School Association
CIS	Council of International Schools
CPAA	Children's Progress Achievement Assessments
CTBS	California Test of Basic Skills
CTP 4	Comprehensive Testing Program
DARE	Drug Abuse Resistance Education
ECAA	Early Childhood Admissions Assessment
ECIS	European Council of International Schools
EPGY	Education Program for Gifted Youth
ERB	Educational Records Bureau
ESHA	European School Heads Association
ESL	English as a Second Language
ETS	Educational Testing Service
FCE	Friends Council on Education
FSL	French as a Second Language
G	Grade(s)
GLSEN	Gay, Lesbian, and Straight Educators Network
hr(s)	hour(s)

HS	High School
IBO	International Baccalaureate Organization
IBSC	International Boys School Coalition
IEP	Individual Education Plan
IMC	Instructional Media Center
ISAL	Independent School Athletic League
ISBOA	Independent Schools Business Officers Assn.
ISEE	Independent Schools Entrance Exam
ISSFBA	Independent Schools of the San Francisco Bay Area
ITBS	Iowa Test of Basic Skills
JESNA	Jewish Education Service of North America
LC-MS	Lutheran Church, Missouri Synod
min.	minute(s)
N/A	Not Available or Not Applicable
N/P	Not provided
NAES	National Association of Episcopal Schools
NAIPS	National Association of Independent Private Schools
NAIS	National Association of Independent Schools
NBOA	National Business Officers Association
NCEA	National Catholic Educational Association
NCGS	National Coalition of Girls Schools
NIPSA	National Independent Private School Association
NLSA	National Lutheran Schools Association
PE	Physical education
PEJE	Partnership for Excellence in Jewish Education
PFS	Personal Financial Statement
PK	Pre-Kindergarten
POCIS	Bay Area People of Color in Independent Schools
PPSL	Peninsula Parochial Sports League
PS	Preschool
SAT	Stanford Achievement Test
SF	San Francisco
SMART	Students Mentoring and Resource Team
SPCAL	South Peninsula Catholic Athletic League
SSAT	Secondary School Admission Test
SSATB	Secondary School Admission Test Board
SSS	School Scholarship Service
TABS	The Association of Boarding Schools
TK	Transitional Kindergarten
WASC	Western Association of Schools and Colleges
WCEA	Western Catholic Education Association

High School Abbreviations

Independent schools
Athenian: The Athenian School (Danville, coed)
Bay School: The Bay School (SF, coed)
Bentley: Bentley School (Lafayette, coed)
Branson: The Branson School (Ross, coed)
Castilleja: Castilleja School (Palo Alto, girls)
College Prep: The College Preparatory School (Oakland, coed)
Convent: Convent of the Sacred Heart High School (SF, girls)
Crystal: Crystal Springs Uplands School (Hillsborough, coed)
Discovery: The Discovery Center School (San Francisco, coed)
Drew: Drew College Preparatory School (SF, coed)
IHS: International High School (SF, coed)
Lick: Lick-Wilmerding High School (SF, coed)
Lycée: Lycée Français La Pérouse (SF & Marin, coed)
MA: Marin Academy (San Rafael, coed)
Marin School: The Marin School (Sausalito, coed)
Menlo: Menlo School, (Atherton, coed)
Mid- Peninsula: Mid- Peninsula High School (Menlo Park, coed)
Sacred Heart: Sacred Heart Preparatory (Atherton, coed)
San Domenico: San Domenico School (San Anselmo, girls)
SF Waldorf: San Francisco Waldorf High School (SF, coed)
Sonoma Academy (Santa Rosa, coed)
Sterne: Sterne School (SF, coed)
Stuart Hall: Stuart Hall High School (SF, boys)
University: University High School, (San Francisco, coed)
Urban: The Urban School of San Francisco (SF, coed)
Wheery: Wheery Academy (Redwood City, coed)
Woodside: Woodside International School (SF, coed)
Woodside Priory: Woodside Priory School, (Portola Valley, coed)

Catholic Schools
Bellarmine: Bellarmine College Preparatory (San Jose, boys)
ICA: Immaculate Conception Academy (SF, girls)
MC: Marin Catholic College Preparatory (Kentfield, coed)
Mercy–Burlingame: Mercy High School (Burlingame, girls)
Mercy–SF: Mercy High School (SF, girls)
Mitty: Archbishop Mitty High School (San Jose, coed)
Moreau: Moreau Catholic High School (Hayward, coed)
Notre Dame: Notre Dame High School (Belmont, girls)
Presentation: Presentation High School (San Jose, girls)

Riordan: Archbishop Riordan High School (SF, boys)
SHCP: Sacred Heart Cathedral Preparatory School (SF, coed)
St. Francis: St. Francis High School (Mountain View, coed)
SI: St. Ignatius College Preparatory (SF, coed)
St. Lawrence: St. Lawrence Academy (Santa Clara, coed)
St. Vincent: St. Vincent de Paul School (Petaluma, coed)
Serra: Junipero Serra High School (San Mateo, boys)

JEWISH SCHOOLS
JCHS: Jewish Community High School of the Bay (SF, coed)
Lisa Kampner Hebrew Academy (SF, coed)

PRIVATE BOARDING SCHOOLS
Andover: Phillips Academy Andover (MA)
Cate: Cate School (CA)
Choate: Choate Rosemary Hall (CT)
Colorado Rocky Mountain School (CO)
Dana: Dana Hall School (MA)
Deerfield: Deerfield Academy (MA)
Dunn: Dunn School (CA)
Ethel Walker: The Ethel Walker School (CT)
Exeter: Phillips Exeter Academy (NH)
George: George School (PA)
Groton: Groton School (MA)
Hotchkiss: The Hotchkiss School (CT)
Lawrenceville: Lawrenceville School (NJ)
Middlesex: Middlesex School (MA)
Midland: Midland School (CA)
Miss Porter's: Miss Porter's School (CT)
Proctor: Proctor Academy (NH)
St. Mark's: St. Mark's School (MA)
St. Paul's: St. Paul's School (NH)
Santa Catalina: Santa Catalina School (CA)
Stevenson: Robert Louis Stevenson School (CA)
Thacher: The Thacher School (CA)

FOREIGN PRIVATE SCHOOLS
Lycée International (Paris, France)
Shawnigan – Shawnigan Lake (British Columbia, Canada

Public Schools
Acalanes: Acalanes High School (Lafayette)
Balboa: Balboa High School (SF)
CAT: City Arts and Technology High School (charter, SF)
Drake: Sir Francis Drake High School (San Anselmo)
El Camino: El Camino High School (South San Francisco)
Galileo: Galileo High School (magnet, SF)
Gateway: Gateway High School (charter, SF)
Leadership: Leadership High School (charter, SF)
Lincoln: Abraham Lincoln High School (SF)
Lowell: Lowell High School (magnet, SF)
MSAT: Marin School of Art and Technology (Novato)
MAT: Metropolitan Arts and Technology (charter, SF)
Novato: Novato High School (Novato)
Oceana: Oceana High School (Pacifica)
Redwood: Redwood High School (Larkspur)
San Marin: San Marin High School (Novato)
San Rafael: San Rafael High School (San Rafael)
SOTA: San Francisco School of the Arts (magnet, SF)
Tamalpais: Tamalpais High School (Mill Valley)
Terra Linda: Terra Linda High School (San Rafael)
Washington: George Washington High School (SF)
Wallenberg: Raul Wallenberg High School (SF)
Westmoor: Westmoor High School (Daly City)

SCHOOLS

Adda Clevenger Junior Preparatory and Theater School for Children

180 Fair Oaks Street (at 23rd) (Mission/Noe Valley)
San Francisco, CA 94110
(415) 824-2240
www.addaclevenger.org

Benjamin Harrison, Director
benjamin.harrison@addaclevenger.org

General

Coed K-8 day school. Founded in 1980. Proprietary. **Member:** N/P. **Enrollment:** Approx. 170. **Average class size:** 15. **Accreditation:** None. **Endowment:** N/P. **School year:** Year-round. **School day:** 8:30 a.m. to 4 p.m. for K; 8:30 a.m. to 4:45 p.m. for G1-4; 8:30 a.m. to 5:30 p.m. for G5-8.

Student Body Ethnicity

"Diverse student body."

Admission

Applications due: For K, Sept.-March; for G1-8 throughout the year on a space-available basis. **Application fee:** $100. **Application process:** Parents attend a Saturday afternoon information meeting hosted by teachers and parents in the fall. They are then invited by appointment to visit when classes are in session. Classroom visits are scheduled Wednesdays from 8:30 to 10 a.m. **No. of applications:** N/P. **No. of K spaces:** 24-30. **Percentage of K class made up of school's preschool class:** N/A. **Admission evaluation requirements for K:** Readiness for a full day (8:30 a.m. to 4 p.m. with rest time, but no nap time) and first grade level curriculum. **Other grades:** Students visit school 3 full days. Teachers evaluate placement and make recommendations based on their observations. Interviews with parents and students are part of this process. **Preferences:** N/P. **What sort of student do you best serve?** "Students of above average learning ability that are focused and eager to learn."

Costs

Latest tuition: $20,000 ($18,000 tuition plus $2,000 fees). **Sibling discount:** Yes. **Tuition includes:** Lunch: No; Transportation: No; Laptop computer: No; Other: Optional extended care. **Tuition increases:** Approx. 2-4% annually, if any. Increases are not automatic. **Other costs:** Approx. $500+ for uniforms, field trips, personal costume items and dance shoes, tickets to professional and high school productions, concert tours/music festivals (G6–8 Concert Group and/or Show Choir), speech tournament fees (Junior High). **Percentage of students receiving financial aid:** None. **Financial aid application deadline:** N/A. **Average grant:** N/A. **Percentage of grants of half-tuition or more:** N/A. **Donations:** The school requests admission donations to the student performances and summer graduation concert.

School's Mission Statement

"Adda Clevenger Junior Preparatory is committed to providing children an education that stimulates, challenges, and inspires them, while offering them the opportunity to discover and realize the potential of their individual gifts and talents. We have designed an environment that ensures all children get more from their time spent in school; by eighth grade, our students are prepared to qualify for admission to college preparatory high schools."

Academic Program

Philosophy: "The academic curriculum, designed to educate children of above-average learning ability, exceeds all California state curriculum requirements and includes all standard, age-appropriate subjects. Students enjoy a well-rounded, challenging curriculum from the very start. Kindergarten students are taught first-grade level subjects at an age-appropriate pace. The highly effective Junior Great Books program is introduced in the second grade. The English language curriculum includes not only standard subjects such as grammar, creative writing, and composition, but offers challenging courses in classical, modern and dramatic literature; in Junior High, students compete in speech tournaments. In kindergarten, children are taught basic math skills; by eighth grade, they complete Algebra 1 and some students enter more advanced, high school level classes. American history is introduced early and included in the curriculum during a comprehensive five-year course, spanning ancient to modern history. • In addition to the academic curriculum, students at Adda Clevenger receive a full performing arts curriculum. Students perform on a full professional stage, in a full range of theatrical productions from Gilbert and Sullivan operettas to Broadway musicals. Each performance is accompanied by the San Francisco Sinfonietta Orchestra. • As members of the Adda Clevenger Youth Chorus of San Francisco, all students at Adda Clevenger receive voice, dance and theater instruction with many opportunities to perform and attend live events. The varied repertoire strengthens each child's performance skills and includes a wide range of styles and genres including classical, sacred, folk, theater, and current popular music." **Foreign languages:** "Spanish and Russian are available after school by separate arrangement." **Computer training:** No. **No. of computers available for students:** N/A. **No. of hours weekly of:** Art- 3; Drama- N/P ("varies according to age"); Music- 5 including theory, performance rehearsals and choral instruction; Computers- N/A; Foreign language- N/A; PE- N/P "daily." **Outdoor education:** N/P. **Grading:** Two formal annual assessment reports sent to parents, both letter and narrative. Letter grades begin in K. **Average nightly homework:** "Age appropriate. Many students complete homework in supervised extended care classes." Posted on the Internet: No. **Percentage of students participating in Johns Hopkins Center for Talented Youth Program:** "None, as it conflicts with our year-round schedule." **Other indicators of academic success:** "Individual assessment by teachers, test scores, acceptance to college preparatory high schools, academic achievement and awards at both high school and college level." **High schools attended by latest graduating class:** Bay, Convent, CSUS, Drew, IHS, Lick, Lowell, Mercy-SF, SHCP, SI, SOTA, Stuart Hall, University, Urban.

FACULTY

Ethnicity: "Diverse." **Percentage of teachers with graduate degrees:** 50%. **Percentage with current California credential:** N/P. **Faculty selection/training:** "Teachers are selected based on experience and special interest in subjects they are hired to teach. They need to be able to work independently and collaboratively, as many of the classes are team taught. All new teachers receive on the job training from faculty members who are experienced with Adda Clevenger teaching methods. Requirements in lieu of credential are BA/MA, significant teaching experience or demonstrated knowledge of assigned subjects, and references." **Teacher/student ratio:** Approx. 1:10 in K-4; approx. 1:15 in G5-8. **Special subject teachers:** "All teachers specialize in the subjects they teach." **Average teacher tenure:** 8 years.

MIDDLE SCHOOL

Description: G5-8. **Teacher/student ratio:** Ranges from 1:7 or 1:24 depending on subject. **Elective courses offered:** N/P. **Achievement**

tracking in: Math, English. **Student social events:** Back to school picnic/swim party; trips to Europe and Ashland, New York; annual Halloween party at Pier 39 and on the Bay; lunches downtown before attending theater.

STUDENT SUPPORT SERVICES

No. of Licensed Counselors on staff: N/P. **Counselor/student ratio:** N/P. **Learning specialists on staff:** None. **Learning differences/ disabilities support:** None. **High school placement support:** A placement counselor assists students and parents. Test prep classes are part of the Math and English courses in the first semester of eighth grade. Students take the SSAT at the end of seventh grade and again in eighth grade.

STUDENT CONDUCT AND HEALTH

Code of conduct: N/P. **Prevention education and awareness addressed in:** "This is part of the social studies/current events curriculum. We have an annual visit from a member of AA who talks about alcohol and drug abuse. This also is covered from time to time by a current events magazine designed for seventh to ninth grade students, which is used in social studies classes. Although we believe sex education is the parents' responsibility, it does enter the classroom whenever a topic such as teen pregnancies, AIDS, etc. is featured in the student news magazine."

ATHLETICS

Sports offered: Tumbling, dance and age-appropriate sports games. **Team play begins in:** "Many students are members of soccer teams organized and coached by Adda Clevenger parents; teams practice after school and compete in local soccer leagues. Team ages currently range from K-G4."

CAMPUS/CAMPUS LIFE

Campus description: "The school is located in a historic nineteen thousand square foot building in San Francisco's Noe Valley/Mission District. On the ground floor there are 4 classrooms, a small library, a large art room, an auditorium and stage. The upper floor has six classrooms, a dance studio, music/chorus room, offices, and a resource room." **Library:** No. **Sports facilities:** Two fenced-in playgrounds with a basketball court. **Theater/Arts facilities:** Auditorium, stage, dance studio, music rehearsal room, art room. **Computer lab:** No. **Science lab:** No. **Lunch program:** No. **Bus service:** No. **Uniforms/dress code:** Uniforms. **Opportunities for community service:** Yes.

EXTENDED DAY

Morning care: Begins at 7:30 a.m. **After-school care:** Until 6 p.m. **Grade levels:** All. G5-8 are in class until 5:30 daily. **Cost:** $32-$232/month. **Drop-in care available:** Yes. **Coverage over major holidays:** No. **Homework help:** Yes. **Snacks:** Not provided. **Staff/student ratio:** N/P. **After-school classes:** For students in G1-4, the school day lasts until 4:45 p.m., then they have homework class, sports or visit the art room. Students in G5-8 are in regularly scheduled academic and performing arts classes until 5:30 p.m. daily.

SUMMER PROGRAMS

The school's 3-week Creative Summer Day Camp (non-academic) is optional, but included in tuition. It involves art, sports, music, dance, drama and rehearsals for the gymnastics demos and musical to be performed for parents on the last day. Children help paint backdrops, make props, etc. **Cost:** Included in tuition.

PARENT INVOLVEMENT

Parent/teacher communication: Newsletters and e-mail. Parent/teacher conferences scheduled at parents' or teachers' request. **Participation requirements:** "Parents are strongly encouraged to support and attend all student performances. There are many opportunities for parent involvement and all are strictly voluntary." **Parent education programs offered?** No.

WHAT SETS THE SCHOOL APART FROM OTHERS

"Adda Clevenger addresses the whole child with a dual curriculum consisting of accelerated academics and performing arts. As members of the Adda Clevenger Youth Chorus, all students at Adda Clevenger have the rare opportunity to perform in concert tours around the world, taking them to legendary venues such as Carnegie Hall and the White House. The poise, presence and self-confidence that our students achieve by graduation set them apart from their peers. Exposure to a wider range of activities and subject areas makes possible the discovery and development of skills and interests that would go unrealized with the limited curriculum and shorter school day of most elementary schools. At Adda Clevenger, children get more from their time spent in school."

HOW FAMILIES CHARACTERIZE SCHOOL

Parent comment(s): "Everything I've learned about child development the last three years has repeatedly convinced me all the ways that Adda is doing it right, and deepened my respect and admiration for the school."

"As parents of a transfer student, we've had the opportunity to see how other schools operate. Adda Clevenger truly puts the child first, creating an environment that nurtures creativity and imagination and fosters a genuine relationship between the child and self, and the child and others. At once traditional and progressive, Adda Clevenger reflects the wonder and diversity of the city we live in."

Student comment(s): "Adda Clevenger is the school where we found our talents on stage and in the classroom, made friends and had fun. Adda Clevenger has become home to many students for over 25 years. It has also become known as one of the best performing arts schools in the Bay Area. "

BRANDEIS HILLEL DAY SCHOOL, MARIN
180 N. San Pedro Road
San Rafael, CA 94903
(415) 472-1833 *fax (415) 491-1317*
www.bhds.org

Mr. Chaim Heller, Head of School
Amy Pearson, Director of Admissions, apearson@bhds.org

GENERAL
Coed K-8 Jewish community day school. Founded in 1963. Independent. Nonprofit. **Member:** CAIS, NAIS, WASC, ERB, BADA, SSAT. **Enrollment:** Approx. 200. **Average class size:** 20. **Accreditation:** CAIS (6-year term: 2006-12). **Endowment:** $8 million. **School year:** Sept.-June. **School day:** 8 a.m. to 2 p.m. for K; 8 a.m. to 3 p.m. for G1-8.

STUDENT BODY ETHNICITY
86% Caucasian, 8% multi-racial, 4% Asian, 1% African American, 1% Native American.

ADMISSION
Applications due: Jan. (call for date). **Application fee:** $85. **Application process:** Applicant families should call the school in Sept. or Oct. to schedule a tour. After submitting the application, a parent interview will be scheduled, as well as a screening date for K students or a shadow date for students for G1-8. **No. of applications:** N/P. **No. of K spaces:** 22-24. **Percentage of K class made up of school's preschool class:** N/A. **Admission evaluation requirements for K:** Screening, recommendations, parent interview. **Other grades:** Test scores, report

cards, school visit, screening. **Preferences:** N/P. **What sort of student do you best serve?** "Students who are intellectually curious and will thrive in a challenging academic program, as well that will reflect our core values: Integrity, Kindness and Service."

COSTS
Latest tuition: $21,735 for K-7, $23,000 for G8. **Sibling discount:** None. **Tuition includes:** Lunch: No; Transportation: No; Laptop computer: No; Other: Books, materials, supplies, field trips, outdoor education and yearbook. **Tuition increases:** N/P. **Other costs:** None. **Percentage of students receiving financial aid:** Approx. 30%. **Financial aid application deadline:** Jan. (call for date). "Financial aid is based on need and school resources." **Average grant:** N/P. **Percentage of grants of half-tuition or more:** N/P. **Donations:** "We encourage support of our school's fundraising through the annual fund, capital campaign, and auctions. The school strives for 100% parent participation in the school's annual fund."

SCHOOL'S MISSION STATEMENT
"The mission of Brandeis Hillel Day School is to serve the Jewish community by providing children with an outstanding academic program in general and Judaic studies within a dynamic and diverse Jewish cultural environment."

ACADEMIC PROGRAM
Philosophy: "We offer a rich, integrated and challenging curriculum: English, math, science, history, Hebrew and Judaic studies, visual and performance arts, technology, athletics and outdoor education. By setting high standards, prioritizing social and emotional skill development led by exceptional teachers, we prepare children to thrive in a rigorous academic environment, instilling a life-long love of learning. Meaningful service learning and outdoor education programs create additional enrichment opportunities. Students are ethical and responsible citizens who leave 8th grade well prepared for high school and are accepted into their top choice of schools." **Foreign languages:** Hebrew. Spanish as an elective. **Computer training:** Yes. "All students have access to a multi-media lab and media information library. Technology is integrated across all subjects and the technology coordinator works with each teacher to find ways to utilize various programs as learning tools. There are also multi media electives where students put together the school yearbook and learn how to shoot and edit video. Students also write a school magazine." **No. of computers available for students:** 60. **No.**

of hours weekly of: Art- 1-2; Drama- 1-2; Music- 1-3; Computers- N/P ("varies"); Foreign language- 4-5; PE- 2-3. **Outdoor education:** G4-8. Venues vary from year to year and have included exploration of the Gold Country, Salt Point, Morrow Bay, Walker Creek, Sequoia Kings Canyon, Washington D.C. and Israel. **Grading:** Varies by grade; letter grades begin in G4. **Average nightly homework:** None in K; 10-20 min. in G1; 20-30 min. in G2; 30-45 min. in G3; 45-50 min. in G4; 1-1.5 hours in G5-6; 2 hrs. in G7-8. Posted on the Internet: Yes. **Percentage of students participating in Johns Hopkins Center for Talented Youth Program:** N/P. **Other indicators of academic success:** "Test scores (ERB), high school acceptances and colleges attended." **High schools attended by latest graduating class:** Bay, Branson, Drew, JCHS, MA, Redwood, Drake, Terra Linda, Urban, University.

FACULTY

Ethnicity: N/P. **Percentage of teachers with graduate degrees:** 50%. **Percentage with current California credential:** N/P. **Faculty selection/training:** Experience, degrees, credentials, professional development, enthusiasm, commitment. **Teacher/student ratio:** 1:9. **Special subject teachers:** Art, music, technology, drama, PE, architecture. **Average teacher tenure:** 10-15 years.

MIDDLE SCHOOL

Description: "Our middle school endeavors to reach students on the academic, social and emotional levels by engaging students in high-level interdisciplinary projects, providing them with leadership opportunities and honing their organizational skills in preparation for high school. By hiring teachers who understand the particular needs of middle school, and by offering a challenging and rigorous program, students become confident, critical thinkers in a positive and safe environment. Commences in G6." **Teacher/student ratio:** 1:9. **Elective courses offered:** Music, art, drama, architecture, multi-media. **Achievement tracking in:** All academic areas. **Student social events:** Dances, a middle school retreat, and joint activities with the school's SF campus.

STUDENT SUPPORT SERVICES

No. of Licensed Counselors on staff: One full-time. **Counselor/student ratio:** N/P. **Learning specialists on staff:** One full-time. **Learning differences/disabilities support:** The resource specialist works with the teachers and the parents to provide the appropriate educational support for students who may need additional help. **High school placement support:** "The high school placement counselor works with G8 students and families to find the best high school fit for each student. Our students consistently get into their top choice of high schools."

STUDENT CONDUCT AND HEALTH
Code of conduct: "The school has a full discipline and behavior policy designed to ensure a safe and positive learning environment for students. Students are expected to behave in ways that promote physical safety and well-being, respect for themselves and others, responsibility for school property and to be sincere, honest and committed learners." **Prevention education and awareness addressed in:** These programs cover substance abuse, sex education, internet safety, health and body image, and harassment.

ATHLETICS
Sports offered: Cross-country, flag football, basketball, track and field. **Team play begins in:** G3 (intramural).

CAMPUS/CAMPUS LIFE
Campus description: "The Marin campus of Brandeis Hillel, set against the mountains in San Rafael, sits on a larger campus with the Marin Jewish Community Center and Congregation Rodef Sholom. The school also has new play structures, new art room and a garden." **Library:** 12,500 volumes; also has 24 wireless laptops, plus computer work spaces. **Sports facilities:** "State of the art gymnasium, outdoor turf sports field, pool." **Theater/Arts facilities:** Yes. Hoytt Theater. **Computer lab:** Yes. **Science lab:** Yes. **Lunch program:** Yes. **Bus service:** No. **Uniforms/dress code:** Dress code. **Opportunities for community service:** Yes.

EXTENDED DAY
Morning care: Begins at 8 a.m. **After-school care:** Until 6 p.m. **Grade levels:** K-5. **Cost:** "Varies." **Drop-in care available:** Yes. **Coverage over major holidays:** No. **Homework help:** Yes. **Snacks:** Provided (organic apples daily). **Staff/student ratio:** 1:10. **After-school classes:** Yes. **Cost:** N/P.

SUMMER PROGRAMS: N/P.

PARENT INVOLVEMENT
Parent/teacher communication: Conferences, website, e-mail, newsletters. **Participation requirements:** "All parents are members of the school's very active parents association through which parents become involved in the school and develop community. While it is not

required to volunteer, most parents find a way to be active in the many committees and opportunities available to support the school." **Parent education programs offered? Yes.**

WHAT SETS THE SCHOOL APART FROM OTHERS

"The project based learning allows greater depth to the knowledge our students receive and provides a forum of excitement around getting work done. Faculty relate curriculum to real life and include many field trips for them to explore their learning outside the classroom. The individual attention given to each student lets each child become confident and creative thinkers, while the many mentoring opportunities provide them leadership skills. Having a language every day is a great advantage for young children in brain development and in helping students succeed in many other areas of the curriculum. Brandeis Hillel Day School's community is characterized by its mutual respect, friendship and shared purpose."

HOW FAMILIES CHARACTERIZE SCHOOL

Parent comment(s): "Our whole family loves Brandeis Marin. It is a school that not only fills the brain, but also, fills the heart. Its size allows individual attention to each student daily. The teachers are the real stars of the school. They are superior. They offer solid academics, but also wonderful non-core classes, such as art, music, multi media, PE and after school sports. I know that our kids will have a strong academic, social and value base to be able to continue at any high school (and beyond) successfully. For many years I have watched the 8th graders give their graduation speeches and every year I am blown away with their poise and confidence."

Student comment(s): "I love going to school. My teachers are really fun and we get to do projects that help me learn more about things." • "I look forward to coming to school every morning to see my friends. I like all the activities we get to do like art projects, math, science and Hebrew. The teachers are really nice and teach us a lot of good information." "It's a great opportunity to experience your culture. My teachers are kind and caring and really prepare me in all my subjects."

Brandeis Hillel Day School San Francisco

655 Brotherhood Way (Lakeshore/Park Merced)
San Francisco, CA 94132
(415) 406-1035 *fax (415) 584-1099*
www.bhds.org

Chaim Heller, Head of School, cheller@bhds.org
Bruce Werber, Head of Campus, bwerber@bhds.org
Tania Lowenthal, Director of Admission, tlowenthal@bhds.org

General
Coed K-8 Jewish community day school. Founded in 1963. Independent. Nonprofit. **Member:** CAIS, BADA, JESNA, ERB and SSAT. **Enrollment:** Approx. 400. **Average class size:** 22. **Accreditation:** WASC/CAIS (6-year term: 2006-12). **Endowment:** $8 million. **School year:** Sept.-June. **School day:** 8:15 a.m. to 3:15 p.m.

Student Body Ethnicity
88% Caucasian, 7% Asian, 4% Latino, 1% African-American.

Admission
Applications due: Jan. 15th. **Application fee:** $85. **Application process:** School tours for K Sept. to Jan. Open houses are held in the fall for K and in winter for middle school. Upon receipt of an application BHDS schedules an admission screening and parent interview. Notifications are mailed on a common date in cooperation with other Bay Area independent schools. **No. of applications:** N/P. **No. of K spaces:** 44. **Percentage of K class made up of school's preschool class:** N/A. **Admission evaluation requirements for K:** Screening, evaluation form. **Other grades:** School visit, test scores, school grades. **Preferences:** N/P. **What sort of student do you best serve?** "A student that thrives in an academically challenging environment and a 'radically kind' social atmosphere."

Costs
Latest tuition: $21,735 for K-7, $23,000 for G8. **Sibling discount:** None. **Tuition includes:** Lunch: No; Transportation: No; Laptop computer: No; Other: Books, materials, supplies, outdoor education trips, yearbook. **Tuition increases:** N/P. **Other costs:** $75 Parent Association

dues. **Percentage of students receiving financial aid:** 30%. **Financial aid application deadline:** Approx. Jan. 31st (call for date). "Financial aid is based on need and the schools' resources." **Average grant:** N/P. Percentage of grants of half tuition or more: N/P. **Donations:** Voluntary donations for the annual fund, capital campaign, and auctions.

SCHOOL'S MISSION STATEMENT
"To serve the Jewish community by providing children with an outstanding academic program in general and Judaic studies within a dynamic and diverse Jewish cultural environment."

ACADEMIC PROGRAM
Philosophy: "We are deeply committed to the intellectual, social, spiritual and physical growth of our students. We expect our children to develop compassion, tolerance and mutual respect for others and we guide them to become responsible citizens in our community and in the world." **Foreign languages:** Hebrew; Spanish as an elective. **Computer training:** Yes. "Technology is used as a tool to help students access the world and enhance their studies. Beginning in G1, all classes have equal lab time. iMac computers, digital scanners and cameras, laser printers and educational software are available to provide opportunities for students to learn." **No. of computers available for students:** One per student in the computer lab and additional laptops for students through the portable "airport." **No. of hours weekly of:** Art- 1-2; Drama- 1-2; Music- 1-2; Computers- N/P ("varies with class and project based curriculum"); Foreign language- N/P ("Hebrew daily, Spanish elective"); PE- 3. **Outdoor education:** "In G4-8, students participate in extended class trips. Our educational mission is to integrate a strong academic and cultural program with a challenging outdoor experience and travel. In the 4th grade students explore California's Gold Country; 5th graders go to the Northern California coast for a science and outdoor camping experience; 6th graders participate in a 4-day outdoor science camp at Yosemite National Park. 7th graders attend the Naturalists at Large camp in Sequoia National Park; in the 8th grade, students take a week-long trip to Israel as a culmination of their Jewish studies coursework." **Grading:** Letter grades begin in G5. **Average nightly homework:** None in K; 10-20 min. in G1; 20-30 min. in G2; 30-45 min. in G3; 45 min.-1 hr. in G4; 1 to 1-1.5 hrs. in G5-6; 2 hrs. in G7-8. Posted on the Internet: Yes, for middle school. **Percentage of students participating in Johns Hopkins Center for Talented Youth Program:** Over 60%. **Other indicators of academic success:** "ERB, Geo Bee." **High schools attended by latest graduating class:** Balboa, Bay, Gateway, IHS, JCHS, Lick, Lincoln, Lowell, Mercy, Oceana, SI, University, SOTA, St. Paul's, Urban.

Faculty

Ethnicity: 76% Caucasian, 10% other, 8% Asian, 6% Latino. **Percentage of teachers with graduate degrees:** N/P. **Percentage with current California credential:** N/P. **Faculty selection/training:** "We hire the best teachers for the job. We recruit from professional organizations. BHDS has an extensive professional development program and all teachers are encouraged to participate." **Teacher/student ratio:** 1:9. **Special subject teachers:** Art, music, drama, PE, library, ESL, computers. **Average teacher tenure:** 7 years.

Middle School

Description: "Commences in G6. We recognize the changing needs of the emerging adolescent. Within our family-like atmosphere with many adults to provide support and nurturance, our students thrive. They continue to consolidate their scholastic achievements and to develop their problem-solving abilities. Our interdisciplinary curriculum weaves together an awareness of past and present connections and future possibilities." **Teacher/student ratio:** 1:9. (class divided into 3 sections for math, English, Hebrew). **Elective courses offered:** Art studio, band, cooking, creative writing, drama, self defense, ethnobotany, journalism, yearbook, debate, track, fitness. **Achievement tracking in:** Language arts, math, social studies, science, Hebrew and Judaic Studies. **Student social events:** Dances, retreats, interaction with other schools through community service.

Student Support Services

No. of Licensed Counselors on staff: One full-time. **Counselor/student ratio:** N/A. **Learning specialists on staff:** The Dean of Faculty whose job it is to work with high achieving students and the ESL teacher. (The Lower School and Middle School have Learning Specialists.) **Learning differences/disabilities support:** "The resource specialist works with students, parents, and staff to provide appropriate education for children identified with specific learning disabilities." **High school placement support:** "The High School Admissions Team assists 8th grade students and parents through the process. The vast majority of our students are accepted by their first and second choices to the finest public and private high schools."

Student Conduct and Health

Code of conduct: "Students are expected to behave in ways that promote physical safety and well-being, respectful to themselves and others, responsible for school property, promote positive learning environment and be sincere, honest and committed learners." **Prevention education and awareness programs:** These programs cover media safety, substance abuse, sex education, sex, health, harassment, and anti-bullying.

ATHLETICS
Sports offered: Cross-country, soccer, volleyball, basketball (boys and girls teams for all) **Team play begins in:** G6 (intramural). Member of BAIAL.

CAMPUS/CAMPUS LIFE
Campus description: "The San Francisco Frank and Jennie Gauss Campus, completed in 1983, opened a state-of the-art building in 2002. Located in a suburban type setting on 2 acres, the site includes the San Francisco Jewish Community Center Preschool and is next to Congregation Beth Israel-Judea. In the new building there are eight classrooms, 2 for K and 6 for G1-3. There are plans to build a cultural art center, cafeteria and new gymnasium." **Library:** The building also houses a 2,800 square foot library and a Judaic Studies room, acoustically designed music room and a multimedia/technology seminar space. The library's collection includes over 25,000 volumes." **Sports facilities:** Gymnasium, sports field. **Theater/Arts facilities:** Yes. **Computer lab:** Yes. **Science lab:** Yes. **Lunch program:** Yes. **Bus service:** Yes. **Uniforms/dress code:** No. **Opportunities for community service:** "We regard service to the community as a BHDS value, as students gain a sense of belonging to a larger community. The goals of our community service program include showing students that one person can make a difference, putting acts of kindness into action through work in our community, promoting student leadership in the school and the community at large."

EXTENDED DAY
Morning care: Begins at 7:45 a.m. **After-school care:** Until 6 p.m. **Grade levels:** K-8. **Cost:** Prepaid options are $750 for 100 hours, $310 for 40 hours, or $170 for 20 hours. **Drop-in care available:** Yes. **Coverage over major holidays:** No. **Homework help:** Yes. **Snacks:** Provided. **Staff/student ratio:** N/P. Middle-school students may stay after school to do their homework, with supervision, free of charge. **After-school classes:** Drama, movie making, gymnastics, cooking/ baking, self-defense, chess, piano/trumpet; painting/drawing/mixed media, magic, Spanish. **Cost:** $200-$350 for 10-week session.

Summer Programs
"Shakespeare Camp, Camp Galileo, and others are offered on campus over the summer. Please contact the school for current offerings." **Cost:** N/P.

Parent Involvement
Parent/teacher communication: Conferences, website, e-mail, voicemail, newsletter. **Participation requirements:** "All parents are members of the Brandeis Hillel Day School Parent Association. The Parent Association is an active organization through which parents become involved, support BHDS and develop community. While it is not required for our parents to volunteer, there are many committees and opportunities to do so - and BHDS is proud of its active parent volunteer culture." **Parent education programs offered?** Yes.

What Sets the School Apart From Others
"In addition to academic excellence, BHDS is committed to educating children to be caring members of the community, to value and appreciate the Jewish heritage and to become ethically responsible human beings."

How Families Characterize School
Parent comment(s): "BHDS is not only a school of academic excellence, it also has soul."
Student comment(s): "I was very well prepared for high school in math, science and language arts. I was also given invaluable social tools to deal with the challenges of high school. My BHDS friends are friends for life."

Cascade Canyon School
2626 Sir Francis Drake Boulevard
Fairfax, CA 94930
(415) 459-3464 *fax (415) 459-6714*
www.cascadecanyonschool.org

Rebecca Hausammann, School Director, rebecca@cascadecanyon.org

General
Coed K-8 day school. Founded in 1981. Independent. Nonprofit. **Member:** N/P. **Enrollment:** Approx. 66. **Average class size:** 14. **Accreditation:** None. **Endowment:** N/A. **School year:** Aug.-June.

School day: 8:30 a.m. to 3 p.m. lower school; 8:30 a.m. to 3:10 p.m. middle school.

STUDENT BODY ETHNICITY
93% Caucasian (non-Latino), 3% Latino, 2% Asian, 2% African American.

ADMISSION
Applications due: Feb. 5, rolling admissions thereafter as space permits. **Application fee:** $85. **Application process:** Parents visit the school and submit an application. Student visits are then scheduled. **No. of applications:** Varies. **No. of K spaces:** 10. **Percentage of K class made up of school's preschool class:** N/A. **Admission evaluation requirements for K:** Student visit; discussion with preschool teacher(s); minimum age requirement of 5 years old; readiness for a full-day program. **Other grades:** Parent-director phone meeting, parent observation of class followed by student visit. **Preferences:** N/A. **What sort of student do you best serve?** "Self-motivated, independent, and cooperative."

COSTS
Latest tuition: $14,238. **Sibling discount:** 10%. **Tuition includes:** Lunch: No; Transportation: No; Laptop computer: No; Other: N/P. **Tuition increases:** Approx. 5% annually. **Other costs:** Approx. $350 for books, $500 other fees. **Percentage of students receiving financial aid:** 9%. **Financial aid application deadline:** Feb. 19th (call for date). **Average grant:** Approx. $4,200. **Percentage of grants of half-tuition or more:** N/A. **Donations:** A minimum of 40 hours of service per family or a $800 donation in lieu of participation; 2 annual fundraisers or $800 in lieu of participation.

SCHOOL'S MISSION STATEMENT
"Cascade Canyon School is dedicated to maintaining a small student/ teacher ratio and to offering an integrated and balanced curriculum that exposes students to the joys of learning as a lifelong pursuit and leads students to become independent thinkers, strong leaders, and active participants in the global community who are respectful of others, flexible in responding to challenge and appreciative of diversity. • We challenge students to think deeply. We engage students in learning. We inspire students to express themselves. We connect students and families to our staff, each other, the school and communities around us."

ACADEMIC PROGRAM
Philosophy: N/P. **Foreign languages:** Spanish, Sign Language. **Computer training:** Yes. Internet Research, Word, Excel, PowerPoint, Photoshop. **No. of computers available for students:** Two in each elementary classroom; 4 in the middle school classrooms, 4 in the library. **No. of hours weekly of:** Art- 1-2; Drama- 1; Music- 1; Computers- N/P (integrated in G5-8); Foreign language- 2-3; PE- 2-3. **Outdoor education:** Varies; includes 2 school-wide overnight trips. **Grading:** "Extensive narrative report with accompanying developmental and standards-based rubric evaluation of progress in every subject, provided twice a year." **Average nightly homework:** 30-90 min. Posted on the Internet: No. **Percentage of students participating in Johns Hopkins Center for Talented Youth Program:** N/A. **Other indicators of academic success:** N/P. **High schools attended by latest graduating class:** Bay, MA, Drake, Marin School of the Arts.

FACULTY
Ethnicity: N/P. **Percentage of teachers with graduate degrees:** 60%. **Percentage with current California credential:** 80%. **Faculty selection/training:** Hiring process, including live teaching sessions; job vacancies posted at Berkeley, Stanford, Mills, Bank Street and Dominican and on edjoin.org; professional development program and BTSA. **Teacher/student ratio:** 1:10 in K, 1:15 in G1-8. **Special subject teachers:** Spanish, science, art, music, theater, sign language, and PE. **Average teacher tenure:** 6 years.

MIDDLE SCHOOL
Description: G5-8. "Integrates project based learning, student exhibitions and community service with core subjects of language arts, math, science and social studies and specialist subjects of Spanish, science, art, music, theater, sign language (elective) and PE." **Teacher/student ratio:** 1:15. **Elective courses offered:** See the specialist subjects listed above. **Achievement tracking in:** None. **Student social events:** Two annual school-wide overnight trips; several annual school-wide performance opportunities and community gatherings; G8 Transitions Program.

STUDENT SUPPORT SERVICES
No. of Licensed Counselors on staff: None. **Counselor/student ratio:** N/A. **Learning specialists on staff:** None. **Learning differences/ disabilities support:** "Academic intervention program." **High school placement support:** Done by Middle School Lead Teacher.

STUDENT CONDUCT AND HEALTH
Code of conduct: N/P. **Prevention education and awareness programs:** Sex and health for G4-8, and sex, health and drugs for G7-8.

ATHLETICS
Sports offered: Soccer, basketball and volleyball. **Team play begins in:** G1 (intramural).

CAMPUS/CAMPUS LIFE
Campus description: "Natural, wooded setting on twenty acres." **Library:** "Over 1,000 books and reference materials." **Sports facilities:** Playground, basketball court. **Theater/Arts facilities:** Outdoor theater, costume and prop department, and an indoor workshop space with a stage. **Computer lab:** No. **Science lab:** Yes. **Lunch program:** Yes. **Bus service:** No. **Uniforms/dress code:** None. **Opportunities for community service:** "Yes."

EXTENDED DAY: None.

SUMMER PROGRAMS: None.

PARENT INVOLVEMENT
Parent/teacher communication: Conferences, website, newsletter, e-mail, written evaluation. **Participation requirements:** A minimum of 40 hours service is required per family. **Parent education programs offered?** Parent Association; Director Focus Groups.

WHAT SETS THE SCHOOL APART FROM OTHERS
"Our uniquely small size and the degree to which that enables us to know, engage and stretch each student; our strong, vibrant and caring community; our experienced and skilled staff; our progressive and balanced program that challenges students to think deeply, construct meaning, and exhibit knowledge."

HOW FAMILIES CHARACTERIZE SCHOOL
Parent comment(s): "Cascade Canyon is a safe, nurturing place for a child to learn and grow. A place that will inspire a lifelong love of learning which is not just strict academic learning to become a good student but learning to become a good friend, a good person, and a good citizen." • "The beauty of Cascade Canyon is the diverse academic and creative environment that engages students continuously. As a parent, I see first hand that my children want to go to school every day. They

know and I know they will be challenged, nurtured, respected and accepted for who they are. They are empowered to speak their thoughts in a supportive environment and they know they are a part of a loving community of peers, teachers and parents. And, as a result of the whole education process, teaching them to be good students as well as good people, they can go out and make a difference in the world."
Student comment(s): N/P.

CATHEDRAL SCHOOL FOR BOYS
1275 Sacramento St. (at Jones next to Grace Cathedral) (Nob Hill)
San Francisco, CA 94108
(415) 771-6600 *fax (415) 771-2547*
www.cathedralschool.net

Canon Headmaster Michael Ferreboeuf, Head of School, ferreboeuf@cathedralschool.net
Cathy Madison, Director of Admission, madison@cathedralschool.net

GENERAL
K-8 boys day school. Founded in 1957. Independent. Episcopal. Nonprofit. **Member:** CAIS, NAIS, NAES, BADA. **Enrollment:** Approx. 268. **Average class size:** 24 in K-4, 16 in G5-8. **Accreditation:** WASC/CAIS (6-year term: 2006-12). **Endowment:** $13 million. **School year:** Sept.-June. **School day:** 8:15 a.m. to 2:30 p.m. for K; 8:15 a.m. to 2:40 p.m. for G1; 8:15 a.m. to 2:40 p.m. for G2; 8:15 a.m. to 3 p.m. for G3-4; and 8:15 a.m. to 3:25 p.m. for G5-8.

STUDENT BODY ETHNICITY
37% Caucasian (non-Latino), 27% Asian, 14% Middle Eastern, 12% Latino, 5% multi-racial, 4% African-American, 1% Native American.

ADMISSION
Applications due: Early Jan. (call for date). **Application fee:** $100. **Application process:** Tours are available 2 weekday mornings from mid-Sept. to mid-Jan. Parent interviews for K applicants are not required but may be requested until Dec. 1. Applicants are screened for developmental readiness on a Saturday in Jan. **No. of applications:** Approx. 150-200. **No. of K spaces:** 24. **Percentage of K class made up of school's preschool class:** N/A. **Admission evaluation requirements for K:** Developmental readiness screening and preschool evaluation. **Other grades:** Requirements include school visit, grades, test scores,

teacher recommendation and reports from specialists when appropriate. Parent interviews are required for G1-8 applicants. **Preferences:** Children of graduates and siblings. **What sort of student do you best serve?** "Boys who are eager and ready to learn."

Costs

Latest tuition: $23,375. **Sibling discount:** None. **Tuition includes:** Outdoor education, field trips, books, art, music and instrumental music lessons (student choice). Lunch: Yes; Transportation: Yes; Laptop computer available at school in G5-8. Other: N/P. **Tuition increases:** Approx. 4.5% annually. **Other costs:** Uniforms (available new or used at onsite school store), school pictures and gym shirts. **Percentage of students receiving financial aid:** 20%. **Financial aid application deadline:** Feb. (call for date). Financial aid is based on need. **Average grant:** $14,400. **Percentage of grants of half-tuition or more:** 60%. **Donations:** Voluntary.

School's Mission Statement

"To provide an excellent education for boys at the elementary level. • To attract a diverse student body of strong academic potential. • To provide a school committed to intellectual inquiry and rigor, centered in the Episcopal tradition, respectful of and welcoming to people of all religious traditions and beliefs. • To develop civic responsibility through exemplary programs of outreach and service. • To create a community bonded by open-heartedness, hope, compassion and concern."

Academic Program

Philosophy: "Cathedral School for Boys, founded in 1957, strives to provide education in the best traditions of the Episcopal Church and in consonance with the mission of Grace Cathedral. We believe that this education is derived from three main sources: the highest academic and personal standards humanely applied; a diverse community united in its concern for the school and for the world; and an active engagement with religion and the spiritual dimension. Academically, the school sets high standards in literacy, basic skills, self-discipline, the joy of learning, and the pursuit of wisdom. We set equally high standards in good behavior, caring, mutual respect, truth-telling and honor, and emphasize these qualities in all aspects of school life. Art, music, drama and physical education are integral parts of the curriculum. We prepare boys to enter demanding secondary schools confidently; we recognize that there are a variety of learning styles and paces among able students, and we try to teach accordingly. Teachers focus on learning styles which are boy-friendly: hands-on, active study which allows for movement and vigor. We affirm the integrity of childhood and the elementary curriculum, and do not try to replicate secondary school studies." **Foreign languages:** Mandarin or Spanish in G5-8. Latin is required in G7-8. **Computer training:** "Integrated into curriculum. A state of the art Tech Lab and Media Center is available; a roving lab of 200 laptops is used in G5-8 classrooms." **No. of computers available for students:** 200 laptops, 40 stand alone. **No. of hours weekly of:** Art- daily for K-4 in classroom and .75 in art studio, for G5-8, 1.5 in art studio; Drama- 1-2 average; Music- 3x/week in Chapel, 1 for K-4 and 2 for G5-8; Foreign language- 3+; PE- 3+. **Outdoor education:** Week-long trips once a year for G5-8; international language trips. **Grading:** A-F, beginning in G6. **Average nightly homework:** "Varies by grade." Nothing assigned Friday is due Monday. Posted on the Internet: Yes. **Percentage of students participating in Johns Hopkins Center for Talented Youth Program:** Varies each year. **Other indicators of academic success:** N/P. **High schools attended by latest graduating class:** Bay, Branson, Bentley, Gateway, IHS, Lick, Lowell, SI, Stuart Hall, University, Groton, Cate, Deerfield, St. Albans, Thacher.

FACULTY
Ethnicity: 81% Caucasian (non-Latino), 10% Asian, 4% Latino, 2% African-American, 2% multi-racial, 1% other. **Percentage of teachers with graduate degrees:** 56%. **Percentage with current California credential:** 98%. **Faculty selection/training:** BA and 3 years experience required. **Teacher/student ratio:** 1:8. **Special subject teachers:** Science, Latin, art, computer, debate, band, music, Mandarin, Spanish, media, counselor, Upper School learning specialist, Lower School learning specialist, chaplain, PE, library, drama, research skills. **Average teacher tenure:** 9 years.

MIDDLE SCHOOL
Description: Begins In G5 when new students are added and then divided into 2 smaller groups. Two homerooms of 15-16 boys transition into a departmentalized schedule in G5. G6-8 are fully departmentalized including double periods once a week in all major disciplines, including art and science. The program is project-based with an emphasis on an integrated curriculum. Each boy has an advisor and meets with his advisor and parents in Parent Teacher conferences. **Teacher/student ratio:** 1:9. **Elective courses offered:** Varies per quarter. Courses have included Jazz Combo, Film Review, Golf, SSAT Prep Verbal, SSAT Prep Math, Digital Video, Strategy Games, Hoops, Bowling, Mah Jong, Creative Writing,

and Guitar Workshop. **Achievement tracking in:** Math G7-8; math enrichment G5-6. **Student social events:** (Coed) Debate Team with Hamlin, Math Olympiad with KDBS, and Invention Convention with Julia Morgan School for Girls. Community Service Projects throughout San Francisco arranged with each of the all girls' schools. Eighth grade dances twice a year with other independent schools; Play Day once a year with 4 other independent schools.

Student Support Services

No. of Licensed Counselors on staff: One full-time. Full-time Chaplain. **Counselor/student ratio:** N/A. **Learning specialists on staff:** Two. **Learning differences/disabilities support:** Parent group and 2 learning specialists on staff; parent education events. **High school placement support:** "The Head of the Upper School is the High School Placement Advisor and works extensively with parents and students to prepare for and manage the process, including SSAT prep, student interview and essay prep and counseling regarding appropriate choices. Students attend both local and boarding schools."

Student Conduct and Health

Code of conduct: "Cathedral School for Boys has very few formal rules. It is assumed that boys will conduct themselves in a manner respectful of the rights of others and appropriate to their own active membership in a school community. Boys are expected to: be mindful of their own and others' safety and well being, taking care to be friendly and kind all around; be respectful of others, of their work and property; be responsible for their belongings and accountable for their work; and courteously cooperate in the maintenance of good order and of an environment conducive to learning. Discipline at CSB is described as 'caring justice.' Caring justice fits the school's desire to create a safe, morally aware environment for all that respects the rights and needs of individuals. We believe that effective discipline combines clear, consistent expectations with compassion and sensitivity towards the unique lives of each boy, and we relate the disciplinary consequences to the action, not the boy." **Prevention education and awareness programs addressed in:** "A human development curriculum is being expanded to include appropriate health education at every grade level, including nutrition, adolescence, sex, drug and alcohol education. Advisory groups made up of 6-7 boys meet every week; outside speakers address these topics; and the physical education program also includes these topics."

ATHLETICS
Sports offered: G5-8 basketball (winter, ISAL), cross-country (fall, ISAL); G6-8 soccer (fall, ISAL), golf (spring, ISAL); G7-8 baseball, volleyball (spring, ISAL). There is a no-cut policy, and there are 2 teams or more per grade level. Golf and volleyball are dependent upon other league participants. **Team play begins in:** G5 (intramural).

CAMPUS/CAMPUS LIFE
Campus description: The north end of campus includes a large building containing 17 classrooms, a library, a science lab, an art studio, and a music studio. **Library:** Contains over 12,000 volumes, 17 computers, a full-time librarian and a full-time assistant. The south end of campus houses a large band room, 2 classrooms, a gym, cafeteria, stage and a large seminar style conference room. **Sports facilities:** Gymnasium, roof playground, Huntington Park. **Theater/Arts facilities:** Large room with a stage for plays, student council speeches, geography and spelling bee, events, Mandarin speech contest, assemblies, and parent education night speakers. **Computer lab:** Yes plus a Media lab. **Science lab:** Yes. **Lunch program:** Yes, included in tuition. "The school lunch program is organic, locally grown with dietary restrictions honored." **Bus service:** No. **Uniforms/dress code:** Uniforms. The school uniform is a blue shirt and grey pants with a navy sweater bearing the school crest. Upper School boys wear a school tie. **Opportunities for Community Service:** Every grade does community service, integrated in concert with each grade's curriculum. Students in G7-8 go off campus once a week for one quarter to various sites, i.e., retirement homes, tutoring in schools, environmental projects. There are food drives, special projects and other opportunities throughout the year that the student body is ready to help with, i.e. Katrina, Haiti.

EXTENDED DAY
Morning care: Begins at 7:30 a.m. **After-school care:** Until 6 p.m. **Grade levels:** K-6 (G7-8 by arrangement). **Cost:** $11/hour for regular care, pre-paid 2 times a year. **Drop-in care available:** Yes with 24 hrs. notice, or in an emergency. **Coverage over major holidays:** No coverage on Labor Day, Thanksgiving Thursday and Friday, President's Day, Martin Luther King, Jr. Day, and Memorial Day. Camps are offered during the 3 school breaks at Christmas, Winter Break in Feb. and Spring Break from 9 a.m.–5 p.m. **Homework help:** Yes, in a supervised study hall. **Snacks:** Provided, organic. **Staff/student ratio:** 1:10. **After-school classes:** Vary each quarter. Might include chess, fencing, violin, Aikido, science exploration, Lego robotics, piano, cooking, theater arts, movie

making. All students may take these classes, but boys in the extended day program have priority. Parents do not pay for extended care during class hours. **Cost:** "Varies."

Summer Programs

"The school offers a full summer program for both boys and girls. Review online and e-mail for additional information." **Cost:** N/P.

Parent Involvement

Parent/teacher communication: "Formal conferences are held twice during the school year, and informally, if necessary. Calls are returned promptly and e-mail is utilized as well. Homework is posted on the website. The website also provides school information, activities, and a newsletter weekly. Lower School teachers also send home a weekly newsletter." **Participation requirements:** N/A. **Parent education programs offered:** "Speakers, workshops and various discussion groups are held throughout the year, and sponsored by the school and the CSB Parent Association. These widely attended events are called Diversity Dialogues and Community Speaker Nights."

What Sets the School Apart From Others

"We are an Episcopal school which means that we are an inclusive community that embraces all religious backgrounds, and is made up of differences of all kinds, ethnic, cultural, and socio-economic. Our families include LGBT families, and many other combinations of loving adults raising children. We have a small ratio of student to teacher with a very intentional and differentiated way in which we teach to boys. Our faculty, who love and understand boys, does extensive continuing education, and we continue to learn from the latest research regarding education and the teaching of boys. The environment is warm, collegial and safe with an atmosphere of support and encouragement for every boy to succeed, finding his strengths, acknowledging his weaknesses, and giving his best."

How Families Characterize School

Parent comment(s): "By far the best aspect of our experience at CSB has been the care my son has received while progressing along his journey to find his personal passions. Expectations for each boy to achieve his absolute potential both as a student and as a human being will be a gift we will always treasure. The tremendous personal investment teachers extend to my son is something I never expected."

Student comment(s): "Whenever I need help in the classroom or outside, my teachers are there. It's hard to say which is my favorite because all my classes rock. Of course explosions in science are way cool."

CHILDREN'S DAY SCHOOL
333 Dolores Street (between 16th and 17th Sts.) (Mission/Castro)
San Francisco, CA 94110
(415) 861-5432 ext. 322 *fax (415) 861-5419*
www.cds-sf.org

Molly Huffman, Head of School
Diane Larrabee, Interim Director of Admission, dianel@cds-sf.org

GENERAL
Coed PS-8 day school. Founded in 1983. Independent. Nonprofit. **Member:** CAIS, NAIS. **Enrollment:** Approx. 335. **Average class size:** 22. **Accreditation:** CAIS (term N/P). **Endowment:** N/A. **School year:** Sept.-June. **School day:** 8:30 a.m. to 2:45 p.m. for K; 8:30 a.m. to 3 p.m. for G1-2; 8:30 to 3:15 p.m. for G3-4; and 8:15 a.m. to 3:30 p.m. for G5-8.

STUDENT BODY ETHNICITY
54% Caucasian (non-Latino), 27% multi-racial, 8% Latino, 7% Asian, 2% African-American, 2% Middle Eastern.

ADMISSION
Applications due: Jan. (call for date). **Application fee:** $75. **Application process:** Attend a tour or an evening open house in Oct.-Dec. Depending on the grade applying for and the number of openings, the applicant and his or her family may be invited for a visit. **No. of applications:** Approx. 100 (K-G8). **No. of K spaces:** Approx. 10-15. Percentage of K class made up of the school's own preschool class: Approx. 70%. **Admission evaluation requirements for K:** Teacher recommendation, student visit, parent interview. **Other grades:** Teacher recommendation(s), school records, student visit, parent interview. **Preferences:** Siblings and children of faculty/staff/trustees. **What sort of student do you best serve?** "The CDS educational and academic environment is designed to meet the needs of a wide range of children. Our students are happy, confident, curious children who are eager to learn. CDS students exhibit a high degree of social responsibility and routinely make a difference in the world around them. They work and learn collaboratively with other

students of all ages and are appreciative and respectful of differences in others. They show caring of themselves, others and their environment and are academically skilled with an average ERB score in the 90th percentile."

Costs

Latest tuition: $22,250. **Sibling discount:** None. **Tuition includes:** Books and all other required instructional expenses. Lunch: No; Transportation: No; Laptop computer: No; Other: N/P. **Tuition increases:** Approx. 5% annually. **Other costs:** None. **Percentage of students receiving financial aid:** 39%. **Financial aid application deadline:** Mid-Jan. (call for date). Financial aid is based on need. **Average grant:** $13,125. **Percentage of grants of half-tuition or more:** 67%. **Donations:** "It is our ongoing goal to encourage wide community ownership and investment in CDS. We rely on voluntary contributions to support our operating budget as well as to fund improvements to our school facility. Parents are encouraged to participate in our Annual Fund and other fundraising initiatives, and we ask that all families contribute at a level consistent with their financial capabilities."

School's Mission Statement

"Children's Day School recognizes that every child is born with unique gifts. Our mission is to develop each student's genius by providing an inspiring environment where challenging academics are inseparable from social, artistic, and physical experiences, and where children of all backgrounds feel safe to be themselves, become avid learners, and strive to make a difference in the lives of others. • Our Values: The Children's Day School community nourishes and celebrates diversity, promotes justice and respect for all people, and aspires to act always with integrity, compassion and generosity."

Academic Program

Philosophy: "Our educational program encourages curiosity, exploration, cooperation, risk-taking and a love of learning. It is integrated across academic disciplines and incorporates a project-based approach in which our students develop academic skills through inquiry and collaboration. Each day, teams of dedicated teachers guide our children to find the fun in every new task and to excel academically as they take increasing responsibility for their education and their future. Our students develop a sense of caring for self, for others, for the community and for the world as they become creative thinkers, skilled mathematicians, accomplished artists, strong writers and rigorous researchers. They graduate confident in their strengths, unafraid to struggle and prepared for the challenges and opportunities that await them." **Foreign languages:** Spanish PS-8. **Computer training:** Part of classroom instruction. **No. of computers available for students:** "Computers/laptops in each classroom." (N/P #). **No. of hours weekly of:** Art- 1-3, depending on grade; Drama- 3 (beginning in G5, offered as an elective); Music- 1-3, depending on grade; Computers- "varies by grade"; Foreign language- Spanish-speaking teacher in PS, 2-2.5 in K-4, depending on grade; 3 in G5-8: PE- 1.5-3 depending on grade. **Outdoor education:** "Varies by grade." **Grading:** A-F; letter grades begin in middle school (G6). **Average nightly homework:** 10 min. in G1; 20 min. in G2; 30 min. in G3; 40 min. in G4; 50-120 min. in G5-8. Posted on the Internet: Yes for G5-8. **Percentage of students participating in Johns Hopkins Center for Talented Youth Program:** N/A. **Other indicators of academic success:** "Our primary focus is daily evaluation in the classroom. Teachers create benchmarks for progress and assemble portfolios of student work to provide parents with concrete assessments of their child's progress in each academic discipline. Written progress reports are prepared 2-3 times a year and parent-teacher conferences are held twice a year. The ERB standardized test is given to students from third through eighth grades." **High schools attended by latest graduating class:** Drew, IHS, Lick, SF Waldorf, University, Urban, Lowell, MAT.

FACULTY

Ethnicity: 75% Caucasian (non-Latino), 9% Latino, 9% multi-racial, 7% Asian. **Percentage of teachers with graduate degrees:** 39%. **Percentage with current California credential:** 28%. **Faculty selection/training:** Bachelor's degree and teaching experience required, master's degree and teaching credential preferred. **Teacher/student ratio:** 1:8. **Special subject teachers:** Spanish, art, music, PE, drama, environmental education, community-based learning (service learning), learning specialists. **Average teacher tenure:** N/P.

MIDDLE SCHOOL

Description: "Our middle school (G5-8) emphasizes academic preparation for high school while continuing to instill in students a passion for learning. Such an emphasis provides students with the tools necessary for critical thinking, academic proficiency and intellectual development. Collaborative and independent study remain constants as students learn to reason in greater depth about increasingly abstract concepts. All middle school students participate in an advisory group once a week. Classes are subject-specific and taught by a math and science teacher and a humanities teacher; environmental education and community based learning are integrated throughout. PE and Spanish are taught to all students, four times a week." **Teacher/student ratio: 1:8. Elective courses offered:** Art, music, drama, photography, publications; Environmental Education. **Achievement tracking in:** N/A. **Student social events:** Dances, student leadership team, athletics, assemblies.

STUDENT SUPPORT SERVICES
No. of Licensed Counselors on staff: None. **Counselor/student ratio:** N/A. **Learning specialists on staff:** Two. **Learning differences/ disabilities support:** "At CDS, we know that all children learn differently. We have as many different kinds of learners as we have students, and we teach accordingly. CDS is committed to meeting a wide range of abilities, stimulating a range of interests and addressing a variety of needs. An effective parent-teacher partnership is critical for a child's success, and at CDS teachers and parents meet regularly to monitor each child's education. Teachers use a variety of methods to meet the needs of their diverse learners, including differentiation, skill development, formative and authentic assessment, and curriculum design. Our Learning Specialists become involved when an additional point of view or expertise seems necessary to help students fulfill their highest academic and social/emotional potential. Services provided by the CDS Learning Specialists include developing and monitoring educational plans, designing and implementing strategies and accommodations, and evaluating students to determine skill development and create support plans. We know that we cannot be effective with all children, but our experience has shown that we can be effective if children are taking responsibility for their own education, and the adults are properly organized to support this effort in ever-increasing degrees of complexity. Our admission process is designed to identify children and families with whom we think we can work effectively." **High school placement support:** "High school placement counseling."

STUDENT CONDUCT AND HEALTH
Code of conduct: "Our students honor three important guidelines for conduct: 1) take responsibility for yourself, as well as the social and physical environment, 2) be respectful at all times, no matter what, 3) use difficult situations to learn and grow. Limit-setting at CDS is the process of teaching and reminding what it takes to be a respectful and respected member of a group." **Prevention education and awareness addressed in:** Health and human sexuality begins in G3. Alcohol and drug education begins in middle school.

ATHLETICS
Sports offered: Coed volleyball, basketball, futsal (intermural). **Team play begins in:** G5 in PSAL.

CAMPUS/CAMPUS LIFE
Campus description: "Located across from historic Mission Dolores in San Francisco and nestled safely in the middle of the block behind Notre Dame Plaza, our campus has one of the largest outdoor schoolyard spaces in San Francisco. Bordered by palm trees, our sunny campus features an organic garden and farm, which is home to chickens and sheep. Equipped with swings, a climbing structure and sandbox, and a basketball court, our campus gives children a safe place to play freely, be themselves and explore the natural environment. The stately, Spanish-colonial style architecture of our main school building offers large, airy classrooms for students in grades K-8 as well as an art studio. The preschool, located in 3 bungalow classrooms adjacent to the farm and garden, has easy access to the large, sunny playground. An additional building adjacent to the main school campus was acquired in 2008 and houses the school library, the music classroom and administrative offices." **Library:** "Contains approx. 7,000 volumes." **Sports facilities:** No. The school uses the gymnasium at the neighboring Columbia Park Boys & Girls Club. **Theater/Arts facilities:** Art studio. Theater performances in neighboring churches or community spaces. **Computer lab:** No. Computers are in all the classrooms. **Science lab:** Yes. **Lunch program:** No. **Bus service:** No. The school is on and near major MUNI lines and BART. **Uniforms/dress code:** None. **Opportunities for community service:** "Service learning at CDS is education in action, combining experiential learning with community service. Guided by teachers and community members, our students address real community needs—both within and outside our own school community—by planning and executing service projects that are carefully tied to curricula. All projects are developmentally appropriate for the age groups involved."

EXTENDED DAY
Morning care: Begins at 7:30 a.m. **After-school care:** Until 6 p.m. **Grade levels:** K-8. **Cost:** Varies; ranges from $2.25 to $11/hour. **Drop-in care available:** Yes. **Coverage over major holidays:** "Some." **Homework help:** Yes. **Snacks:** Provided. **Staff/student ratio:** 1:10. **After-school classes:** "An integral component of our school community and open to all students in the Bay Area, our extended day program provides a comfortable, fun place for children to spend time after school. Taking full advantage of our protected acre of land, experienced teachers create

a dynamic environment that is fun and engaging, and provides ample time for play. Children may choose from a wide variety of organized, age-appropriate activities including enrichment classes taught by CDS teachers, community teachers and instructors from accredited local organizations such as chess, movie-making, gymnastics, science, art, yoga." **Cost:** "Varies."

Summer Programs
Open to all students in the Bay Area, the school offers four 2-week sessions for children in PS-8. Each session has a different theme. Each session includes outdoor activities and field trips. **Cost:** "Varies."

Parent Involvement
Parent/teacher communication: Two scheduled parent-teacher conferences/year, website, weekly all-school and classroom newsletters, regular e-mail, telephone and in-person communication. **Participation requirements:** "Parents are encouraged, but not required, to participate in the CDS community in some capacity during the school year. By getting involved, parents have the opportunity to develop deeper relationships with other parents and families, with their child's teachers and with the CDS staff. Plus, it's fun." **Parent education programs offered?** "Yes."

What Sets the School Apart From Others
"Preparing young people academically is the central function of all schools. At CDS, we believe that academic performance is not education itself, but the result of education, and that education is a process of leading each child's unique genius out into the world in ever widening circles of personal challenge and social complexity. We have established a culture of diversity in which children spend less time and energy trying to 'measure up' and instead—with our guidance—focus on discovering their own gifts, passions and unique genius. It is our goal at CDS to guide each child's unique genius out into the world. It is also our goal that in so doing, all of our students will: love learning; take responsibility for themselves, their community and the environment around them; think critically and creatively; show respect for themselves and others; and be academically prepared."

How Families Characterize School
Parent comment(s): "CDS instills an excitement and enthusiasm for learning simply by making it so much fun. I love that my daughter loves to go to school and feels such pride in the school." • "The teachers are great—knowledgeable, warm and caring professionals."

Student comment(s):
"The best part of CDS is the great teachers." • "CDS is a place where you can express yourself, learn to the fullest and have people around who support you. The education lets you work how you want to, and the teachers really want you to succeed." • "CDS is a school where you are allowed to express yourself. Teachers listen to you and your ideas, and students treat you the way you want to be treated. Everyone is respectful and everyone is respected." • "CDS is amazing. I've had so many good experiences here. I love this school; they let you be yourself."

CHINESE AMERICAN INTERNATIONAL SCHOOL
Main Campus: 150 Oak Street (between Gough and Franklin Sts.) (Hayes Valley)
San Francisco, CA 94102
(415) 865-6000 *fax (415) 865-6089*
Pre-K Campus: 42/52 Waller Street (at Octavia)
San Francisco, CA 94102
(415) 655-9362
www.cais.org

Dr. Jeff Bissell, Head of School
Linda Vann-Adibé, Director of Admission, lv_adibe@cais.org

GENERAL
Coed PK-8 day school. Founded in 1981. Independent. Nonsectarian. Nonprofit. **Member:** NAIS, CAIS, BADA. **Enrollment:** Approx. 460. **Average class size:** 18 in Pre-K, 19 in K, 19 in G1-5, 20 in G6-8. **Accreditation:** WASC (6 year term: 2008-14). **Endowment:** N/P. **School year:** Sept.-June. **School day:** 8.45 a.m.-3.15 p.m. for Pre-K; 8:30 a.m. to 3:30 p.m. for K; 8 a.m. to 3 p.m. for G1-5; and 8 a.m. to 3:30 p.m. for G6-8.

STUDENT BODY ETHNICITY
43% Asian/Asian American, 35% multi-racial, 20% Caucasian (non-Latino), 1% Latino, 1% African-American.

ADMISSION
Applications due: Dec. (call for date). **Application fee:** $100. **Application process:** Admission events, Tour/information session, application and evaluation of applicants. **No. of applications:** N/P. Percentage of class made up of school's preschool class: 66%. **Admission**

evaluation requirements for K: Evaluation and current school/teacher recommendations. **Other grades:** One-day visit, evaluation, current school/teacher recommendations. **Preferences:** Siblings. **What sort of student do you best serve?** "CAIS welcomes all families interested in providing and supporting their children with a Mandarin immersion and multicultural learning experience."

COSTS

Latest tuition: $21,010. **Sibling discount:** None. **Tuition includes:** Lunch: No; Transportation: No; Laptop computers: Yes; Other: Morning extended care from 7.30 a.m. **Tuition increases:** "Annually" (N/P %). **Other costs:** $250 Outdoor Education fee for G6-8. **Percentage of students receiving financial aid:** Approx. 25%. **Financial aid application deadline:** Mid-Jan. (call for date). Financial aid is based on need. **Average grant:** $7,400. **Percentage of grants of half-tuition or more:** N/P. **Donations:** N/P.

SCHOOL'S MISSION STATEMENT

"Our mission at Chinese American International School is to educate students for academic excellence, moral character, and international perspective through immersion in American and Chinese culture and language."

ACADEMIC PROGRAM

Philosophy: "The CAIS program prepares students to be bilingual, biliterate and bicultural when they graduate; demonstrate intellectual curiosity that inspires a lifelong love of learning; act with civility and compassion, and respect diverse beliefs and cultures; contribute to society, family, and peers out of a sincere desire to be of service, and exhibit diligence, resiliency, integrity and self respect; be committed to preserving the global environment and improving the human condition." **Foreign languages:** Mandarin. **Computer training:** Yes. **No. of computers available for students:** Computers and laptops are available in each class. **No. of hours weekly of:** Art- 1; Music- 1; Computers- 1; Foreign language- N/P ("students spend half of the day with an English-speaking teacher and the other half with a native, Mandarin Chinese-speaking teacher"); PE- 2. **Outdoor education:** "Yes." **Grading:** Letter grades begin in G6. **Average nightly homework:** "Appropriate for grade level starting in G1." Posted on the Internet: Yes. Percentage of students participating Johns Hopkins Center for Talented Youth Program: N/P. **Other indicators of academic success:** "Our students have placed first numerous times in MATHCOUNTS competitions, science fairs, and

Chinese speech contests." **High schools attended by latest graduating class:** N/P. High schools admitted: University, Lick, Lowell, SI, IHS, Urban, Drew, Bay, SHCP, MA, SOTA.

FACULTY

Ethnicity: 57% Asian/Asian American, 42% Caucasian (non-Latino), 1% multi-racial. **Percentage of teachers with graduate degrees:** N/P. **Percentage of teacher with current California credential:** N/P. **Faculty selection/training:** "Ongoing professional development." **Teacher/student ratio:** 1:9 in PreK-K, 1:9 in G1-5, 1:13 in G6-8. **Special subject teachers:** Art, music and movement, science, computer technology, Chinese brush painting, drama. **Average teacher tenure:** N/P.

MIDDLE SCHOOL

Description: In middle school (G6-8), students spend 35% in Mandarin each day—in a combined Chinese Humanities program. The remaining core subjects—English Humanities, Mathematics, and Science are taught in English by specialists. Students also attend classes in computer technology, art, music, dance, PE. **Teacher/student ratio:** 1:13. **Elective courses offered:** Chinese brush painting, Chinese dance, Chinese Music Ensemble, Art, Music, Computer Technology in G7-8, and an annual Shanghai Student Exchange Program for G8 in which CAIS students live with their Chinese host families for 2 weeks and host their Chinese "buddies" who stay with them in San Francisco. **Achievement tracking in:** N/P. **Student social events:** An elected student government organizes student dances and spirit days, celebrations of cultural events, and community service in partnership with the school.

STUDENT SUPPORT SERVICES

No. of Licensed Counselors on staff: One full-time and one part-time. **Counselor/student ratio:** N/P. **Learning specialists on staff:** "Two Reading Specialists and one bilingual Learning Specialist. Chinese language Support (CLA) and English language Support (ELA) programs in place." **Learning differences/disabilities support:** "The Students Services department ensures that all children are fully supported. Students requiring special accommodations to the program will have a Student Services Plan to ensure that the child receives consistent support from his/her teachers and parents. The school's program ensures that children who are able to manage their personal learning styles thrive best at CAIS." **High school placement support:** "The CAIS High School Placement Office provides information about local and national high schools; guides students and parents towards appropriate school choices; facilitates attendance to local fairs and events; acts as a liaison between parents, students and high school personnel; and ultimately advocates for students."

STUDENT CONDUCT AND HEALTH
Code of conduct: "CAIS students are taught to appreciate differences, respect diversity, be honest, be kind, be respectful, and be safe." **Prevention education and awareness addressed in:** "The school has a middle school advisory class with a small group environment where pre-teen topics can be discussed openly with the guidance of an advisor. Health Education with an outside specialist in G5-8. Outside speakers present topics such as Internet safety."

ATHLETICS
Sports offered: Volleyball, basketball, handball, softball, soccer, swimming, cross-country, triathlon, futsal. **Team play begins in:** K.

CAMPUS/CAMPUS LIFE
Campus description: The International Schools Campus is located at the corner of Oak and Franklin Streets and is home to CAIS, FAIS, and IHS. A new separate PK Campus was opened in Sept. 2009 at 42/52 Waller Street, about a 10 minute walk from main campus. **Library:** Two libraries. Staffed with a Library Media Specialist. Contains 14,950 titles with 17,370 holdings, 3,250 of which are Mandarin Chinese titles, including 125 videotapes and 200 DVDs. **Sports facilities:** Gymnasium. **Theater/Arts facilities:** One Art Studio and a Performing Art Studio. **Computer lab:** Yes. **Science lab:** Yes, 3. **Lunch program:** Yes, vendor provided. **Bus service:** No. **Uniforms/dress code:** None. **Opportunities for community service:** "The main goal of the CAIS community service program is to establish a tradition of giving back to one's community. The program is facilitated through advisory classes and curriculum projects in middle school. Students are encouraged to initiate their own community service activities. Emphasis is placed on serving the local Chinese-speaking community."

EXTENDED DAY
Morning care: Begins at 7:30 a.m. **After-school care:** Until 6 p.m. **Grade levels:** PK-8. **Cost:** $250/month, $80/week, $20/day. **Drop-in care available:** Yes. **Coverage over major holidays:** Yes. **Homework help:** Yes. **Snacks:** Provided for PK and K. **Staff/student ratio:** 1:10. **After-school classes:** "Examples of enrichment program include

Chinese and Western cultural classes, visual and performing arts, chess, math games, martial arts, pottery, dance, music." **Cost:** Approx. $250/10 week session.

SUMMER PROGRAMS

"Mandarin Immersion Camp gives students an opportunity to begin, develop and utilize their Mandarin-speaking abilities through immersion-based activities such as singing, Chinese calligraphy, dance, arts and crafts, martial arts, cooking, and everyday conversation. Students with little or no Mandarin skills are welcome."

PARENT INVOLVEMENT

Parent/teacher communication: Two Parent/Teacher conferences are available per year and as needed. Weekly classroom communication via Thursday Envelope. Parents and staff receive Thursday Flash, a semimonthly newsletter sent via e-mail. **Participation requirements:** Each parent is expected to contribute a minimum of 20 volunteer hours per student per year, and to contribute financially to the annual fund. **Parent education programs offered?** Yes.

WHAT SETS THE SCHOOL APART FROM OTHERS

"CAIS is the nation's leader in pre-collegiate Mandarin Chinese and English language immersion education. As an independent elementary and middle school, it offers immersion education in Mandarin Chinese and English to students from PK (age 3) through eighth grade. Most schools and weekend programs teach Chinese language arts only. CAIS teaches the core subjects—math, social studies and language arts—in both English and Mandarin. By learning through instruction in each language for half of each day, CAIS students learn to speak, read, write and understand both English and Mandarin Chinese fluently."

HOW FAMILIES CHARACTERIZE SCHOOL

Parent comment(s): "We loved CAIS when we were touring the school. We love it more now that we are part of the CAIS community. The teachers are amazing and have exceeded all our expectations. Our daughter loves CAIS too and we are in awe of how much she has learned." • "The kids really take to learning Mandarin. I'm a parent who doesn't speak Chinese at all, but my daughter has learned to do her Chinese homework independently, in school and without me. I'm very proud when I hear her speak Chinese–our friends who live in China tell me her accent is perfect."

Student comment(s): "My experience at CAIS has been a wonderful and wholesome journey of fun and education. I really enjoyed having a one on one conversation with teachers during independent study. The teachers are very open, and it is comfortable speaking about my own opinions or asking questions. I also enjoy how CAIS gives me a lot of options in trying new things and in doing what I do best during wheel classes. For instance, I wasn't really sure about taking brush painting class, but when I tried it out, I loved it. I have had a great time attending CAIS and I hope that everyone enjoys their own journey at CAIS too!" "CAIS has a great, fun, supportive, and unique environment to learn and grow. Through the years I've actually looked forward to and been excited about school. Learning a new language has been amazing, and it is a treasure I will always value."

CONVENT OF THE SACRED HEART ELEMENTARY SCHOOL

2222 Broadway (between Webster and Fillmore) (Pacific Heights)
San Francisco, CA 94115
(415) 563-2900 *fax (415) 929-6928* (Admissions)
www.sacredsf.org

Anne Wachter, RSCJ, Head of School, wachter@sacredsf.org
Pamela Thorp, Director of Admission, thorp@sacredsf.org

GENERAL

Girls K-8 day school. Founded in 1887. Independent, Catholic. Convent of the Sacred Heart Elementary School along with Stuart Hall for Boys, Convent of the Sacred Heart High School and Stuart Hall High School, is one of the four Schools of the Sacred Heart in San Francisco. Nonprofit. **Member:** CAIS, Network of Sacred Heart Schools, NAIS, NCGS, NCEA, ERB, CASE, BADA. **Enrollment:** 324. **Average class size:** 15-20. **Accreditation:** CAIS/WASC (6-year term: 2005-11), Network of Sacred Heart Schools. **Endowment:** $12 million. **School year:** Sept.-June. **School day:** 8:15 a.m. to 2:45 p.m. Mon.-Thurs. for K. Dismissal for G1-8 is staggered between 3 p.m. and 3:30 p.m. Friday dismissal for K is 2 p.m. and for G1-8 is staggered between 2:15 p.m. and 2:45 p.m.

STUDENT BODY ETHNICITY
"22% students of color."

ADMISSION

Applications due: Mid-Dec. for K, for G1-8, early Jan. (call for dates). **Application fee:** $100. **Application process:** Parent tours are held 2 hours on a weekday morning beginning in late Sept. The Head of School meets with parents for a question and answer period during the tour. Parents are also invited to meet with the Head of School when their child attends the playgroup activity. **No. of applications:** N/P. **No. of K spaces:** 40. **Percentage of K class made up of school's preschool class:** N/A. **Admission evaluation requirements for K:** Applicants must be 5 years old by Aug. 1. Assessment for readiness to begin the full-day program offered by the school includes both an individual screening and a playgroup date. Preschool evaluations are also part of each child's application. **Other grades:** Includes a parent tour, teacher recommendation, previous grades and testing. **Preferences:** Siblings receive priority consideration. **What sort of student do you best serve?** "Students and families who will support the school's Mission Statement."

COSTS

Latest tuition: $23,750. **Sibling discount:** None. **Tuition includes:** Lunch: No; Transportation: No; Laptop computer: No; Other: N/P. **Tuition increases:** Approx. 6% annually; **Other Costs:** Approx. $200 for K uniform including shoes. Uniforms are also available through school's thrift shop, Seconds-To-Go. **Percentage of students receiving financial aid:** 11%. **Financial aid application deadline:** Jan. (call for date). Financial aid is based on need. **Average grant:** N/P. **Percentage of grants of half-tuition or more:** N/P. **Donations:** Parents are solicited to participate in annual giving; participation is voluntary.

SCHOOL'S MISSION STATEMENT

"Founded in 1887 as an independent Catholic school, Schools of the Sacred Heart, San Francisco, carry on the educational mission of the Religious of the Sacred Heart. We share with the other members of the nationwide Network of Sacred Heart Schools five common goals and the commitment to educate to: A personal and active faith in God; A deep respect for intellectual values; A social awareness which impels to action; The building of community as a Christian value; Personal growth in an atmosphere of wise freedom. A K-12, four-school complex, Schools of the Sacred Heart, San Francisco offer the unique experience of single-sex education within a coed community. Students are expected to achieve their highest level of scholarship while learning to assume leadership roles as responsible, compassionate and contributing members of society."

ACADEMIC PROGRAM

Philosophy: "Convent students are engaged in a process designed to encourage experimentation, introspection and effort. Rigorous academics in a collaborative atmosphere create an optimal learning environment. The curriculum between and within grade levels is clearly defined and articulated, enabling students to move from grade to grade experiencing continuity, growth and a sense of appreciation for and knowledge of their own individual learning styles. The emphasis is always on the student as an individual with her unique gifts and talents to explore and contribute. Learning takes place both in and out of the classroom, providing the intellectual impetus that stimulates achievement." **Foreign languages:** French, Spanish beginning in G3. Latin is mandatory in G6. **Computer training:** Yes, K-8. **No. of computers available for students:** Approx. 175 "state-of-the-art computers." Computers are located in the Unkefer Computer Lab, the elementary school library and laptop carts in each building. **No. of hours weekly of:** Art- N/P; Drama- N/P; Music- N/P; Computers- N/P; Foreign language- N/P, PE- N/P. **Outdoor education:** "Yes." **Grading:** Narrative reports in K-5. Letter grades in G6-8. **Average nightly homework:** "Varies by grade." Posted on the Internet: Yes, G6-8. **Percentage of students participating in Johns Hopkins Center for Talented Youth Program:** N/P. **Other indicators of academic success:** "Convent Elementary School graduates are well prepared for their high school experience. They maintain high academic standards and participate in the full life of high school including sports, clubs and leadership roles in student government." **High schools attended by latest graduating class:** Convent, Lick, University, SI, SHCP, Thacher, Branson, MA, Redwood, IHS, Drew.

FACULTY

Ethnicity: N/P. **Percentage of teachers with graduate degrees:** 61%. **Percentage with current California credential:** N/P. **Faculty selection/training:** "Experience, college degree and/or credential. Professional teacher development is an integral part of the school's program." **Teacher/student ratio:** 1:10 in the Lower Form; 1:15-20 in the Middle Form. **Special subject teachers:** Art, music, computers, religion, foreign language, music, PE and the after-school program, which includes private instrumental music lessons in piano, violin, guitar. **Average teacher tenure:** 9 years.

MIDDLE SCHOOL

Description: "The core curriculum builds on knowledge gained in the Lower Form, moving the students into increasingly comprehensive and rigorous academic study. Writing, both creative and expository, is emphasized in all subject areas. Convent students build upon their experience in a science lab and the scientific method of discovery. All students complete Algebra 1 in the G8. Collaboration between the departments enhances in-depth studies. The values of citizenship continue to be stressed through the Goals and Criteria of Sacred Heart Education. A strong esprit de corps defines the atmosphere for students and faculty within each classroom and across the school. Departmentalization begins in G7." **Teacher/student ratio:** 1:15-20. **Elective courses offered:** No. **Achievement tracking in:** None. **Student social events:** With Stuart Hall for Boys: Dances, drama club and the after-school program including orchestra.

STUDENT SUPPORT SERVICES
No. of Licensed Counselors on staff: One full-time and 1 part-time consultant. **Counselor/student ratio:** N/P. **Learning specialists on staff:** One full-time and 2 part-time. **Learning differences/disabilities support:** "Educational resources as needed." **High school placement support:** The Head of School and Dean of the Middle Form counsel students and their families.

STUDENT CONDUCT AND HEALTH
Code of conduct: "As articulated in the Goals and Criteria of Sacred Heart Schools." **Prevention education and awareness addressed in:** Health classes mandatory in K-8.

ATHLETICS
Sports offered: Volleyball, cross-country, basketball, soccer, golf, fitness. **Team play begins in:** G5 (intermural). Convent Elementary School belongs to the Bay Area Interscholastic Athletic League (BAIAL) and the Catholic Youth Organization (CYO).

CAMPUS/CAMPUS LIFE
Campus description: Convent Elementary School occupies the former Grant House and Herbst House and is located on the same campus as Stuart Hall for Boys and Convent High School. Stuart Hall High School is located several blocks away at Pine and Octavia. **Library:** Houses 27,600 volumes including fiction, non-fiction and reference books, periodicals, audiobooks, videos, DVDs and computers. **Sports facilities:** Gymnasium with a basketball court and running track. **Theater/Arts facilities:** Two theaters. The Syufy Theater is used for school presentations including plays, musical presentations and guest

lectures. The Siboni Arts and Science Center houses all the art, music and science classrooms for Convent Elementary School, Stuart Hall for Boys and Convent High School. **Computer lab:** Yes. **Science lab:** Yes. **Lunch program:** Yes. **Bus service:** No. **Uniforms/dress code:** Uniforms. **Opportunities for community service:** "From its inception, Sacred Heart education has had a deep and abiding commitment to social service. Convent Elementary School students involve themselves in community service through classroom projects, fundraisers and active on-site work. The development of social awareness and the expectation to become involved in responsible social action is an integral part of the Sacred Heart program for all students. Community service cultivates a spirit of cooperation and collaboration and fosters a comprehension of leadership today and tomorrow."

EXTENDED DAY
Morning care: Begins at 7:30 a.m. **After-school care:** Until 6 p.m. (coed). **Grade levels:** K-4. **Cost:** No charge for a.m. care. For a 5 p.m. pick up, $3,400/year; for a 6 p.m. pickup, $4,400/year. **Drop-in care available:** Yes. **Coverage over major holidays:** No. **Homework help:** Yes. **Snacks:** Provided. **Staff/student ratio:** Average 1:10. **After-school classes:** Coed for students in K-8, these have included Italian, robotics, fencing, art, sports, chess, gymnastics, cooking, creative writing, SSAT preparation and debate club. The after-school program for middle school students is available on a drop-in basis at no charge until 6 p.m. Music lessons are also available. **Cost:** "Varies."

SUMMER PROGRAMS
Classes are coeducational and include sports camp for G3-8 and academic and enrichment classes for G7-8. **Cost:** "Varies."

PARENT INVOLVEMENT
Parent/teacher communication: Conferences are scheduled twice yearly and as needed. Parents also utilize e-mail, the Schools' website, eThursday Notes and Lower Form monthly grade level newsletters. **Participation requirements:** Parents are encouraged to volunteer for activities assisting with the Schools' annual fundraising activity auction/ dinner and Saturday family-fest, creating gift items for the boutique as well as assisting with phoning and mailings. Parents also volunteer to help on class field trips and in the school library. **Parent education programs offered?** Yes.

What Sets the School Apart From Others

"Among the oldest independent schools in California, Schools of the Sacred Heart are a part of a worldwide network of Sacred Heart Schools having their beginnings in the Society of the Sacred Heart founded in Paris in 1800. Our independent Catholic school draws on the rich tradition of Sacred Heart education worldwide, including strong intellectual challenge, faith development, social awareness and growth of the individual as a community member. Convent Elementary School offers the benefits of single sex education in a coed environment and prepares girls to assume leadership responsibilities as intelligent, compassionate, self-confident and contributing members of society."

How Families Characterize School

Parent comment(s): "Convent is a very loving and welcoming community. My children have received an excellent education. The teachers are very involved and build great relationships with the students."

Student comment(s): "I love my classes and my friends at school. My teachers are very nice. It's fun to have the Stuart Hall boys next door."

Corpus Christi School

75 Francis Street (at Alemany Blvd.) (Outer Mission)
San Francisco, CA 94112
(415) 587-7014 *fax (415) 587-1575*
www.corpuschristisf.org

Sister Martina Ponce, Head of School, fmaccsf@aol.com

General

Coed K-8 parochial day school. Founded in 1928 under the supervision of the Salesian Fathers and the tutelage of the Sisters of St. Joseph of Orange. Since 1974 supervised by Salesian Sisters of St. John Bosco. Catholic. Nonprofit. **Member:** N/P. **Enrollment:** Approx. 200. **Average class size:** 22-25. **Accreditation:** WASC (6-year term: 2010-16). **Endowment:** N/P. **School year:** Aug.-June. **School day:** 8 a.m. to 3 p.m.

Student Body Ethnicity

56% Asian, 33% Latino, 1% Caucasian (non-Latino), 1% other, 1% African-American, 8% multi-racial.

ADMISSION

Applications due: Jan.-Aug. (call for date). **Application fee:** $50. **Application process:** Kindergarten applicants are tested on a set Saturday and on weekdays for those not able to come on the set date; G1-8 have whole day classroom visits. **No. of applications:** 50. **No. of K spaces:** 35. **Percentage of K class made up of school's preschool class:** N/A. **Admission evaluation requirements for K:** Test. **Other grades:** Test, school records and school visit. **Preferences:** Siblings. **What sort of student do you best serve?** "Students who want to learn."

COSTS

Latest tuition: $4,700. **Sibling discount:** Yes (amount N/P). **Tuition includes:** Lunch: No; Transportation: No; Laptop computer: Yes; Other: None. **Tuition increases:** Less than 1% annually. **Other costs:** Approx. $380 for general fee and $100 for registration fee. **Percentage of students receiving financial aid:** 48%. **Financial aid application deadline:** Approx. Feb. 28 (call for date) for Archdiocese of San Francisco and April 15 (call for date) for the BASIC Fund. Financial aid is based on need. **Average grant:** N/P. **Percentage of grants of half-tuition or more:** 50%. **Donations:** N/P.

SCHOOL'S MISSION STATEMENT

"Corpus Christi Catholic School is dedicated to the service and nurturance of the young in all its forms: academic/intellectual, spiritual/psychological, moral/social, and physical. We strive to promote human and Gospel values, educating in the Salesian method of joy, friendliness and sense of belonging. We celebrate the ethnic diversity of the various communities with whom we work and strive to ensure a safe, supportive environment for children to grow and learn, inspired by the attitude of 'Hand in Hand, Together We Can.'"

ACADEMIC PROGRAM

Philosophy: "Corpus Christi Catholic School draws enlightenment and inspiration from the life example and educational method of St. John Bosco, upon which the Salesian charism is founded. The philosophy finds its deepest roots in this educational system, which focuses on reason, religion, and loving-kindness which helps create a positive attitude of joy and friendliness together with a firm insistence that students demonstrate personal responsibility, discipline, academic excellence, and respect towards all God's creation. • The goal of Corpus Christi Catholic School is to engage in the holistic development of each student, the academic/intellectual, spiritual/psychological, moral/social and physical. The teachers, as the key facilitators of learning, encourage the students to reach their potential to become active and responsible citizens, as well as responsible stewards of all God's creation. **Foreign languages:** N/P. **Computer training:** N/P. **No. of computers available for students:** 80 laptops. **No. of hours weekly of:** Art- .75; Drama- none; Music- .75; Computers- N/P ("varies, with classes having access to computer lab and 4 mobile laptop classroom labs each with 20 computers"); Foreign language- none; PE- 1. **Outdoor education:** "Yes." **Grading:** A-F, beginning in G1. **Average nightly homework:** "1-2 hrs. and more for G6-8." Posted on the Internet: Yes for G1-8. **Percentage of students participating in Johns Hopkins Center for Talented Youth Program:** N/A. **Other indicators of academic success:** "1) to provide for Curriculum Planning for Language Arts Skills Enhancement; 2) to provide moral and spiritual formation of the family; 3) to create a strategic plan for the school." **High schools attended by latest graduating class:** SI, SHCP, Riordan, Mercy-SF, ICA, Notre Dame, Westmoor, Lowell, El Camino, Serra, Lincoln.

FACULTY
Ethnicity: 60% Caucasian (non-Latino), 30% Asian, 10% Latino. **Percentage of teachers with graduate degrees:** 95%. **Percentage with current California credential:** 90%. **Faculty selection/training:** "Degree." **Teacher/student ratio:** 1:21. **Special subject teachers:** Five (subjects N/P). **Average teacher tenure:** N/P.

MIDDLE SCHOOL
Description: G6-8, departmentalized. **Teacher/student ratio:** 1:30. **Elective courses offered:** N/P. **Achievement tracking in:** Accelerated math and reading; online Alex Math program. **Student social events:** "Five per year."

STUDENT SUPPORT SERVICES
No. of Licensed Counselors on staff: N/A. **Counselor/student ratio:** N/A. **Learning specialists on staff:** One. **Learning differences/ disabilities support:** N/P. **High school placement support:** N/P.

STUDENT CONDUCT AND HEALTH
Code of conduct: "Written in the Family and Student Handbooks." **Prevention education and awareness programs addressed in:** "Taught informally by the homeroom teachers."

ATHLETICS
Sports offered: Basketball, volleyball, baseball. **Team play begins in:** G3.

CAMPUS/CAMPUS LIFE
Campus description: "The school is a 2-story building with 9 spacious classes." **Library:** Yes, computerized with scanning system (N/P volumes). **Sports facilities:** The school has 3 yards. The upper yard has 3 basketball courts with a removable volleyball court; the middle yard has 2 basketball courts with a removable volleyball court; and the lower yard has 4 basketball courts. **Theater/Arts facilities:** N/P. **Computer lab:** Yes, 2. **Science lab:** Yes. **Lunch program:** $4/lunch. **Bus service:** No. **Uniform/dress code:** Uniforms. **Opportunities for community service:** Yes.

EXTENDED DAY
Morning care: Students may arrive by 7 a.m. **After-school care:** Until 6 p.m. **Grade levels:** K-8. **Cost:** $8 flat fee from 3-6 p.m. and $15 flat fee from 1-6 p.m. **Drop-in care available:** Yes. **Coverage over major holidays:** No. **Homework help:** Yes for K-8. **Snacks:** Provided. **Staff/student ratio:** 1:10. **After-school classes:** Math and reading. **Cost:** N/P.

SUMMER PROGRAMS
The school offers a summer program with math and language arts classes. **Cost:** $500 for 5 weeks.

PARENT INVOLVEMENT
Parent/teacher communication: Conferences, website, e-mail, newsletter. **Participation requirements:** Parents and guardians are required to participate in the parent-teacher conferences held twice a year. **Parent education programs offered:** Parent education and technology programs are offered during monthly parent meetings.

WHAT SETS THE SCHOOL APART FROM OTHERS
"We are in the heart of the Mission District. The School is involved in community service projects throughout the year."

HOW FAMILIES CHARACTERIZE SCHOOL
Parent comment(s): "Great family spirit reigns."
Student comment(s): "Everyone knows everybody."

THE DISCOVERY CENTER SCHOOL

1442 Fulton Avenue
San Francisco, CA 94117
(415) 724-7458
www.dcssf.com

Jan Taylor, Head of School and Officer of Admissions, jantaylor2007@
gmail.com

GENERAL
Coed K-12 day school. Founded in 1970. Independent. Proprietary. **Member:** N/A. **Enrollment:** Approx. 90. **Average class size:** 12. **Accreditation:** NIPSA (N/P term). **Endowment:** N/A. **School year:** Sept.-June. **School day:** 8:30 a.m. to 3 p.m.

STUDENT BODY ETHNICITY
60% Caucasian (non-Latino), 10% Asian, 10% Latino, 5% African-American, 10%, multi-racial; 5% other.

ADMISSION
Applications due: Rolling admissions. **Application fee:** $100. **Application process:** N/P. **No. of applications:** N/P. **No. of K spaces:** 24. **Percentage of K class made up of school's preschool class:** N/A. **Admission evaluation requirements for K:** Visit and screening. **Other grades:** Grades, interview, testing, screening. **Preferences:** None. **What sort of student do you best serve?** "Students with motivated parents."

COSTS
Latest tuition: $9,000. **Sibling discount:** 50%. **Tuition includes:** Lunch: No; Transportation: "Some"; Laptop computer: No; Other: Snack. **Tuition increases:** N/A. **Other costs:** Approx. $300 for books and supplies. **Percentage of students receiving financial aid:** 20%. **Financial aid application deadline:** On-going. Financial aid is based on: N/P. **Average grant:** $4,500. **Percentage of grants of half-tuition or more:** 25%. **Donations:** Voluntary.

SCHOOL'S MISSION STATEMENT
"The Discovery Center School provides a caring and positive learning environment while preparing each student for college."

ACADEMIC PROGRAM

Philosophy: "Each student is an individual with unique talents, achievements, and capabilities. With that in mind, a full traditional comprehensive program is offered. Each student is provided the maximum chance for success." **Foreign languages:** Spanish, French. **Computer training:** Yes. **No. of computers available for students:** N/P. **No. of hours weekly of:** Art- 5; Drama- 2; Music- 3; Computers- 5; Foreign language- 5; PE- 5 ("varies"). **Outdoor education:** "Once yearly." **Grading:** A-F, beginning in K. **Average nightly homework:** 1 hour. Posted on the Internet: N/P. **Percentage of students participating in Johns Hopkins Center for Talented Youth Program:** N/P. **Other indicators of academic success:** "97% of graduates have continued on to the best colleges and universities world-wide." **High schools attended by latest graduating class:** Serra, Drew, Lick, Lowell, Wherry.

FACULTY

Ethnicity: 50% Caucasian (non-Latino), 20% Asian, 20% Latino, 10% African-American. **Percentage of teachers with graduate degrees:** 75%. **Percentage with current California credential:** 90%. **Faculty selection/training:** "Credential, experience, in-house." **Teacher/student ratio:** 1:12. **Special subject teachers:** 3 (subjects N/P). **Average teacher tenure:** 8 years.

MIDDLE SCHOOL

Description: "Comprehensive program, college preparatory." **Teacher/student ratio:** 1:12. **Elective courses offered:** "Enrichment in all areas." **Achievement tracking in:** All subject areas. **Student social events:** Parties, dances, performances.

STUDENT SUPPORT SERVICES

No. of Licensed Counselors on staff: One. **Counselor/student ratio:** 1:12. **Learning specialists on staff:** N/A. **Learning differences/disabilities support:** N/A. **High school placement support:** "The Discovery Center School has an excellent reputation and assists placing students in the best high schools. In addition, students may continue on at DCS to finish high school in the college preparatory program."

STUDENT CONDUCT AND HEALTH

Code of conduct: "We expect respect shown to students, teachers and parents." **Prevention education and awareness programs:** "We encourage abstinence in drugs, sex, etc., while informing students in all areas."

ATHLETICS: N/P.

CAMPUS/CAMPUS LIFE
Campus description: "Although DCS is not church affiliated, we have rented rooms above a large church." **Library:** N/P. **Sports facilities:** N/P. **Theater/Arts facilities:** The school uses the main building for theater performances. **Computer lab:** No. **Science lab:** No. **Lunch program:** No. "We encourage students to bring lunch." **Bus service:** "Some." **Uniforms/dress code:** "Casual dress code." **Opportunities for community service:** "Work on campus or at another private school site."

EXTENDED DAY
Morning care: Begins at 7 a.m. **After-school care:** Until 6 p.m. **Grade levels:** All. **Cost:** $9/day. **Drop-in care available:** Yes. **Coverage over major holidays:** Yes. **Homework help:** Yes. **Snacks:** Provided. **Staff/student ratio:** 1:12. **After-school classes:** Art, music, etc. **Cost:** Included in $9/day.

SUMMER PROGRAMS
Summer Odyssey runs from June through Aug. It includes a combination of academics and activities including field trips. **Cost:** $200/week plus field trip entrance fees, if any.

PARENT INVOLVEMENT
Parent/teacher communication: Conferences, website, e-mail, newsletter, phone. **Participation requirements:** None. **Parent education programs offered?** No.

WHAT SETS THE SCHOOL APART FROM OTHERS
"The school accomplishes the task of preparing each student for college. The atmosphere is positive and supportive. The result is a happy, well-educated individual. We have small class sizes and caring teachers. The rules harken back to the 50s where students led more simple lives and kids could be kids."

HOW FAMILIES CHARACTERIZE SCHOOL
Parent comment(s): "The best!"
Student comment(s): "This is our home."

Ecôle Notre Dame des Victoires (NDV)

659 Pine Street (at Grant Avenue) (Chinatown/Financial District)
San Francisco, CA 94108
(415) 421-0069 *fax (415) 421-1440*
www.ndvsf.org

Mary Ghisolfo, Principal, principal@ndvsf.org
Desiree Almendares, Director of Admissions, admissions@ndvsf.org

General

Coed K-8 parochial day school. Founded in 1924. Roman Catholic. Nonprofit. **Member:** NCEA. **Enrollment:** Approx. 280 students. **Average class size:** 32. **Accreditation:** WCEA/WASC (6-year term: 2008-14). **Endowment:** N/P. **School year:** Aug.-June. **School Day:** 8:10 a.m. to 2:20 p.m. for K; 8:10 a.m. to 3:20 p.m. for G1-8.

Student Body Ethnicity

56% Caucasian, 18% multi-racial, 11% Asian, 5% Latino, 4% Filipino, 3% Chinese, 3% other Asian.

Admissions

Applications Due: Dec. 10 for K; open for G1-8. **Application process:** For K, school tour, one-on-one assessment, large group visit, and preschool evaluation. **Application fee:** $100. **No. of applications:** N/P. **No. of K spaces:** 30. Percentage of K class make up of school's preschool class: N/A. **Admission evaluation requirements for K:** Assessment, school visit and tour, preschool evaluations. **Other grades:** School tour, entrance test on basic skills, transcript from previous school and teacher evaluation. **Preferences:** Siblings, NDV Parish members, Roman Catholic. **What sort of student do you best serve?** "We serve a diverse community of learners whose families value a faith-based curriculum in the Roman Catholic tradition. The community spirit is highly valued by all parents. Students who academically perform at grade level or above are encouraged to apply. We educate the whole child supporting each child's spiritual, intellectual, emotional, social and physical growth."

Costs

Latest tuition: $7,293. **Sibling discount:** Yes (amount N/P). **Tuition includes:** Lunch: No; Transportation: No; Laptop computer: No; Other: N/P. **Tuition increases:** Approx. 5-6% annually. **Other costs:** Plus aide fee ($900 for K-2 and $500 for G3-5, annually); enrollment fee of $955 for K, $455 for families newly enrolling in G1-8, and $355 for returning families; approx. $25 for supplies; and $150 for uniforms. **Percentage of students receiving financial aid:** N/P. **Financial aid application deadline:** Call for date. Financial aid is based on need. **Average grant:** $1,000. Percentage of grants at half tuition or more: N/P. **Donations:** "Annual Giving Program asks each family to make a $600 donation to the church, and fundraisers include a Jog-a-thon, Mission Carnival, Bal de Paris, and Les Amis de NDV Annual Campaign."

SCHOOL'S MISSION STATEMENT
"Ecôle Notre Dame des Victories is a Catholic elementary school founded in 1924 by the Marist Fathers and is located near the financial district of San Francisco. We embrace the values of the Marists and the Sisters of St. Joseph of Orange and continue our tradition of teaching the French language and culture. As a faith-filled community, the faculty and staff of NDV are committed to nurturing our students spiritually, academically, emotionally, socially and physically. We support a diverse group of learners who endeavor to develop an inclusive and compassionate world vision."

ACADEMIC PROGRAM
Philosophy: "Ecôle Notre Dame des Victories continues its long tradition of excellence that offers a strong academic program to all students. Over the years our students realize their individual potential and become active and productive citizens who live out their Christian values. They leave our school with confidence. We look forward to the years ahead, where we as a staff can strengthen our commitment to offering a strong Catholic education to all who enter our learning community." **Foreign languages:** French K-8. **Computer training:** Yes. Number of computers available to students: 18 in the lab, 2-3 in the classrooms. Interactive white boards in several classrooms. **No. of hours weekly of:** Art- .5.; Drama- N/P; Music- .5 K-G; Computers- .75; Foreign language- 3+. **Outdoor education:** G6 attends the 5-day, 5-night Yosemite Institute Program at Yosemite National Park. **Grading:** A-F, beginning in G3. **Average nightly homework:** 20-30 min. in G1; 20-40 min. in G2-3; 35-55 min. in G4; 45-60 min. in G5; 60-90 min. in G 6; and 60-110 min. in G7-8. Posted on the Internet: Yes for G6-8. **Percentage of students participating in Johns Hopkins Center for Talented Youth Program:** 2%. **Other indicators of academic success:** "NDV ITBS test scores are in the top 5% in the SF Archdiocese. Its Academic Decathlon team has regularly taken first, second or third place in the competition. NDV graduates matriculate to top private and public academic high

schools, many placing into Advanced Placement courses." **High schools attended by latest graduating class:** SHCP, Lick, SI, IHS, Lowell, Convent, Stuart Hall, Bay, University, Urban, Moreau, Acalanes.

FACULTY

Ethnicity: 99% Caucasian (non-Latino), 1% Filipino. **Percentage of teachers with graduate degrees:** 45%. **Percentage with current California credential:** 100%. **Faculty selection/training:** Successful elementary school teaching experience, minimum BA degree, ability to support mission of the school, preference given to practicing Roman Catholics. **Teacher/student ratio:** 2:32 in K-2; 2:35 in 3-5; 1:35 in G6-8. **Special subject teachers:** Science, music, library, PE, computers, art, drama, French. **Average teacher tenure:** 12 years.

MIDDLE SCHOOL

Description: G6-8 are departmentalized in math, English, social studies, science, French, library, and language arts. **Teacher/student ratio:** 1:35. **Elective courses offered:** None. **Achievement tracking in:** Math, science, English/literature, social studies, religion. **Student social events:** Age-appropriate field trips, G8 Confirmation retreat, Family Picnic, CCCYO Sports, Viking soccer, Father-Daughter Dinner Dance, Mother-Son SF Giants baseball event, Mission Carnival, Choral Festival, performance at Davies Symphony Hall, various field trips to SFMOMA, American Conservatory Theater, Randall Museum, Christmas and Spring Music Concerts, Art Show, Coyote Point Museum, California Academy of Sciences, de Young Museum, Family Masses & receptions, Class Masses & receptions, Villa Sinfonia Winter and Spring Concerts, SF Ballet, Asian Art Museum, City Hall & ATT Park tours, St. Mary's Cathedral, Cable Car Museum, Immigration Center/Angel Island, Chinatown Walking Tour, Conservatory of Flowers GGP, Marin Museum of American Indians, Legion of Honor, Oakland Museum, Jack London State Park, Crissy Field Study, Chabot Space and Science Center, Marin Science Institute.

STUDENT SUPPORT SERVICES

No. of Licensed Counselors on staff: One part-time. **Counselor/student ratio:** 1:280, **Learning specialists on staff:** One part-time 3 days/week. **Learning differences/disabilities support:** "NDV uses a Student Success Team (SST) approach which helps with identifying students who are struggling academically or behaviorally. The SST process supports struggling students, thereby improving the child's academic, spiritual, social and emotional well-being. The classroom teacher, along with the school's learning specialist, principal, vice principal, and parents will collaborate in order to support and assist the student, thus enabling the child to become successful." **High school placement support:** Eighth grade teacher and principal.

STUDENT CONDUCT AND HEALTH

Code of Conduct: "Discipline within Notre Dame des Victories is considered an aspect of moral guidance and not a form of punishment. It is a means of training the students to take control of their own choices and to assume responsibility for their own actions. Our main purpose at NDV is to learn and to grow both individually and also as a Catholic Christian Community. At NDV, the expectation is that relationships are based on mutual respect, inclusion, safety and effective communication." **Prevention education and awareness addressed in:** Family Life Education, Health Education (PE and science), vision and hearing screening, and life skills classes provided by the counselor. The RISE Program (Respect, Include, Safety and Effective Communication) supports the learning community by teaching students conflict management skills.

ATHLETICS

Sports offered: Soccer, basketball, girls volleyball. **Team play begins in:** K.

CAMPUS/CAMPUS LIFE

Campus description: "Ecôle Notre Dame des Victories (NDV) is a vibrant downtown San Francisco school with the spirit of a close-knit community. On-going refurbishment throughout the building has included the office relocation to the auditorium entrance and the creation of the St. Peter Chanel Chapel on the first floor, which has helped to beautify and maintain a safe learning environment. The outdoor courtyard has been recently updated with new basketball backboards and raised gardens." **Library:** Yes. Primary and G3-8 libraries (N/P volumes). Book collection accessed through computer accessed card catalog. **Sports facilities:** Gymnasium. **Theater/Arts facilities:** Theater and Art room. **Computer lab:** Yes. **Science lab:** Yes. **Lunch program:** Yes. **Bus service:** None. "The school is located in downtown San Francisco with easy access to many major bus lines, BART and the Cable Car." Uniform/dress code: Uniforms. **Opportunities for community service:** "Students in G8 are required to complete 30 hours of service prior to graduation which may include working with people in soup kitchens, rest homes, and peer tutoring. The school community sponsors food drives, clothing drives, toiletry drives, penny races, bake sales, dinners, and a variety of other community outreach activities that support national and international emergencies that arise."

Extended Day
Morning Care: Begins at 7:20 a.m. **After-school care:** Until 6 p.m. Grades levels: For K-5, NDV Extension Program and for G6-8, Junior High After School. **Cost:** $40/mo. for morning care; $195/mo. for after care. **Drop-in care available:** No. **Coverage over major holidays:** No. **Homework help:** Yes. **Snacks:** Provided. **Staff/student ratio:** 8:11. **After-school classes:** Knitting, pottery, watercolor, French, guitar. **Cost:** N/P.

Summer Programs
Middle School Summer Program for students entering G6-8. Two weeks in Aug. **Cost:** $475.

Parent Involvement
Parent/teacher communication: Parent-teacher conferences, school and teachers' websites, Wednesday newsletter, e-mail, Powerschool G6-8. **Participation requirements:** 36 hours per year for 2 parent families and 18 hours for single parents. **Parent education programs offered?** Yes.

What Sets the School Apart from Others
"In addition to offering a rigorous academic program, all grades receive instruction in the French language and culture on a daily basis. A wide variety of fine arts activities are offered including formal art instruction, violin, cello and piano. Cultural field trips are planned on a regular basis which allows our students to develop an appreciation for the arts, sciences and history. A strong sense of community nurtures family and student relationships in a downtown environment."

How Families Characterize School
Parent comments(s): "NDV provides a safe Catholic environment for the children, a variety of activities and daily French class. NDV teachers are caring and a strong sense of community is nurtured. Students are offered excellent instruction and have the security to explore their potential." "NDV has a stellar extra-curricular music program, excellent location for working parents, an involved principal, a clean environment and provides a solid preparation for high school."
Student comment(s): "NDV creates a good and conducive learning

environment. Teachers are always willing to help you better understand concepts and make it fun at the same time." • "I think the teachers are nice and they help us learn and they make me look forward to going to school and learning."

FRENCH-AMERICAN INTERNATIONAL SCHOOL
150 Oak Street (between Gough and Franklin) (Hayes Valley)
San Francisco, CA 94102
(415) 558-2080 *fax (415) 558-2065*
www.frenchamericansf.org

Jane Camblin, Head of School, janec@frenchamericansf.org
Andrew Brown, Director of Admission, andrewb@frenchamericansf.org

GENERAL
Coed PK-8 day school and International High School. Founded in 1962. Independent. Nonprofit. **Member:** The College Board, CAIS, CIS, NAIS, ECIS. **Enrollment:** Approx. 650 (PK3-8). **Average class size:** 16. **Accreditation:** WASC/CAIS, CIS, AEFE ("full term"). **Endowment:** $5.2 million. **School year:** Sept.-June. **School day:** 8:20 a.m. to 3:15 p.m.

STUDENT BODY ETHNICITY
64% Caucasian (non-Latino), 15% multi-racial, 9% Asian, 8% African-American, 3% Latino, 1% other.

ADMISSION
Applications due: Dec. 15. **Application fee:** $100. **Application process:** Campus visit, appointment with Admission Director, and completed application. No. of K applications: Approx. 140. **No. of K spaces:** Approx. 18. **Percentage of K class made up of school's preschool class:** 75%. **Admission evaluation requirements for K:** General readiness screening, confidential recommendation and letter of recommendation. **Other grades:** After K, French competence is necessary. Applicants must provide report cards or dossiers and test scores if appropriate. Applicants to grades above K take part in a day-long evaluation and class visit. **Preferences:** "Diversity is a key element in the mission of the FAIS. Our younger children are being immersed—psychologically and emotionally—in diversity just as they are being immersed in language. It is a point of pride that a FAIS education is international, multilingual and open to the world. We actively recruit families representing a

multiplicity of nationalities who are native speakers of languages from all around the globe. We actively seek students from racially, culturally and socio-economically diverse families. Our family configurations are multifarious too. We welcome single parent, gay and lesbian, divorced and separated, as well as adoptive and foster families. From the very beginning our students rub shoulders with others who reflect an astonishing variety of attitudes, religions and political persuasions. We think they learn more because of this, and gain a profound understanding of the richness of the human experience." **What sort of student do you best serve?** "Bright, social children from diverse backgrounds whose parents are very supportive of bilingualism, strong academics and a global outlook."

Costs
Latest tuition: $20,810 for PK-5, $22,500 for G6-8. **Sibling discount:** None. **Tuition includes:** Lunch: No; Transportation: No; Laptop computer: No; Other: Textbooks and most field trips. **Tuition increases:** Approx. 4% annually. **Other costs:** "Less than $1,000 in other fees for overnight trips, book clubs, supplies and the like." **Percentage of students receiving financial aid:** Approx. 30%. **Financial aid application deadline:** Jan. 15. Financial aid is based on need. **Average grant:** N/P. **Percentage of grants of half-tuition or more:** N/P. **Donations:** "Our advancement department is very active soliciting voluntary donations for the annual fund, capital campaign, auctions, etc."

School's Mission Statement
"Guided by the principles of academic rigor and diversity, the French-American International School offers programs of study in French and English to prepare its graduates for a world in which the ability to think critically and to communicate across cultures is of paramount importance."

Academic Program
Philosophy: "Our curriculum is based on the core program of the French Ministry of Education. In PK-2 the program is taught by immersion, 80% in French and 20% in English. In G3-5 we emphasize balanced bilingualism and a transfer of competencies between the 2 languages. The ratio changes to 50% French and 50% English. Most children enter PK3, PK4 and K without previous knowledge of French." **Foreign languages:** French, Spanish, Chinese, Italian, German and Latin. **Computer training:** Yes. Weekly classes PK4-9. **No. of computers available for students:** Approx. 200. **No. of hours weekly of:** Art- 1

or more; Drama- 1+; Music- 1+; Computers- 1+; Foreign language-N/P; PE- 3 or more. **Outdoor education:** Field trips and week long overnights. **Grading:** Skills assessment. Number grades begin in G4. **Average nightly homework:** "Varies." Posted on the Internet: Yes. Accessed by a password-protected parent portal." **Percentage of students participating in Johns Hopkins Center for Talented Youth Program:** N/P. **Other indicators of academic success:** "Year after year, at the end of G4 our global ERB scores are several points above the independent school norms in all criteria. This is empirical evidence that a bilingual program does not sabotage learning in English. Our French standardized tests far exceed national averages in France." **High schools attended by latest graduating class:** IHS, Lick, University, Urban, Lowell, Andover, Exeter.

FACULTY
Ethnicity: 80% Caucasian (non-Latino), 6% Asian, 4% African-American, 4% multi-racial, 4% other, 2% Latino. **Percentage of teachers with graduate degrees:** 90%. **Percentage with current California credential:** 30% (more than 60% are credited by the French Ministry of Education). **Faculty selection/training:** "In general we seek experienced international educators with at least 3 years experience. We have a generous professional development budget." **Teacher/student ratio:** Approx. 1:16. **Special subject teachers:** Art, music, theatre, computers, PE, third languages. **Average teacher tenure:** Approx. 5 years.

MIDDLE SCHOOL
Description: "The Middle School offers a bilingual course of study in French and English from G6-8. Our curriculum encourages personal growth enriched by academic rigor, the ability to listen and to understand, and an awareness and openness towards the outside world. Students entering the Middle School must have a high level of literacy in French." **Teacher/student ratio:** 1:18. **Elective courses offered:** Art, music, theatre, computers, PE, Chinese, Spanish, Italian, German. **Achievement tracking in:** All subjects. **Student social events:** Exchange visits, regular dances, concerts, performances, community service celebrations.

STUDENT SUPPORT SERVICES
No. of Licensed Counselors on staff: Four. **Counselor/student ratio:** 1:30. **Learning specialists on staff:** Three. **Learning differences/disabilities support:** "Strategies are developed as a result of external diagnostic testing and are handled in-house." **High school placement**

support: "85% of Middle School graduates continue on to our own International High School. Full and active support for applications to 'colleague' high schools is in place."

STUDENT CONDUCT AND HEALTH

Code of conduct: "The Middle School is a peaceful and studious academic community where each individual shows respect for and is respected by others. There is a Code of Conduct for both the Middle and Lower Schools." **Prevention education and awareness addressed in:** The school's counselors provide health, social (and parenting) education school-wide, most often featuring outside experts.

ATHLETICS

Sports offered: Basketball, soccer, volleyball, cross-country, baseball. **Team play begins in:** N/P.

CAMPUS/CAMPUS LIFE

Campus description: "Expansive 6 floor campus occupying an entire city block in the heart of San Francisco's civic and cultural corridor." **Library:** Two libraries containing print, video and DVD selections in 3 languages—English, French and Chinese. There is a reference section, periodicals and computer stations for on-line research (N/P volumes). **Sports facilities:** "One of the best gymnasiums in the city adjacent to large outside spaces. Sports fields, tennis courts and pool are contracted offsite." **Theater/Arts facilities:** Adjacent new Arts Building on Page Street. **Computer labs:** Three. **Science labs:** Five. **Lunch program:** Voluntary at extra cost. **Bus service:** No. **Uniforms/dress code:** "Respectful dress code." **Opportunities for community service:** "A wide range of opportunities are available beginning in G2."

EXTENDED DAY

Morning care: Begins at 7:30 a.m. **After-school care:** Until 6 p.m. **Grade levels:** All. **Cost:** "Varies." **Drop-in care available:** Yes. **Coverage over major holidays:** Yes, but not the winter vacation. **Homework help:** Available in 2 languages. **Snacks:** Provided. **Staff/ student ratio:** 1:8. **After-school classes:** A variety of classes including fencing, music, photography, art. **Cost:** $120+/class.

SUMMER PROGRAMS

"We are a premier location for both fun and rigorous bilingual summer programs. Our programs offer students age three through 8th grade the unique opportunity to learn, enhance and expand their language skills in a fun, creative atmosphere. Our mission is to develop self-confidence in written and verbal language skills and to foster an awareness of the cultural diversity within our international community." **Cost:** "Varies."

Parent Involvement

Parent/teacher communication: "Regular parent-teacher conferences, website, e-mail, newsletters. 'Very active' Parent Associations and room parent network." **Participation requirements:** "Twelve hours is the minimum requested volunteer commitment by the school. Many parents do much more. Whole-hearted, parental involvement is key to supporting the immersion process." **Parent education programs offered?** Yes.

What Sets the School Apart From Others

"The French-American International School offers world-class bilingual education in the heart of San Francisco. At FAIS we offer the better of two educational worlds—we are both the largest PreK-12 independent school in the Bay Area and a fully-accredited, French public school. Our own International High School experience culminates in a two-year baccalaureate program. We are one of very few schools in the world offering both the International Baccalaureate and the French Baccalaureate."

How Families Characterize School

Parent comment(s): "If you want your child to be completely bilingual by age eight, to rub shoulders with people of widely varying national and socioeconomic backgrounds, and to become immersed in a sophisticated and content-rich academic environment, then this is the place for you. The kids work hard, the pace is intense, but they seem to have a great time and their horizons are wider than those of many others their age."

Student comment(s): "The acquisition of facts is not the priority, knowledge is not the issue, but understanding is, and understanding goes beyond just dates, and laws, and formulas. This reminds me of a Calvin and Hobbes strip, in which Calvin complains that, in school, 'for some reason they'd rather teach us stuff that any fool can look up in a book.' Fortunately, the experience at IHS is different; the things we learn are not self sufficient, but they depend on the thought that is put behind them, the idea that drives them. As Calvin knew, any fool can look up facts in a book. Our teachers know this as well, which is why with each fact we learn, we are not assimilating, but reacting, understanding, and thinking."

GREENWOOD SCHOOL

17 Buena Vista Avenue
Mill Valley, CA 94941
(415) 388-0495 *fax (415) 388-6895*
www.greenwoodschool.org

Robert Schiappacasse, School Director, robert@greenwoodschool.org
Vicki Seastrom, Director of Admission, vicki@greenwoodschool.org

GENERAL

Coed PS-8 day school. Founded in 1992, Nonprofit. **Member:** N/P. **Enrollment:** 150. **Average class size:** 17. **Accreditation:** N/P. **Endowment:** None. **School year:** Sept.-June. **School day:** 8:25 a.m. to 3:05 p.m.

STUDENT BODY ETHNICITY: N/P.

ADMISSION

Applications due: For PS-K, the last Friday in Jan.; rolling for G1-8. **Application fee:** $75. **Application process:** School visit, submit the application form, parent introduction form, teacher recommendation form, application fee. **No. of applications:** 75. **No. of K spaces:** 22. **Percentage of K class made up of school's preschool class:** N/A, 2010 first year of preschool program. **Admission evaluation requirements for K:** Application, teacher recommendation, family interview with staff and faculty. **Other grades:** Application, teacher recommendation, family interview with staff and faculty and 2-3 day student visit with prospective class. **Preferences:** Siblings. **What sort of student do you best serve:** "Students whose parents feel that they will thrive in Greenwood's Waldorf-Inspired curriculum and school culture."

COSTS

Latest tuition: $5,998-$14,995 for PS; $14,995 for K; $16,795 for G1-5; $17,395 for G6-8. **Sibling discount:** Yes, 15% second child, 20% third child. **Tuition includes:** Lunch: No; Transportation: Yes. Morning bus service available from San Anselmo, San Rafael, Greenbrae, and Corte Madera $4/ride. Laptop computer: No; Other: N/A. **Tuition increases:** Approx. 5% annually. **Other costs:** $250 one time enrollment fee, $1,000 one time deposit refundable upon graduation or withdrawal with written notice; tuition refund plan $435 for K, $487 for G1-5, $505 for G6-8; incidental and optional fees include but not limited to bus fee, hot lunch, extended day care, vacation camp, class field trips, musical instrument rental, and tuition service fee. **Percentage of students receiving financial aid:** 33%. **Financial aid application deadline:** Last Friday in Jan. Financial aid is based on need. **Average grant:** 20% of tuition. **Percentage of grants of half-tuition or more:** N/P. **Donations:** Greenwood School families are asked to participate in annual fundraising to the extent that they are able.

SCHOOL'S MISSION STATEMENT

"Greenwood School is a Waldorf-inspired community of families and teachers who share a passionate commitment to the education of the whole person."

ACADEMIC PROGRAM

Philosophy: "Greenwood's integrated approach to academics is rigorous and dynamic. Whether the subject is math, history, science, language arts, ecology, world language, our Waldorf-trained faculty brings it to life. Academic subjects are further enlivened and integrated through story, drama, singing, painting, orchestra, movement games, and handwork. An essential characteristic of the Waldorf curriculum is its developmental orientation. Children are taught subjects at each stage of their development in ways that are most receptive to them. Our unhurried and measured approach to learning concentrates on the physical, emotional, and intellectual foundations of literacy - resulting in students who grow more confidently into each academic stage of their development." **Foreign languages:** Spanish G1-8; Mandarin or Arabic Introduction G1-4. **Computer training:** G6-8. **No. of computers available for students:** N/P. **No. of hours weekly of:** Art- N/P; Drama-N/P; Music- N/P; Computers- N/P; Foreign language- N/P; PE- N/P. **Outdoor education:** One day per week, 4-5 periods for each grade. Overnight class trips beginning in G3. **Grading:** Letter grades beginning in G6. **Average nightly homework:** Approx. 30 min. in G4; 30-45 min. in G5; 60 min. in G6; 60-90 min. in G7-8. Posted on the Internet: N/P. **Percentage of students participating in Johns Hopkins Center for Talented Youth Program:** N/A. **Other indicators of academic success:** "Greenwood School's Waldorf-inspired curriculum enables students not simply to learn, but to experience and internalize what they learn, education from within. Children emerge from their years at Greenwood prepared, aware of their own capabilities, happy, enthusiastic and fully engaged with the world in which they live. Graduates have attended a wide range of Bay Area private and public high schools as well as colleges and universities." **High schools attended by latest graduating class:** SF Waldorf, MA, Urban, Tamalpais, Redwood.

FACULTY

Ethnicity: N/P. **Percentage of teachers with graduate degrees:** 70%. **Percentage with current California credential:** N/P. **Faculty selection/training:** Waldorf certified. **Teacher/student ratio:** Ranges from 1:9 to 1:24 depending on grade. **Special subject teachers:** Music, orchestra, Eurythmy, poetry, Spanish, Arabic, Mandarin, nature and environmental studies, drama, handwork, woodwork, games and PE, gardening. **Average teacher tenure:** 5 years.

MIDDLE SCHOOL

Description: G6-8, **Teacher/student ratio:** 1:12 **Elective courses offered:** Afterschool electives include circus arts, Taiko drumming, soccer, Mandarin, gardening, and others. **Achievement tracking in:** Standardized testing in G7-8. **Student social events:** Seasonal Festivals and Winter Faire, grade appropriate field trips, annual overnight class trip beginning in G3, dance for G7-8, seasonal orchestra recitals, concerts, plays.

STUDENT SUPPORT SERVICES

No. of Licensed Counselors on staff: N/A. **Counselor/student ratio:** N/A. **Learning specialists on staff:** Learning Support Director and additional part-time specialist. **Learning differences/disabilities support:** Learning Support Program for students identified with learning challenges that integrates Waldorf developmental insight with expertise in contemporary educational therapy. **High school placement support:** Eighth grade faculty and staff.

STUDENT CONDUCT AND HEALTH

Code of conduct: "Student conduct guidelines are intended to create a shared understanding among teachers, parents, and students about the standards of conduct in our school community and they set forth the consequences to be expected in cases of misconduct. The rules are derived from the following three principles; 1) respect for all human beings, animals, and nature, and a willingness to do nothing that might harm others or one's self; 2) respect for all school and personal property and a commitment to do nothing to damage any physical property; and 3) respect for the guidance provided by teachers and staff, realizing that they are responsible for the well-being of all the school's students." **Prevention education and awareness addressed in:** Family life, drug awareness, and health education are incorporated into the curriculum.

ATHLETICS

Sports offered: "Competitive games which are tied to the curriculum such as a Greek Pentathlon and Medieval Games take place with Bay Area Waldorf schools. **Team play begins in:** G5 (intermural).

CAMPUS/CAMPUS LIFE

Campus description: "The Greenwood School Main Campus is located in the heart of Mill Valley in an historical 3 story school building. The preschool campus is located a short distance down Blithedale at the corner of Sycamore and East Blithedale Ave." **Library:** No. **Sports facilities:** Gymnasium. **Theater/Arts facilities:** Performance stage. **Computer lab:** No. **Science lab:** No. **Lunch program:** Yes. Vegetarian hot lunch is offered varied days during the week. **Bus service:** Greenwood School offers morning bus service from San Anselmo, Greenbrae, Corte Madera and San Rafael - $4/ride. **Uniforms/dress code:** Dress code. **Opportunities for community service:** Students in G8 are required to complete 35 hours of community service in the form of a project connected with the community in an ecological/environmental studies approach. During the spring, each child presents their environmental service project to the greater community.

EXTENDED DAY

Morning care: None. **After-school care:** Until 5:30 p.m. **Grade levels:** K-8. **Cost:** $8/advance reservation, $12 drop-in. **Drop-in care available:** Yes. **Coverage over major holidays:** No, however occasional camps are offered during school breaks. **Homework help:** Yes. **Snacks:** Provided. **Staff/student ratio:** 1:6-1:12. **After-school classes:** Soccer, Taiko drumming, Mandarin, woodworking, circus arts, cooking, gardening, art. **Cost:** $12-$25/class.

SUMMER PROGRAMS

The summer camp programs are available for K-8 during selected weeks of the summer vacation. **Cost:** "Varies."

PARENT INVOLVEMENT

Parent/teacher communication: Parent-teacher conferences, class parent meetings every 6 weeks, parent circle meetings monthly, school website, e-mail, weekly newsletter, voicemail. **Participation requirements:** While not required, community participation is certainly encouraged. **Parent education programs offered?** Yes.

What Sets the School Apart From Others

"Waldorf-inspired Education—The Kindergarten, elementary and middle school children of Greenwood School undertake their educational journey in an environment that nurtures, inspires, and prepares them for the changing road ahead. Our experienced, Waldorf trained teachers are committed to academic excellence and to addressing the emotional, intellectual, and physical needs and capabilities of children at each crucial stage of their development. We believe that a Waldorf-based education unfolding in an atmosphere of true innovation creates an exceptional learning environment for children. Academics, movement, and fine and practical arts combine in a multidisciplinary curriculum that enables students not simply to learn, but to experience and internalize what they learn—education from within. Greenwood School also boasts a one of a kind Nature and Environmental Studies Program where one day each week class unfolds in the field. The scope of the curriculum varies according to what is developmentally appropriate to each age group. Children have the opportunity to experience class held in a redwood grove, at Slide Ranch or Green Gulch, coastal farm settings near Muir Beach or on one of many field trips exploring the biologically diverse and rich landscape of the Bay Area."

How Families Characterize School

Parent comment(s): "The Greenwood School is an amazing school. As we raise our children in the 21st century a strong environmental education is essential. The environmental education program is amazing. The school's values are aligned with the programs. It is a 'green' school with recycling, composting, organic everything. They honor universal spirituality and educate the soulfulness of the children through nature. They have a wonderful gardening program, an award winning Poetry program. The students at Greenwood School have won the 'River of Words' poetry contest multiple times. The students at Greenwood School spend a day a week out in nature using the environment as the classroom for learning. They have a strong strings program throughout the grades. I highly recommend this school." • "A wonderful school that treats each child with reverence and love, while guiding them towards becoming confident, social, and capable human beings. Each teacher carries a deep knowledge and understanding of the developing child and a passion for working with young children and their families. Care for the environment and for one another are an inherent part of this program, with its natural materials, organic foods, and composting/gardening program. What a gift it has been to be part of the Greenwood's early childhood and grade school."

Student Comment(s): "On a daily basis I notice many qualities and characteristics I have taken away from my experiences at Greenwood. One of the greatest lessons is how open minded I am today. Through many of the experiences I had at Greenwood, such as nature day, handwork, woodworking, gardening, poetry, etc. I was exposed to such a wide variety of possibilities and choices for life. I carried this out with me into the world. I now know that in every situation that I get into, I am capable of doing anything I want with it and becoming whatever I want."

THE HAMLIN SCHOOL
2120 Broadway (between Webster and Buchanan) (Pacific Heights)
San Francisco, CA 94115
(415) 922-0300 *fax (415) 674-5409*
www.hamlin.org

Wanda M. Holland Greene, Head of School, holland_greene@hamlin.org
Lisa Lau Aquino '81, Director of Admission, aquino@hamlin.org

GENERAL
Girls K-8 day school. Founded in 1863. Independent. Nonprofit. **Member:** NAIS, CAIS, NCGS. **Enrollment:** Approx. 400. **Average class size:** "10-22." **Accreditation:** CAIS (6-year term: 2006-12). **Endowment:** $12 million. **School year:** Sept.-June. **School day:** 8:15 a.m. to 2 p.m. for K; 8:15 a.m. to 3:15 p.m. for G1-8.

STUDENT BODY ETHNICITY:
"40% students of color."

ADMISSION
Applications due: Mid-Dec. for K, mid-Jan. for G1-8 (call for dates). **Application fee:** $100. **Application process:** A completed application, parent interview, student visit, and a nonrefundable $100 application fee are required elements of the admission process. "Hamlin encourages families to visit our school, discuss our program, and tour our buildings." **No. of applications:** 200+. **No. of K spaces:** 44. **Percentage of K class made up of school's preschool class:** N/A. **Admission evaluation requirements for K:** Student screening and visit, preschool teacher evaluation, parent interview. **Other grades:** Student visit, school records, teacher recommendations, ISEE exam for G5-8, parent interview. **Preferences:** Siblings. **What sort of student do you best serve?**

"The Hamlin School best serves girls who are motivated, hardworking and eager to learn. We offer a challenging academic program in an environment of encouragement and support."

Costs
Latest tuition: $24,775. **Sibling discount:** None. **Tuition includes:** Lunch: No; Transportation: No; Laptop computer: No; Other: Textbooks, field trips, outdoor education programs, yearbook. **Tuition increases:** Approx. 3-5% annually. **Other costs:** Approx. $30-$150 for uniforms. **Percentage of students receiving financial aid:** 22%. **Financial aid application deadline:** Jan./Feb. (call for date). Financial aid is based on need. **Average grant:** $12,000. **Percentage of grants of half-tuition or more:** 60%. **Donations:** Voluntary. Include time, annual fund, capital campaign, parent association events.

School's Mission Statement
"For well over a century, the mission of The Hamlin School has been 'to educate girls and young women to meet the challenges of their time.' The program at Hamlin aims to develop the intellect, the character, and the citizenship of each girl to prepare her to face the future with courage and confidence. • Hamlin offers a challenging academic program in an environment of encouragement and support. Students master the skills that provide a foundation for life-long learning as well as the habits of speculation, inquiry, and critical thinking. Our methods are both experiential and collaborative, promoting engagement and creativity. Hamlin students graduate knowing how to learn, appreciating the value of industry, and possessing a love of knowledge. • Hamlin is committed to be an inclusive community where diversity is a component of excellence and all members of the community are respected. We welcome and benefit from the perspectives that emerge from a diversity of ethnicity, culture, religion, socioeconomic status, learning style, sexual orientation, and family structure. The participation of all is important to the health of the community. • Hamlin cultivates leadership skills in every young woman and promotes the importance of service to others, both within and beyond our community. Through mutual respect, honesty, and kindness, we impress upon our students the importance of personal integrity and ethical decision-making. • In the tradition of Sarah Dix Hamlin, we inspire girls to find the best in themselves and to contribute with energy and distinction to the world around them."

ACADEMIC PROGRAM

Philosophy: "See Mission Statement." **Foreign languages:** French, Spanish. **Computer training:** Yes. **No. of computers available for students:** 72 plus 25 wireless laptops. **No. of hours weekly of:** Art- 1.5-2.5 in K-4, 3-4 in G5-8; Drama- K-4 after-school program, 3-4 in G5-8 (elective); Music- 1.5-2.5 in K-4, 1.5-3 in G5-8; Computers- .75- 1.5 in K-8; Foreign language- .75-2.5 in K-4, 3-4 in G5-8; PE- 1.5-2.5 in K-4, 3-4 in G5-8. **Outdoor education:** Field trips in every grade. Overnight trips begin in G3. **Grading:** A-F, beginning in G5. **Average nightly homework:** "Varies." Posted on the Internet: No. **Percentage of students participating in Johns Hopkins Center for Talented Youth Program:** N/P. **Other indicators of academic success:** N/P. **High schools attended by latest graduating class:** Bay, Branson, Convent, CSUS, Deerfield, Drew, Exeter, IHS, Lick, Lowell, MA, Miss Porter's, SI, University, Urban.

FACULTY

Ethnicity: "25% of color." **Percentage of teachers with graduate degrees:** 50%. **Percentage with current California credential:** N/P. **Faculty selection/training:** Graduate degree preferred; minimum 3 years head teaching experience. **Teacher/student ratio:** 1:7. **Special subject teachers:** Art, music, dance, drama, French, Spanish, technology, library, PE. **Average teacher tenure:** 15 years.

MIDDLE SCHOOL

Description: The middle school spans G5-8. The program is entirely departmentalized and is on a 6 day rotation. **Teacher/student ratio:** 1:7. **Elective courses offered:** Drama, dance, yearbook, computer, music. **Achievement tracking in:** French, math. **Student social events:** Culture club, debate club, community service, literary magazine, student government.

STUDENT SUPPORT SERVICES

No. of Licensed Counselors on staff: Two part-time. Daily advising program. **Counselor/student ratio:** 1:200. **Learning specialists on staff:** Two. **Learning differences/disabilities support:** Individual and group support for mild to moderate learning differences. **High school placement support:** High school placement counselor.

STUDENT CONDUCT AND HEALTH

Code of conduct: "The Hamlin Creed, written by Hamlin students, embodies the values of the entire community. The Creed guides the interactions among students, faculty, and family. Be respectful; Be responsible; Be caring; Be honest; Be positive." **Prevention education and awareness programs offered in:** The school's program covers drug and alcohol awareness, smoking, health and human sexuality education, body image, media literacy, self-defense, and harassment.

ATHLETICS
Sports offered: Volleyball, basketball, soccer, cross-country, running club, softball, futsal. **Team play begins in:** G5 (intermural).

CAMPUS/CAMPUS LIFE
Campus description: Hamlin's campus, overlooking the San Francisco Bay, consists of 3 buildings, including its historic main building. The campus includes 20 classrooms, 2 science labs, and 2 dining rooms. **Library:** 13,000 volumes, 9 computers. **Sports facilities:** Gymnasium, small "field," rooftop playground, climbing wall. **Theater/Arts facilities:** Gymnasium/theater, 2 music rooms, ceramics room. **Computer lab:** Yes. **Science lab:** Yes. **Lunch program:** Yes. **Bus service:** No. **Uniforms/ dress code:** Uniforms. **Opportunities for community service:** Multiple opportunities through the Lend-A-Hand program for families and students; Middle School community service program.

EXTENDED DAY
Morning care: Begins 7 a.m. **After-school care:** Until 6 p.m. **Grade levels:** K-8. **Cost:** $10/hour. **Drop-in care available:** Yes. **Coverage over major holidays:** Yes. **Homework help:** Yes. **Snacks:** Provided. **Staff/student ratio:** 1:8. **After-school classes:** The school's After School Academy includes a variety of non-academic classes such as creative dance, theater, carpentry, fencing and more. **Cost:** Approx. $20/ class.

SUMMER PROGRAMS
"Sports and outdoor education program is offered to current Hamlin students. In addition for incoming Hamlin Kindergarten girls we have Cubs Club which is filled with arts and crafts, drama, games, imaginative play and more." **Cost:** N/P.

PARENT INVOLVEMENT
Parent/teacher communication: Conferences, phone, e-mail, newsletter, website folder. **Participation requirements:** "Parents are an integral part of the school, and we encourage all of our parents to become involved with the Hamlin community. Through the Parents

Association, parents are on campus helping in the lunchroom and the library, preparing for numerous Hamlin community events, organizing community service projects, or helping with school fundraisers. You can also find parents reading stories in the classrooms, driving on field trips, sharing a particular expertise as a guest speaker in the classroom, and so much more." **Parent education programs offered?** Yes.

WHAT SETS THE SCHOOL APART FROM OTHERS: N/P.

HOW FAMILIES CHARACTERIZE SCHOOL
Parent comment(s): "Academic, nurturing, inclusive, visionary."
Student comment(s): "Engaging, caring, community, responsibility."

HOLY NAME OF JESUS SCHOOL
1560 40th Avenue (at Lawton) (Outer Sunset District)
San Francisco, CA 94122
(415) 731-4077 *fax (415) 731-3328*
www.holynamesf.com

Mrs. Judy Cosmos, Principal, judycosmos@gmail.com

GENERAL
Coed K-8 parochial day school. Founded in 1941. Catholic. Nonprofit. **Member:** NCEA. **Enrollment:** Approx. 360. **Average class size:** 25. **Accreditation:** WASC (6-year term: 2009-15). **Endowment:** N/P. **School year:** Aug.-June. **School day:** 8 a.m. to 3 p.m.

STUDENT BODY ETHNICITY
40% Chinese, 26% multi-racial, 15% Caucasian, 9% other Asian, 7% Filipino, 2% Hispanic, 1% African-American.

ADMISSION
Applications due: Rolling admissions. **Application fee:** $50. **Application process:** Applications are available online or from the school office. Submit the application, a small photo of the child, the application fee, a copy of the birth certificate, a copy of the baptismal certificate (if applicable), and a copy of his/her immunization records to the school office either in person or by mail. A Preschool Evaluation Form will be sent to preschools of K applicants. Once all paperwork has been submitted, the child will be scheduled for a test/evaluation. Parents are usually notified within one week of testing as to whether

their child is accepted. **No. of applications:** N/P. **No. of K spaces:** 30. **Percentage of K class made up of school's preschool class:** N/A. **Admission evaluation requirements for K:** Preschool evaluation form, screening and school visit. **Other grades:** Prior or current report cards, test scores, evaluation test. **Preferences:** Siblings, Catholic parishioners, other qualified children. **What sort of student do you best serve?** "Holy Name welcomes enthusiastic children who want a culturally diverse environment to learn and grow academically, socially, physically and emotionally."

Costs

Latest tuition: $5,500 (parish contributing) - $6,600 (non-supporting). **Sibling discount:** Yes. **Tuition includes:** Lunch: No; Transportation: No; Laptop computer: No; Other: N/A. **Tuition increases:** Approx. 5% annually. **Other costs:** Registration fee $350; Parent Guild fee $30; Sacrament fee (G2-8) $40; graduation fee (G8) $75; G7 outdoor education $350. **Percentage of students receiving financial aid:** 8%. Financial aid is based on need and provided through the Archdiocese of San Francisco and the Basic Fund. **Financial aid application deadline:** April. **Average grant:** N/P. **Percentage of grants of half-tuition or more:** N/P. **Donations:** 30 service hours per family.

School's Mission Statement

"Holy Name School is a Catholic school committed to offering its students a strong spiritual foundation and a solid academic education. Each student is expected to achieve his or her highest level of scholarship while learning values to help them become compassionate, contributing and responsible members of society."

Academic Program

Philosophy: "We, the faculty of Holy Name School, are committed to providing a quality Catholic education for each student. We believe that this education is vital to the formation of a responsible, maturing Christian child. We strive: 1) To form a Catholic community; 2) To form a Christian community; 3) To teach and demonstrate Christian values emphasizing respect for the rights and dignity of every person; 4) To support and supplement the family as the educators of their children; 5) To show concern for the well-being, the progress and the individual needs of each child; 6) To develop the whole child spiritually, intellectually, physically, socially, culturally and emotionally; 7) To develop each child's potential and creativity." **Foreign languages:** Cantonese, Mandarin after school. **Computer training:** Yes. **No. of computers available for**

students: Three in each classroom, 35 laptops in Technology Center. **No. of hours weekly of:** Art- 1; Drama- N/P; Music- 1; Computers- 1: Foreign language- N/P; PE- 1. **Outdoor education:** "One week in G7." **Grading:** N/P. **Average nightly homework:** 25 min. in G1-2; 45 min. in G3-4; 60-90 min. in G5-6; 90-120 min. in G7-8. Posted on the Internet: No. **Percentage of students participating in Johns Hopkins Center for Talented Youth Program:** 10%. **Other indicators of academic success:** "Successful participation in numerous contests, Math Counts participation, accepted into prestigious high schools." **High schools attended by latest graduating class:** Lick, University, Lowell, SI, SHCP, Riordan, Mercy, Lincoln, Washington.

FACULTY
Ethnicity: Caucasian 71%, Hispanic 11%, Chinese 7%, Filipino 7%, multi-racial 4%. **Percentage of teachers with graduate degrees:** 63%. **Percentage with current California credential:** 93%. **Faculty selection/training:** N/P. **Teacher/student ratio:** 1:25. **Special subject teachers:** Art, music, computers, PE. **Average teacher tenure:** 12 years.

MIDDLE SCHOOL
Description: G7-8 departmentalized. Junior high students rotate between classrooms and are taught by 8 different teachers for various subjects. **Teacher/student ratio:** 1:30. **Elective courses offered:** High School Entrance Exam preparation classes are offered to 8th grade students. **Achievement tracking in:** N/P. **Student social events:** G8 Christmas dance, Valentine's Day dance, graduation dance. K-8 classroom celebrations (parents invited) for major holidays.

STUDENT SUPPORT SERVICES
No. of Licensed Counselors on staff: One Educational Counselor. **Counselor/student ratio:** 1:360. **Learning specialists on staff:** Two part-time. **Learning differences/disabilities support:** Learning specialists and work modifications accompanied by a modified report card. **High school placement support:** "The junior high teacher and principal offer guidance on choosing the best high school for each student."

STUDENT CONDUCT AND HEALTH
Code of conduct: "A code of conduct and disciplinary measures are clearly stated in the Holy Name School Parent Handbook." **Prevention education and awareness addressed in:** Project Choice, a drug, alcohol,and tobacco awareness program, is presented by the National

Council on Alcoholism and Other Drug Addictions–Bay Area to students in G4-6. An officer for the San Francisco Police Department speaks to G7-8 about drugs. Sex, health and harassment are covered in the curriculum provided by the Archdiocese of San Francisco.

ATHLETICS
Sports offered: Basketball, boys soccer, boys baseball; girls volleyball. **Team play begins in:** G3.

CAMPUS/CAMPUS LIFE
Campus description: "A multi-faceted facility." **Library:** "A new library within the school building" (N/P volumes). **Sports facilities:** A large gymnasium. **Theater/Arts facilities:** The school uses the gymnasium, which has a large stage, audio system and stage lighting. **Computer lab:** Yes. **Science lab:** Yes. **Lunch program:** Optional hot or cold lunches. **Bus service:** No. **Uniforms/dress code:** Uniforms. **Opportunities for community service:** Junior high students are required to perform 10 hours of community service.

EXTENDED DAY
Morning care: Begins at 7 a.m. **After-school care:** Until 6 p.m. **Grade levels:** K-8. **Cost:** $220/mo. **Drop-in care available:** Yes. **Coverage over major holidays:** N/P. **Homework help:** Yes. **Snacks:** Provided. **Staff/student ratio:** 1:10. **After-school classes:** Mandarin, Cantonese, Art of Self-Discipline, piano, chess, Conservatory of Music for advanced students. **Cost:** "Varies."

SUMMER PROGRAMS
Summer school is offered to students registered with Holy Name School entering K-8. **Cost:** For the Academic Program (8 a.m.-11 a.m.), $500 for 5 weeks (not available on a weekly basis); for Summer Camp (11 a.m.-2 p.m.), $ 75/week or $300 for 5 weeks; for Recreation Camp (2 a.m.-6 p.m.), $100/week or $500 for 5 weeks; entire program (all 3 programs) (8 a.m.-6 p.m.) $1,000 for 5 weeks.

PARENT INVOLVEMENT
Parent/teacher communication: Parent-teacher conferences, website, Tuesday Parent Bulletin. **Participation requirements:** Families are required to give 30 service hours, participate in the scrip program, and support the school fundraisers. **Parent education programs offered?** Yes.

What Sets the School Apart From Others
"Holy Name School has a warm, nurturing staff that genuinely cares for their students. Holy Name provides a culturally diverse environment in which students learn and grow academically, socially, physically and emotionally."

How Parents/Students Characterize the School
Parent comment(s): "Holy Name School is one of the best kept secrets in San Francisco." • "My child is so happy at this school. I wish I had brought him here sooner." • "The school is very welcoming and friendly." "I am amazed at all the activities at this school."
Student comment(s): "I love it; it's the best!" • "It's totally awesome; the teachers are great." • "Oh, I really think it's been great for me. I got into one of the best high schools!"

Katherine Delmar Burke School
7070 California Street (at 32nd Avenue) (Sea Cliff)
San Francisco, CA 94121
(415) 751-0177 *fax (415) 666-0535*
www.kdbs.org

Kim Wargo, Head of School, kim@kdbs.org
Renee Thompson, Director of Admissions, renee@kdbs.org
Mary Jizmagian, Associate Director of Admissions, mary.j@kdbs.org

General
Girls K-8 day school. Founded in 1908, Independent, Nonprofit. **Member:** NAIS, CAIS, NCGS, NBOA, ISBOA, ERB, BADA. **Enrollment:** Approx. 400. **Average class size:** N/P. **Accreditation:** CAIS (6-year term: 2006-12). **Endowment:** $11.5 million. **School year:** Sept.-June. **School day:** 8:30 a.m. to dismissal at 2:15 p.m. to 3:20 p.m. for K-4; 8:15 a.m. to 3:30 p.m. for G5-8.

Student Body Ethnicity
70% Caucasian (non-Latino), 12% Asian, 12% multi-racial, 3% Latino, 3% African-American.

Admission
Applications due: Dec. 15. **Application fee:** $100. **Application process:** "The thorough application process begins in Sept. and

continues through the fall and winter; responses are mailed to applying families in mid-March. Families begin to get to know the school by attending the Admissions Preview (open house) and a tour. Burke's gets to know each applicant through her visit to campus, teacher and school recommendations, transcripts, and age/grade-appropriate admissions testing." **No. of applications:** Approx. 170. **No. of K spaces:** 44. **Percentage of K class made up of school's preschool class:** N/A. **Admission evaluation requirements for K:** Group visit, individual screening, preschool evaluations, parent tour, parent interview; **Other grades:** Admissions test (ISEE) for applicants to G5-8, student visit, teacher recommendations, transcript, parent tour, parent interview. **Preferences:** Siblings. **What sort of student do you best serve?** "We serve a wide range of students who have the common characteristic of being ready and eager to learn."

Costs
Latest tuition: $24,200 for K-4; $25,000 for G5-8. **Sibling discount:** N/A. **Tuition includes:** Lunch: No; Transportation: No; Laptop computer: No. Other: Books, fees, and outdoor education. **Tuition increases:** Approx. 4-6% annually. **Other costs:** Uniforms cost $123 in the Lower School, $136 in the Upper School. **Percentage of students receiving financial aid:** Approx. 22%. **Financial aid application deadline:** mid-Jan. (call for date.) Financial aid is based on need. **Average grant:** $11,700. Percentage of grants of half tuition or more: 51%. **Donations:** Voluntary.

School's Mission Statement
"'Educate, Encourage, and Empower Girls.' Burke's prepares able, motivated girls for academic challenge, life in community, and a lifelong love of learning. Burke's celebrates childhood as the best preparation for adulthood, enabling girls to take risks and become confident in whom they are. Burke's embraces individual and cultural differences, teaching that each girl can make a difference in her world."

Academic Program
Philosophy: "We provide a deeply engaging and challenging program that inspires each student to excel both in and out of the classroom. We nurture curious, critical thinkers who are confident in their ideas and their ability to express them. Our skillful and dedicated teachers and staff create a cooperative, collaborative environment that fosters independence, responsibility and respect for self and others." **Foreign languages:** French, Spanish, Mandarin. **Computer training:** Beginning

in K. **No. of computers available for students:** 133. **No. of hours weekly of:** Art- 1.5; Drama- .75; Music- 1.5; Computers- 1.5; Foreign language- 2-3 G5-8; PE- 3. **Outdoor education:** "Yes, begins in G3." **Grading:** A-F, beginning in G5 in addition to qualitative feedback. **Average nightly homework:** Formal homework begins in G2 when students are expected to spend approximately thirty minutes a night on this work. The amount of homework increases incrementally each year. G8 completes approximately 2-3 hours of homework each night. Posted on the Internet: No. **Percentage of students participating in Johns Hopkins Center for Talented Youth Program:** 9%. **Other indicators of academic success:** "Performance as reported by high schools." **High schools attended by latest graduating class:** Bay, Branson, Cate, Convent, Deerfield, Drew, Dunn, IHS, Lick, Lowell, MA, Marin School, Menlo, Redwood, SHCP, SI, University, Taft, Thacher, Urban.

FACULTY
Ethnicity: 78% Caucasian (non-Latino), 11% Asian, 5% Latino, 5% African-American, 1% other. **Percentage of teachers with graduate degrees:** 45%. **Percentage with current California credential:** 80%. **Faculty selection/training:** The school seeks candidates with relevant teaching experience and at least a BA degree. **Teacher/student ratio:** 1:7. **Special subject teachers:** Art, community service and service learning, drama, library, music, science, PE and athletics, technology. **Average teacher tenure:** 11 years.

MIDDLE SCHOOL
Description: Burke's Upper School begins in G5. **Teacher/student ratio:** 1:8. **Elective courses offered:** Art, drama, chorus, journalism, photography, newspaper, cooking, sewing, calligraphy, needlepoint, yearbook. **Achievement tracking in:** Math beginning in G7. **Student social events:** Independent school dances in G8.

STUDENT SUPPORT SERVICES
No. of Licensed Counselors on staff: One part-time. **Counselor/student ratio:** N/P. **Learning specialists on staff:** Three full-time. **Learning differences/disabilities support:** N/P. **High school placement support:** The school has a full-time High School Placement Counselor.

STUDENT CONDUCT AND HEALTH
Code of conduct: "The school works in partnership with its families. Parents and school share responsibility for helping students learn how to behave individually and in communities. In addition, the school holds

the responsibility for creating a positive school climate in which respect for self and community helps us all be equally free to grow, learn, and to develop as individuals. At Burke's, we emphasize the importance of respecting the differences in others. Deliberate unkindness has no place at Burke's or anywhere else. The school strives to maintain a climate of honesty and trust." (An expanded and detailed description of 'conditions of enrollment' is contained in the Burke's Handbook and is provided to every school family.) **Prevention education and awareness addressed in:** "These areas are covered in virtually every grade with a special emphasis in the G8 Science curriculum. Girls study reproductive health which includes anatomy, sexually transmitted infections, sexual decision-making, and birth control. G7-8 meet with a visiting drug and alcohol abuse prevention educator."

ATHLETICS
Sports offered: Volleyball, cross-country, basketball, soccer, softball in G7-8. **Team play begins in:** Club G5, and Varsity and Junior Varsity in G7.

CAMPUS/CAMPUS LIFE
Campus description: "Our unique 3½ acre campus in the city of San Francisco contributes to a vibrant academic climate and welcoming atmosphere. Our expansive outdoor campus encourages physical and intellectual exploration and wellness." **Library:** "State-of-the-art 5,500 square foot library and technology resource center contains a collection of over 32,000 volumes and 15 computers." **Sports facilities:** Gymnasium, large grass playing field, 2 outdoor climbing structures, sports court and 2 multi-purpose courtyards. **Theater/Arts facilities:** Five music, art and drama studios. **Computer lab:** Two desktop labs and 2 laptop virtual labs. **Science lab:** Two. **Lunch program:** Yes. **Bus service:** No. **Uniforms/dress code:** Uniforms. **Opportunities for community service:** "Burke's students learn firsthand about making a positive and meaningful impact on their peers, school and greater community. Each grade level participates in age-appropriate community service projects that reinforce the values of citizenship and responsibility. Examples of our partner organizations/projects are Haight-Ashbury Food Program, SPCA, campus recycling, Breast Cancer Awareness, disaster-relief, local schools, and senior centers."

EXTENDED DAY
Morning care: Begins at: 7:30 a.m. **After-school care:** Until 6 p.m. **Grade levels:** K-8. **Cost:** No charge for a.m. care; p.m. care is $8/hour.

Drop-in care available: Yes. **Coverage over major holidays:** No. **Homework help:** Available informally in G2-4. Study Hall is available for girls in G5-8 and the supervisor is available to answer questions. **Snacks:** Provided. **Staff/student ratio:** Approx. 1:12. **After-school classes:** A variety of classes such as chess, debate, karate, dance, technology, art exploration, ceramics, violin, piano, singing, drama, painting, knitting. **Cost:** $20/hour.

SUMMER PROGRAMS
Burke's offers a summer camp for children entering K for 2 weeks in June. The camp offers a variety of activities in one-week modules such as art, sports, cooking, and hands-on science projects. Burke's also offers other summer camp opportunities for students in grades K-8. Opportunities vary from year to year. **Cost:** "Varies."

PARENT INVOLVEMENT
Parent/teacher communication: "Because girls learn and thrive when families and schools work together, Burke's provides both formal and informal opportunities for parents to support their daughter's education. In addition to regular written progress reports and parent-teacher conferences, there are scheduled parent education meetings throughout the year. The school also publishes a weekly newsletter called Tuesday Notes. Information is also posted on the Burke's website and school-wide e-mail messages are sent as needed and appropriate." **Participation requirements:** "Burke's expects our parents to participate in parent-teacher conferences. Parents are also encouraged to become active in the Parents' Association by volunteering to help with projects on or off campus or from their homes." **Parent education programs offered?** Yes.

WHAT SETS THE SCHOOL APART FROM OTHERS
"Burke's offers a rigorous academic program in a school culture that fosters individual growth and learning through the exploration of childhood."

HOW FAMILIES CHARACTERIZE SCHOOL
Parent comment(s): "Burke's is a strong and caring community. The combination of excellent academics, creative arts, athletics, service to community, and character development is outstanding. We are proud of our daughter's academic achievements and equally happy with the fine young woman that she is becoming."
Student comment(s): "Burke's has taught me not only what 4 x 2 is or

how to write a paragraph, but also to have confidence in my education and my ability to think for myself."

KITTREDGE SCHOOL

2355 Lake Street (at 25th Avenue) (Richmond District)
San Francisco, CA 94121
(415) 750-8390 *fax (415) 751-2011*
www.kittredge.org

Peter Lavaroni Head of School, lavaroni@kittredge.org

GENERAL

Coed K-8 day school. Founded in 1944. Independent. Proprietary. **Member:** NIPSA. **Enrollment:** Approx. 85. **Average class size:** 14. **Accreditation:** NIPSA (7-year term: 2004-11). **Endowment:** N/A. **School year:** Sept. -June. **School day:** 8:30/8:40 a.m. to 3 p.m.

STUDENT BODY ETHNICITY: N/P.

ADMISSION

Applications due: Approx. Jan. 10 (call for date). **Application fee:** $75. **Application process:** "Parents/guardians must attend an open house or tour the school before submitting an application. The completed application with the application fee must be returned to the school. Current school records and recommendations must be completed by the prior school and sent to Kittredge before a visit for the child is arranged. Children applying for K will be evaluated during a play date/screening arranged by the school in Jan. Children applying for G1-8 will spend a full school day at Kittredge in their current grade. Decisions are mailed early March in accordance with the BADA calendar. Parents will be expected to respond within a week's time by returning the completed contract with deposit." **No. of applications:** Approx. 35. **No. of K spaces:** 7 (K and G1 are combined into a class of 14). **Percentage of K class made up of school's preschool class:** N/A. **Admission evaluation requirements for K:** Recommendations from the child's preschool, a play date/ screening. Students must be 5 years old by the first day of school. **Other grades:** Parents must have the child's current school complete and return the student recommendation forms and record release form. Selected students will spend a full school day at Kittredge where they will be assessed for appropriate fit. The principal will administer a short achievement test during the student's visit day. **Preferences:** Siblings may be evaluated and accepted early. **What sort of student do you best serve?** "We serve children who will thrive in a small environment that is both academically challenging and nurturing."

COSTS
Latest tuition: $14,500 for K-5, $15,300 for G6-8. **Sibling discount:** 10% for youngest sibling. **Tuition includes:** Lunch: No; Transportation: No; Laptop computer: No; Other: Books and most supplies. **Tuition increases:** Approx. 5% annually. **Other costs:** Approx. $300 for G7-8 outdoor education, yearbook, some sports teams and after school classes. **Percentage of students receiving financial aid:** 5%. **Financial aid application deadline:** Call for date. Financial aid is based on need. **Average grant:** N/P. **Percentage of grants of half-tuition or more:** N/P. **Donations:** N/A.

SCHOOL'S MISSION STATEMENT
"Kittredge School's mission is to offer its students challenging academics in a warm and nurturing environment."

ACADEMIC PROGRAM
Philosophy: "Kittredge School is structured, friendly and productive. We believe in recognizing the worth and dignity of students and faculty alike while creating an atmosphere where strong academic goals are combined with supportive human interaction. Kittredge School recognizes the need for educating the whole child. Students receive weekly instruction in fine arts, music and drama as well as Spanish three times a week. The school also provides a daily formal physical education program. Kittredge School recognizes the necessity of self-discipline in order for a student to progress to his/her maximum potential. The goal is to help each student recognize his/her obligations to appropriate citizenship. Through published standards and effective modeling by concerned teachers, students learn the balance between freedom and responsibility. Kittredge School expects and requires students to exercise appropriate self-discipline and to respect people and property, providing a safe environment for each student to develop his/her individuality." **Foreign languages:** Spanish. **Computer training:** N/P. **No. of computers available for students:** 40. **No. of hours weekly of:** Art- 1; Drama- 1.5; Computers- 1-3; Foreign language- 2-3; PE- 2.5. **Outdoor education:** Varies by grade. G7-8 have an annual week-long trip to Yosemite Institute. **Grading:** A-F, beginning in G4. **Average nightly homework:** Varies from 15-20 min. in K to 1.5-2.5 hours in G8. Posted on the Internet: "Some." **Percentage of students participating**

in Johns Hopkins Center for Talented Youth Program: 28% in upper grades. **Other indicators of academic success:** Test scores and school placements. **High schools attended by latest graduating class:** Bay, Urban, University, Drew, SOTA, Lowell, Stuart Hall.

FACULTY
Ethnicity: 60% Caucasian (non-Latino), 10% Asian, 10% multi-racial, 20% other. **Percentage of teachers with graduate degrees:** 67%. **Percentage with current California credential:** 80%. **Faculty selection/training:** "Kittredge hires classroom teachers that hold teaching credentials, usually from California. Experience and advanced degrees are a plus. Kittredge School searches for teachers that want to work in the environment as described in our philosophy." **Teacher/student ratio:** Approx. 1:14. **Special subject teachers:** Art, performing arts, Spanish, PE. **Average teacher tenure:** 10 years.

MIDDLE SCHOOL
Description: G6-8. Classes are team-taught by several core teachers. **Teacher/student ratio:** 1:15 maximum. **Elective courses offered:** N/P. **Achievement tracking in:** Math with algebra or pre-algebra. **Student social events:** The school participates in all independent school dances.

STUDENT SUPPORT SERVICES
No. of Licensed Counselors on staff: None. **Counselor/student ratio:** N/A. **Learning specialists on staff:** None. **Learning differences/disabilities support:** "Kittredge School's small classes allow its teachers to support children with learning differences by working with them, their parents and the specialists secured by the families from outside of school. Teachers are made aware of the recommendations for the students with identified differences and implement as many as possible. Though Kittredge School is not designed specifically for students with learning differences, many such students have thrived because of the concern and care offered by the teachers, the staff and the other students, and by the diligence of the teachers to challenge each student appropriately." **High school placement support:** "A high school counselor with 25 years experience with local high schools."

STUDENT CONDUCT AND HEALTH
Code of conduct: "Kittredge School places a high priority on students assuming responsibility for their behavior and treating others with respect. Students are expected to be courteous, cooperative, honest, well mannered and considerate. Behavior that conflicts with these values is

not condoned and will be subject to counseling and possible disciplinary action." **Prevention education and awareness addressed in:** "Kittredge students are exposed to prevention education and awareness in grade appropriate curriculum."

ATHLETICS
Sports offered: Cross-country, volleyball, basketball, futsal. **Team play begins in:** G6 (intermural).

CAMPUS/CAMPUS LIFE
Campus description: Kittredge School's entire campus is situated in a converted 3-story house in the Richmond District of San Francisco. **Library:** "Each classroom has its own library of grade-appropriate books." (N/P volumes) **Sports facilities:** The school uses city playgrounds and rents local gyms for sport events. **Theater/Arts facilities:** The school rents local theaters. **Computer lab:** Yes. **Science lab:** No. **Lunch program:** No. **Bus service:** No. **Uniforms/dress code:** Dress code. **Opportunities for community service:** The Kittredge School Parent Association offers opportunities for students and their families to participate voluntarily throughout the community. Kittredge School holds special community service days for the whole school and for individual classes.

EXTENDED DAY
Morning care: Begins at 7:45 a.m. **After-school care:** Until 6 p.m. **Grade levels:** "All, but most appropriate for K-6." **Cost:** $280 a month. **Drop-in care available:** Yes. **Coverage over major holidays:** Yes. **Homework help:** Yes. **Snacks:** Provided. **Staff/student ratio:** 1:8. **After-school classes:** Varies each semester. **Cost:** N/P.

SUMMER PROGRAMS
"The Kittredge School Summer Program is six weeks long and emphasizes the basic skills of mathematics, reading and all forms of English language arts. Our small class size (15 students max.) allows each teacher to engage the students in a variety of activities designed to enrich their academic foundation and keep them involved and interested in learning. Extended Day is available where supervised study, recreational and educational activities are provided in conjunction with the morning academic program." **Cost:** The morning program (9 a.m.-1 p.m.) costs $1,150 without extended care or, with extended care (7:45 a.m. to 6 p.m.), $1,650.

PARENT INVOLVEMENT

Parent/teacher communication: "Communication between parents and teachers is important at Kittredge. Day-to-day informal communication is made easier by the student/teacher ratio and relatively small size of the school. The administration publishes a weekly newsletter to keep parents informed of the happenings around the school and each teacher hosts a classroom website with current information posted for parents. Formal communication includes 2 scheduled parent-teacher conferences. Report cards are issued four times a year, at the end of the quarter and semester periods. A back-to-school night is held one evening each September. The Parents' Association meets once a month." **Participation requirements:** "Though there are no formal requirements, parents are expected to conduct themselves in a responsible manner with their interactions with the school. They are to reinforce the school rules with their children and take an active role in their child's personal development." **Parent education programs offered?** "The school and the parent association offer opportunities for parents to meet specialists and members of the Kittredge School faculty and staff to share information."

WHAT SETS THE SCHOOL APART FROM OTHERS

"Small size and intimacy."

HOW FAMILIES CHARACTERIZE SCHOOL

Parent comment(s): "Recently, I was asked about what we think about Kittredge. As I went on and on listing the virtues of the school, I realized something I had not noticed before, that there are no bullies at the school. I don't know how Kittredge does it—I suspect by establishing a kind and courteous environment with clear expectations for student behavior—but they do!" • "Kittredge has been a hugely positive element in my daughter's life. The small family-like environment has supported her (and her family as well) in her formative years. My daughter has become a self-confident and contributive student who cares about her classmates, teachers and studies. The challenging academics have continued to shape her strong work ethic."

Student comment(s): "This is a school where it is cool to be nice." "Kittredge is a very good school. The best part of the 'Kittredge experience' is the teachers. The teachers are animated and seem to like their job a lot, probably because of the small class sizes. The teachers try their hardest to make the kids in this school want to learn."

Krouzian-Zekarian-Vasbouragan Armenian School

825 Brotherhood Way (between Lake Merced & 19th Avenue)
San Francisco, CA 94132
(415) 586-8686 *fax (415) 586-8689*
www.kzv.org, kzvoffice@kzv.org

Mrs. Grace Andonian, Principal, gandonian@kzv.org

General

Coed PS-8 day school. Founded in 1980. Private. Nonprofit. Religious.
Member: N/P. **Enrollment:** Approx. 120. **Average class size:** 12.
Accreditation: WASC (6-year term: 2009-15). **Endowment:** $1.5
million. **School year:** Aug.-June. **School day:** 8:15 a.m. to 3:35 p.m.

Student Body Ethnicity

90% Caucasian (non-Latino), 5% Latino, 5% other.

Admission

Applications due: April (call for date). **Application fee:** $200.
Application process: Interview. **No. of applications:** N/P. **No. of K
spaces:** 22. **Percentage of K class made up of school's preschool
class:** 80%. **Admission evaluation requirements for K:** Screening.
Other grades: School transcript, teacher recommendations, testing,
school visit. **Preferences:** N/P. What student do you best serve? N/P.

Costs

Latest tuition: $6,615. **Sibling discount:** Yes. **Tuition includes:** Lunch:
No; Transportation: No; Laptop computer: No; Other: None. **Tuition
increases:** Approx. 10% annually. **Other costs:** Registration fee $225;
approx. $500 for books; $150 uniforms; $200 other fees. **Percentage
of students receiving financial aid:** 30%. **Financial aid application
deadline:** April (call for date). Financial aid is based on need. **Average
grant:** $1,000. **Percentage of grants of half-tuition or more:** None.
Donations: Each family is required to participate in the various activities
and fundraisers organized by the PTA.

School's Mission Statement

"The Armenian Schools under the jurisdiction of the Western Prelacy
of the Armenian Apostolic Church firmly believe in the importance of
education and academic excellence, the development of national character

and the heritage of the Armenian people, language, culture, traditions and religion. Our schools strive to: • Provide educational opportunities that will develop positive universal values, academic, social and emotional skills that will guide, prepare and encourage our students to become viable Armenian-American citizens to better serve mankind.• Instill students with Armenian spirit within a wholesome environment in order to ensure their commitment to traditional Armenian values, secure future growth, promote their involvement in the rebuilding process of Armenia and the perpetuation of her independence, based upon principals of democracy, equality, justice and economic prosperity."

ACADEMIC PROGRAM

Philosophy: "As an Armenian American day school, KZV offers a structured curriculum consistent with the California state standards and its philosophy and goals. The KZV school curriculum is designed to prepare students for their education beyond elementary and middle school grades. The core curriculum consists of the following courses: language arts (English and Armenian), mathematics, science, and social studies. Students also receive instruction in computer science, art, health, physical education and music. • Students are given opportunities to demonstrate and develop their artistic abilities in drama, speech, dance, voice and arts and crafts, by participating in school pageants and programs. Religion is an integral part of the KZV curriculum. Armenian Church history, Bible stories, Armenian Church liturgy and sacraments, as well as ethical and moral ideas and values are explored. The annual Literature and Science Fairs provide additional opportunities for students to research, develop, problem solve, and display unique projects pertaining to literature and science. Our seventh grade class has the special opportunity to visit Armenia, during the summer. **Foreign languages:** Armenian. **Computer training:** N/P. **No. of computers available for students:** 18. **No. of hours weekly of:** Art- 1; Drama- 1; Music- 1; Computers- 1; Foreign language- 10; PE- 2. **Outdoor education:** "Yes." **Grading:** A-F, beginning in G3. **Average nightly homework:** Varies by grade. 20-30 min. plus reading in G1-2; 30-90 min. plus reading in G3-4; 20-30 min. per subject for 5 academic subjects in G5-6; 30-40 min. per subject in G7-8. Posted on the internet: G6-8. **Percentage of students participating in Johns Hopkins Center for Talented Youth Program:** None. **Other indicators of academic success:** "Quality of students work, SAT10 scores, GPAs, success of our alums in high school." **High schools attended by latest graduating class:** Lowell, SI, SHCP, Mercy-SF, Mercy-Burlingame, Riordan.

FACULTY
Ethnicity: 90% Caucasian (non-Latino), 5% Asian, 5% other. **Percentage of teachers with graduate degrees:** 15%. **Percentage with current California credential:** 50%. **Faculty selection/training:** Experience and degree. **Teacher/student ratio:** 1:10. **Special subject teachers:** Armenian, art, music, computers. **Average teacher tenure:** 7 years.

MIDDLE SCHOOL
Description: G6-8, departmentalized. **Teacher/student ratio:** 1:10. **Elective courses offered:** None. **Achievement tracking in:** "Beginning G6." **Student social events:** "Some."

STUDENT SUPPORT SERVICES
No. of Licensed Counselors on staff: One part-time. **Counselor/student ratio:** N/P. **Learning specialists on staff:** No. **Learning differences/ disabilities support:** Yes. **High school placement support:** Yes.

STUDENT CONDUCT AND HEALTH
Code of conduct: "The school is committed to a physically and emotionally safe and secure learning environment. Discipline is the training that develops character, self control, efficiency, and orderliness. It is the key to good conduct, consideration, and respect for the rights of others. The school places emphasis upon teaching and reinforcing appropriate behavior in order to establish and maintain a positive learning environment. Specific goals of the discipline policy are the following: establish a safe productive learning environment free of hate speech that ensures the safety of all students, teachers and staff, promote self-direction, motivation, and a sense of responsibility among students, cultivate mutual respect among students, teachers, administration, and parents. **Prevention education and awareness addressed in:** Health class.

ATHLETICS
Sports offered: N/P. **Team play begins in:** G3 (intramural).

CAMPUS/CAMPUS LIFE
Campus description: N/P. **Library:** Yes. **Sports facilities:** Outdoor courts. **Theater/Arts facilities:** Yes, with stage. **Computer lab:** Yes. **Science lab:** No. **Lunch program:** Yes. **Bus service:** No. **Uniforms/ dress code:** N/P. **Opportunities for community service:** Yes.

Extended Day

Morning care: Begins at 7:45 a.m. **After-school care:** Until 6 p.m. **Grade levels:** All. **Cost:** PS, $10/hour; K-8, $8/hour. **Drop-in care available:** No. **Coverage over major holidays:** No. **Homework help:** Yes. **Snacks:** Not provided. **Staff/student ratio:** 1:10. **After-school classes:** Chess, music, traditional dance, team sports. **Cost:** N/P.

Summer Programs

The school offers "Hye Em Yes" Bay Area Summer Day Camp for children ages 6-14 years and Nabasdag (The Rabbit) Play Camp for children ages 2½-5 years. **Cost:** $150/session, $250/both sessions. $125 discount for the second child, and $100 for a third child.

Parent Involvement

Parent/teacher communication: Conferences, meetings, telephone, websites, e-mail, progress reports, newsletter. **Participation requirements:** 40 hours per family. **Parent education programs:** None.

What Sets the School Apart From Others

"The Krouzian-Zekarian-Vasbouragan Armenian School endeavors to provide an educational environment of the highest quality in which students are educated, through a bilingual curriculum to become Armenian Americans confident in their identity and heritage, proficient in their languages, appreciative of their cultures, and well prepared as members of American Society. High academic standards stressing sound study skills, and development of good character and self-discipline are coupled with the commitment to developing the whole child in a Christian and family-like atmosphere. • KZV Armenian School, believes in the uniqueness of each individual. The educational effort focuses on the process of "learning to learn" by fostering the love of learning. Among the basic elements encouraged by faculty are inquisitiveness, exploration, experimentation, creativity, intuition, imagination, and logical thinking, each in its appropriate place and time.• This school believes in developing the whole person and, therefore, encourages its students to develop as well-rounded individuals with a wide variety of extracurricular interests and achievements that help them exercise leadership, cooperation, and caring for the overall welfare of the school and its community. • The students of this school also acquire a strong sense of Armenian ancestry and Christian values. These values permeate their lives not only while they are at this school, but also long after they have left it."

How Families Characterize School
Parent comment(s): "Family oriented."
Student comment(s): "Dynamic."

The Laurel School

350 9th Avenue (Clement and Geary) (Inner Richmond District)
San Francisco, CA 94118
(415) 752-3567 *fax (415) 752-6870*
www.thelaurelschool.com

Andrea Montes, Head of School, amontes@thelaurelschool.com
Roberta Rodriguez-Havens, Director of Admissions,
rhavens@thelaurelschool.com

General
Coed PK-8 day school. Founded in 1969. Independent. Nonprofit.
Member: N/P. **Enrollment:** Approx. 85. **Average class size:** 9.
Accreditation: N/P. **Endowment:** N/A. **School year:** Sept.-June.
School day: 8:30 a.m. to 3 p.m. Mon.-Thurs.; 8:30 a.m. to 1:30 p.m. Fri.

Student Body Ethnicity: N/P.

Admission
Applications due: Call for date. **Application fee:** $100. **Application process:** "Contact the school." **No. of applications:** N/P. **No. of K spaces:** 9. **Percentage of K class made up of school's preschool class:** N/A. **Admission evaluation requirements for K:** School visit, teacher evaluation and parent interview. **Other grades:** School visit, grades, test scores, recommendations. **Preferences:** N/P. **What sort of student do you best serve?** "Laurel School's best fits are: 1) Children who are shy and benefit from a small, nurturing learning environment; 2) Children whose strengths lie in their learning, but have difficulty fitting in socially; 3) Typically developing children who benefit from small class sizes and have a chance to develop leadership skills; 4) Children who struggle with their learning, but do not qualify for Special Education services through their school districts; 5) Children who need extra time to find their voices and whose voices will be heard at Laurel; 6) Children who need an individualized learning program due to diagnoses of Language Based Learning Disabilities, Non-Verbal Learning Disabilities, Sensory Integration Dysfunction, ADD/ADHD, or other related conditions."

Costs

Latest tuition: $22,500. **Sibling discount:** 10%. **Tuition includes:** Lunch: No; Transportation: No; Laptop computer: Yes; Other: N/P. **Tuition increases:** Approx. 10% annually. **Other costs:** Approx. $100 for uniforms, $100 for other fees. **Percentage of students receiving financial aid:** 30%. **Financial aid application deadline:** Call for date. Financial aid is based on need. **Average grant:** N/P. **Percentage of grants of half-tuition or more:** N/P. **Donations:** Voluntary.

School's Mission Statement

"The Laurel School is dedicated to cultivating the individual potential of each child in a community that practices mutual respect, embraces diversity, and inspires a life-long love of learning."

Academic Program

Philosophy: "The key to unlocking your child's academic, emotional, and social growth is understanding who he/she is and how he/she learns. The Laurel School's individualized teaching approach recognizes the whole child. We focus on the unique abilities and learning style of each child and develop specific strategies for learning and personal achievement." **Foreign languages:** None. **Computer training:** N/P. "Macintosh." **No. of computers available for students:** 40. **No. of hours weekly of:** Art- 1; Drama- 1; Music- 1; Computers- N/P; Foreign language- N/A; PE- N/P ("daily"). **Outdoor education:** N/P. **Grading:** A-F, beginning in G6. **Average nightly homework:** Individualized for each student. Posted on the Internet: No. **Percentage of students participating in Johns Hopkins Center for Talented Youth Program:** N/P. **Other indicators of academic success:** N/P. **High schools attended by latest graduating class:** Drew, SHCP, Riordan, Stuart Hall, Marin School, Waldorf, Mid-Peninsula, Mercy-SF, Sterne School.

Faculty

Ethnicity: N/P. **Percentage of teachers with graduate degrees:** 17%. **Percentage with current California credential:** N/P. **Faculty selection/training:** N/P. **Teacher/student ratio:** 1:9. **Special subject teachers:** Art, music, science, drama, movement/dance, PE. **Average teacher tenure:** 8 years.

Middle School

Description: "Middle school is from G6-8. The program follows a traditional middle school model with students transitioning to a variety of classrooms for each subject area. The emphasis is on individualizing academic programs." **Teacher/student ratio:** 1:9. **Elective courses offered:** Study skills, keyboarding, high school preparation. **Achievement tracking in:** N/P. **Student social events:** Four dances per year, Student Council, Year End Graduation Trip.

STUDENT SUPPORT SERVICES

No. of Licensed Counselors on staff: One. **Counselor/student ratio:** N/P. **Learning specialists on staff:** N/P. **Learning differences/ disabilities support:** "The majority of our teachers have Special Education training and backgrounds." The G5 students participate with the Jonathan Mooney, "Eye to Eye" Program. Speech and language therapy available. **High school placement support:** Advisor.

STUDENT CONDUCT AND HEALTH

Code of conduct: "Students are expected to conduct themselves in an appropriate manner at all times. They should show courtesy to all faculty, staff, and other students. Each teacher has his/her own classroom rules which the administration supports." **Prevention education and awareness addressed in:** N/P.

ATHLETICS

Sports offered: N/P. **Team play begins in:** G3 through CYO team.

CAMPUS/CAMPUS LIFE

Campus description: "A safe and secure urban setting with many neighborhood resources just out our front doors." **Library:** The school uses the newly renovated Richmond branch of the San Francisco Public Library, across the street from the school. **Sports facilities:** Gymnasium. **Theater/Arts facilities:** Auditorium. **Computer lab:** Yes. **Science lab:** Yes. **Lunch program:** Yes. **Bus service:** Yes. **Uniforms/dress code:** Uniforms. **Opportunities for community service:** Graduation requirements include 30 hours of community service.

EXTENDED DAY

Morning care: Begins at 8 a.m. **After-school care:** Until 6 p.m. **Grade levels:** All. **Cost:** $8/hour. **Drop-in care available:** Yes. **Coverage over major holidays:** No. **Homework help:** Yes. **Snacks:** Provided. **Staff/ student ratio:** 1:10. **After-school classes:** Study Hall for middle school students daily. **Cost:** N/A.

Summer Programs

"The Laurel school created a program designed for kids who learn differently and need an alternative environment than the typical camp. Our 1:5 ratio staff to camper ratio ensures each child gets the attention. The school offers a 4-week summer program with academic emphasis on reading, language arts, math, social skills group, occupational therapy, sport skills." **Cost:** Approx. $1,300 for each 2-week session.

Parent Involvement

Parent/teacher communication: Conferences, e-mail, and newsletter. **Participation requirements:** Thirty hours for 2 parent families and 20 hours for single parent families are required. **Parent education programs offered?** Yes.

What Sets the School Apart From Others

"Top 10 Reasons Why Laurel School is Unique: 1) Small class size and a low student to teacher ratio allow each teacher the time to understand and best teach each child; 2) Each student's diverse gifts, talents, and challenges are celebrated in a positive way; 3) Families and educators work together to create an inclusive school community where each student truly feels a sense of belonging; 4) The needs of each student are met through the small class size and individualized curriculum; 5) At Laurel every teacher knows every child; 6) Each student is a full and participating member of the Laurel School community; 7) Teachers confer and collaborate to meet each child's educational physical, and social needs; 8) The entire class benefits from the collaboration of the classroom teachers and outside specialists because all children have different learning styles; 9) Laurel has a flexible curriculum. Programs are adapted and accommodations take place seamlessly throughout the school as needed; 10) Laurel School is a small school where positive changes can quickly happen. New programs are embraced and introduced. There is no bureaucracy to slow program implementation."

How Families Characterize School

Parent comment(s): "Our child was caught between the cracks of the public school system. We found the Laurel School. Now he loves school, works extremely hard, and has made tremendous progress."
Student comment(s): "The Laurel School is like a second home—a big family. There's acceptance of each other's differences."

LISA KAMPNER HEBREW ACADEMY

645 14th Avenue (at Balboa) (Richmond District)
San Francisco, CA 94118
(415) 752-7333 *fax (415) 752-5851*
www.hebrewacademy.com

Rabbi Pinchas Lipner, Head of School, info@hebrewacademy.com
Mimi Real, Ph.D., Director of Admission, info@hebrewacademy.com

GENERAL

Coed Jewish PS-8 day school. Founded in 1969. Independent. Jewish. Nonprofit. **Member:** Torah Umesorah. **Enrollment:** Approx. 100. **Average class size:** 12. **Accreditation:** None. **Endowment:** N/P. **School year:** Sept.-June. **School day:** 8:30 a.m. to 3:36 p.m.

STUDENT BODY ETHNICITY

96% Caucasian (non-Latino), 2% Asian, 2% African American.

ADMISSION

Applications due: Rolling admissions. **Application fee:** $50. **Application process:** School visit and interview, application form, references, testing administered at school. **No. of applications:** N/P. **No. of K spaces:** N/P. **Percentage of K class made up of school's preschool class:** 75%. **Admission evaluation requirements for K:** School visit, interview with Preschool Director. **Other grades:** School visit, interview, references, application form, testing. **Preferences:** "Jewish by Jewish law or by acceptable conversion." **What sort of student do you best serve?** "We want students who want to be active in and contribute to a learning community that has high intellectual and moral standards. We value a positive attitude towards learning, personal creativity, kindness and moral strength. We value students who want to contribute to their families, their community and the Jewish people."

COSTS

Latest tuition: N/P. **Sibling discount:** "On case-by-case basis." **Tuition includes:** Lunch: K only; Transportation: No; Laptop computer: No; Other: N/P. **Tuition increases:** N/P. **Other costs:** Approx. $250 for books, $600 other fees (building fund). **Percentage of students receiving financial aid:** 88%. **Financial aid application deadline:** None. Financial aid is based on need. **Average grant:** N/P. **Percentage of grants of half-tuition or more:** N/P. **Donations:** N/P.

School's Mission Statement

"Our campus is a place for a learning partnership with the strong and simple family values of love and respect for one another. In a world of increasing turbulence, the Hebrew Academy is a safe place. Every student is valued for his or her own potential. We provide a morally structured but accepting environment. Our success rate is high: our students enter universities, Yeshivas and careers of their choice. Educating a child is a responsibility best shared between the home and school. The Hebrew Academy is a Jewish day school, which strives to provide an excellent academic and Jewish education. We endeavor to expose our children to an intensive appreciation of their religious and ethical responsibilities. The creation of the State of Israel is one of the seminal events in Jewish history. Recognizing the significance of the State and its national institutions, we seek to instill in our students an attachment to the State of Israel and its people as well as a sense of responsibility for their welfare. Our goal is to develop knowledgeable, independent, proud Jews who will contribute to their Jewish and general communities. We are guided by the Biblical injunction: 'Train up a child in the way he should go and when he is old he will not depart from it.' (Proverbs 22:6)."

Academic Program

Philosophy: "See Mission Statement." **Foreign languages:** Hebrew. **Computer training:** None. **No. of computers available for students:** None. **No. of hours weekly of:** Art- N/P; Drama- N/P; Music- N/P; Computers- none; Foreign language- 3.3; PE- 1.5. **Outdoor education:** N/P. **Grading:** VG-U; A-F, beginning in G6. **Average nightly homework:** "Varies by grade." Posted on the Internet: No. **Percentage of students participating in Johns Hopkins Center for Talented Youth Program:** None. **Other indicators of academic success:** "Our students perform exceptionally well on standardized tests. Our curriculum is one grade level above that in public schools." **High schools attended by latest graduating class:** 98% of school's 8th graders continue at Hebrew Academy High School, Lowell, JCHS.

Faculty

Ethnicity: 100% Caucasian. **Percentage of teachers with graduate degrees:** 75%. **Percentage with current California credential:** 75%. **Faculty selection/training:** BA or BS required plus further study; experience required. **Teacher/student ratio:** 1:10. **Special subject teachers:** Hebrew, Judaic studies. **Average teacher tenure:** 14 years.

Middle School
Description: G7-8, departmentalized. **Teacher/student ratio:** 1:12. **Elective courses offered:** None. **Achievement tracking in:** Reading, language skills, math, social studies, science. **Student social events:** N/P.

Student Support Services
No. of Licensed Counselors on staff: One part-time; **Counselor/ student ratio:** N/P. **Learning specialists on staff:** None. **Learning differences/disabilities support:** Reading specialist, G1-4. **High school placement support:** "Most students remain at Lisa Kampner Hebrew Academy."

Student Conduct and Health
Code of conduct: "Spelled out in Parent/Student Handbook." **Prevention education and awareness addressed in:** "Included in curriculum."

Athletics
Sports offered: No organized sports teams. **Team play begins in:** N/A.

Campus/Campus Life
Campus description: "A modern stucco building in a quiet park-like residential neighborhood close to Golden Gate Park." **Library:** "Spacious and airy, with approx. 7,000 volumes that include secular and Judaic works in both English and Hebrew." **Sports facilities:** Full-sized gymnasium/multi-purpose room, outdoor basketball area. **Theater/Arts facilities:** The school has a stage where middle and high school students put on annual productions. **Computer lab:** No. **Science lab:** Yes. **Lunch program:** Yes but "partial." **Bus service:** No. **Uniforms/dress code:** Dress code. **Opportunities for community service:** Not required until high school.

Extended Day
Morning care: N/A. **After-school care:** Until 6 p.m. **Grade levels:** K-6. **Cost:** "Varies." **Drop-in care available:** No. **Coverage over major holidays:** No. **Homework help:** Yes. **Snacks:** Provided in K only. **Staff/ student ratio:** 1:4. **After-school classes:** None until high school. **Cost:** N/P.

Summer Programs: None.

Parent Involvement

Parent/teacher communication: Parents are kept informed through conferences and newsletters. **Participation requirements:** Attendance at school functions and plays. **Parent education programs offered?** No.

What Sets the School Apart From Others

"The Lisa Kampner Hebrew Academy is a remarkable school with exceptional students. We provide a morally structured but accepting environment. Our success rate is high: our students enter universities, Yeshivas and careers of their choice. Our standards are high, and we look for students with the ability to reach their personal and academic goals. The relationships between faculty and students are unique in their depth, friendship and mutual respect. The Lisa Kampner Hebrew Academy is a school where academic, creative and personal potential are fulfilled and lifetime relationships are forged. Each student is part of a close knit and outstanding whole whose well-being is the focus of our highly trained and caring faculty."

How Families Characterize School

Parent comment(s): "Academically rigorous and outstanding. My children couldn't get a better education. And I know my children are safe and are learning good moral values and learning to be good Jews. Also, everyone knows the reputation of the school for getting its students into good universities."

Student comment(s): "Hebrew Academy is like a family; you feel the warmth and closeness the minute you walk through the front door." • "I wish I could stay at the Hebrew Academy forever."

Live Oak School

1555 Mariposa Street (across from Jackson Park) (Potrero Hill)
San Francisco, CA 94107
(415) 861-8840 *fax (415) 861-7153*
www.liveoaksf.org

Virginia Paik, Interim Head of School, virginia_paik@liveoaksf.org
Tracey Gersten, Director of Admission, admissions@liveoaksf.org

General

Coed K-8 day school. Founded in 1971. Independent. Nonprofit. **Member:** NAIS, CAIS, BADA. **Enrollment:** Approx. 260. **Average

class size: 22 in lower school, 2 class sections per grade of 17 each in middle school. **Accreditation:** CAIS (term N/P). **Endowment:** "Seeded." **School year:** Sept.-June. **School day:** 8:30 a.m. to 3:15 p.m.

STUDENT BODY ETHNICITY
70% Caucasian (non-Latino), 18% multi-racial, 4% Latino, 4% Asian, 3% African American, 1% other.

ADMISSION
Applications due: Dec. for K, Feb. for middle school (check website for dates). **Application fee:** $85. **Application Process:** Tour, application, student visit/screening, parent interview. **No. of applications:** 180. **No. of K spaces:** 22. **Percentage of K class made up of school's preschool class:** N/A. **Admission evaluation requirements for K:** School visit and screening, parent interview and current school recommendation/ evaluation. **Other grades:** The other entry point for the school is G6, where the school normally has 16 middle school spaces open. Students applying for G6 participate in a school visit and screening, and submit current school recommendation, evaluation and records, and ISEE scores. Spaces are available in other grades by attrition and applicants to those grades should submit an application and submit school records and school recommendation/evaluation, and a student visit including screening/assessment will be scheduled if a space becomes available. **Preferences:** Siblings. **What sort of student do you best serve?** "With a focus on differentiated instruction, and on preparing students to be powerful learners and problem solvers, Live Oak serves a wide range of students well. We know our students well as individuals, allowing them to achieve their full potential through academic risk taking, opportunities for creative expression, and active community involvement. As a family school, Live Oak welcomes families who want to participate and to create a partnership between home and school, and who want their children to grow up to be who they are meant to be."

COSTS
Latest tuition: $22,200. **Sibling discount:** None. **Tuition includes:** Lunch: No; Transportation: Van service; Laptop computer: No; Other: Field trips, annual camping trip, books. **Tuition increases:** Approx. 3-6% annually. **Other costs:** $500 per family work assessment fee and $1,000 capital deposit fee for first 3 years (waived for families receiving tuition assistance); $550 for G8 trip to Washington, D.C. **Percentage of students receiving financial aid:** 29%. **Financial aid application deadline:** Jan. (see website for date). Financial aid is based on financial

need. **Average grant:** 52%. **Percentage of grants of half-tuition or more:** N/P. **Donations:** Voluntary.

School's Mission Statement

"Live Oak School supports the potential and promise of each student. We provide a strong academic foundation, develop personal confidence and the ability to collaborate with others, inspire students to act with compassion and integrity, and nurture a passion for learning to last a lifetime."

Academic Program

Philosophy: "Live Oak's compelling and rigorous curriculum is designed to prepare students for high school and for life. In addition to core subjects, we emphasize development of positive values and life skills. Inspired by educational theory and rooted in practical application, we foster a learning environment that challenges and engages our students, and that nurtures, encourages, and celebrates each student's exploration and growth. We understand that childhood is a time to explore, to try new things, to open doors, and to learn about learning. We place a balanced emphasis on art, music, drama, physical education, the humanities and sciences, promoting integration and connectedness within the curriculum. Our teachers teach at the forefront of learning theory as a result of a deep commitment to ongoing professional development and lifelong learning, tapping into students' natural curiosity to actively engage them in learning. They know our students well and differentiate instruction, capitalizing on student strengths and interests in order to foster success in meeting academic goals. They design a rigorous curriculum relevant to the group and responsive to the individual. Our students learn through direct experience and hands-on exploration, working cooperatively with their peers to communicate, negotiate and problem solve. We create a challenging, supportive environment so our students can take the academic risks that expand their thinking. We forge a partnership between school and home, and families participate actively in the life of the school. We create and nurture a diverse K-8 community, embracing our similarities and differences and encouraging the sharing and valuing of our unique backgrounds. Our community cultivates open-mindedness, responsibility, compassion and integrity, and strives to reflect the values it seeks to instill in its children. Our graduates leave Live Oak as knowledgeable, articulate human beings, eager and ready for the challenges ahead, and with self-esteem, confidence, and a sense of responsibility to themselves and their community." **Foreign languages:** Spanish. **Computer training:** Yes. **No. of computers available for students:** 23 in computer lab; 20 laptops, 90 in classrooms and library. **No. of hours weekly of:** Art- 2; Drama- 1 (G6-8); Music- 2; Computers- N/P; Foreign language- 2-4 (G4-8); PE- 2-3. **Outdoor education:** "Yes, G4-8." **Grading:** K-5 narratives, comments. Letter grades begin in G6. **Average nightly homework:** 1-2 hours depending on grade level and student. Posted on the Internet: Yes. **Percentage of students participating in Johns Hopkins Center for Talented Youth Program:** 45% are eligible, 10% participate. **High schools attended by latest graduating class:** Bay, Drew, IHS, Lick, Lowell, MA, Riordan, SHCP, SOTA, SI, Stuart Hall, University, Urban.

FACULTY
Ethnicity: 73% Caucasian, 13% African-American, 10% Asian, 3% Latino, 1% other. **Percentage of teachers with graduate degrees:** "48% (teachers and staff)." **Percentage with current California credential:** 38%. **Faculty selection/training:** Experience, degree, training. **Teacher/ student ratio:** 1:6 in the lower school, 1:5 in the middle school. **Special subject teachers:** Art, music, drama, computers. **Average teacher tenure:** 7 years.

MIDDLE SCHOOL
Description: Departmentalized. Begins in G6 with 2 sections of approx. 17 students each in G6-8. **Teacher/student ratio:** 1:5. **Elective courses offered:** Courses vary each trimester and have included French, drama, athletics, debate, public speaking, podcasting, cooking, Student Council, yearbook, photography, creative writing, book group. **Achievement tracking in:** Spanish. Advanced Spanish is available for native Spanish speakers and students coming from Spanish immersion schools. **Student social events:** Dances, school events.

STUDENT SUPPORT SERVICES
No. of Licensed Counselors on staff: None. **Counselor/student ratio:** N/A. **Learning specialists on staff:** One full-time, 1 part- time. **Learning differences/disabilities support:** "Learning Specialists, well-trained faculty." **High school placement support:** High School Placement Counselor.

STUDENT CONDUCT AND HEALTH
Code of conduct: "Live Oak's behavioral expectations are known well by the students and are reinforced as part of the culture of the school. We have high expectations for student behavior." **Prevention education and awareness addressed in:** Drug education, sex education, middle school advisory program.

ATHLETICS
Sports offered: Volleyball, cross-country, basketball, futsal. **Team play begins in:** G5.

CAMPUS/CAMPUS LIFE
Campus description: Newly renovated, 3-story urban campus. **Library:** "Beautiful library that houses 8,000 volumes." **Sports facilities:** Half court gymnasium, courtyard playground, public park across the street from the school. UCSF Mission Bay gymnasium is used as "home court" for after school athletics; students are driven there in school van. **Theater/ Arts Facilities:** Grand Hall with stage and theatrical lighting and sound system, music room, art studio. **Computer lab:** Yes, 23 workstations, plus 20 laptops, and an additional 90 computers in classrooms. **Science lab:** Two. **Lunch program:** Yes. **Bus service:** Yes. Morning bus service from Sea Cliff, Pacific Heights and Cow Hollow, school van from Noe Valley and Cole Valley. **Uniforms/Dress code:** No. **Opportunities for community service:** "Yes, integrated into program."

EXTENDED DAY
Morning care: Begins at 7:30 a.m. **After-school care:** Until 6 p.m. **Grade levels:** K-8. **Cost:** $7/hour pre-purchased, **Drop-in care available:** Yes, $9/hour. **Coverage over major holidays:** Yes. **Homework help:** Yes. **Snacks:** Provided. **Staff/student ratio:** Approx. 1:8. **After-school classes:** Variety which can include Mandarin, Italian, Aikido, golf, drama, Lego engineering, ceramics, science, music, fencing, chess, guitar, and piano. **Cost:** $185-$375/10 weekly classes (tuition assistance available).

SUMMER PROGRAMS
The school's 8-week summer program, Summer Oaks, is open to the public and provides a theme-based program for children in K-2, and a wide variety of course offerings for children in G3-8. **Cost:** $150-$275 per week.

PARENT INVOLVEMENT
Parent/teacher communication: Conferences, e-mail, phone, and newsletter. **Participation requirements:** Parents of students in the Lower School are required to volunteer 60 hours per year; Middle School parents volunteer 30 hours per year; 50% of the required number for single parent families. **Parent education programs offered?** Yes.

What Sets the School Apart From Others

"We nurture a small, strong community where students are known well—by classmates, faculty, parents and themselves. We enjoy an inclusive, diverse environment that celebrates differences. By knowing children well, we inspire, support, and challenge them to be powerful lifelong learners with the courage to be change makers and leaders who are well prepared for success in our rapidly changing world. Live Oak puts children at the center of all we do, providing access and challenge for every student, supporting deep thinking, self-expression and new perspectives. We value joy and humor, and in it find the willingness to learn from our mistakes, the desire to take healthy risks, and the curiosity of childhood."

How Families Characterize School

Parent comment(s): "We love Live Oak because we get strong academics and a rich creative arts program while still having a warm environment and close-knit community where my child is known well and appreciated for the individual he is. Live Oak supports his brain, his heart and his creative spirit, and gives him the room to soar as high as he can."

Student comment(s): "I think Live Oak offers a strong academic core but allows you to go above and beyond. It also helps you with problems, too. It's about making sure you get to your personal best."

Lycée Français La Pérouse, The French School

San Francisco Primary School campus (PK-5):
755 Ashbury Street (at Frederick) (Haight-Ashbury)
San Francisco, CA 94117
(415) 661-5232 *fax (415) 661-0945*
www.lelycee.org

San Francisco Secondary School campus (G6-12)
1201 Ortega Street (at 19th Avenue)(Sunset)
San Francisco, CA 94122
(415) 661-5232

Marin County Primary School campus (PK-5)
330 Golden Hind Passage
Corte Madera, CA 94925
(415) 661-5232 *fax (415) 924-2849*

Frédérick Arzelier, Head of School, farzelier@lelycee.org
Isabelle Desmole, Director of Admission, idesmole@lelycee.org

GENERAL

Coed PS-12 French day school (with all subjects taught in French and extensive English). Founded in 1967. Independent. Nonsectarian. Nonprofit. **Member:** CAIS/WASC, AEFE, BADA. The San Francisco campus includes a lower school which is Preschool (beginning at age 3) through G12; the Corte Madera (Marin County) campus includes preschool (beginning at age 2.5) through G5. **Enrollment:** Approx. 900. **Average class size:** 15-20. **Accreditation:** WASC/CAIS, French Ministry of Education (term N/P). **Endowment:** None. **School year:** Sept.-June. **School day:** 8:15 a.m. to 3:15 p.m.

STUDENT BODY ETHNICITY

"The school has 31 nationalities represented. 60% are French (26% French, 30% French-U.S., 4% French-other) plus 34% Americans and 6% other nationalities."

ADMISSION

Applications due: Jan. (call for date). **Application fee:** $100 per child. **Application process:** Visits by appointment and open houses held throughout the year (see website). Students coming from other French schools or the French system are automatically admitted to grade level based on their report cards. Non-French speaking students are welcome to apply up to K. **No. of applications:** N/P. **No. of K spaces:** 15. **Percentage of K class made up of school's preschool class:** 75%. **Admission evaluation requirements for K:** None, open enrollment. **Other grades:** Two+ years of grade reports, recommendations, and a student/parent meeting. **Preferences:** French citizens, siblings, alumni from a Lycée Français. **What sort of student do you best serve?** "Internationally minded, academically oriented, future contributing citizen of the world."

COSTS

Latest tuition: $11,650 for part-time PS, $17,400 for PS-5, $18,450 for G6-9. **Sibling discount:** 10%. **Tuition includes:** Lunch: No; Transportation; No; Laptop computer: No. Other: N/P. **Tuition increases:** Approx. 3% annually. **Other costs:** None. **Percentage of students receiving financial aid:** Approx. 25%, French citizens are eligible for grants from the French government. **Average grant:** $2,000. **Percentage of grants of half-tuition or more:** 60%. Fifty-five percent of French government grants to French nationals, 5% of Lycée grants. **Financial aid application deadline:** March (call for date). Financial aid is based on need. **Donations:** Voluntary.

SCHOOL'S MISSION STATEMENT

"The Lycée Français La Pérouse provides international-minded families of the greater Bay Area an academically-rigorous curriculum in a French/ English fully bilingual environment. Based on the French national education system, the Preschool-12 innovative program prepares students for completion of the educational requirements of both France and the United States and provides an excellent preparation for both European and North American colleges and universities. The diverse and international nature of the student body and faculty fosters a spirit of community and prepares students to be contributing citizens of the world."

ACADEMIC PROGRAM

Philosophy: "The Lycée Français La Pérouse is a French international school, with classes from the 'petite section de maternelle' (2 years before K) through G12. Students receive an academically rigorous education, learning all the subjects of a French school, complemented by the English education commensurate with their year in school. The Lycée is a full immersion school, where students learn all their subjects in French, except for English and U.S. history." **Foreign languages:** French, English, 3rd language in G6 (German, Spanish or Mandarin). **Computer training:** "The SF campuses are equipped with both a computer lab and a teaching center dedicated to teaching on the Internet and taking advantage of the many French educational programs available through the Internet." **No. of computers available for students:** Two computer labs and 20 wireless classroom laptops. **No. of hours weekly of:** Art- 1; Drama- 1; Music- 1; Computers- 1; Foreign language- 6; PE- 2. **Outdoor education:** N/P. **Grading:** "The Lycée uses the French system of grading on a scale of 0 to 20, complemented by written evaluations. The French system is more rigorous than American grading and is known and respected by American colleges and universities." **Average nightly homework:** 30-60 min. in G1-5; 60-90 min. in G6-9. Posted on the Internet: Yes. **Percentage of students participating in Johns Hopkins Center for Talented Youth Program:** N/P. **Other indicators of academic success:** N/P. **High schools attended by latest graduating class:** Lycée.

FACULTY

Ethnicity: 95% Caucasian (non-Latino), 1% Asian, 1% Latino, 1% African-American, 1% multi-racial, 1% other. **Percentage of teachers with graduate degrees:** "The French Ministry of Education sends certified teachers from France for 1-4 years, while other French teachers are hired locally. Yearly evaluations are held by French officials. English and U.S. history teachers hold California teaching credentials. In-service days are held on an on-going basis as well as continuing education." **Percentage with current California credential:** 100% of English teachers. **Faculty selection/training:** See above. **Teacher/student ratio:** 1:5. **Special subject teachers:** Art, music, computer science, American math, ESL, FSL (French as a Second language). **Average teacher tenure:** N/P.

MIDDLE SCHOOL

Description: "Beginning in G6 each subject is taught by a specialist and Spanish and German are added to the curriculum. Science is expanded to include biology, geology, chemistry, and physics. Students also study English literature, U.S. and world history and geography in English. At the conclusion of G9 students take the 'Brevet des Colleges' examination in French, mathematics and history." **Teacher/student ratio:** 1:9. **Elective courses offered:** Theater, drawing, music, sports. **Achievement tracking in:** N/P. **Student social events:** "Various."

STUDENT SUPPORT SERVICES

No. of Licensed Counselors on staff: Two. **Counselor/student ratio:** N/P. **Learning specialists on staff:** Two. **Learning differences/ disabilities support:** N/P. **High school placement support:** N/P.

STUDENT CONDUCT AND HEALTH

Code of conduct: Disciplinary policy for drug/alcohol use, improper language and sexual/racial harassment in school regulations. **Prevention education and awareness addressed in:** "Civic education from G6-10; sex education through biology class; support systems specific to middle school students. " A psychologist is on site 3 hours per week.

ATHLETICS

Sports offered: Basketball, volleyball, cross-country, soccer, softball. **Team play begins in:** G6 (G1 for soccer).

Campus/Campus Life
Campus description: In 1996, Lycée moved into a 42,000 sq. ft. building at the site of the former St. Agnes School for the San Francisco primary campus. The building has been extensively remodeled to include 3 floors of classrooms, computer, a music room, an extensive library with a rooftop terrace (open only to the upper grades), and a greenhouse. In 2007, the Lycée acquired the building of the former Conservatory of Music for its new secondary school campus. The building has been extensively remodeled and includes newly equipped science labs, computer room, a 400-seat auditorium, 2 patios, and a French/English library. **Library:** Yes, on each campus. **Sports facilities:** N/P. **Theater/Arts facilities:** Auditorium on the secondary campus. **Computer lab:** Yes. **Science lab:** Yes. **Lunch program:** Yes. **Bus service:** From the Peninsula, $2,000/year round trip, and from the North Bay, $1,800/year round trip. **Uniforms/dress code:** N/P. **Opportunities for community service:** Yes.

Extended Day
Morning care: Available on a need basis. **After-school care:** Until 6 p.m. **Grade levels:** All. **Cost:** $7/hour. **Drop-in care available:** Yes. **Coverage over major holidays:** No. **Homework help:** Yes, 4 days a week. **Snacks:** Provided. **Staff/student ratio:** N/P. **After-school classes:** The school offers after-school classes, changing on a trimester basis. **Cost:** N/P.

Summer Programs
"The Lycée Français La Pérouse offers a unique and exciting 4-week summer camp for children from the ages of 5 to 13. The summer camp, which focuses on bilingualism and theater, takes place under the sun in Corte Madera. The various programs have been designed to address the creative and playful side of children, all in an educational environment. Participants are filmed during their activities and field trips. A DVD capturing every moment of discovery and emotional occasion is offered at the end of the summer camp. Transportation from San Francisco is provided for a fee. Activities vary depending on age, but include picnics on Angel Island, rock climbing, and days at the beach. The camp is from 9 a.m. to 3 p.m. with extended care from 8 a.m. and to 6 p.m." **Cost:** $300/session with extended care costing $5/hour.

Parent Involvement
Parent/teacher communication: Students receive 3 report cards a year. Parent/teacher conferences are 3 times a year, 2 held on a one-on-one

basis. One class council per trimester is held with all teachers, student delegates, parent delegates, and the administration. **Participation requirements:** Parents are expected to participate in fundraising by contributing financially to the Annual Appeal and volunteering 10 hours a year, by assisting in organizing the annual auction, gardening, painting, or by lodging or sponsoring a student. Parents are encouraged to serve on committees of the Board of Directors and to seek election to the Board or School Council. Other volunteer opportunities are available including a French market in June at the Marin campus, translating, library help, and newsletter publication. **Parent education programs offered?** Yes. "Cross-cultural workshops; U.S. college panel discussions with alumni; a French educational system counselor from France available annually; lectures and discussions on bilingualism, communication, safety and other issues."

WHAT SETS THE SCHOOL APART FROM OTHERS

"The Lycée belongs to a network of over 400 French schools worldwide and receives financial support from the French government. Founded in 1967 by parents, the Lycée is an academic institution accredited by the French Ministry of Education. The Lycée's students have access to any other French school at their own grade level. As a result of the high quality English curriculum, students are also qualified to enter an American school at or above their grade level and are fully prepared to enter European or North American colleges and universities."

HOW FAMILIES CHARACTERIZE SCHOOL

Parent comment(s): "I believe that the Lycée is educating tomorrow's world leaders. Who else can be better prepared to face this international world than our own children, who at age eight can already tell us how a French person's approach is different from an American's and that neither one is better, they are just different?" • "The environment is so positive. It's obvious that the instructors have a vision. They are well prepared to carry out their mission, and they are secure in their role. I like the fact that my son's teachers have such excellent morale."
Student comment(s): N/P.

MARIN CHRISTIAN ACADEMY

1370 S. Novato Boulevard
Novato, CA 94947
(415) 892-5713
www.visitmca.org

Christopher R. Mychajluk, Head of School, cmychajluk@visitmca.org
Heather Freeman, Director of Admission, hfreeman@visitmca.org

GENERAL

Coed PS-8 day school. Founded in 1979. Christian. Nonprofit. **Member:** ACSI. **Enrollment:** Approx. 200. **Average class size:** 15. **Accreditation:** ACSI (N/P term). **Endowment:** N/P. **School year:** Sept.-June. **School day:** 8:30 a.m. to 3 p.m.

STUDENT BODY ETHNICITY: N/P.

ADMISSION

Applications due: Rolling admissions. **Application fee:** $250. **Application process:** Forms, testing, interview, report cards, and test scores. **No. of applications:** N/P. **No. of K spaces:** 18. **Percentage of K class made up of school's preschool class:** 85%. **Admission evaluation requirements for K:** Testing and interviewing. **Other grades:** Testing, interview. **Preferences:** Sibling. **What sort of student do you best serve?** "MCA best serves the student that excels in an environment that is challenging, structured, and safe."

COSTS

Latest tuition: $5,500-$12,000. **Sibling discount:** 7%. **Tuition includes:** Lunch: No; Transportation: No; Laptop computer: No; Other: No. **Tuition increases:** Approx. 7% annually. **Other costs:** Approx. $190 for books, $30-200 other fees. **Percentage of students receiving financial aid:** 10%. **Financial aid application deadline:** "Third round April 15th, then based on fund availability." Financial aid is based on need. **Average grant:** $2,500. **Percentage of grants of half-tuition or more:** 90%. **Donations:** Voluntary.

SCHOOL'S MISSION STATEMENT

"Marin Christian Academy is dedicated to high spiritual and academic standards that address the development of the whole child—spiritual, mental, social, physical and emotional."

Academic Program
Philosophy: "Christian." **Foreign languages:** Spanish. **Computer training:** Yes. **No. of computers available for students:** 45. **No. of hours weekly of:** Art- 1; Drama- N/P; Music- 1 (seasonal); Computers- 1.5; Foreign language- 1.5; PE- 1.5. **Outdoor education:** "Camp." **Grading:** A-F, beginning in K. **Average nightly homework:** .5 hr. in K-3; .75 hr. in G4-5; 1-2 hrs. in G6-8. **Posted on the Internet:** Yes. **Percentage of students participating in Johns Hopkins Center for Talented Youth Program:** N/P. **Other indicators of academic success:** "SAT scores and well-balanced students." **High schools attended by latest graduating class:** MC, Novato, San Marin, Branson, St. Vincent.

Faculty
Ethnicity: N/P. **Percentage of teachers with graduate degrees:** 25%. **Percentage with current California credential:** 98%. **Faculty selection/training:** Degree and experience. **Teacher/student ratio:** 1:15. **Special subject teachers:** English, math, science, art, computers, choir. **Average teacher tenure:** 10 years.

Middle School
Description: G6-8. **Teacher/student ratio:** 1:16. **Elective courses offered:** Drama, computers, home economics, Spanish. **Achievement tracking in:** All subject areas. **Student social events:** N/P.

Student Support Services
No. of Licensed Counselors on staff: None. **Counselor/student ratio:** N/A. **Learning specialists on staff:** One. **Learning differences/ disabilities support:** N/P. **High school placement support:** Letters of recommendation provided. "Pastors and Youth Ministers are available for student/parent counseling."

Student Conduct and Health
Code of conduct: "The code of conduct is designed to promote peace and maintain order and mutual respect." **Prevention education and awareness addressed in:** Abstinence education and awareness programs.

Athletics
Sports offered: Basketball, wrestling, golf, volleyball, track. **Team play begins in:** N/P.

Campus/Campus Life
Campus description: "The School is conveniently located right off the highway. Facilities enable the full development of a child. Internet, video, and TV installed in each room." **Library:** "Accredited with 2,800 volumes." **Sports facilities:** Multi-purpose room, sports fields. **Theater/Arts facilities:** Theater/Drama room and stage. **Computer lab:** Yes. **Science lab:** Yes. **Lunch program:** Yes. **Bus service:** No. **Uniforms/dress code:** Dress code. **Opportunities for community service:** Yes.

Extended Day
Morning care: Begins at 6:30 a.m. **After-school care:** Until 6 p.m. **Grade levels:** All. **Cost:** Varies. **Drop-in care available:** Yes. **Coverage over major holidays:** Preschool only. **Homework help:** Yes. **Snacks:** Provided. **Staff/student ratio:** 1:20. **After-school classes:** Piano, band, Spanish, golf. **Cost:** N/P.

Summer Programs
"MCA Summer Day Camp provides an exciting and fun time that will include games, crafts, field trips, computer, drama classes and Bible devotion times in a warm, healthy, Christian environment." **Cost:** $500 monthly.

Parent Involvement
Parent/teacher communication: Conferences, e-mail, weekly newsletter, website and Renweb teacher/parent/student academic software. **Participation requirements:** 10 hours. **Parent education programs offered?** Yes.

What Sets the School Apart From Others
"We provide a safe environment that challenges each student to develop fully in areas of mind, body, and spirit."

How Families Characterize School
Parent comment(s): "My daughter is a graduate of UC-Berkeley. Recently she told me how thankful she was that I sent her to Marin Christian Academy because the study habits, learning skills and academics she learned were very important to her success in college."
Student comment(s): "MCA was an excellent foundation for the rest of my academic career. Not only did teachers instruct me about history, math, and English, but also they taught me life skills and values that are still a part of who I am today. It was where I learned how to learn."

Marin Country Day School

5221 Paradise Drive
Corte Madera, CA 94925-2107
(415) 927-5900 *fax (415) 924-1082*
www.mcds.org

Lucinda Lee Katz, Head of School, llkatz@mcds.org
Jeff Escabar, Director of Admission, jescabar@mcds.org

General
Coed K-8 day school. Founded in 1956. Independent. Nonprofit. **Member:** NAIS, CAIS, ASCD, ESHA, CASE, GLSEN, POCIS, ABADO, BADA, ISBOA, NBOA. **Enrollment:** Approx. 560. **Average class size:** 18. **Accreditation:** CAIS (6-year term: 2010-16). **Endowment:** $13 million. **School year:** Sept.-June. **School day:** 8:20 a.m. to 3 p.m. (dismissal for K is 2 p.m.).

Student Body Ethnicity
73% Caucasian (non-Latino), 13% multi-racial, 7% Asian, 4% African-American, 2% Latino, 1% other.

Admission
Applications due: Dec. (call for date). **Application fee:** $100. **Application process:** Applicant families should visit the website at www.mcds.org and follow the prompts on the admission tab. The scheduling of a Community Visiting tour, the first step in the admission process, followed by submitting an application, is all completed online. School visits and applications are only available the year prior to the date the student would enter the school. After submitting the application, both a parent appointment and an evaluation date will be scheduled by the admission office. For grades other than K, the evaluation date will be a Saturday in early Feb. Applicants to G6-8 will spend a day visiting campus. Main entry points are K and G6; admission to other grades is by attrition only. **No. of applications:** 200+ for K and 50-70 for G6. **No. of K spaces:** 54. **Percentage of K class made up of school's preschool class:** N/A. **Admission evaluation requirements for K:** Screening/school visit, preschool recommendations. **Other grades:** School transcript, teacher recommendations, testing, school visit. **Preferences:** Siblings. **What sort of student do you best serve?** "Students who demonstrate the capacity and motivation to affirm the school's core values and to find success in a comprehensive and challenging program."

Costs

Latest tuition: Indexed tuition is $500-$23,030 for K-2; $500-$23,775 for G3-5; and $500-$26,715 for G6-8. **Sibling discount:** None. **Tuition includes:** Lunch: Yes; Transportation: No; Laptop computer: No; Other: Books and educational materials, outdoor education, field trips, laboratory fees, yearbooks, athletic uniforms. **Tuition increases:** Approx. 5% annually. **Other costs:** None. **Percentage of students receiving financial aid:** 25%. **Financial aid application deadline:** Jan. (call for date). Financial Aid (Indexed tuition) is based on need. **Average grant:** $15,900. **Percentage of grants of half-tuition or more:** 72%. **Donations:** "The school raises annually $1.8 million in Annual Giving. The school relies on voluntary giving to support the operating budget. We strive for 100% participation from families currently in school and gifts of any size are appreciated. The school also solicits donations for capital projects and the endowment."

School's Mission Statement

"Our school is a community that inspires children to develop a love of learning, thoughtful perspectives and a diversity of skills; nurtures in each of them a deep sense of respect, responsibility and compassion; and challenges them to envision and work toward a better world."

Academic Program

Philosophy: "Through a broad, balanced and personally challenging curriculum that values the arts, music, physical education and experience in the outdoors in addition to traditional academic disciplines, a skilled and caring faculty seeks to develop every student's potential. Such basic skills as thinking, communicating, creating and collaborating are reinforced in every aspect of a child's experience. Because of the school's low student-teacher ratios, 9:1, teachers know students and their parents well. The close relationship among teachers and students nurtures confidence, respect for differences, a willingness to take risks, and pride in the school community. The school is organized around core values of respect, responsibility and compassion. An MCDS education is active and engaging; teachers employ many strategies and methods to accommodate a variety of learning needs and styles, with close collaboration among teachers to build bridges among disciplines." **Foreign languages:** Spanish, Mandarin. **Computer training:** Yes. **No. of computers available for students:** 150+. **No. of hours weekly of:** Art- 1.4; Drama- .75 G6-8; Music- 1.4; Computers- N/P; Foreign language- 2.75 (G3-4), 2 (G5), 3.3 (G6-8); PE- 2.75. **Outdoor education:** "Yes." **Grading:** Progress reports K-5, letter grades beginning in G6. **Average

nightly homework: Occasional in G1-2; 20-60 min. plus reading in G3-6; 20-30 min. per subject for 5 academic subjects in G6; 30-45 min. per subject in G7-8. Posted on the Internet: Yes. **Percentage of students participating in Johns Hopkins Center for Talented Youth Program:** N/P. **Other indicators of academic success:** "Quality of student work, GPAs, success of our alums in high school." **High schools attended by latest graduating class:** Bay, Branson, Cate, Deerfield, Drew, Exeter, Galileo, Lick, MA, Redwood, SI, Stevenson, Tamalpais, Thacher, University, Urban.

Faculty

Ethnicity: 80% Caucasian (non-Latino), 9% Asian, 7% Latino, 3% African-American, 1% multi-racial. **Percentage of teachers with graduate degrees:** 44%. **Percentage with current California credential:** N/P. **Faculty selection/training:** Experience, degree; continuing professional development. **Teacher/student ratio:** 1:9. **Special subject teachers:** Spanish, Mandarin, art, music/drama, technology, PE, library. **Average teacher tenure:** 17 years.

Middle School

Description: "MCDS Upper School (G5-8) is an engaging environment in which hard work and caring, responsible behavior are the norm. The program allows students to further discover who they are; acquire fundamental, lifetime learning skills and attitudes; become critical and creative thinkers; explore various interests and talents—intellectual, artistic and physical—and grow and develop into empowered young people eager to contribute to making the world a better place, now and in the future. In sixth grade, the school admits new students to expand the size of the class so that returning students can make new friends and the school can broaden its course offerings. Upper School students begin the day in grade-level homerooms (G5 remains in self-contained classrooms) supervised by a faculty advisor, who also serves as liaison with parents. G6-8 are departmentalized and students travel between classes to study English, social studies, math, science, Spanish, Mandarin, visual and performing arts, and physical education. Tutorials and activity periods are provided. Many students stay at school after dismissal to play on athletic teams or to participate in drama, music, supervised study hall or other elective activities." **Teacher/student ratio:** 1:9. **Elective courses offered:** "Varies." **Achievement tracking in:** Math. **Student social events:** "Varies."

Student Support Services

No. of Licensed Counselors on staff: Two. **Counselor/student ratio:** 1:280. **Learning specialists on staff:** Seven. **Learning differences/ disabilities support:** "Student Support Services members work with parents and teachers to develop strategies to best support students' learning, and directly with students, individually and in small groups. Grades 6-8 use the Transitions Program." **High school placement support:** Provided by the Secondary School Placement Counselor, Upper School Division Head, Dean of Students, and eighth grade faculty.

Student Conduct and Health

Code of conduct: "The guiding principle for all behavior begins with our core values: respect, responsibility and compassion. We believe that honoring these values creates a safe, purposeful environment where the important work of teaching, learning and growing can take place. School rules are designed to provide a healthy, safe and friendly learning environment for all children. Clear expectations and developmentally appropriate consequences when expectations are not honored help ensure that standards of behavior and performance are reasonable, consistent and enforced fairly. An appropriate consequence is one that helps the student contribute something positive to the community in return. In G6-8, a system of 'marks' helps monitor behavior. It is the responsibility of all MCDS teachers and staff to model and to be aware of appropriate behavior—to praise, support and reward student behavior when it is consistent with our core values, and to identify it and assign the appropriate consequence when it is not. Very serious behavior violations require an individual approach, beginning with a full discussion with the student and a careful investigation of the incident. Parents and/or guardians are involved in the process. In extremely serious cases, the Division Head will work with the Head of School in determining the appropriate course of action. In extreme situations, suspension and even expulsion may be considered. The school and parents must work together to ensure that MCDS is a safe and caring environment for all children." **Prevention education and awareness addressed in:** "Drug/alcohol education is provided through workshops. The G6 curriculum incorporates a body image/eating disorders program, which allows students to receive the information at an age when it is most likely to be meaningful, but timely enough to be primarily preventative. Sixth grade also takes part in a series of workshops designed to help them develop the tools to deal with the challenges and stresses of academic and social life typical of the age group. Small groups meet for activities and discussions aimed at broadening their understanding of the human brain, natural reactions to stress, and ways to cope. In seventh grade, students study body image, sexuality and AIDS awareness in the context of human biology. AIDS education is also part of the eighth grade curriculum. Parent education opportunities are also offered in these areas."

ATHLETICS
Sports offered: Soccer, basketball, volleyball, softball, cross-country, track and field. **Team play begins in:** G6 (intermural).

CAMPUS/CAMPUS LIFE
Campus description: "MCDS is located on 35 naturally beautiful acres which begin at the Bay and run up the hills of Ring Mountain, where the school property abuts the Marin County Open Space District. Low, simple frame buildings fit naturally into their setting. The athletic fields, playgrounds, gardens, informal study areas and marine science dock all invite interaction with the outdoors. The structures accommodate classrooms, a Learning Resource Center (library/technology), science laboratories, a computer laboratory, separate music and art buildings, a performing arts auditorium, gymnasium, multipurpose room and offices." **Library:** 28,000+ volumes, 80 periodicals, on-line catalog, electronic database subscriptions, multiple computer stations. **Sports facilities:** Gymnasium, 2 sports fields. **Theater/Arts facilities:** Performing Arts Building, stage in gymnasium, 2 music and 3 art rooms. **Computer lab:** Yes, and 4 mobile labs. **Science lab:** Yes. **Lunch program:** Yes. **Bus service:** Yes. **Uniforms/dress code:** Dress code. **Opportunities for community service:** Service Learning curriculum in K-8; Community Service Club in G6-8; 8th grade Community Service Days; family community service program.

EXTENDED DAY
Morning care: Begins at 8 a.m. **After-school care:** Until 6:15 p.m. **Grade levels:** K-5; study hall/after-school activities in G6-8. **Cost:** Up to $20/day (indexed at rate of tuition). **Drop-in care available:** Yes. **Coverage over major holidays:** No. **Homework help:** Yes. **Snacks:** Provided. **Staff/student ratio:** Varies by attendance; average 1:13. **After-school classes:** The school's after-school activities program (ASAP) varies by semester. Classes may include cooking, martial arts, sports, chess, arts and crafts, and nature adventure. Individual and group music instruction is also available (Forte). **Cost:** N/P.

SUMMER PROGRAMS
"Beyond Borders is a summer enrichment program that draws on the transformative power of creating an intentional community of diverse

cultures, ethnicities and economic backgrounds. • Fourth through sixth graders from the San Francisco Bay Area broaden their perspectives and deepen cultural literacy by engaging in story-sharing, service learning, visual arts, technology and music. Each day features an ensemble block where they apply the skills they are learning in various performances: puppetry, animations, film, improvisations and plays. • Through shared experiences and creative endeavors, Beyond Borders fosters self-awareness and self-respect along with a spirit of collaboration and respect for the dignity of others." • The program is offered in two 3-week sessions. Participants can choose either session or attend both. **Cost:** Based on a sliding scale. Bus transportation is provided. • In addition to Beyond Borders, Marin Country Day School hosts a variety of summer opportunities that vary each year. **Cost:** Varies.

PARENT INVOLVEMENT
Parent/teacher communication: Conferences, progress reports, meetings, roundtables, website, e-mail, telephone, online newsletter. **Participation requirements:** "MCDS expects that families will support the school as actively as individual circumstances permit. The school offers a wide variety of volunteer opportunities with differing time commitments and locations." **Parent education programs offered?** Yes.

WHAT SETS THE SCHOOL APART FROM OTHERS
"Marin Country Day School is a warm, inclusive community guided by core values of respect, responsibility and compassion. The school is dedicated to helping children become excellent learners and good people, motivated to make a difference in the world. Service learning and character education are integral elements of the program. MCDS is committed to the principles and practices of diversity throughout the school community. The curriculum is broad-based and personally rigorous, including a thorough grounding in the traditional academic disciplines as well as art, athletics, drama, music and outdoor education. Teachers work collaboratively in developing an active program that encourages students to question, to reason and to make connections. The classroom atmosphere is highly participatory, with teachers acting as coaches and mentors who encourage students' exploration, discovery and reflection. Perhaps the school's most enduring characteristic is its vibrant spirit—of students, families, teachers and staff engaged in working together to make Marin Country Day School a good place for children."

Marin Horizon School
305 Montford Avenue
Mill Valley, CA 94941
(415) 388-8408 *fax (415) 388-7831*
www.marinhorizon.org

Rosalind Hamar, Head of School, rhamar@marinhorizon.org
Sharman M. Bonus, Director of Admission, admissions@marinhorizon.org

General
Coed PS–8 day school. Founded in 1977. Independent. Nonprofit. **Member:** NAIS, CAIS, IMC, BADA, BAMA. **Enrollment:** Approx. 285. **Average class size:** N/P ("Maximum class size: 24"). **Accreditation:** CAIS (6-year term 2009-15) and State of California preschool license. **Endowment:** $285,000. **School year:** Sept.-June. **School day:** 8:40 a.m. to 2 p.m. for PreK and K; 8:20 a.m. to 2:45 - 3:30 p.m. for G1-8.

Student Body Ethnicity
71% Caucasian (non-Latino), 9% Asian, 6% multi-racial, 6% African-American, 6% Latino, 2% unreported.

Admission
Applications due: Early to mid-Jan. (call for date). **Application fee:** $75. **Application process:** Interested families should contact the admissions office in Sept. or early Oct. to request a tour and application packet for the following academic year. After attending a tour or open house and submitting an application, a parent appointment and student visit date will be scheduled. **No. of applications:** 30 for K. **No. of K spaces:** 10 -12. **Percentage of K class made up of school's preschool class:** 60-80%. **Admission evaluation requirements for K:** Screening, school visit, teacher recommendations, parent questionnaire about student. **Other grades:** Assessment, previous report cards/grades, standardized test scores, school visit, teacher recommendations, parent questionnaire about student. **Preferences:** N/P. **What sort of student do you best serve?** "Students who have the ability to support the school's mission can work independently and cooperatively in the classroom and have the desire to be successful in a challenging program."

Costs

Latest tuition: $13,860-$24,190 depending on grade level. **Sibling discount:** None. **Tuition includes:** Lunch: No; Transportation: No; Laptop computer: No; Other: Field trips and outdoor education camp. **Tuition increases:** Approx. 7% annually. **Other costs:** "Annual capital deposit of $1,000 per child is required for PK-7. The maximum accrued deposit is $10,000 per child or $15,000 per family whichever is the lesser amount. The principal is returned to the family the Sept. following the graduation or permanent withdrawal of their child from school." **Percentage of students receiving financial aid:** 20%. **Financial aid application deadline:** Jan. (call for date). Financial aid is based on need. **Average grant:** $12,990. **Percentage of grants of half-tuition or more:** 65%. **Donations:** "Voluntary giving is critical to support the operating budget. For over 10 years, MHS has achieved 100% participation by trustees, faculty, administration and parents in the annual fund."

School's Mission Statement

"Our mission is to challenge students to be self-reliant thinkers and lifelong learners. We inspire academic excellence, nurture students' natural love of learning, and encourage them to be confident, creative individuals who are responsible to each other, the community, and the world."

Academic Program

Philosophy: "Marin Horizon School offers a challenging academic curriculum that prepares its graduates to succeed in school and in life. Our program offers traditional core disciplines—cultural studies, language arts, science, mathematics, and fine arts—within an enriched and interdisciplinary approach. Specialists provide instruction in Spanish, visual and performing arts, music, library, media, science and physical education. Children are encouraged to work at their highest academic potential. Our curriculum is integrated and interdisciplinary, focusing on the inter-connection of everything in the world. Our curriculum is organized in a spiral so that ideas and concepts that are introduced to young children are revisited and revisited with greater detail and complexity as children mature. Our program is solidly grounded in multicultural studies and celebration of diversity in its many manifestations. Our program addresses the 'whole child' and we are as concerned about their social, emotional, physical, and creative development as we are about their academic growth. We consciously work with children on their decision-making processes and their interactions with others. We teach and encourage a conflict resolution approach to disagreements."

Foreign languages: Spanish PK-8; language immersion trips to Spanish-speaking countries are offered to Middle School students in the summer. **Computer training:** Yes. **No. of computers available for students:** 56. **No. of hours weekly of:** Depends on grade level. In general, Art- 2-3; Drama- 0-1; Music- 1-2; Computers- N/P; Foreign language- 1-5; PE- 1.5-3. **Outdoor education:** One week for elementary and middle school students on an environmental studies trip. Middle School students also take a weekly class in outdoor education, which culminates in backpacking/camping trips on Mt. Tamalpais. **Grading:** Matrix progress reports with narratives. Percentages beginning G6. **Average nightly homework:** "Ranges by grade level from 20 min. to 2 hours." Posted on the Internet: No. **Percentage of students participating in Johns Hopkins Center for Talented Youth Program:** N/P. **Other indicators of academic success:** "High school acceptances, individual work/achievements of students, individual progress reports." **High schools attended by latest graduating class:** Bay, Branson, Convent, Drew, Tamalpais, MA, SHCP, San Domenico, SI, Stuart Hall, Urban, University.

FACULTY
Ethnicity: 77% Caucasian (non-Latino), 11% Asian, 6% Latino, 6% African-American. **Percentage of teachers with graduate degrees:** 35%. **Percentage with current California credential:** "All head teachers and co-teachers hold Montessori and/or state elementary teaching credentials." **Faculty selection/training:** Experience, education and philosophical fit. **Teacher/student ratio:** 1:9. **Special subject teachers:** Art, Spanish, music, technology, PE, media literacy and research. **Average teacher tenure:** 11 years.

MIDDLE SCHOOL
Description: "Our middle school, which includes G6-8, provides a bridge between the academic foundation of the elementary years and the increased challenges students will encounter in high school and beyond. It is intentionally small—not more than 72 students—because of the value of a small community for early adolescents. MHS provides an educational environment where students are well known personally and academically by their teachers, and can receive the kind of guidance they need at this time of vulnerability and great change in their lives. The middle school is departmentalized. The three-year interdisciplinary rotations—U.S. history and government, Europe and Africa in the Middle Ages, and Japan and the Pacific Rim—include language arts, humanities, geography and fine arts. In addition, each year there is a

middle school simulation that synthesizes and deepens each student's understanding of what they have learned. These simulations include a 7-scene murder mystery presentation of Murder in Londinium entwining Celtic and Pax Romana cultures, a mock trial trying Harry S. Truman for crimes against humanity in Hiroshima and Nagasaki, or team creations of Rube Goldberg machines and the spirit of innovation that led to the U.S. Industrial Revolution. Science and math are also integrated into these major projects. Mathematics includes mastery of computation, problem solving, introductory algebra, and geometry. Science includes biology, physical science, chemistry, and physics. Other offerings include computer technology, Spanish, health, and PE." **Teacher/student ratio:** 1:7. **Elective courses offered:** "Varies." **Achievement tracking in:** N/P. **Student social events:** Limited social events.

STUDENT SUPPORT SERVICES
No. of Licensed Counselors on staff: One part-time. **Counselor/ student ratio:** N/P. **Learning specialists on staff:** One full-time, 3 part-time. One part-time occupational therapist on staff. A sensory motor program is conducted for K and followed through G1 if appropriate. **Learning differences/disabilities support:** "MHS provides a Learning Support Program to support the success of students who need additional academic support. This program includes regular direct support from a LSP teacher, classroom observations, and regular communication between parents, teachers, and outside specialists retained by the family. Parents of students who are placed in this program by the school are assessed an additional fee while the student is in the program." **High school placement support:** "During the fall semester, the high school preparation course is taught to support students and their families in the skills and strategies helpful in the application and decision making process. The course includes SSAT preparation, assessment skills to determine appropriate 'matches' between student and school, and interviewing techniques."

STUDENT CONDUCT AND HEALTH
Code of conduct: "The school has behavioral guidelines that are universal and each class establishes class rules. In addition there are accountability policies for both the elementary grades and middle school. To avoid behavioral problems, the school offers conflict resolution training and instruction through Advisory Group meetings." **Prevention education and awareness addressed in:** Drug, alcohol, and sex education is addressed through weekly health classes. There is a no tolerance disciplinary policy for drug/alcohol use, improper language and sexual/

racial harassment. Support systems specific to middle school students include counseling by teachers and guidance counselor, individually and through advisory groups.

ATHLETICS
Sports offered: Soccer, basketball, flag football. **Team play begins in:** G3 (intermural), G4-8 for cross-country meets, basketball, track and field, flag football, soccer.

CAMPUS/CAMPUS LIFE
Campus description: MHS is situated in the Homestead Valley neighborhood of Mill Valley on 2.5 acres with access to Marin County fields and open space. **Library:** On campus, 5,000 volume library and adjacent computer lab, staffed by a full-time librarian. **Sports facilities:** Playground and adjacent grass field. **Theater/Arts facilities:** Outdoor amphitheater. Theatrical productions are held at nearby theaters. **Computer lab:** No. **Science lab:** Yes. **Lunch program:** Yes. "Organic hot lunch offered for nominal fee." **Bus service:** From Greenbrae, Corte Madera, Mill Valley and San Francisco. Carpooling is strongly encouraged. **Uniforms/dress code:** Dress code. **Opportunities for community service:** "MHS's community service program is widely recognized. Our students of all ages, their parents, and teachers work together on various community service projects and directly contribute to more than 20 different non-profit and community service organization throughout the year. Students have collected and delivered over 30,000 pounds of food in the last 10 years to the Marin Community Food Bank, worked on projects with the seniors at The Redwoods, and participated in neighborhood and local clean-up days."

EXTENDED DAY
Morning care: Begins at 7:30 a.m. **After-school care:** Until 6 p.m. **Grade levels:** PK-8. **Cost:** $8/hr. Annual plans available. **Drop-in care available:** Yes. **Coverage over major holidays:** "Limited." **Homework help:** Yes. **Snacks:** N/P. **Staff/student ratio:** 1:12 or fewer. **After-school classes:** Available for students in PS-G8. Classes frequently include cooking, chess, Irish step dancing, Capoeira, drama, guitar, gymnastics, yoga, baseball, soccer. **Cost:** Varies.

SUMMER PROGRAMS
Summer Camp sessions run approx. 6 consecutive weeks usually in late-June through early Aug. The camp offers programs for 3- to 9-year-olds with a counselor to camper ratio of 1:8. Activities include

cooking, swimming, gardening, magic, theatre and art with field trips every Friday. Swimming and gymnastics are offered for ages 4 and up. Two-week Spanish immersion camp available for G4-8. **Cost:** "Varies depending on the number of days per week and number of weeks per summer enrolled. Extended care is also provided from 8-9 a.m. and 3-5:30 p.m. for a per hour fee."

Parent Involvement

Parent/teacher communication: Parent/teacher conferences and written progress reports twice a year; class notes; e-mail communications; weekly school newsletter; website. **Participation requirements:** Parents are strongly encouraged to participate in many aspects of the MHS community including but not limited to trustees, board committees, Parent Board officers, class parents, special programs, field trips, and chaperones. **Parent education programs offered?** Throughout the year, speakers are invited to discuss issues involved in parenting with the MHS community and the broader community. Topics such as adoption perspectives, earthquake preparedness and adolescence are presented.

What Sets the School Apart From Others

"MHS offers a Montessori-inspired curriculum with strong curricular focus on multiculturalism, the environment, and community service. In addition to basic skill development, academic preparation emphasizes research, writing, and presentation skills across the curriculum. Teachers are 'facilitators of learning' more than 'dispensers of knowledge.' Different learning styles are acknowledged via a mix of teaching and learning strategies ranging from hands-on projects to seminars and presentations."

How Families Characterize School

Parent comment(s): "What's special about Marin Horizon? Well, first, I love that the curriculum is holistic and explores the natural connections between disciplines. I was also struck by how energized and engaged the students and faculty are, and that the school fosters independent and critical thinking."

Student comment(s): "It's uncommon that one school can produce so many brilliant minds but MHS does so by teaching children how to teach themselves at a young age. Being equipped at six to structure work and apply focus and tenacity to a task, helped me to establish strong study habits at nine and further maturing those skills throughout middle school, educationally preparing myself for the high school work load. I truly cannot thank the MHS community enough. But I try, in any endeavor I involve myself, knowing it is truly a reflection of those who helped me get where I am now. To some MHS is just a school, for others their home away from home, but for me it will always be the community that truly helped prepare me for life."

MARIN MONTESSORI SCHOOL
Lower Campus:
5200 Paradise Drive
Corte Madera, CA 94925
(415) 924-5388 *fax (415) 924-5305*
www.marinmontessori.org

Upper Campus (G7-8):
1 St. Vincent's Drive
San Rafael, CA 94903

Emerson Johnson, Head of School
Katrina Schlude, Director of Admission, kschlude@marinmontessori.org

GENERAL
Coed PS-8 day school. Founded in 1963. Independent. Nonprofit. **Member:** AMI, POCIS, BADA, ISBOA, ABADO. **Enrollment:** Approx. 230. **Average class size:** 25 in Primary (2.5 to 6 yrs.), 30 in Elementary (6-12 yrs.), 20 in Junior High-Erdkinder (12-15 yrs.). **Accreditation:** AMI (term N/P). **Endowment:** N/P. **School year:** Sept.-June. **School day:** 8:30 a.m. to 11:45 a.m. for Toddler/Primary half-day; 8:30 a.m. to 2:55 p.m. for Toddler/Primary full-day; 8:30 a.m. to 3 p.m. for Elementary and Junior High.

STUDENT BODY ETHNICITY
82% Caucasian (non-Latino), 8% Asian, 6% multi-racial, 2% African-American, 2% Latino.

ADMISSION
Applications due: Jan. (call for date). **Application fee:** $75. **Application process:** Attend an open house scheduled on a Saturday in Oct. or Jan. and a school tour scheduled between Oct. and Feb. Family visits/classroom visits are by invitation. **No. of applications:** 130. **No. of K spaces:** 4-5. **Percentage of K class made up of school's preschool class:** 80%. **Admission evaluation requirements for K:** Classroom visit and preschool recommendation form. **Other grades:**

School records, current teacher recommendations, classroom visit, and screening in some cases. **Preferences:** Siblings. **What sort of student do you best serve?** "The Montessori education is designed to meet the developmental needs—intellectual, emotional, social, and physical—of all children. The Montessori education nurtures the development of the 'whole child' and encourages curiosity, love of learning, internal motivation, and independent thought through self-direction."

COSTS

Latest tuition: $14,720 for Primary half-day, $20,090 for Primary full-day, $20,390 for Elementary, $21,420 for Junior High. **Sibling discount:** None. **Tuition includes:** Lunch: No; Transportation: No; Laptop computer: No; Other: No. **Tuition increases:** Approx. 2-5% annually. **Other costs:** None. **Percentage of students receiving financial aid:** 25%. **Financial aid application deadline:** Jan. (call for date). Financial aid is based on need. **Average grant:** $11,350. **Percentage of grants of half-tuition or more:** 64%. **Donations:** "Voluntary annual giving is encouraged to support the school's operating budget. The school also solicits donations during capital campaigns and to fund special projects. We welcome giving at all levels and strive for 100% participation from our currently enrolled families."

SCHOOL'S MISSION STATEMENT

"The mission of Marin Montessori School, in adherence to the principles of the Association Montessori Internationale (AMI) as envisioned by Dr. Maria Montessori, is to nurture the development of each child in our diverse community to his or her fullest potential – an independent, responsible, compassionate, learned individual who thinks critically and realizes clearly his or her role in the world. Thus our mission is to provide education for life."

ACADEMIC PROGRAM

Philosophy: "MMS provides an authentic Montessori education for children from 18 months to 15 years old. We encourage every child to discover and reach his or her fullest individual potential so that he or she is prepared to contribute to, thrive in, and help to create a better world. As children progress through the school, from toddler to young adult, their growth is exponential, as each year's learning concretely, logically, and consistently builds upon lessons learned in previous years. • The toddlers (18 months to 3 years old) learn and explore language, music, movement, art, practical life activities, and fine and gross motor skills in a beautiful and safe environment, especially built for them. Led by a teacher and an assistant, they develop a trust in self and in others, building self esteem through purposeful activities in a loving, supportive community. • In the Primary classrooms (2 ½ to 6 years old), children are introduced to all aspects of the world. They explore history, geography, math, language, biology, art, and music through individualized lessons and self-directed work with the classroom materials, developing self-confidence, initiative, and concentration. The Primary classroom is a multi-age classroom, an essential element of Montessori education where the older children (5- and 6-year-olds) are the classroom leaders and act as role models. Younger children are interested in learning and emulating their older peers. The result is a deep sense of caring and respect for each other. • MMS's exciting, innovative, and scientifically-proven approach to intellectual development continues in the Elementary level where children pursue their growing quest for knowledge. MMS emphasizes 'high order' skills—the ability to research information, interpret it, connect it to information already obtained, and analyze its importance. Collaborative projects are common as each member contributes his or her own talents and knowledge. MMS students challenge themselves and set high expectations for their quality of thoughts, work, and mastery of intellectual content and skills." **Foreign languages:** Spanish G4-8. **Computer training:** Yes. **No. of computers available for students:** One in each elementary classroom, computer lab in Junior High plus additional laptops for field work. **No. of hours weekly of:** Art- N/P; Drama- N/P; Music- N/P; Computers- N/P; Foreign language- N/P; PE- 3+. **Outdoor education:** "Integrated daily." **Grading:** Narrative evaluations, no grades. **Average nightly homework:** At least 30 min. of reading each night; other homework is only given as needed for areas of challenge. Posted on the Internet: No. **Percentage of students participating in Johns Hopkins Center for Talented Youth Program:** N/A. **Other indicators of academic success:** "Each year our students are admitted to the most respected high school programs in the Bay Area. Students and parents report that in high school, the children continue to be very self-disciplined and passionate about completing their assigned projects to their fullest potential." **High schools attended by latest graduating class:** Urban, Drake. (The school's junior high had its first graduating class of 3 students in 2010.)

FACULTY

Ethnicity: N/P. **Percentage of teachers with graduate degrees:** 64%. **Percentage with current California credential:** N/P. **Faculty selection/training:** "Rigorous AMI teacher training, experience, and continued professional development." **Teacher/student ratio:** 1:23.

Special subject teachers: PE, art, music, outdoor education. **Average teacher tenure:** 10 years.

MIDDLE SCHOOL

Description: "MMS offers a unique land-based Junior High program, offering G7-8 students the opportunity to learn and work in the beauty and tranquility of nature. The program reflects Maria Montessori's curricular design for meeting the developmental needs of the age group through a combination of rigorous intellectual development and experiential learning. MMS's adolescents apply their academic skills to the task of creating an ecologically sound and sustainable learning environment where they explore human interactions and interdependence with nature.
• This experiential learning environment provides purposeful courses of study and is designed to enable young adults to be equipped with the confidence, knowledge, and skills to prosper in the real world. The adolescents balance their days with a blend of theoretical and rigorous academic work and relevant practical experience. Their learning process thus becomes less about acquisition and memorization and more about interpretation, analysis, and synthesis of information. Lessons on economics, environmental sciences, and the arts are acquired through collaborative hands-on work, while their intellects are developed through reading, community discussion, and enriching interactions with art, music, and nature. Through internship, service, and real work in a community context, combined with a rigorous academic curriculum, MMS students develop a strong sense of self in preparation for entering high school. Igniting the adolescent's passion for learning becomes the catalyst to understanding the power of human potential and one's contribution as a global citizen. **Teacher/student ratio:** 1:5. **Elective courses offered:** "Varies." **Achievement tracking in:** N/P. **Student social events:** "Varies."

STUDENT SUPPORT SERVICES

No. of Licensed Counselors on staff: None. **Counselor/student ratio:** N/A. **Learning specialists on staff:** One learning specialist consultant. **Learning differences/disabilities support:** "We work with a learning specialist who observes, tests, and consults with faculty and parents to evaluate learning challenges and create a plan to better support the child by implementing customized interventions and accommodations for his/her learning in the classroom as well as recommending additional tutoring/support when needed. **High school placement support:** By the Secondary School Placement Counselor, Director of Education, and Junior High-Erdkinder faculty.

Student Conduct and Health

Code of conduct: "Grace and courtesy are the cornerstones of our community that is built on caring, respect, and consideration of others. Grace is harmony between mind and body. Courtesy is the harmony between oneself and others. Grace and courtesy are natural expressions of a community, and when they are implemented and modeled by all members of the community, a harmonious environment is created that promotes the welfare of all." **Prevention education and awareness addressed in:** "Peace education, environmental consciousness, and healthy nutrition/sound body education."

Athletics

Sports offered: "Team sports, track and field, yoga, movement, skating, in the PE program and after-school classes." **Team play begins in:** G1.

Campus/Campus Life

Campus description:

Lower Campus (Toddler-G6): "Five buildings nestled around a beautiful bay estuary just east of Ring Mountain Open Space Preserve in Corte Madera. Campus includes classrooms, fields, multi-purpose room, multiple gardens student use, and offices." **Library:** "Each classroom has its own comprehensive library, and when more resources are required, students regularly organize outings to our local public library as a means to encourage and support their engagement as active members of our local community." **Sports facilities:** One large field, one small field, one paved court for basketball and hockey/skating. **Theater/Arts facilities:** A multi-purpose room with stage facilities. **Computer lab:** No. **Science lab:** "Extensive science equipment in all elementary classrooms." **Lunch program:** No. **Bus service:** No. **Uniforms/dress code:** "Appropriate school dress." **Opportunities for community service:** Yes.

Upper Campus: (G7-8): "Located on the picturesque St. Vincent's campus in San Rafael. Campus includes classrooms, science lab, computer lab, library/study, industrial kitchen, art and music facilities, auditorium/gymnasium, gardens, and outdoor space for classes and sports." **Library:** Extensive on-site library. **Sports facilities:** Auditorium/ gymnasium, fields, paved open space, running trails, and access to tennis courts and pool. **Theater/Arts facilities:** Large auditorium, multi-purpose room with stage. **Computer lab:** Yes. **Science lab:** Yes. **Lunch program:** No. **Bus service:** Yes. **Uniforms/dress code:** "Appropriate school dress." **Opportunities for community service:** "There are many opportunities for community service, both required as part of the curriculum, structured by adults, and created by the students, within our own school environment, greater Bay Area communities, and the world at large."

EXTENDED DAY
Morning care: Begins at 7:30 a.m. **After-school care:** Until 6 p.m. **Grade levels:** PK-8 **Cost:** $9.50/hour reserved; $10/hour drop-in. **Drop-in care available:** Yes. **Coverage over major holidays:** Yes. **Homework help:** N/P. **Snacks:** Provided. **Staff/student ratio:** Maximum of 1:12. **After-school classes:** Optional after-school classes are available for Primary and Elementary. Offerings have included: Spanish, cooking, soccer, nature exploration, yoga/movement, art, skating, chess, creative writing. **Cost:** "Varies."

SUMMER PROGRAMS
Summer camps offered for students enrolled at MMS. A variety of half-day and full-day camps are available from late June to early Aug., and can include instruction on art, movement, geography, nature, science, sports, Spanish. **Cost:** "Varies."

PARENT INVOLVEMENT
Parent/teacher communication: Two formal parent/teacher conferences each year. Continual parent-teacher communication as needed throughout the year. Parents are encouraged to schedule classroom observations at will, based on availability. Parents are encouraged to use e-mail and phone to contact the teacher with any questions, concerns, or important information. Classroom newsletters and the weekly school bulletin are also important sources of information. **Participation requirements:** Parents are expected to attend Back to School Night, 3 Parent Education events, 2 Parent/Teacher Conferences, and to observe their child's classroom a minimum of once a year. It is expected that parents will support the school through a vast array of volunteer opportunities each year. **Parent education programs offered?** Yes.

WHAT SETS THE SCHOOL APART FROM OTHERS
"The greatest gift of a Montessori education is that each child is given the chance to build a strong sense of self, a passion for lifelong learning, the self-discipline to make good choices, and a respect for the Earth and his fellow human beings. Each environment is designed to provide the balance between freedom and responsibility that allows the child to not only learn what is 'required,' but to go far beyond that as s/he follows his/her interests and passions. S/he will possess all the tools necessary

for leading a successful and worthwhile life that contributes to the world around him/her."

HOW FAMILIES CHARACTERIZE SCHOOL: N/P

MARIN PREPARATORY SCHOOL

117 Diamond Street (at Castro)
San Francisco, CA 94114
Phone (415) 865-0899 *fax (415) 241-7831*
www.marinpreparatoryschool.org

Flora Mugambi-Mutunga, Interim Head of School
Cameron Story, Director of Admission, camerons@marinpreparatory.org

GENERAL
Coed Junior K-8 day school. Founded in 2009. Independent. Nonprofit. **Member:** N/P. **Enrollment:** Approx. 52 in 2010 in JK-1 to grow to 200. **Average class size:** Approx. 14-16. **Accreditation:** N/A (School is new). **Endowment:** N/A. **School year:** Sept.-June. **School day:** 8:30 a.m. to 3:30 p.m.

STUDENT BODY ETHNICITY
"30% students of color."

ADMISSION
Applications due: Rolling admissions. **Application fee:** $100. **Application process:** School tours and open houses are offered during the day and in the evening. Individual tours are available. Process includes application, teacher recommendation, parent interview, and student visit. **No. of applications:** Approx. 100 for JK-1. **No. of K spaces:** 32. **Percentage of K class made up of school's JK class:** 37%. **Admission evaluation requirements for K:** Developmentally and emotionally ready. **Other grades:** The school is adding one grade per year until reaching 8th grade. **Preferences:** Children and families that appreciate and will benefit from a developmentally appropriate, progressive approach to education within an interactive Spanish infused environment. **What sort of student do you best serve?** N/P.

COSTS
Latest tuition: $18,700-$20,000. **Sibling discount:** None. **Tuition includes:** Lunch: No. Transportation: No. Laptop computer: No; other:

N/P. **Tuition increases:** Approx. 3-5% annually. **Other Costs:** None. **Percentage of students receiving financial aid:** 10%. **Financial aid application deadline:** Call for date. Financial aid is based on need. **Average grant:** N/P. **Percentage of grants of half-tuition or more:** N/P. **Donations:** "Welcomed and appreciated."

SCHOOL'S MISSION STATEMENT

"Marin Preparatory School is an independent, non-profit, coeducational school, offering classes from junior kindergarten through 8th grade. Our Mission is to provide opportunities for students to achieve their personal best, become positive responsible community members, and to embrace learning in a warm and productive environment. We endeavor to provide a progressive, Spanish infused educational program that embraces interactive thinking with an experiential curriculum, while nurturing the individual strengths and needs of a diverse student population. Our goal is to stimulate a lifelong desire to seek knowledge, and to build a strong sense of community among students, faculty, and parents. At Marin Preparatory, we strive to make the ordinary, extraordinary."

ACADEMIC PROGRAM

Philosophy: "Children learn best by doing, not by merely being told what to do. Our unique hands on, project based approach to education provides a challenging and engaging learning experience for all our students. Guided by outstanding teachers, our students are encouraged to share knowledge with their peers. They are asked to present the result of their work and in doing so make a better connection with the 'how' and the 'why.' In the adult world, we have long incorporated active learning by engaging the services of interns to learn by doing. When it has come to teaching, however, most schools have followed the philosophies of mass education, established in a different era, with a different need and focus. We have treated a child's mind as an empty vessel which needed to be filled. We have told them how to do something, but didn't let them have experience of doing it. In today's high tech world, where information is only a few key strokes away, learning through experience and fully understanding the concepts that support, initiate, or conclude is more important than ever. Marin Preparatory School is a knowledge based school, rather than a data based school. It is a place where students are encouraged to take chances and where there is no fear of failure. As students are empowered to learn and explore, they gain confidence and enthusiasm for the process. They form a community of learners. Children learn in many different ways and through many different modalities. At Marin Preparatory school we embrace the rich variety of learning styles, and teachers work with students to help them reach their unique potential. It is our goal to provide our students the tools for creative problem solving and global citizenship, by using 21st century teaching methods and thinking." **Foreign languages:** Spanish. **Computer training:** Yes. **No. of computers available for students:** N/P. **No. of hours weekly of:** Art- 3; Music- 2; Computers- N/P; PE- 5. Progress Reports: Every 4 weeks, narrative beginning in JK. **Average nightly homework:** "Four nights per week, less than 30 minutes per night." Posted on the Internet: N/P. **Percentage of students participating in John Hopkins Center for Talented Youth Program:** N/A. **Other indicators of academic success:** "Student work and self confidence with the material." **High schools attended by latest graduating class:** N/A. First graduating class will be in 2018.

FACULTY
Ethnicity: 33% Latino. **Percentage of teachers with graduate degrees:** 50%. **Percentage with current California credential:** N/P. **Faculty selection/training:** Faculty selection is based on level of education, experience and philosophy. **Teacher/student ratio:** 1:8. **Special subject teachers:** N/A. **Average teacher tenure:** N/A.

MIDDLE SCHOOL: N/A (no middle school yet).

STUDENT SUPPORT SERVICES
"Available as needed."

STUDENT CONDUCT AND HEALTH
Code of Conduct: "We are a community of respect." **Prevention education and awareness addressed in:** N/P.

ATHLETICS
Sports offered: N/P. **Team play begins in:** "Team sports will be added beginning in G3."

CAMPUS/CAMPUS LIFE
Campus description: "Like some other independent schools that have grown and moved on, Marin Preparatory School is starting out in a charming former parish school building in the Castro. The building has 3 floors with 10 bright and airy classrooms, 2 large meeting spaces and 9 individual offices." **Library:** "Growing." **Sports facilities:** Facilities close to the school are rented as needed. **Theater/Arts facilities:** Facilities close to the school are rented as needed. **Computer lab:** No.

Science lab: No. **Lunch program:** Yes. **Bus service:** No. **Uniforms/dress code:** Dress code. **Opportunities for community service:** "At Marin Preparatory School global citizenship is part of daily life. Each student takes part in community or global social service projects and parents are invited to join with children in service activities. Children become good citizens by working collaboratively and deciding how they can make a difference."

EXTENDED DAY
Morning care: Begins at 7:30 a.m. **After-school care:** Until 6 p.m. **Grade levels:** JK-3. **Cost:** $6,000 annually. **Drop-in care available:** Yes. **Coverage over major holidays:** Yes. **Homework help:** "If and when applicable." **Snacks:** Provided. **Staff/student ratio:** 1:10. **After-school classes:** None currently. **Cost:** N/A.

SUMMER PROGRAMS
Exploraciones is a unique, Spanish infused, summer experience for children entering K-G2. The program offers a new language experience with a different adventure every week, for nine weeks. Campers will have the opportunity to learn Spanish through experiencing firsthand all the amazing things our city has to offer. Throughout the summer, campers will become explorers of many engaging themes such as animals, science, food, and the beach, including many exciting field trips and a variety of hands on experiences. Campers will also experience a taste of Latin American culture while exploring the Mission District, and taking a virtual viaje to several Spanish speaking countries. **Cost:** "Varies."

PARENT INVOLVEMENT
Parent/teacher communication: "Daily and on-going. Progress reports are provided every 4 weeks." **Participation requirements:** "Voluntary and welcomed." **Parent education programs offered?** "We will be offering Spanish language for adults. Other topics will be offered when appropriate."

WHAT SETS THE SCHOOL APART FROM OTHERS
"Marin Preparatory School offers children and their families an exceptional cross-cultural learning environment that fosters high standards of academic success. With Spanish language and Latino culture infused into the curriculum, children grow to appreciate worlds beyond their own. Marin Preparatory School encourages children to develop a sense of citizenship, both local and global, while preparing

for the next steps in their academic careers. Marin Preparatory School is affiliated with Marin Day Schools and both are part of the Bright Horizons community."

HOW FAMILIES CHARACTERIZE SCHOOL
Parent comment(s): "Like many San Francisco families we went through the challenging private/public school kindergarten application process. How wonderful to find Marin Prep! The dedication and ability to focus on each child as an individual is amazing. In addition to the Spanish infusion, the science curriculum is hands on and amazing. Everyone is devoted to the child's education, the school community, the welfare of the other children and the children are having tons of fun in the process. The school makes a point of being part of a neighborhood and is in a great old school building with children's art on display everywhere."
Student comment(s): Current students have said: "When I started kindergarten I didn't have any friends, now I have a school full of friends." • "When I started the year, I was afraid to ask questions, now I ask lots of questions." • "In kindergarten, I was afraid to speak in front of a large group, now I feel more comfortable speaking in front of a group."

MARIN PRIMARY & MIDDLE SCHOOL
20 Magnolia Avenue
Larkspur, CA   94939
(415) 924-2608 *fax (415) 924-9351*
www.mpms.org

Julie Elam, Head of School
Donna Fanfelle and Erin Murphy, Co-Directors of Admission,
dfanfelle@mpms.org

GENERAL
Coed PS-8 day school. Founded in 1975. Independent. Nonprofit. **Member:** CAIS, BADA. **Enrollment:** Approx. 370. **Average class size:** 24. **Accreditation:** WASC/CAIS (N/P term). **Endowment:** $400,000. **School year:** Sept.-June. **School day:** 8:15 a.m. to 3:15 p.m.

STUDENT BODY ETHNICITY
84% Caucasian (non-Latino), 11%, multi-racial, 3% other, 1% Asian, 1% African-American.

ADMISSION
Applications due: Approx. Jan. 14 (call for date). **Application fee:** $75. **Application process:** "Campus tour for parents, preliminary and formal applications, transcripts (if applicable), teacher recommendations, school visit or screening, attendance at one of the 3 admission coffees. **No. of applications:** Approx. 188. **No. of K spaces:** 25. **Percentage of K class made up of school's preschool class:** 48%. **Admission evaluation requirements for K:** In house screening, teacher recommendations, transcripts (if applicable), tour for parents. **Other grades:** N/P. **Preferences:** Sibling. **What sort of student do you best serve?** "MP&MS best serves families who are committed to and believe in the mission and philosophy of the school."

COSTS
Latest tuition: $19,650 for JK, $20,900 for K, $21,400 for G1-4, $22,750 for G5-7, $23,050 for G8. **Sibling discount:** None. **Tuition includes:** Lunch: No; Transportation: Yes; Laptop computer: No; Other: Includes field trips and books. **Tuition increases:** Approx. 4% annually. **Other costs:** Other costs vary yearly. **Percentage of students receiving financial aid:** 22%. **Financial aid application deadline:** Approx. Jan. 14 (call for date). Financial aid is based on need. **Average grant:** $13,135. **Percentage of grants of half-tuition or more:** 70%. **Donations:** "Voluntary but strongly encouraged."

SCHOOL'S MISSION STATEMENT
"At Marin Primary & Middle School we make education meaningful, while encouraging pride in self, respect for others, and enthusiasm for learning. • We treasure childhood. We honor and enjoy children's natural curiosity, competence, and exuberance. We teach to reach children. Using teams of teachers and educational methods tailored to how children learn best, we connect with our students, build trusting relationships, and make learning relevant, memorable and fun. We teach children to reach. Asking not 'how smart is the child' but 'how is the child smart,' we guide our students to see their full potential, and we equip them to pursue it with passion and purpose. • We inspire children to make a difference. We value academic excellence, personal integrity, and community action, and encourage our students to become informed, engaged, and ethical global citizens."

ACADEMIC PROGRAM
Philosophy: N/P. **Foreign languages:** Spanish. **Computer training:** Yes. **No. of computers available for students:** 75. **No. of hours**

weekly of: Art- 1.5; Drama- 1; Music- 1.5; Computers- N/P; Foreign language- N/P; PE- 3. **Outdoor education:** Curriculum guided trips to the Discovery Museum, San Francisco Symphony, Guide Dogs for the Blind, Clem Miller Environmental Education Center in Point Reyes, Mendicino, Yosemite, Washington State, Gold Country, Marin Headlands. Optional trips to Ecuador and Washington D.C. **Grading:** A-F, beginning in G4. **Average nightly homework:** "Varies. Homework policy determined by teams of teachers." Posted on the Internet: Yes. **Percentage of students participating in Johns Hopkins Center for Talented Youth Program:** N/P. **Other indicators of academic success:** "Secondary school and college placement record." **High schools attended by latest graduating class:** Branson, MA, MC, Urban, Marin School, University, SOTA, MSAT, Bay.

FACULTY
Ethnicity: 83% Caucasian (non-Latino), 7% Latino, 6% "international," 2% Asian, 2% multi-racial. **Percentage of teachers with graduate degrees:** 18%. **Percentage with current California credential:** 28%. **Faculty selection/training:** N/P. **Teacher/student ratio:** 1:6. **Special subject teachers:** Art, music, woodworking, drama, PE, Spanish, technology. Extensive after-school elective program; Outdoor Education center. **Average teacher tenure:** 15 years.

MIDDLE SCHOOL
Description: Integrated subjects through G8. **Teacher/student ratio:** 1:7. **Elective courses offered:** "We have integrated specialist courses: art, music, band, instrumental music, chorus, physical education, woodworking, Spanish, outdoor education center program for all grades. After school electives include: Foreign language, woodworking, technology, music, drama, homework lab, creative writing, art, team sports including boys and girls flag football, boys and girls basketball, cross-country, and track and field. **Achievement tracking in:** N/P. **Student social events:** Barbecues, theatrical productions, Annual Sock Hop, International Day, Grandparents and Special Friends Day, Harvest Festival, buddy program, Literary Day, Book Fair, community service projects.

STUDENT SUPPORT SERVICES
No. of Licensed Counselors on staff: One. **Counselor/student ratio:** "N/A." **Learning specialists on staff:** Five. **Learning differences/ disabilities support:** "The school honors learning differences in all its students. Teachers routinely integrate classroom and testing

accommodations into their daily structures and routines. The school's Learning Resource Center has a well-defined and flexible program of skill-building and curriculum support across the primary and middle grades. Prospective students with identified learning disabilities are admitted to the school based on class composition and whether their individual needs can be met." **High school placement support:** "There is extensive support from the Eighth Grade teachers and the Administration. Aid in the secondary school admission process begins during the spring of G7."

STUDENT CONDUCT AND HEALTH

Code of conduct: "Six rules to live by: Be kind, Be respectful, Be an active listener, Be safe, Be accountable, Give your personal best." **Prevention education and awareness addressed in:** "Included in life skills classes taught to all Middle School students. Special programs, assemblies and various presenters are part of this curriculum."

ATHLETICS

Sports offered: Cross-country, track and field, soccer, basketball, flag football. **Team play begins in:** G5 (inter/intramural).

CAMPUS/CAMPUS LIFE

Campus description: "The campus includes large classrooms, a multipurpose room used for bi-weekly all-school assemblies, an expansive Library Media Center, an Outdoor Education Center, an Integrated Subjects Projects Lab, an Art room, a Music room, 2 fields and access to public tennis courts." **Library:** Library/media center with 20,000 volumes. **Sports facilities:** Tennis courts, baseball field, basketball court. **Theater/Arts facilities:** Multi-purpose and art room. **Computer lab:** "Yes. The entire campus has wireless connection." **Science lab:** Yes. **Lunch program:** Yes. **Bus service:** From San Francisco. **Uniforms/ dress code:** Dress code. **Opportunities for community service:** Extensive community service opportunities on campus and in the greater area are available to students. Each Middle School student is required to complete community service hours annually.

EXTENDED DAY

Morning care: Begins at 7:30 a.m. **After-school care:** Until 6 p.m. **Grade levels:** PreK-8. **Cost:** Approx. $7.50/hour. Free playground supervision before morning class time. **Drop-in care available:** Yes. **Coverage over major holidays:** No. **Homework help:** A homework lab for Middle School students is available at an extra cost. A homework room is also available for Primary and Middle School students at an additional cost. **Snacks:** Provided. **Staff/student ratio:** 1:6. **After-school classes:** Woodworking, art, instrumental music lessons, team sports, technology instruction, drama, Garage Band, chess, Legos, science, tennis and RC cars. **Cost:** Varies from $200-$285/semester depending on class time and materials involved.

SUMMER PROGRAMS
"Summer camp is in session from mid-June to early Aug. Camp is for students entering PK-7. Camp includes extensive elective opportunities including model car building, surfing, cooking, field trips to amusement parks, sports." **Cost:** Based on number of weeks attended. Drop-in attendance is available depending on space availability.

PARENT INVOLVEMENT
Parent/teacher communication: "Conferences, website, e-mail, Friday newsletter, extensive report cards/progress reports." **Participation requirements:** Twenty voluntary hours per year. **Parent education programs offered?** Speaker Series events and many other opportunities are offered throughout the year. Parent involvement is highly important and encouraged.

WHAT SETS THE SCHOOL APART FROM OTHERS
"At Marin Primary & Middle School, we believe childhood is a time to be treasured. We believe that children respond best to kindness, encouragement and mutual respect. We also recognize that relationships, relevance and high standards are critical to successful education. MP&MS students are challenged to develop a lifelong passion for learning that includes equal measures of wonder and rigorous inquiry. We teach our children to learn with and from each other, and we teach the group to respect the individual."

HOW FAMILIES CHARACTERIZE SCHOOL
Parent comment(s): "Marin Primary & Middle School truly values my child for who she is." • "The teachers at MP&MS care about and understand my child." • "My child loves to come to school." • "MP&MS doesn't just say they educate the whole child, they really do it!"
Student comment(s): "At MP&MS, my teachers care about who I am." "I left MP&MS more than ready for high school. MP&MS gave me the gift of knowing how I learn and what my individual strengths are."

Marin Waldorf School

755 Idylberry Road
San Rafael, CA 94903
(415) 479-8190 ext. 102 *fax (415) 479-9921*
www.marinwaldorf.org

Jean Bowler, Administrator, Jeanbowler@marinwaldorf.org
Nick Broad, Director of Admission, outreach@marinwaldorf.org

General

Coed PS-8 day school. Founded in 1972. Independent. Nonprofit. **Member:** N/P. **Enrollment:** Approx. 230. **Average class size:** 22. **Accreditation:** AWSNA (term N/P.) **Endowment:** N/P. **School year:** Sept.-June. **School day:** 8:15 a.m. to 3:15 p.m.

Student Body Ethnicity

81% Caucasian (non-Latino), 5% Asian, 5% multi-racial, 5% other, 2% Latino, 2% African-American.

Admission

Applications due: "March then rolling admissions for remainder of year." **Application fee:** $75. **Application process:** Parents are strongly encouraged to take a tour, submit the application packet available online, and schedule an interview. **No. of applications:** 75+. **No. of K spaces:** 44. **Percentage of K class made up of school's preschool class:** 85%. **Admission evaluation requirements for K:** Application and interview. **Other grades:** Application, teacher recommendation form, interview, class visit. **Preferences:** Sibling, prior Waldorf school attendance. **What sort of student do you best serve?** "We seek students who are academically strong, well-rounded, inquisitive, and enthusiastic about learning."

Costs

Latest tuition: $14,000 for K; $16,600 for G1-8. **Sibling discount:** 25%. **Tuition includes:** Lunch: No; Transportation: No; Laptop computer: No; Other: N/A. **Tuition increases:** Approx. 3% annually. **Other costs:** $500 enrollment fee; approx. $50 musical instrument fees. **Percentage of students receiving financial aid:** 34%. **Financial aid application deadline:** Feb. (call for date). Financial aid is based on need. **Average grant:** "Varies." **Percentage of grants of half-tuition or more:** N/P. **Donations:** Voluntary.

School's Mission Statement

"The mission of the Marin Waldorf School is to provide an education that will prepare children to fulfill their highest potential as free human beings energized by a life-long joy for learning. Recognizing the spiritual nature of the human being, we bring into practice the educational principles of Rudolf Steiner in a way that reflects their relevance for an ever-changing and socially diverse world. Each stage of a child's development is supported by activities that engage the mind, fire the imagination, and strengthen the will in order to develop capacities and skills that can serve an evolving humanity."

Academic Program

Philosophy: "At Marin Waldorf School, we celebrate academic excellence, cultivate artistic expression, and help our students develop life-long practical skills. We do this by stimulating their love of learning, channeling their idealism, and deepening their sense of social responsibility." **Foreign languages:** Spanish, German. **Computer training:** Yes in G7-8. **No. of computers available for students:** N/A. **No. of hours weekly of:** Art- 6; Drama- 4: Music- 6; Computers- N/A; Foreign language- 4; PE- 4. **Outdoor education:** 4. **Grading:** Portfolio Assessment, written evaluations. Letter grades beginning in G6. **Average nightly homework:** In G4-8, 45-90 min. Posted on the Internet: No. **Percentage of students participating in Johns Hopkins Center for Talented Youth Program:** N/A. **Other indicators of academic success:** "N/A." **High schools attended by latest graduating class:** MA, Branson, San Domenico, Bay, SF Waldorf, MC.

Faculty

Ethnicity: 90% Caucasian (non-Latino), 10% African-American. **Percentage of teachers with graduate degrees:** 25%. **Percentage with current California credential:** N/P. **Faculty selection/training:** 100% Full Waldorf Teacher Training, plus minimum of a BA. **Teacher/student ratio:** 1:20. **Special subject teachers:** Art, instrumental music, PE, movement, choir, foreign language, gardening, handwork, woodwork. **Average teacher tenure:** 8 years.

Middle School

Description: "In Middle School (G6-8) we promote academic excellence, deepen emotional and social intelligence, and further develop practical skills to prepare our students for high school and beyond. The middle school curriculum builds upon the interest and enthusiasm of the earlier years, introducing the full range of subjects, which are now taught in a demanding, but interesting way, inspiring the intellect, stirring the emotions, and physically challenging the capacities of adolescents. Middle School students study math, language arts, chemistry, physics, biology, Spanish, geography, history, music, art, handwork, woodwork, physical education, movement, speech, gardening, drama. Students also go on regular educational field trips. The highest academic standards are expected of the students." **Teacher/student ratio:** 1:20. **Elective courses offered:** "N/A." **Achievement tracking in:** Math, Spanish. **Student social events:** "Numerous."

STUDENT SUPPORT SERVICES
No. of Licensed Counselors on staff: None. **Counselor/student ratio:** N/A. **Learning specialists on staff:** One. **Learning differences/ disabilities support:** N/A. **High school placement support:** "N/A."

STUDENT CONDUCT AND HEALTH
Code of conduct: "Yes." **Prevention education and awareness addressed in:** Health class.

ATHLETICS
Sports offered: Track and field, basketball, soccer. **Team play begins in:** G6.

CAMPUS/CAMPUS LIFE
Campus description: "Eleven acres, large playing fields, school garden, large classrooms." **Library:** "5,000 volumes." **Sports facilities:** Soccer pitch field and multipurpose field. **Theater/Arts facilities:** Amphitheater. **Computer lab:** No. **Science lab:** No. **Lunch program:** Yes, organic lunch program. **Bus service:** No. **Uniforms/dress code:** Dress code. No commercial logos allowed. **Opportunities for community service:** "Yes, varies by class and age."

EXTENDED DAY
Morning care: None. **After-school care:** Until 5:30 p.m. **Grade levels:** PS-8. **Cost:** N/P. **Drop-in care available:** Yes. **Coverage over major holidays:** No. **Homework help:** No. **Snacks:** Provided. **Staff/student ratio:** 1:4. **After-school classes:** None. **Cost:** N/A.

SUMMER PROGRAMS
"Magic Forest Summer Camp, for children ages 3-6 years. Crafts, gardening, traditional games, nature walks, puppetry. Camp includes three, 2-week sessions from 8:30 a.m. to 12:45 p.m." **Cost:** $475/session.

Parent Involvement
Parent/teacher communication: Parent/teacher conference and 2 written evaluations. **Participation requirements:** Parents are asked to give 15 hours of volunteer time every year. **Parent education programs offered?** Yes.

What Sets the School Apart From Others
"Our educational community (and it really is a community) our students, faculty, parents, alumni and, of course, our demanding curriculum -- all work in concert to help each student become smart and skilled and capable of not just meeting—but embracing—life's challenges. Over 900 Waldorf schools internationally."

How Families Characterize School
Parent comment(s): "I have so appreciated my son's education at Marin Waldorf School. He has had a stable and healthy environment for learning and he loves to come to school to be in his class with friends he has known for years and a teacher who knows him well."
Student comment(s): "My Waldorf education has challenged me to think for myself and to reach new heights both academically and personally. Marin Waldorf School was able to give me a nourishing relationship with my education and has ultimately given me a stronger sense of self, and the confidence to accomplish anything."

Megan Furth Catholic Academy
2445 Pine Street
San Francisco, CA 94115
(415) 346-9500 *fax (415) 346-8001*
www.meganfurthacademy.org

Nicole McAuliffe, Principal, nmcauliffe@meganfurthacademy.org

General
Coed K-8 parochial day school. Megan Furth Catholic Academy opened in 2005 as a result of the merging of two Catholic elementary schools: Sacred Heart (founded in 1905) and St. Dominic's (founded in 1929). **Member:** NCEA. **Enrollment:** Approx. 110. **Average class size:** 14. **Accreditation:** WASC/WCEA (N/P term). **Endowment:** N/P. **School year:** Aug.-June. **School day:** 8:30 a.m. to 4 p.m.

STUDENT BODY ETHNICITY
61% African-American, 17% Filipino, 14% other, 8% Latino.

ADMISSION
Applications due: April 1st. **Application fee:** $35. **Application process:** Grade level assessment, previous school questionnaire, transcripts. **No. of applications:** N/P. **No. of K spaces:** 25. **Percentage of K class made up of school's preschool class:** N/A. **Admission evaluation requirements for K:** Screening, school visit and tour, preschool recommendations. **Other grades:** Entrance test, transcript, previous school teacher questionnaire. **Preferences:** Siblings, current MFCA family recommendations. **What sort of student do you best serve?** N/P.

COSTS
Latest tuition: $3,000. **Sibling discount:** $500. **Tuition includes:** Lunch: No; Transportation: No; Laptop computer: No; Other: N/P. **Tuition increases:** None. **Other costs:** $100 pre-registration deposit; approx. $300 registration fee; uniforms. **Percentage of students receiving financial aid:** 85%. **Financial aid application deadline:** April 15 for most programs. Financial aid is based on need. **Average grant:** $1,000. **Percentage of grants of half-tuition or more:** 50%. **Donations:** "A financial agreement stipulates that families will raise $400 in school sponsored fundraisers such as the walkathon, candy sale, e-script, holiday gift sale, among other opportunities."

SCHOOL'S MISSION STATEMENT
"We graduate students who are confident, academically prepared to succeed in the bay area's best high schools and who believe and practice our values every day of their lives."

ACADEMIC PROGRAM
Philosophy: "Students in K-8 follow a comprehensive standards-based curriculum in the areas of religion, language arts, science, math, and social studies. Students are challenged in an array of academic subjects that require the use of critical thinking skills to engage them in problem-solving activities that will assist in preparing them for the next level of their education. A progressive curriculum connects new learning to their prior knowledge. Students are challenged through differentiated instructional opportunities throughout the curriculum." **Foreign languages:** Spanish. **Computer training:** Yes. **No. of computers available for students:** 25 in lab. **No. of hours weekly of:** Art- .5; Drama- 6 hours per semester;

Music- .5; Computers- 2+; Foreign language- 2+; PE- 1. **Outdoor education:** One full day with Yosemite Institute at the Marin Headlands. **Grading:** A-F, beginning in G3. **Average nightly homework:** 20-30 min. for G1; 20-40 min. for G2-3; 35-55 min. for G4; 45-60 min. for G5; 60-90 min. for G6; and 60-110 min. for G7-8. Posted on the Internet: "Optional for teachers." **Percentage of students participating in Johns Hopkins Center for Talented Youth Program:** 1%. **Other indicators of academic success:** N/P. **High schools attended by latest graduating class:** Riordan, SHCP, Lick, ICA, Mercy-SF, Marin School, Urban. 70% of graduates attend private Catholic high schools.

FACULTY
Ethnicity: 90% Caucasian (non-Latino), 8% Latino, 2% Asian. **Percentage of teachers with graduate degrees:** 60%. **Percentage with current California credential:** 100%. **Faculty selection/training:** Successful elementary school experience, degree, compatibility with mission of school, preferably a practicing Roman Catholic. **Teacher/ student ratio:** 1:14. **Special subject teachers:** Science, music, PE, computers, drama, Spanish. **Average teacher tenure:** 5 years.

MIDDLE SCHOOL
Description: G6-8, departmentalized in math/science and English/ Social Studies in G7-8. **Teacher/student ratio:** 1:15. **Elective courses offered:** None. **Achievement tracking in:** Math, science, English/ literature, social studies, religion. **Student social events:** N/P.

STUDENT SUPPORT SERVICES
No. of Licensed Counselors on staff: One part-time. **Counselor/ student ratio:** 1:110 **Learning specialists on staff:** Reading specialist 5 days per week. **Learning differences/disabilities support:** Speech and language services. **High school placement support:** Part-time High School Admissions Coordinator. "A member of the junior high faculty serves as a high school counselor who meets with students once a week for eight to ten weeks, conducts 'mock interviews' and works with parents to prepare families for the secondary school application process."

STUDENT CONDUCT AND HEALTH
Code of conduct: N/P. **Prevention education and awareness addressed in:** Family Life Education, Health Education.

ATHLETICS
Sports offered: Basketball through the CYO. **Team play begins in:** "G3 play basketball and cheer leading. Students beginning in G1 may participate in pep squad."

CAMPUS/CAMPUS LIFE
Campus description: N/P. **Library:** No. Classes walk to a nearby public library. **Sports facilities:** None. **Theater/Arts facilities:** None. **Computer lab:** Yes. **Science lab:** No. **Lunch program:** No. **Bus service:** None. The school is located in an area providing access to various MUNI points around the city. **Uniforms/dress code:** Uniform. "Students are expected to be clean and neatly groomed during the school day and properly attired at school." **Opportunities for community service:** Students in G8 are required to complete 20 hours of community service before graduation. The school community sponsors toy drives, food drives, special fundraising for international emergencies and an annual coat drive for the homeless.

EXTENDED DAY
Morning care: Begins at 7 a.m. **After-school care:** 4 p.m.-6 p.m. **Grade levels:** K-8. **Cost:** Morning care is free. After school is $100 a month. **Drop-in care available:** Yes. **Coverage over major holidays:** No. **Homework help:** Yes. "A large number of University of San Francisco volunteers tutor and provide homework help." **Snacks:** Provided. **Staff/student ratio:** 1:2. **After-school classes:** N/P. **Cost:** N/P.

SUMMER PROGRAMS: None.

PARENT INVOLVEMENT
Parent/teacher communication: Parent-teacher conferences, school website, e-mail, weekly newsletter, voicemail, required parent volunteers, Parent-Teacher Association. **Participation requirements:** 30 hours of service per year. **Parent education programs offered?** "Through Catapult Learning."

WHAT SETS THE SCHOOL APART FROM OTHERS
"Healthy interactions among teachers, students, parents, shareholders and the greater community abound as Megan Furth Academy does actively represent itself as a Catholic school. The new direction of the Megan Furth Academy as a union of St. Dominic and Sacred Heart schools is supported by regular collaboration of Dominican Fathers and Dominican Sisters with prayer and personnel. Megan Furth Academy

benefits from the support of two pastors, one from St. Ignatius and one from St. Dominic's, as well as a committed group of founders who wanted to maintain a high-quality, low-cost Catholic education in the Western Addition. • Megan Furth Academy's use of a professionally acceptable assessment process has been highly effective. Data drives their instruction and curriculum choices. The school's regular use of Edusoft allows teachers to do frequent benchmark testing every 6-8 weeks, to disaggregate scores, and inform shareholders like parents and the Board of Regents. • The rich cultural and environmental opportunities tapped by Megan Furth Academy—from the public library to the symphony, museums and Golden Gate National Recreation Area—enrich student personal and academic growth and provide opportunity to integrate the SLEs into the academic program. • Megan Furth Academy has kept tuition affordable. Per student spending averages $16,300 but tuition per student is $3,000. Assistance by outside organizations is provided for those families who cannot afford the $3,000. Tuition per student has remained the same ($3,000) for the past five years."

HOW FAMILIES CHARACTERIZE SCHOOL: N/P.

MISSION DOLORES CATHOLIC SCHOOL
3321 - 16th Street (at Church) (Upper Market)
San Francisco, CA 94114
(415) 861-7673 *fax (415) 861-7620*
www.missiondolores.org

Andreina Gualco, Head of School and Director of Admission, agualco@ missiondolores.org

GENERAL
Coed K-8 parochial day school. Founded in 1893. Catholic. Nonprofit. **Member:** NCEA. **Enrollment:** Approx. 200. **Average class size:** 25. **Accreditation:** WASC/WCEA (6-year term: 2007-13). **Endowment:** N/P. **School year:** Aug.-June. **School day:** 8 a.m. to 3 p.m.

STUDENT BODY ETHNICITY
50% Latino, 19% multi-racial, 14% Asian, 12% African-American, 4% Caucasian (non-Latino), 1% Native American.

ADMISSION

Applications due: Rolling admissions. **Application fee:** $30.
Application process: "Once application is completed students are asked to come in for a screening. We administer a readiness test to K and G1 students." **No. of applications:** 30. **No. of K spaces:** 25. **Percentage of K class made up of school's preschool class:** N/A. **Admission evaluation requirements for K:** Preschool recommendation; screening. **Other grades:** "Students applying for G2-8 are asked to come and spend a day at school; we also require grades, test scores, and recommendations." **Preferences:** Sibling, Catholic. **What sort of student do you best serve?** "We do not have services for children with some special needs."

COSTS

Latest tuition: $5,100 for participating Catholic families or $6,500 for non-participating. **Sibling discount:** Yes. **Tuition includes:** Lunch: No; Transportation: No; Laptop computer: No; Other: N/P. **Tuition increases:** Approx. 5% annually. **Other costs:** Approx. $330 registration fees; $150 uniforms; $100 graduation fees (G8 only). **Percentage of students receiving financial aid:** 67%. **Financial aid application deadline:** April 15. Financial aid is based on need. **Average grant:** $500. **Percentage of grants of half-tuition or more:** 50%. These are grants given by the BASIC Fund or Guardsman not the school itself. **Donations:** "$120 (candy sale)."

SCHOOL'S MISSION STATEMENT

"We, the community of Mission Dolores School, a part of the evangelization ministry of Mission Dolores Parish, base our philosophy of education on our belief in the fundamental dignity and uniqueness of the individual as created in God's image. We acknowledge the presence of Jesus in the sacramental and ministerial life of the Church. We believe Catholic education is a process of growth that engages the student in every dimension of his/her life—spiritual, intellectual, emotional, social, cultural, and physical. Our school complements and supports the efforts of parents/guardians, who are the primary educators of their children. •
It is our mission to facilitate the development of the whole person. We strive to provide a balanced curriculum in a nurturing environment where students are challenged: to integrate the Gospel values of love, peace, justice, and service in their everyday lives; to develop their abilities to think independently and to make free and responsible choices in the light of Christian values; to embrace their individual differences and cultural diversity; to appreciate all the wonders of God's creation; and to value responsible stewardship for the earth and its people."

ACADEMIC PROGRAM
Philosophy: N/P. **Foreign languages:** Spanish; French G6-8. **Computer training:** Yes. **No. of computers available for students:** 18 in lab; 2-4 in each classroom. **No. of hours weekly of:** Art- 1; Drama- none; Music- .5; Computers- 1; Foreign language- N/P; PE- 1-1.5. **Outdoor education:** G6. **Grading:** A-F, beginning in G3. **Average nightly homework:** "Varies by grade level." Posted on the Internet: Yes. **Percentage of students participating in Johns Hopkins Center for Talented Youth Program:** None. "[Students participate in various summer programs including]: Aim High at Urban; Summerbridge at University (G6-8), and at SF Day School (G4-5); Magis at SI." **Other indicators of academic success:** "90-100% of students applying to private high schools are accepted." **High schools attended by latest graduating class:** SI, Lowell, Stuart Hall, Convent, SHCP, Riordan, Mercy-Burlingame, Lick, Leadership, Wallenberg.

FACULTY
Ethnicity: 70% Caucasian (non-Latino), 20% Asian, 10% Latino. **Percentage of teachers with graduate degrees:** 70%. **Percentage with current California credential:** 100%. **Faculty selection/training:** Experience, degree. **Teacher/student ratio:** 1:25. **Special subject teachers:** Choir, PE, art (G6-8). **Average teacher tenure:** 6 years.

MIDDLE SCHOOL
Description: "Commences in G6, departmentalized." **Teacher/student ratio:** 1:25. **Elective courses offered:** N/P. **Achievement tracking in:** Algebra G8. **Student social events:** N/P.

STUDENT SUPPORT SERVICES
No. of Licensed Counselors on staff: One part-time. **Counselor/student ratio:** N/P. **Learning specialists on staff:** N/P. **Learning differences/ disabilities support:** N/P. **High school placement support:** N/P.

STUDENT CONDUCT AND HEALTH
Code of conduct: "Available in handbook." Prevention, education and awareness programs addressed in: Integrated in science, social studies, physical education, religion curriculum.

ATHLETICS
Sports offered: Basketball, girls volleyball. **Team play begins in:** G3.

Campus/Campus Life
Campus description: N/P. **Library:** Yes (N/P volumes). **Sports facilities:** Gym. **Theater/Arts facilities:** Auditorium. **Computer lab:** Yes. **Science lab:** N/P. **Lunch program:** Yes. **Bus service:** No. **Uniforms/dress code:** Uniforms. **Opportunities for community service:** Yes for G7-8.

Extended Day
Morning care: Begins at 7 a.m. **After-school care:** Until 6 p.m. **Grade levels:** K-8. **Cost:** $3/hour. **Drop-in care available:** Yes. **Coverage over major holidays:** No. **Homework help:** Yes. **Snacks:** Provided. **Staff/student ratio:** 1:20. **After-school classes:** Choir G5-8. **Cost:** $50/year.

Summer Programs
"Five week program."

Parent Involvement
Parent/teacher communication: Conferences, website, e-mail, newsletter. **Participation requirements:** 30 hours per year. **Parent education programs offered?** Yes.

What Sets the School Apart From Others
"Mission Dolores is a truly diverse school. Our school population truly reflects the diversity of San Francisco. Not only do our students represent a United Nations of cultures, they also come from various economic classes, family situations and they have different learning styles and abilities. Our children, parents and staff do not only appreciate the differences, they celebrate and embrace the diversity that makes Mission Dolores unique!"

How Families Characterize School
Parent comment(s): "My child is receiving a quality Catholic education in a supportive family environment."
Student comment(s): "Mission Dolores School not only prepared me to succeed in the challenging academic environment at St. Ignatius College Preparatory, but it also taught me that we are citizens of the world and success is measured not only in grades but in service and outreach to all people——those like us and those who are different."

MONTESSORI DE TERRA LINDA

620 Del Ganado Road
San Rafael, CA 94903
(415) 479-7373 *fax (415) 479-5394*
www.mdtl.org

Mary Yahnke, Head of School, mary@mdtl.org

GENERAL

Coed PS-6 day school. Founded in 1970. Independent. Nonprofit. **Member:** AMI, Green School Alliance, San Rafael Chamber of Commerce, Center for Volunteer and Nonprofit Leadership of Marin. **Enrollment:** Approx. 130. **Average class size:** 24. **Accreditation:** "AMI Recognized" (N/P term). **Endowment:** None. **School year:** Aug.-June. **School day:** 8:30 a.m. to 3 p.m.

STUDENT BODY ETHNICITY

79% Caucasian (non-Latino), 12% Asian, 4% other, 3% Latino, 2% multi-racial.

ADMISSION

Applications due: Jan. (call for date) **Application fee:** $70. **Application process:** Open house, tour/observation, child visit. **No. of applications:** 60. **No. of K spaces:** "Varies." **Percentage of K class made up of school's preschool class:** 75%. **Admission evaluation requirements for K:** Screening, school visit, teacher recommendations. **Other grades:** Same as for K. **Preferences:** Sibling, Montessori transfers. **What sort of student do you best serve?** "Creative and independent learners."

COSTS

Latest tuition: $13,375. **Sibling discount:** No. **Tuition includes:** Lunch: No; Transportation: No; Laptop computer: No; Other: N/A. **Tuition increases:** Approx. 4-5% annually. **Other costs:** Outdoor education, trips. **Percentage of students receiving financial aid:** 18%. **Financial aid application deadline:** Feb. (call for date). Financial aid is based on need. **Average grant:** $7,500. **Percentage of grants of half-tuition or more:** 90%. **Donations:** "Voluntary through our Annual Fund and Auction."

School's Mission Statement

"MdTL is a diverse community of teachers, parents and children working together for the education of the child, utilizing the methods of Maria Montessori. We serve children ages 2-12, providing a rich learning environment based upon the belief that all children can reach their personal and academic potential. • MdTL believes that the genuine cooperation of parents, students and educators combines to provide an effective and highly successful experience. Engaging and applying our core values, we work to develop responsible and caring students who are self-motivated and who respect themselves, their peers and their surroundings. • Core Values: We share a respect for self, others, our world and our environment; We teach students independence, critical thinking and social grace and courtesy; We strive to instill in our students a love of learning; We teach the students through hands-on, individualized experiences; We believe all adults in our community are role models."

Academic Program

Philosophy: "Maria Montessori's philosophy is based on the physical, academic, social and emotional developmental needs of the child and values respectful, compassionate communication and relationships between children and adults." **Foreign languages:** Spanish. **Computer training:** Integrated in the elementary curriculum. **No. of computers available for students:** 4. **No. of hours weekly of:** Art- 5+; Drama- N/P; Music- 3+; Computers- N/P; Foreign language- 3; PE- 5. **Outdoor education:** "Varies." **Grading:** Annual Progress Reports begin in K. **Average nightly homework:** 30 min. Posted on the Internet: No. **Percentage of students participating in Johns Hopkins Center for Talented Youth Program:** N/A. **Other indicators of academic success:** Stanford Achievement and OLSAT tests begin in G3. **High schools attended by latest graduating class:** N/A. Montessori de Terra Linda currently goes through the 6th grade. Some of the schools our students have continued on to are Saint Mark's School, San Domenico School, and St. Isabella's.

Faculty

Ethnicity: 71% Caucasian (non-Latino), 24% Latino, 5% other. **Percentage of teachers with graduate degrees:** 29%. **Percentage with current California credential:** "N/A." **Faculty selection/training:** AMI Credential, BA, experience. **Teacher/student ratio:** 1:10. **Special subject teachers:** Music, Spanish, art. **Average teacher tenure:** 9 years.

MIDDLE SCHOOL: N/A.

STUDENT SUPPORT SERVICES
No. of Licensed Counselors on staff: None. **Counselor/student ratio:** N/A. **Learning specialists on staff:** None. **Learning differences/ disabilities support:** None. **High school placement support:** N/A (school goes to G6).

STUDENT CONDUCT AND HEALTH
Code of conduct: "Montessori philosophy inspires respect and compassion for others. Conflict resolution curriculum is part of the Montessori philosophy and begins in preschool." **Prevention education and awareness addressed in:** At all levels, as appropriate, within the daily curriculum.

ATHLETICS
Sports offered: Softball, track, volleyball, soccer, basketball, hiking, swimming. **Team play begins in:** G1 (intramural).

CAMPUS/CAMPUS LIFE
Campus description: "Beautifully landscaped gardens surround the campus located within easy walking distance to the grocery store, post office, restaurants, coffee shop, and bus service." **Library:** "Within the classrooms." (N/P volumes.) **Sports facilities:** Basketball, grassy field, sports fields within walking distance, pool at recreation center 1/2 block away. **Theater/Arts facilities:** Multi-purpose building. **Computer lab:** "In classrooms." **Science lab:** No. **Lunch program:** No. **Bus service:** No. **Uniforms/dress code:** Dress code. "Conservative dress." **Opportunities for community service:** Yes.

EXTENDED DAY
Morning care: Begins at 7:30 a.m. **After-school care:** Until 5 p.m. **Grade levels:** K-6. **Cost:** $8/hour. **Drop-in care available:** Yes. **Coverage over major holidays:** No. **Homework help:** Yes. **Snacks:** Provided. **Staff/student ratio:** 1:10. **After-school classes:** Yes, these include art and science classes. **Cost:** $90 for a 6-week session.

SUMMER PROGRAMS
"Weekly programs are available for current and incoming students." **Cost:** N/P.

Parent Involvement

Parent/teacher communication: Conferences, website, e-mail, weekly bulletins and quarterly newsletters. **Participation requirements:** 24 hours of volunteering per family; 12 hours for single parents). **Parent education programs offered?** Yes.

What Sets the School Apart From Others

"Our school has a warm and welcoming community for both the students and the parents. Modeling care and respect for each other is a community effort."

How Families Characterize School

Parent comment(s): "Responsive to parents' needs." • "Safe and caring school."
Student comment(s): "Loving, supportive teachers." • "Learning is fun and exciting."

Mount Tamalpais School

100 Harvard Avenue
Mill Valley, CA 94941
(415) 383-9434 *fax (415) 383-7519*
www.mttam.org

Dr. Kate Mecca, Head of School, kmecca@mttam.org
Daphne Edwards Opperman, Director of Admission, dedwards@mttam.org

General

Coed K-8 day school. Founded in 1976. Independent. Nonprofit. **Member:** CAIS, WASC, BADA, ISBOA, NAIS. **Enrollment:** Approx. 272. **Average class size:** 16. **Accreditation:** CAIS/WASC (6-year term: 2005-11). **Endowment:** "$3.5 million+." **School year:** Aug.-June. **School day:** 8 a.m. to 3 p.m.

Student Body Ethnicity

75% Caucasian (non-Latino), 6% Asian, 6% Latino, 4% African-American, 3% other.

Admission

Applications due: Jan. (call for date). **Application fee:** $150. **Application process:** Parents must visit, go on a group tour, and meet with the Admissions Director and Head of School. Students are screened following receipt of application, which includes 3 reference/recommendation forms to be sent separately. Applicants to G2-8 must spend a full school day on campus during which time they are interviewed and participate in criterion-referenced testing in core subjects. **No. of applications:** Approx. 250 for K. **No. of K spaces:** 24-32. **Percentage of K class made up of school's preschool class:** N/A. **Admission evaluation requirements for K:** Screening, school visit, minimum of 3 recommendations (one of which must come from the child's current teacher or preschool team/director); parent interview, student interview and observation, admission test scores, copy of certified birth record, photograph. **Other grades:** "Standardized test results, transcript, school visit, student interview, parent interview, at least 3 recommendations, one of which must come from the child's current teacher, writing sample, work portfolio, etc." **Preferences:** "Siblings and legacies do receive some preference." **What sort of student do you best serve?** "MTS seeks to enroll students who are enthusiastic, motivated learners who will thrive in a strong academic program that emphasizes individual growth, creativity, exploration, and character development, within an integrated spiraling curriculum."

COSTS

Latest tuition: $22,350. **Sibling discount:** None. **Tuition includes:** Lunch: No; Transportation: No; Laptop computer: No; Other: No. **Tuition increases:** Approx. 3-7% annually. **Other costs:** Approx. $100 for specific textbooks in G6-8; approx. $100 for uniforms; $25-$125 other fees. **Percentage of students receiving financial aid:** Approx. 20%. **Financial aid application deadline:** Jan. (call for date). Financial aid is based on need; applications made through SSS. **Average grant:** "Varies." **Percentage of grants of half-tuition or more:** 85%. **Donations:** "Annual donations are expected to the Annual Fund, Faculty Fund, as well as to the Building Fund and/or Capital Campaign or Endowment Fund when school is engaged in an active campaign. Donations of goods and/or services and attendance at the annual Auction Gala fund raising event are strongly encouraged and appreciated."

SCHOOL'S MISSION STATEMENT

"Mount Tamalpais School is an independent, coeducational school serving students in Kindergarten through Grade 8. Mount Tamalpais School is dedicated to the active pursuit of knowledge and to integrity, community service and fairness. We want our students to embrace diversity, honoring the value of each individual's heritage, strengths, choices, feelings and ideas. We strive to celebrate the human spirit by being responsible members of our families, our school, our community and our world. We are committed to a strong, innovative, interactive, multidisciplinary curriculum designed to challenge and enlighten, and to teachers who serve as guides and role models for our students. The school's program, atmosphere and overall environment have been designed to encourage the development of the whole child, with an emphasis on creativity, strong academic preparation, values, emotional growth, personal and social skills, effective thinking and problem solving capabilities, with attention to individual strengths and diversity of learning styles. Mount Tamalpais School places equal emphasis on the academic and social development of each student within a community that esteems family, the pursuit of personal excellence, the perpetuation of valued traditions, and the development of a strong moral code. Mount Tamalpais School is strongly committed to the partnership of home and school on behalf of each individual student."

ACADEMIC PROGRAM

Philosophy: "Mount Tamalpais School seeks to provide students with a strong academic foundation and to foster genuine enthusiasm for lifelong learning through an intellectually stimulating and challenging program. Working within a departmentalized curriculum with teachers who are specialists in their subject areas helps to instill a love of learning and develops students who are inquisitive, thoughtful, determined, independent, intellectually curious, creative thinking and well-integrated human beings. It is our goal to include the mastery of skills and concepts at each grade level in each subject while integrating query, investigation, problem solving and higher level thinking skills. We also want students to challenge themselves, to grow in creativity, to question, to seek information, to work well independently and with others in a cooperative and collaborative manner. It is also our hope that each student will find and explore their own individual strengths and creative outlets and will be committed to contribute to the greater good." **Foreign languages:** Mandarin, French and Spanish in K-5, French or Spanish, plus Latin in G6-8, plus Mandarin or Japanese in G6-8. **Computer training:** K-8. **No. of computers available for students:** 140. **No. of hours weekly of:** Art- 1.5+; Drama- 1+; Music- 1.5+; Computers- 1.5+; Foreign language- 3-5+; PE- 5+. **Outdoor education:** G4-8. **Grading:** G1-3 evaluation. G4-8 A-F. **Average nightly homework:** Approx. 20 min. in G1-2 to approx. 1 hour + in G8. Posted on the Internet: No. **Percentage of students participating in Johns Hopkins Center for Talented Youth Program:** 3-5%. **Other indicators of academic success:** "Honor Roll each trimester (B+ 91% average)." **High schools attended by latest graduating class:** Branson, University, SI, MA, Convent, Stuart Hall, Urban, Thacher, MC, Groton.

FACULTY

Ethnicity: 85% Caucasian (non-Latino), 6% other, 4% multi-racial, 2% Latino, 2% African-American, 1% Asian. **Percentage of teachers with graduate degrees:** 70%. **Percentage with current California credential:** 75%. **Faculty selection/training:** Degree, credential, graduate degree, experience, specialized training in subject area. **Teacher/student ratio:** 1:8. **Special subject teachers:** Art, art history, dance, drama, technology, PE, music, choral, instrumental, musical theatre, health, character development, debate, etiquette, geography, current events, yoga. **Average teacher tenure:** 13 years.

MIDDLE SCHOOL

Description: G6-8, departmentalized in all grades and all subjects. **Teacher/student ratio:** 1:8; 1:12 for some classes. **Elective courses offered:** "Trimester rotation, single or double blocks depending on the course—art, dance, drama, computers and music, current events, IT, creative writing, animation, computers (all in addition to regularly scheduled classes in most of these subjects.)" **Achievement tracking in:** "Math only, according to learning style, G5-8." **Student social events:** Student Council functions and events, Spirit Days, Junior High dances.

STUDENT SUPPORT SERVICES

No. of Licensed Counselors on staff: One in counseling capacity; also teaches and serves in other roles. **Counselor/student ratio:** N/P. **Learning specialists on staff:** Three. **Learning differences/disabilities support:** "Two full-time Learning Specialists who work with students individually and in small groups, with teachers and with parents. Students participate in differentiated instruction and receive extended time on tests. Particular students may have their schedules and/or their subject requirements modified if/when appropriate. One learning specialist works specifically with higher achieving students who benefit from additional enrichment activities." **High school placement support:** Dean of Students/G8 Homeroom teacher and Head of School lead the secondary school admission process for students and families in G8. This process begins in G7 with a spring meeting to help explain and organize the high school admission calendar for the eighth grade year.

Student Conduct and Health

Code of conduct: "Students are expected to respect themselves, their school, the environment and others." **Prevention education and awareness addressed in:** "Our comprehensive Health Education program includes specific units on decision making, eating disorders, stereotypes, drugs, alcohol, subliminal advertising, personal choices, gender bias and sexual harassment issues."

Athletics

Sports offered: Cross-country (G3-8), volleyball (G6-8), soccer (G6-8), basketball (G2-8), track and field (G3-8), lacrosse (G3-8), **Team play begins in:** G2.

Campus/Campus Life

Campus description: "MTS is located on more than 12 acres in Mill Valley, 15 minutes north of San Francisco. We are close to the Pacific Ocean, the Bay, and Highway 101 and Shoreline Highway Route 1. The beautiful campus includes a large playing field (full soccer field overlaid by 2 baseball diamonds and a peripheral track), a smaller grass circle area, and a 1+ acre Cypress Grove outdoor learning area." **Library:** "The Rappoport Library Learning Center incorporates 2,500+ square feet including a small instructional classroom and individual student work stations. There is a dedicated computer mini-lab within the library, and our entire computer system is networked and wireless. The library houses more than 18,000 books, plus reference materials and online resources. There are 12 permanent student computer stations, 2 faculty/staff computer stations and unlimited laptop access within the library." **Sports facilities:** The 15,000+ sq. ft. Founder's Hall includes a full gymnasium/theatre, a dance/gymnastics room, a piano room, and a music room, in addition to 2 small instrumental instruction rooms and a hospitality kitchen. **Theater/Arts facilities:** See above. **Computer lab:** The main computer lab houses 22 student workstations and 2 faculty/ staff work stations. There are several mini labs throughout the school, plus 3 laptop carts and an Alpha Smart cart of 20 each. All teachers have desktop or laptop computers at their desks; all access is wireless and networked. **Science lab:** Two dedicated science lab classrooms and a connecting shared work study/office space serve students in K-8 and the Science Department teachers. **Lunch program:** Yes. **Bus service:** Yes. **Uniforms/dress code:** Uniforms. **Opportunities for community service:** "Community service learning opportunities are woven within curriculum and explored as well through Student Council-sponsored activities. All students in G6-8 have specific community service projects each year of middle school that are done outside of school time. These assignments must be direct service with bona fide non-profit programs, especially those that serve children, the elderly, the environment, or special needs populations."

EXTENDED DAY
Morning care: Begins at 7:30 a.m. **After-school care:** Until 6 p.m. **Grade levels:** K-8. **Cost:** $10/hour prepaid in $100 increments. **Drop-in care available:** Daily with credit card on file. **Coverage over major holidays:** No. **Homework help:** Yes. **Snacks:** Provided. **Staff/student ratio:** 1:10 max. **After-school classes:** "Full range of classes each trimester, including dance, sewing, science adventures, computers, chess, brain games, art, rock climbing, etc." **Cost:** All classes are $175 for twelve sessions.

SUMMER PROGRAMS
The school currently offers 2 summer enrichment courses, each from 9 a.m. to 3 p.m. Sports camp lasts 2 weeks; students may sign up for a single week or for both. Drama camp lasts 2 weeks and students sign up for both weeks, as the program culminates in a Shakespeare production. **Cost:** $375 for 2 weeks, including t-shirts and snacks.

PARENT INVOLVEMENT
Parent/teacher communication: Conferences, website, e-mail, telephone, personal interaction, newsletter. **Participation requirements:** 60 hours per year per family. **Parent education programs offered?** Yes.

WHAT SETS THE SCHOOL APART FROM OTHERS
"We are a small, personalized, dynamic school and we are departmentalized. Our teachers work in their main areas of interest, training and expertise. We are committed to individualized, small group instruction and to helping each student maximize his/her potential. Because students and teachers work together over a range of years (primary, middle grades, junior high) they develop close, meaningful relationships which extend beyond the classroom."

HOW FAMILIES CHARACTERIZE SCHOOL
Parent comment(s): "Parents are committed, participatory and involved. They are supportive of faculty, staff and administration, and they value the strength and closeness of the school community. Parents also appreciate their interaction with teachers and the level of personal, individualized care and attention given to their children."

Student comment(s): "Students love their school and love their teachers. Students enjoy the wide range of classes offered and appreciate the personal attention and close interaction with faculty and staff."

THE NEW VILLAGE SCHOOL
100 Ebbtide Avenue, Suite 144
Sausalito, CA 94965
(415) 289-0889 *fax (415) 789-5504*
www.theNewVillageSchool.org

Meinir Davies, Head of School and Director of Admissions,
meinir@theNewVillageSchool.org

GENERAL
Coed K-6 day school to grow to a K-8 in 2012/2013. Founded in 2009. Independent. Nonprofit. **Member:** N/P. **Enrollment:** "Approx. 40 students, growing mindfully by 10-15 students each year." **Average class size:** 8. **Accreditation:** N/A (new school). **Endowment:** N/A. **School year:** Aug.-June. **School day:** 8:30 a.m. to 3:10 p.m.

STUDENT BODY ETHNICITY: N/P.

ADMISSION
Applications due: Jan. (call for date). **Application fee:** $75. **Application process:** "Applicant families should visit the website and follow the information under the Admission tab. After visiting our website, the first step in the admission process is to attend an Open House or school tour, followed by submitting an application. Once the application is received, a parent/child meeting will be set up. Following the conversation, applicants (other than K) will spend 1 to 3 days visiting the school. Following the visiting days, another conversation will take place with the parent and teachers. Following that conversation, the parents will meet with New Village School parent representatives." **No. of applications:** 25+ for K and 15+ for other grades. **No. of K spaces:** 10. **Percentage of K class made up of school's preschool class:** N/A. **Admission evaluation requirements for K:** Meeting with teachers, Student Characterization form (from preschool teacher). **Other grades:** Meeting with teachers, visiting days, Student Characterization form (from current teacher). **Preferences:** Siblings. **What sort of student do you best serve?** "We serve students and families who are aligned with the values of the New Village School and are seeking an innovative approach to education."

COSTS
Latest tuition: $14,995 for K-6. **Sibling discount:** 10%. **Tuition includes:** Lunch: No; Transportation: No; Laptop computer: N/A; Other: Educational materials, outdoor education. **Tuition increases:** Approx. 5% annually. **Other costs:** Taiko drumming (G2+, $700/yr); overnight class trips (G4-8). **Percentage of students receiving financial aid:** 70%. **Financial aid application deadline:** Jan. (call for date). Tuition assistance is based on need. **Average grant:** 30%. **Percentage of grants of half-tuition or more:** 18%. **Donations:** "The school relies on voluntary giving to support the operating budget. We strive for 100% participation from families currently in school and gifts of any size are appreciated."

SCHOOL'S MISSION STATEMENT
"With full measures of love, respect, rigorous academic challenge, music, community and fresh air, the New Village School cultivates an atmosphere in which children can remain inquisitive and are allowed to become deeply capable and responsible. Their renewable inner resources will help them thrive in a profoundly changing world."

ACADEMIC PROGRAM
Philosophy: "We have created a new extended family: the new village. This is a place in which parents feel safe in the knowledge that everyone feels responsible for everyone's well-being. Our neighborhoods as we once knew them have changed and our school addresses the need for community. In that way our school is a portable neighborhood and our children are raised in a community of caring individuals. In the classroom, we have created a natural extended family. We do not always separate the children artificially by grades. Indeed, all the children interact with each other at various points throughout the day. We believe in long-term relationships. Children respond with feelings of camaraderie, commitment, and a profound sense of trust. Teachers benefit from the time and ability to deeply understand and come to know the children, as well as how best to help them develop their abilities. Finally, the New Village is a community of learners—children and adults—who never give up trying to discover even more about ourselves. Because of this, we strive to create an atmosphere in which everyone feels safe to be vulnerable, honest and authentic." **Foreign languages:** Spanish, Mandarin, Arabic. **Computer training:** None. **No. of computers available for students:** N/A. **No. of hours weekly of:** Art- 4; Drama- 1.5.; Music- 1.5; Computers- N/A; Foreign language- 6; PE- 3.5. **Outdoor education:** "Yes." **Grading:** Written reports. (N/P

grade). **Average nightly homework:** 15-30 min. in G4; 30-60 min. in G5-8. Posted on the Internet: No. **Percentage of students participating in Johns Hopkins Center for Talented Youth Program:** N/A. **Other indicators of academic success:** "Quality of student work, ability of students to thrive in diverse settings." **High schools attended by latest graduating class:** N/A (school currently is K-6).

FACULTY
Ethnicity: 43% Asian, 29% Caucasian (non-Latino), 14% Latino, 14% African-American. **Percentage of teachers with graduate degrees:** 29%. **Percentage with current California credential:** "N/A." **Faculty selection/training:** Experience, degree; continuing professional development. **Teacher/student ratio:** 1:9. **Special subject teachers:** Spanish, Mandarin, Arabic, Taiko drumming, handwork, movement, gardening, music. **Average teacher tenure:** "N/A because school is new."

MIDDLE SCHOOL
Description: "At the New Village School, the emerging adolescent enters a Middle School that is dedicated to providing an education that understands and embraces their stage of development. Caring adults and a nurturing environment meet their needs for both independence and a sense of belonging. In the Middle School emerging critical thinking faculties are directed toward observing the natural world from a scientific standpoint. The critical value of artistic expression is experienced as a dynamic interplay of knowledge of self and the world. The school is dedicated to providing an education that acknowledges and encourages the development of the child as a whole human being focusing on all aspects of their development. Along with high academic standards and lifetime skills, our education addresses the growing inner life of the child. Our student goals reflect this unique perspective. The goals for our students are: Academic and critical thinking skills; self-confidence; flexibility and independent thinking; experiential knowledge; balance of thinking, feeling and willing; awakened inner life through creative processes; sense of reverence, beauty and wonder; appreciation of differences; strong inner moral compass; recognition of individuality, sense of self, and task in life. **Teacher/student ratio:** 1:9. **Elective courses offered:** "Varies." **Achievement tracking in:** N/A. **Student social events:** "Varies."

STUDENT SUPPORT SERVICES
No. of Licensed Counselors: N/A. **Counselor/student ratio:** N/A. **Learning specialists:** N/A. **Learning differences/disabilities support:** Teaching team. **High school placement support:** Teaching team.

STUDENT CONDUCT AND HEALTH
Code of conduct: "Self-respect, respect for others and respect for the environment. A very strong emphasis is placed upon the building of relationships between the child and his/her teacher, the child and the other children and the child and the content of each lesson. Thus learning becomes truly meaningful and each child's motivation remains an inner one." **Prevention education and awareness addressed in:** "The curriculum of the G6-8 addresses prevention education and awareness issues. Awareness of the body and how all the organs work together to allow life to exist are subjects in anatomy. Human sexuality and the ability to have balance and healthy relationships to ourselves and others are examined in physiology. The human body is further studied so that the students have a thorough and clear picture of their bodies and a good understanding of how to keep the body healthy. The question of sexuality, reproduction and all the implications of this is a part of the classroom conversations and these questions are addressed as they come up so that the students feel comfortable coming to the teachers with any theme that is causing them unease or distress of any kind. The emphasis is on prevention and preparation."

ATHLETICS
Sports offered: N/P sports. "The sports program at the New Village School is integrated into the curriculum. Our daily movement activities, which begin in kindergarten, include exercises that build self-confidence, balanced strength and promote collaboration and team building. In G5, students work toward a proficiency in their physical movements in order to participate in pentathlon." **Team play begins in:** G6.

CAMPUS/CAMPUS LIFE
Campus description: "The New Village School is located on 17 acres in Sausalito. The classrooms are beautifully appointed and have a great deal of natural light and space." **Library:** No. **Sports facilities:** Gymnasium, large sports field, track, basketball court. **Theater/Arts facilities:** No. **Computer lab:** No. **Science lab:** No. **Lunch program:** No. **Bus service:** No. **Uniforms/dress code:** Dress code. **Opportunities for community service:** Classroom Without Walls curriculum in K-6, to also be extended to K-8; Community Service project planned for G8.

EXTENDED DAY
Morning care: Begins at 8 a.m. **After-school care:** Until 5:30 p.m. **Grade levels:** N/P. **Cost:** Up to $20/day. **Drop-in care available:** Yes. **Coverage over major holidays:** No. **Homework help:** Yes. **Snacks:** Provided. **Staff/student ratio:** "Varies by attendance." **After-school classes:** Varies, including cooking, drumming, sports, arts and crafts, physical activities, nature adventures. **Cost:** "Varies."

SUMMER PROGRAMS
Summer programs vary from year to year, but are available for all grades. Themes may include: Outdoor Adventures; Spanish Immersion with crafts, cooking and dancing; Musical Theater Camp. **Cost:** "Varies."

PARENT INVOLVEMENT
Parent/teacher communication: Conferences, end-of-year reports, individual parent meetings, monthly class meetings, website, e-mail, telephone, newsletter. **Participation requirements:** "The New Village School invites families to support the school with volunteer activities as actively as individual circumstances permit. The school offers a wide variety of volunteer opportunities with differing time commitments." **Parent education programs offered?** Yes.

WHAT SETS THE SCHOOL APART FROM OTHERS
"The New Village School provides sustainable education for the 21st century. What is Sustainable Education? Organic farmers know that if they only take nourishment from the soil and simply replenish it with chemical fertilizers, the food grown in that soil is neither healthy nor nourishing. The soil ends up completely depleted. The same can be said for human beings. That is why the children at New Village School are received with interest and respect. It's why we offer nourishing content to help them expand their inner horizons and create colorful inner landscapes. With such a foundation, they will have a much better chance of responding to the challenges of a twenty-first century life with its highly volatile developments. We find that children who haven't been given the time and tools to develop inner strength become dependent on entertainment and consumerism in order to define and give meaning to their existence. Yet children who are continually nourished, like the soil lovingly tended by an organic farmer, feel free to expand and develop their unique personas. They can regenerate themselves when they are depleted. And when life's challenges arise—and they always do—these children can deal with them by calling on their own inner responses. The education at the New Village School offers children tools to develop

themselves in a way that will enable them to retain the vitality of body, mind and spirit."

Our Lady of the Visitacion School

795 Sunnydale Avenue (at Sawyer) (Visitacion Valley)
San Francisco, CA 94134
(415) 239-7840 *fax (415) 239-2559*
www.olvisitacion.com

Mrs. Maxie O'Rourke, Principal, visitacionsf@yahoo.com

General

Coed K-8 parochial day school. Founded in 1964. Catholic. Nonprofit. **Member:** WASC/WCEA (N/P term). **Enrollment:** Approx. 241. **Average class size:** Approx. 27. **Accreditation:** WASC/WCEA (6 year term 2006-12). **Endowment:** N/P. **School year:** Aug.-June. **School day:** 8:10 a.m. to 3 p.m.

Student Body Ethnicity: N/P.

Admission

Applications due: "Students accepted until classes are filled." **Application fee:** $65. **Application process:** Readiness testing, school visit, and tour, preschool recommendations. **No. of applications:** N/P. **No. of K spaces:** 25. **Percentage of K class from preschool class:** N/A. **Admission evaluation requirements for K:** Individual screening. **Other grades:** School tour, individual evaluation by grade level teacher, transcript and interview with principal. **Preferences:** N/P. **What sort of student do you best serve?** "We accept those students who are respectful, caring, and love God. They should be willing to work to the best of their ability. Our students are not test scores, but individuals who are challenged to persevere and set personal goals for success."

Costs

Latest tuition: $4,100. **Sibling discount:** Yes. **Tuition includes:** N/P. **Tuition increases:** N/P. **Other costs:** $200 school fees. **Percentage of students receiving financial aid:** N/P. **Financial aid application deadline:** N/P. Financial aid is based on need. **Average grant:** N/P. **Percentage of grants of half-tuition or more:** N/P. **Donations:** N/P.

SCHOOL'S MISSION STATEMENT

"It is the mission of Our Lady of the Visitacion School to provide its diverse student population with the educational opportunities for academic achievement that are necessary to fulfill the basic Archdiocesan elementary curriculum requirements for entrance into secondary school. All learning experiences are fostered within a faith community that has as its model the person and Gospel of Jesus Christ. Animated by the spirit of St. Vincent de Paul, St. Louise de Marillac and St. Elizabeth Ann Seton, education and teaching are seen as the vision of service that manifests the Daughters of Charity's consecration to God, to the Church and to the Community and the vision of service."

ACADEMIC PROGRAM

Philosophy: "The curriculum follows the guidelines set forth by the Archdiocesan and California State Standards. The faculty endeavors to provide a curriculum that challenges all students to reach their full potential. It recognizes the diversity of the school community and strives to create graduates who are well-rounded students with an understanding of the Catholic faith and Vincentian values, the significance of service to God and their community, and a love for learning that will last a lifetime. It is supplemented with art, music, physical education, and technology."
Computer training: Yes. **No. of computers available for students:** There are 31 laptop computers on a mobile laptop cart and 2-3 computers are in the classroom. **No. of hours weekly of:** Art- 1; Drama- N/P; Music- N/P; Computers- N/P ("varies"); Foreign language- N/P; PE- 2. **Outdoor education:** N/P. **Grading:** A-F. **Average nightly homework:** 20 min. in K-2; 30-40 min. in G3-4; 45-60 min. in G5-6; 60-90 min. in G7-8. Posted on the Internet: N/P. **Percentage of students participating In the Johns Hopkins Center for Talented Youth:** N/P. **Other Indicators of success:** "Many of our alumni bring their children to the school for education. Graduates have commented that they felt confident when they entered their first freshman class in high school because they knew that they had been fully prepared for high school by their teachers." **High schools attended by latest graduating class:** SHCP, Riordan, SI, ICA, Mercy-Burlingame, Mercy-SF, Lowell, Oceana.

FACULTY

Ethnicity: N/P. **Percentage of teachers with graduate degrees:** 30%. **Percentage with current California credential:** N/P. **Faculty selection/training:** By interview, college. **Teacher/student ratio:** 1:27. **Special subject teachers:** 2. **Average teacher tenure:** 15 years.

MIDDLE SCHOOL

Description: G6-8 are departmentalized in the subjects of language arts, social studies, math and science. "Students are challenged to demonstrate their understanding of concepts through student designed projects." **Teacher/student ratio:** 1:27. **Achievement tracking in:** N/P. **Elective courses offered:** N/P. **Student social events:** N/P.

STUDENT SUPPORT SERVICES

No. of Licensed Counselors on staff: One full-time. **Counselor/student ratio:** 1:241. **Learning specialists on staff:** Three. **Learning differences/disabilities support:** "One Title IA Math Resource Specialist and we offer language arts remediation and after school math tutoring. In addition there are vision and auditory screenings." **High school placement support:** Provided by 8th grade teacher and Principal.

STUDENT CONDUCT AND HEALTH

Code of conduct: "Students are expected to learn the self-discipline skills that are a part of the Discipline with Purpose Program. The program is developmentally based and each student thereby learns to take responsibility for his own actions. All students and staff members are expected to treat each other with love and compassion." **Prevention and awareness addressed in:** N/P.

ATHLETICS

Sports offered: Baseball, basketball, volleyball. **Team play begins in:** N/P.

CAMPUS/CAMPUS LIFE

Campus description: N/P. **Library:** "Yes." (N/P # volumes.) **Sports facilities:** Yes. **Theater/Arts facilities:** N/P. **Computer Lab:** No. **Science lab:** Yes. **Lunch program:** Three times a week. **Bus service:** Close to public transportation- T-Rail, #8, and 9 lines. **Uniforms/dress code:** Dress code. **Opportunities for Community Service:** Christian service projects.

EXTENDED DAY

Morning care: Begins at 6:50 a.m. **After school care:** Until 6 p.m. **Grade levels:** N/P. **Cost:** N/P. **Drop in care available:** Yes. **Coverage over major holidays:** No. **Homework help:** Yes. **Snacks:** No. **Staff/student ratio:** N/P. **After school classes:** After school art and music classes are available. **Cost:** "Varies."

SUMMER PROGRAMS: N/P.

PARENT INVOLVEMENT
Parent/Teacher Communication: Parent/teacher conferences, school website, e-mail weekly newsletter (available on-line). **Participation requirements: "Yes." Parent education programs offered?** N/P.

WHAT SETS THE SCHOOL APART FROM OTHERS
"Our Lady of the Visitacion School is blessed with the presence of the Daughters of Charity. Their charism has been present in the school since 1964. The Sisters work side by side with other staff members to serve the students in the compassionate and loving ways that St. Louise de Marillac and St. Vincent de Paul did 150 years ago. The school is a welcoming faith-based learning community for all those who are a part of it."

HOW FAMILIES CHARACTERIZE SCHOOL
Parent comment(s): "OLV has a very caring staff dedicated to motivating students to learn, raising the bar, while incorporating high standards in an extremely supportive environment. It is a loving community rich in Christian values." • "The school is to be commended for initiating Christian service projects, a respectful and caring faculty, family environment, and diverse student population. OLV provides an affordable education, focus on preparing students for high school, attentiveness to requests of parents, and positive parent involvement."
Student comment(s): "I enjoy being a part of a small school community. We all appreciate our teachers who encourage us to express our talents." • "The teachers work hard to make learning fun and enjoyable." • "We are thankful for the financial help given to families." • "We really appreciate the extracurricular activities offered by the school."

PRESIDIO HILL SCHOOL
3839 Washington Street (btwn. Maple and Cherry) (Presidio Heights)
San Francisco, CA 94118
(415) 751-9318 *fax (415) 751-9334*
www.presidiohill.org

Scott Duyan, Head of School, scott_duyan@presidiohill.org
Laura Novia, Director of Admission & Financial Assistance,
laura_novia@presidiohill.org

GENERAL

Coed TK-8 day school (Transitional K is for students turning 5 between June 1 and December 2). Founded in 1918. Independent. Nonprofit. **Member:** NAIS, CAIS, BADA. **Enrollment:** Approx. 197. **Average class size:** 12 in TK, 17 in K-5, 14 in G6-8. **Accreditation:** CAIS (6-year term: 2007-12). **Endowment:** None. **School year:** Sept.-June. **School day:** 9 a.m. to 3 p.m. for TK-2; 8:30 a.m. to 3-3:25 p.m. for G2-8.

STUDENT BODY ETHNICITY

56% Caucasian (non-Latino), 20% multi-racial, 9% Asian, 9% Latino, 6% African-American.

ADMISSION

Applications due: Jan. (call for date). **Application fee:** $75. **Application process:** Tour or attend open house, application fee, student evaluation form, play date. **No. of applications:** 180 (TK-8). **No. of K spaces:** 8-10. (No. of TK spaces: 12). **Percentage of K class made up of school's TK class:** 50-60%. **Admission evaluation requirements for TK and K:** See above. **Other grades:** Parent application, student application (G6-8), student visit (G1-8), current teacher evaluation, 2 years of school records. **Preferences:** Siblings. **What sort of student do you best serve?** "We look for families who understand and support our school mission and core values, who will thrive in our program, and who will enrich our vibrant community through their contribution to the multicultural fabric of our school. Children who thrive at Presidio Hill have a natural curiosity, find motivation from within rather than through extrinsic rewards, take an active role in learning, and enjoy a cooperative, socially interactive setting and activity-based projects."

COSTS

Latest tuition: $20,975 for TK-3, $22,250 for G4-8. **Sibling discount:** None. **Tuition includes:** Lunch: No; Transportation: No; Laptop computer: No; Other: Before school care beginning at 8 a.m. **Tuition increases:** Approx. 3-6%. **Other costs:** Approx. $250. **Percentage of students receiving financial aid:** 22%. **Financial aid application deadline:** Jan. (call for date). Financial aid is based on need. **Average grant:** $15,000. **Percentage of grants of half-tuition or more:** 75%. **Donations:** "Voluntary. The school expects families to give at least 24 hours of volunteer service each year. Many families give more than this and others give their time in a capacity that best suits their family life."

School's Mission Statement

"When we ask ourselves what we want for our children, we may reply:
• A school in which our children will be happy
• Teachers who call forth their capacity to imagine, inquire and care
• The company of students who advocate for themselves and others
• A curriculum of integrated academics that inspires curiosity, critical thinking, cooperative learning and global stewardship
• A place where the companionship of their peers fosters community life and helps each carry a just share of responsibility within and beyond the walls of the school
• Caring connections throughout the fabric of community life that ensure• all children are known and appreciated for their unique traits
• An environment where progress is measured not only by personal success but also by the success of all
• A school that mirrors and embraces the mosaic that is San Francisco
• A place where children permanently fall in love with learning
Presidio Hill School ~ Opening Minds Since 1918"
(See school website for a description of the origin of the mission statement)

Academic Program

Philosophy: "Our child-centered curriculum encompasses the arts, sciences and humanities. The mathematics and science programs not only build skills but also give students opportunities to use creative concepts in life situations. The language arts curriculum is literature-based throughout the grades with a school-wide emphasis on writing fluency. Critical thinking and research skills are emphasized in social studies as students learn to question information sources and develop an understanding of historical contexts. Appreciating one's responsibility in the local and global community is reinforced through service learning projects in every grade. Other curricular areas, integrated with the core subjects, include art, music, Spanish, and physical education. Presidio Hill School is committed to meeting students' individual needs in small classes with cooperative, hands-on learning." **Foreign languages:** Spanish. **Computer training:** Yes. **No. of computers available for students: 18. No. of hours weekly of:** Art- 1-2; Drama- 1-2: Music- 1-2; Computers- N/P; Foreign language- 2-4; PE- 2-3. **Outdoor education:** "Yes." **Grading:** Evaluations in K-5; evaluations/grades in G6-8. **Average nightly homework:** 20-60 min. in the lower grades and 1-2 hrs. in middle school. Posted on the Internet: "This varies according to teacher and student interest or need." **Percentage of students participating in Johns Hopkins Center for Talented Youth Program:** N/P. **Other**

indicators of academic success: "Students are being evaluated on a daily basis on all of their academic, social, emotional and physical skills right in the classroom. Through hands-on learning the students learn not only how to take tests but also how to apply their knowledge to everyday situations. Presidio Hill School graduates get into and attend top high schools in the Bay Area and beyond. They are self-advocates and they expect and seek out relationships with their teachers." **High schools attended by latest graduating class:** Bay, Bentley, Convent, Drew, Gateway, IHS, JCHS, Lick, Lowell, MA, Mercy, SHCP, SI, SOTA, University, Urban, Washington.

FACULTY

Ethnicity: 74% Caucasian (non-Latino), 8% multi-racial, 7% African-American, 7% Latino, 4% Asian. **Percentage of teachers with graduate degrees:** 40%. **Percentage with current California credential:** 50%. **Faculty selection/training:** "Minimum of a Bachelor's degree, experience, and a rigorous hiring process that involves a committee, a national search organization, telephone interviews, teaching observation, reference checks." **Teacher/student ratio:** 1:8. **Special subject teachers:** Art, music, drama, PE, Spanish. **Average teacher tenure:** 7 years. Average teaching experience is 13 years.

MIDDLE SCHOOL

Description: "Beginning in G6, Presidio Hill offers an entry point for a minimum of 12 new students every year. We have 2 sections of each grade, with 14-16 students per class and 28-32 students per grade. The middle school shares the same mission and philosophy as the younger grades and offers departmentalized classes." **Teacher/student ratio:** 1:8. **Elective courses offered:** "Art, music, drama, PE; G6-8 also take life skills and elective classes. **Achievement tracking in:** N/A. "It is not practiced at Presidio Hill. Our middle school is small enough to meet the individualized needs of students without tracking. Spanish, however, is grouped according to achievement level." **Student social events:** School dances are regularly arranged in collaboration with partner schools in the area.

STUDENT SUPPORT SERVICES

No. of Licensed Counselors on staff: None. **Counselor/student ratio:** N/A. **Learning specialists on staff:** Three part-time. **Learning differences/disabilities support:** The learning specialists are responsible for conducting screenings, providing small group classes and individual tutoring, meeting with outside specialists or tutors, and working with the parents and teachers to keep everyone informed about the student's needs. **High school placement support:** The high school placement counselor helps prepare students for standardized testing and counseling throughout the high school application process. This includes a weekly class as well as individual family meetings.

STUDENT CONDUCT AND HEALTH

Code of conduct: "Respect and responsibility are the guiding principles for the choices students must make. We teach students that their actions have consequences and guide them in making appropriate choices. Choices that diminish or violate these principles are met with consequences appropriate to the particular situation." **Prevention education and awareness addressed in:** "These programs are part of various classes and parent education evenings on a regular basis."

ATHLETICS

Sports offered: Cross-country, volleyball, basketball and futsal in G6. Intramural sports are offered in TK-5. **Team play begins in:** TK intramural, G6 intermural.

CAMPUS/CAMPUS LIFE

Campus description: "The campus is over 17,000 square feet and was extensively renovated in 2001, more than doubling the facility and expanding every classroom. We have 3 play yards and use Julius Kahn Park in the Presidio as an extension of our own building." **Library:** Yes, with more than 1,000 volumes and 4 computers. **Sports facilities:** "Rooftop yard and fields throughout the city." **Theater/Arts facilities:** "Dedicated rooms for music, drama, art, and the Susan Andrews Theatre." **Computer lab:** No. **Science lab:** Yes. **Lunch program:** No. **Bus service:** No. **Uniforms/dress code:** None. **Opportunities for community service:** "Community service and service learning are deeply embedded in the history and curriculum at every grade level, guided by the principles of equity and justice."

EXTENDED DAY

Morning care: Begins at 8 a.m. **After-school care:** Until 6 p.m. **Grade levels:** All. **Cost:** Approx. $12/hour (with financial assistance available) for after-school care; morning care is free. **Drop-in care available:** $14/hr. **Coverage over major holidays:** "We offer child care during some holidays and breaks." **Homework help:** Yes. **Snacks:** Provided. **Staff/student ratio:** 1:8. **After-school classes:** "We offer after-school enrichment classes each semester. The classes and costs range each session, and a current sampling are always available through the admissions office." **Cost:** N/P.

Summer Programs: N/P.

Parent Involvement

Parent/teacher communication: Parent-teacher conferences 2-3 times per year. Every teacher e-mails a weekly classroom letter in the school-wide weekly e-mail. Hard copies are also available. "Parents and teachers share a warm relationship and communicate often." **Participation requirements:** Parent participation is a minimum of 24 hours a year and the school understands that families give their time to the extent they can. **Parent education programs offered?** "We offer a variety of programs with topics such as progressive education, social media, sex education and bullies; we provide many opportunities for parents to discuss child development and parenting."

What Sets the School Apart From Others

"It's the spirit of the place that really differentiates Presidio Hill. You sense it in the energy of the students, the history of the building, the warmth of the teachers, the dedication of the staff, and the commitment of the families."

How Families Characterize School

N/P. "The best way to know how the parents and students characterize the school is to visit and ask them directly. We have an admission process that encourages applicant families to get to know our school through visits to the classroom, conversations with our teachers, and ample contact with our current families. We encourage questions and provide many opportunities to do so."

Ring Mountain Day School

70 Lomita Drive
Mill Valley, CA 94941
(415) 381-8183 ext. 35 *fax (415) 381-8484*
www.ringmountain.org

Dr. Nancy Diamonti, Head of School,ndiamonti@ringmountain.org
Daisy Cassidy, Director of Admissions, dcassidy@ringmountain.org

GENERAL
Coed PS-8 day school. Founded in 1976. Independent. Nonprofit. **Member:** Provisional Member of CAIS, NAIS. **Enrollment:** Approx. 120. At full capacity will have approx. 135-150. **Average class size:** 12. **Accreditation:** Currently applying for WASC and CAIS. **Endowment:** N/P. **School year:** Sept.-June. **School day:** 8:30 a.m. to 3:15 p.m.

STUDENT BODY ETHNICITY
68% Caucasian (non-Latino), 11% Latino, 8% other, 5% African-American, 4% multi-racial, 4% Asian.

ADMISSION
Applications due: Call for date. **Application fee:** $100. **Application process:** Tour, application, teacher recommendation form, copy of student records, student visit. **No. of applications:** N/P. **No. of K spaces:** 12. **Percentage of K class made up of school's preschool class:** 40%. **Admission evaluation requirements for K:** Teacher recommendation, school visit and screening. **Other grades:** Tour, application, teacher recommendation, student records, student visit. **Preferences:** Sibling. **What sort of student do you best serve?** "Most students, as we teach to the individual child."

COSTS
Latest tuition: $20,800 for K-4, $21,400 for G5-6, $21,700 for G7-8. **Sibling discount:** None. **Tuition includes:** Lunch: No; Transportation: No; Laptop computer: Yes; Other: N/P. **Tuition increases:** Approx. 3% annually. **Other costs:** Approx. $500 for materials; for outdoor education trips, fees are approx. $200 for G3-4 and approx. $1,500 for G5-8. **Percentage of students receiving financial aid:** 15%. **Financial aid application deadline:** Call for date. Financial aid is based on need. **Average grant:** N/P. **Percentage of grants of half-tuition or more:** 50%. **Donations:** Voluntary for Annual Fund, Auction.

SCHOOL'S MISSION STATEMENT
"Ring Mountain Day School's student-centered program creates a dynamic learning environment to stimulate creative thinking, motivate academic excellence and instill a lifelong desire to learn. Small class size enables our faculty to apply an individualized, integrated and rigorous instructional approach that inspires students to realize their talents, strengths, dreams and capabilities. The curriculum emphasizes problem solving in real-life situations, promoting comprehensive understanding of academics and the arts. Students develop overall self-awareness and

sense of personal responsibility to their communities: family, school, and the diverse world in which they live."

ACADEMIC PROGRAM

Philosophy: "A John Dewey, progressive, project-based learning environment where our goals are [to]: - Develop and nurture a love of learning with an emphasis on problem solving, creativity and process. - Achieve mastery of math and language skills through integrated multi-discipline curriculum instruction. - Provide individualized instruction in a multi-age classroom with teaching methods that maximize the benefits of interaction and collaboration among the children and faculty. - Expose children to art, music, dance and drama. - Promote appreciation of cultural diversity and global awareness through cultural immersion and outreach - Encourage children to develop age appropriate physical skills stressing good sportsmanship and teamwork. - Help children develop confidence in themselves, demonstrate respect for others and assume responsibility for their own actions." **Foreign languages:** Spanish. **Computer training:** Computer electives offered in Middle School; a technology teacher is on staff as needed for special projects. **No. of computers available for students:** 20 multi-media computers and 30 laptops. **No. of hours weekly of:** Art- 2; Drama- 2; Music- 2; Computers- N/P; Foreign language- 4; PE- 2. **Outdoor education:** "Done throughout the year." **Grading:** A-F, beginning in G5. Students are evaluated twice each year with 2 parent/teacher conferences and written evaluations through G4. **Average nightly homework:** Approx. 10 min. per grade, including reading (thus 10-15 min. for K; 80-90 min. for G8). Posted on the Internet: Yes. **Percentage of students participating in Johns Hopkins Center for Talented Youth Program:** 10%. **Other indicators of academic success:** ERB Scores. **High schools attended by latest graduating class:** Bay, SI, MA, Branson, MC, University, Urban, Stevenson.

FACULTY

Ethnicity: 80% Caucasian (non-Latino), 15% other, 5% Latino. **Percentage of teachers with graduate degrees:** 75%. **Percentage with current California credential:** 80%. **Faculty selection/training:** "Experience, degrees, interview with selection committee that also consists of other teachers, observation of sample lesson." **Teacher/ student ratio:** "No more than 1:15 but oftentimes they work in pods of 7 or 1:8. **Special subject teachers:** Spanish, art, music, drama, dance, PE, computers. **Average teacher tenure:** 7 years.

MIDDLE SCHOOL
Description: "Commences in G5. Discussion based teaching based on the Harkness Table model at Phillips Exeter Academy, Exeter, N.H." **Teacher/student ratio:** "No more than 1:12. Teachers are formally trained by Exeter teachers." **Elective courses offered:** Varies each quarter but has included Student Council, photography, academic chess, sports, media, student newspaper, computers. **Achievement tracking in:** All subjects. **Student social events:** Back To School Pizza Night, Thanksgiving Circle, Spring Concert, Middle School dances, Spirit Week, annual school play, Earth Day Celebration, all school Angel Island End of the Year Picnic, annual Student Art Show, Step-Up Celebration/ Graduation Picnic in the Park.

STUDENT SUPPORT SERVICES
No. of Licensed Counselors on staff: N/P. **Counselor/student ratio:** N/P. **Learning specialists on staff:** None. **Learning differences/ disabilities support:** "We accept children with a wide range of learning styles; however, we don't have a learning resource specialist on staff so we determine 'goodness of fit' on a case-by-case basis." **High school placement support:** "We do SSAT preparation starting in G7. If a student is applying to a private high school they work directly with our Head of School and the High School Counselor. If they are going to a public high school we provide counseling support to make sure the students and families know about the resources that are available to them. Ninety-eight percent of our graduates have been accepted to their first choice high school."

STUDENT CONDUCT AND HEALTH
Code of conduct: "We have high expectations for our students, and the Middle School students are expected to be good role models and leaders. The four guiding principles for behavior are attentive listening, mutual respect, appreciation/no put downs, and right to pass." **Prevention education and awareness addressed in:** "Education on drugs, sex, health and harassment primarily begins in G5."

ATHLETICS: N/P.

CAMPUS/CAMPUS LIFE
Campus description: "Located in a suburban setting and surrounded by a residential neighborhood, Ring Mountain's new campus has a remodeled interior. Renovations to the existing building include a new science center, an expanded technology laboratory, multimedia, science

and Spanish language labs; a multipurpose room; and an art studio with a low-fire kiln and a dark room. The facility is surrounded by grassy playing fields and also features a state of the art turf soccer field, basketball court, outdoor playground and play structure, and in 2006, a space for a community garden and courtyard amphitheater. The campus backs up to public open space, which gives it a country feel." **Library:** Yes. **Sports facilities:** Multi-purpose room, sports field, basketball and volleyball court, playground, access to Bay Trail. **Theater/Arts facilities:** "We have a performing arts program on site which includes drama, dance and music." **Computer lab:** Yes. **Science lab:** Yes. **Lunch program:** An optional hot lunch program is available, catered by School Foodies. **Bus service:** To/from San Francisco. **Uniforms/dress code:** Dress code. **Opportunities for community service:** "There is a commitment to service learning school wide."

EXTENDED DAY
Morning care: Begins at 8 a.m. **After-school care:** Until 6 p.m. **Grade levels:** K-8. **Cost:** No charge for morning care. After-school care is $25/day. **Drop-in care available:** Yes. **Coverage over major holidays:** No. **Homework help:** Yes if needed, before school, at recess and lunch and after school as well. **Snacks:** Not provided. **Staff/student ratio:** 1:4. **After-school classes:** "Classes vary each quarter. They have included Science Adventures, academic chess, Aikido, French, lacrosse, Mom & Me Mosaic Classes, cooking, and drama, etc." **Cost:** "Varies."

SUMMER PROGRAMS
"The school sometimes offers summer camps, which are typically one-week camps for PS-G1. Past programs have included Science Adventures, and art and crafts." **Cost:** N/P.

PARENT INVOLVEMENT
"There are many ways to get involved that include working with the Parent Association. There are many events throughout the year that require parent participation including the Annual Walkathon, Book Fair, Teacher Appreciation, Annual Auction/Dinner & Dance and the Annual Art Show." **Parent/teacher communication:** Newsletter, weekly class letters, website, e-mail, conferences, Bagel Breakfasts with Head of School, Back to School Night and Annual State of the School Meetings. **Participation requirements:** Twenty hours per family per year. **Parent education programs offered?** Yes.

What Sets the School Apart From Others
"Ring Mountain Day School offers small class size with individualized instruction, project-based learning, multi-aged environment, dynamic learning environment with a heart in the arts."

How Families Characterize School
Parent comment(s): "Ring Mountain Day School is Marin's hidden gem." • "The community has welcomed our family with open arms." "Ring Mountain gave my child the tools she needed to be successful in high school."
Student comment(s): "I never thought learning could be so fun!" • "I never thought of myself as a scholar." • "Ring Mountain is a place where I feel safe." • "RMDS is like my family."

St. Anne School
1320 14th Avenue (between Irving and Judah) (Inner Sunset)
San Francisco, CA 94122
(415) 664-7977 *fax (415) 661-7904*
www.stanne.com

Mr. Thomas C. White, Principal, white@stanne.com

Coed K-8 parochial day school. Founded in 1920. Catholic. **Member:** WCEA. **Enrollment:** Approx. 500. **Average class size:** 32. **Accreditation:** WASC (6-year term: 2006-12). **Endowment:** $1.8 million. **School year:** Aug.-June. **School day:** 8:10 a.m. to 2:50 p.m. for K-3, 8:10 a.m. to 3:05 p.m. for G4-8.

Student Body Ethnicity
50% Asian, 35% Caucasian (non-Latino), 8% Latino, 5% multi-racial, 2% African-American.

Admission
Applications due: Rolling admissions. **Application fee:** $50. **Application process:** N/P. **No. of applications:** 100. **No. of K spaces:** 70. **Percentage of K class made up of school's preschool class:** N/A. **Admission evaluation requirements for K:** Screening. **Other grades:** Test. **Preferences:** Sibling, in-parish Catholics, out-of-parish Catholics, non-Catholics. **What sort of student do you best serve?** N/P.

Costs
Latest tuition: $5,400 (participating) - $6,800 (non-Catholics). **Sibling discount:** Yes. **Tuition includes:** Lunch: No; Transportation: No; Laptop computer: No; Other: N/P. **Tuition increases:** N/P. **Other costs:** N/P. **Percentage of students receiving financial aid:** 5%. **Financial aid deadline:** Feb. (call for date). Financial aid is based on need. **Average grant:** N/P. **Grants of half-tuition or more:** N/P. **Donations:** N/P.

School's Mission Statement
"St. Anne School Community is committed to carrying out the ministry of Jesus Christ in the education of the youth we serve. We seek to evangelize and strengthen faith formation in partnership with the family and parish. We value the cultural diversity of our school and welcome the unique gift each student contributes to our school community. We seek to develop the whole person, fostering spiritual, intellectual, physical, and psychological growth in a Catholic environment of peace, security, and love."

Academic Program
Philosophy: "St. Anne School strives to challenge the students in a caring and nurturing environment helping them reach their full potential." **Foreign languages:** None. **Computer training:** Yes. **No. of computers available for students:** 96. **No. of hours weekly:** Art- 1; Drama- N/P; Music- .75; Computers- .75; Foreign language- N/A; PE- .75. **Outdoor education:** "Yes, G6." **Grading:** A-F, beginning in G3. **Average homework:** "Varies." Posted on the Internet: No. **Percentage of students in Johns Hopkins Talented Youth Program:** None. **Other indicators of academic success:** N/P. **High schools attended by latest graduating class:** Lowell, SI, Riordan, SHCP, Mercy, ICA.

Faculty
Ethnicity: 95% Caucasian (non-Latino), 5% Asian. **Percentage of teachers with graduate degrees:** N/P. **Percentage with current California credential:** 98%. **Faculty selection/training:** N/P. **Teacher/ student ratio:** 1:30. **Special subject teachers:** "Two." (subjects N/P) **Average teacher tenure:** 15-25 years.

Middle School: N/P.

Student Support Services
No. of Licensed Counselors on staff: One part-time. **Counselor/student ratio:** N/P. **Learning specialists on staff:** Two. **Learning differences/ disabilities support:** N/P. **High school placement support:** N/P.

Student Conduct and Health
Code of conduct: "Discipline/behavior policy." **Prevention education and awareness addressed in:** Youth Aware Life Skills Program.

Athletics
Sports offered: N/P. **Team play begins in:** G3 (intermural).

Campus/Campus Life
Campus description: N/P. **Library:** The school's library has 7,000 volumes and 4 computers. **Sports facilities:** N/P. **Theater/Arts facilities:** Moriarty Hall. **Computer lab:** Yes. **Science lab:** Yes. **Lunch program:** Yes. **Bus service:** No. **Uniforms/dress code:** Uniforms. **Opportunities for community service:** Yes.

Extended Day
Morning care: Begins at 7 a.m. **After-school care:** Until 6 p.m. **Grade levels:** All. **Cost:** Varies; contact school. **Drop-in care available:** Yes. **Coverage over major holidays:** No. **Homework help:** Yes. **Snacks:** Provided. **Staff/student ratio:** 1:25. **After-school classes:** Chinese school, karate, ballet, academic chess. **Cost:** "Varies."

Summer Programs: N/P.

Parent Involvement
Parent/teacher communication: Conference, website, e-mail, weekly newsletters. **Participation requirements:** N/P. **Parent education programs offered?** Yes.

What Sets the School Apart From Others
"The dynamics between the students and faculty, the involvement of the parents, and the involvement within the parish make St. Anne a special community. The dedication of our parents and staff to our precious children is very evident in the friendly and positive energy that they radiate."

How Families Characterize School
Parent comment(s): "Our school staff offers a strong educational program for my child." • "We looked at all the schools in the area and are extremely happy that our children are at St. Anne School."
Student comment(s): "I love my teachers." • "When I need some help I can always count on help from my teachers."

Saint Brigid School

2250 Franklin Street (at Broadway) (Pacific Heights)
San Francisco, CA 94109
(415) 673-4523 *fax (415) 674-4187*
www.saintbrigidsf.org

Sister Carmen Santiuste, RCM, Head of School, principal@saintbrigidsf.org
Director of Admission, office@saintbrigidsf.org

General

Coed K-8 Archdiocesan day school. Founded in 1888. Catholic.
Nonprofit. **Member:** N/P. **Enrollment:** Approx. 270. **Average class
size:** 30. **Accreditation:** WASC (6-year term: 2003-09). **Endowment:**
N/P. **School year:** Late Aug. to mid-June. **School day:** Begins at 8 a.m.
Dismissal is 2:45 p.m. for K-2; 2:55 p.m. for G3-5; and 3 p.m. for G6-8.

Student Body Ethnicity

43% Asian, 20% multi-racial, 11% Latino, 11% Caucasian (non-Latino),
10% other, 5% African-American.

Admission

Applications due: Dec. for K, March for G1-7. **Application fee:** $100.
Application process: Begins in Dec. for K. Application forms available
at the school or may be downloaded on its website. A K readiness test
is given to all K applicants. **No. of applications:** Approx. 60-70. **No. of
K spaces:** 35. **Percentage of K class made up of school's preschool
class:** N/A. **Admission evaluation requirements for K:** "We expect the
child to be ready for a full day Kindergarten work—follow directions,
stay on task, etc. We seek children who pass our entrance test, who
are cooperative and behave well, and who have a desire to perform
to the best of their abilities." **Other grades:** An entry test given to all
transferring students in March; school visits are held during Open House
and Catholic Schools Week in Jan. Individual tours may be arranged. Call
to schedule. **Preferences:** Siblings, Catholics. **What sort of student do
you best serve?** "Families looking for a caring, nurturing school family
that strives daily to live out the gospel values."

Costs

Latest tuition: $5,900. **Sibling discount:** None. **Tuition includes:**
Lunch: No; Transportation: No; Laptop computer: No; Other: N/A.
Tuition increases: Approx. 3-5% annually. **Other costs:** Approx. $250

for uniforms, $500 registration fee, PTG fee $75. **Percentage of students receiving financial aid: 20%. Financial aid application deadline:** April (call for date). Financial aid is based on need. **Average grant:** N/P. **Percentage of grants of half-tuition or more: 6%. Donations:** Voluntary for scholarship fund.

SCHOOL'S MISSION STATEMENT

"St. Brigid School, in partnership with each family, educates and develops the whole child by teaching the principles of the Catholic faith and by providing a solid academic education. We foster an environment that brings us together as a caring, nurturing school family. We provide the opportunity and motivation for a child to develop spiritually, intellectually, physically, and socially."

ACADEMIC PROGRAM

Philosophy: "St. Brigid School's curriculum is well known for having strong academic standards. In addition to the traditional classes, students have weekly classes in music, computer, science lab, Spanish, and PE. Additional services available to all students are a fully staffed library, school counselor, and reading specialist." **Foreign languages:** Spanish G1-8. **Computer training:** "Students K-8 are taught technology with skills progressing as they move up through the grades." **No. of computers available for students: 60. No. of hours weekly of:** Art- 1; Drama-1; Music- 1; Computers- N/P; Foreign language- N/P; PE- 1. **Outdoor education:** "Grades 5-6." **Grading:** A-F, beginning in G3. **Average nightly homework:** "Varies with grade." Posted on the Internet: Yes. **Percentage of students participating in Johns Hopkins Center for Talented Youth Program:** "40% of G7 & G8; 60% participate in the UC Irvine Talent Search." **Other indicators of academic success:** "Students usually get accepted in the high school of their choice." **High schools attended by latest graduating class:** Convent, SI, Stuart Hall, Lowell, Riordan, Washington, SOTA, ISA, Mercy-SF, Galileo.

FACULTY

Ethnicity: 60% Caucasian (non-Latino), 34% Latino, 6% other. **Percentage of teachers with graduate degrees: N/P. Percentage with current California credential: 100%. Faculty selection/training:** N/P. **Teacher/student ratio: N/P. Special subject teachers:** Music, PE, computer, science, Spanish, math (G6-8), social studies (G6-8). **Average teacher tenure:** N/P.

MIDDLE SCHOOL
Description: G6-8. **Teacher/student ratio:** 1:35. **Elective courses offered:** N/P. **Achievement tracking in:** N/P. **Student social events:** N/P.

STUDENT SUPPORT SERVICES
No. of Licensed Counselors on staff: One. **Counselor/student ratio:** 1:270. **Learning specialists on staff:** Two. **Learning differences/disabilities support:** N/P. **High school placement support:** N/P.

STUDENT CONDUCT AND HEALTH
Code of conduct: "The Code of Christian Conduct in the Parent-Student Handbook reiterates that it shall be an expressed condition of enrollment that the parent/guardian of a student shall also conform to the standards of conduct that are consistent with the Christian principles of the school." **Prevention education and awareness addressed in:** Health, taught as a core subject.

ATHLETICS
Sports offered: Basketball and soccer for boys; volleyball and basketball for girls. **Team play begins in:** G3.

CAMPUS/CAMPUS LIFE
Campus description: The campus, which spans a block from Franklin Street to St. Brigid's Church on Van Ness, includes 2 buildings with 9 classrooms, library, computer lab, science lab, music room, extended program room, cafeteria, auditorium, and office. **Library:** Library with 20,000 print volumes. **Sports facilities:** School yard. **Theater/Arts facilities:** School Auditorium. **Computer lab:** Yes. **Science lab:** Yes. **Lunch program:** Yes. **Bus service:** No. **Uniforms/dress code:** Uniforms. **Opportunities for community service:** N/P.

EXTENDED DAY
Morning care: None. **After-school care:** Until 6 p.m. **Grade levels:** K-8. **Cost:** $1,800/year (to 4 p.m.), $2,340/year (to 5 p.m.), and $2,970/year (to 6 p.m.). **Drop-in care available:** Yes. **Coverage over major holidays:** No. **Homework help:** Yes. **Snacks:** Provided. **Staff/student ratio:** N/P. **After-school classes:** Piano and other musical instruments, dance (ballet, hip-hop), Karate, other languages (Mandarin, Japanese). **Cost:** N/P.

SUMMER PROGRAMS: None.

PARENT INVOLVEMENT
Parent/teacher communication: Conferences, website, e-mail, monthly newsletter, Wednesday Folder. Parent/teacher conferences are required in the first quarter of the school year. Parents may request evening conferences through the individual teachers. **Participation requirements:** 20 hours per family or 10 hours per parent. **Parent education programs offered?** Yes, Active Parenting class every other year, Drug Education Parent Night, and Sacraments Program.

WHAT SETS THE SCHOOL APART FROM OTHERS
"St. Brigid School is distinguished by the involvement of its diverse parent community and the communications it maintains among parents, teachers, staff, and students. Academic study is complemented with field trips and cultural and environmental enrichment activities. Apart from high academic scores and achievement scores, the school plant itself is kept in excellent condition. St. Brigid School is one of the few schools that has many religious on its staff [including] Sisters of the Immaculate Conception [and a] Sister of the Presentation."

HOW FAMILIES CHARACTERIZE SCHOOL
Parent comment(s): "Very clean and well maintained, very good academic program, prepares the students well for high school."
Student comment(s): "Caring and lots of support."

ST. CECILIA SCHOOL
660 Vicente Street (corner of 18th Ave.) (Parkside/Sunset District)
San Francisco, CA 94116
(415) 731-8400 *fax (415) 731-5686*
www.stceciliaschool.org

Sister Marilyn Miller, S.N.J.M., Principal, mmiller@stceciliaschool.org

GENERAL
Coed K-8 parochial day school. Founded in 1930. Catholic. Nonprofit. **Member:** N/P. **Enrollment:** Approx. 600. **Average class size:** 30. **Accreditation:** WASC/WCEA (N/P term). **Endowment:** N/P. **School year:** Aug.-June. **School day:** 8 a.m. to 3 p.m. for G1-8; 8 a.m. to 11:45 a.m. for morning K; 11:25 a.m. to 3 p.m. for afternoon K.

STUDENT BODY ETHNICITY
66% Caucasian (non-Latino), 22% Asian, 11% Latino, 1% African-American.

ADMISSION
Applications due: Applications available in the beginning of Dec. (call for date). **Application fee:** $50. **Application process:** Kindergarten open houses begin in Oct. **No. of applications:** Approx. 120. **No. of K spaces:** 70. **Percentage of K class made up of school's preschool class:** N/A. **Admission evaluation requirements for K:** Age appropriate language and readiness for reading and math learning; preschool experience for development of social and group learning skills; age appropriate screening. Applicants must be 5 years old by Sept. 1. **Other grades:** N/P. **Preferences:** Siblings, Catholics who are members of the parish, Catholics from other parishes, non-Catholics. **What sort of student do you best serve?** N/P.

COSTS
Latest tuition: Ranges from $4,975 (participating Catholics) to $5,880 (non-participating). **Sibling discount:** 30%. **Tuition includes:** Lunch: No; Transportation: No; Laptop computer: No; Other: N/P. **Tuition increases:** Approx. 6% annually. **Other costs:** N/P. **Percentage of students receiving financial aid:** 10%. **Financial aid application deadline:** Call for date. Financial aid is based on need. **Average grant:** "Varies each year depending on funds available." **Percentage of grants of half-tuition or more:** N/P. **Donations:** No contributions are required.

SCHOOL'S MISSION STATEMENT
"St. Cecilia School is a Catholic elementary school of the Archdiocese of San Francisco, whose purpose is to develop students who are active Christians, life-long learners, and responsible citizens."

ACADEMIC PROGRAM
Philosophy: "St. Cecilia School is a Catholic elementary school dedicated to the religious, academic, social, psychological, cultural, and physical development of each individual. St. Cecilia School is committed to providing instruction and opportunities in a Catholic community of faith which will lead the children to pray, to serve and respect others, and to make Christian choices. Parents, as primary educators, and teachers, as facilitators of learning, work together to provide a quality education that assists students in developing their unique capabilities and prepares them to become responsible citizens. Students develop intellectually by

participating in age-appropriate and meaningful activities. As life-long learners, students develop the skills of effective communication and problem-solving to help them face the challenges of the future." **Foreign languages:** N/P. **Computer training:** "Highly developed technology program integrating the curriculum and technology." **No. of computers available for students:** "Numerous wireless laptops in the classrooms." **No. of hours weekly of:** Art- 1; Drama- N/P ("an elective"); Music- .5 hour of classroom singing (instrumental lessons available); Computers- 1; Foreign languages- N/P; PE- 1. **Outdoor education:** N/P. **Grading:** "According to the Archdiocesan guidelines and scale." **Average nightly homework:** 1 hour. Posted on the Internet: Some grades. **Percentage of students participating in Johns Hopkins Center for Talented Youth Program:** N/P. **Other indicators of academic success:** Junior High Honors Program, high standardized test scores. **High schools attended by latest graduating class:** SI, SHCP, Mercy-SF, Mercy-Burlingame, Serra, Riordan, Convent, Stuart Hall, Lick, Lowell, Lincoln, Washington, SOTA, CAT, Academy of Arts and Science.

FACULTY

Ethnicity: 99% Caucasian (non-Latino), 1% Asian. **Percentage of teachers with graduate degrees:** 30%. **Percentage with current California credential:** 100%. **Faculty selection/training:** Experience, degree, credential. **Teacher/student ratio:** 1:25. **Special subject teachers:** Music, computer, PE, drama. **Average teacher tenure:** 13 years.

MIDDLE SCHOOL

Description: G6-8, departmentalized. **Teacher/student ratio:** 1:25. **Elective courses offered:** N/P. **Achievement tracking in:** N/P. **Student social events:** N/P.

STUDENT SUPPORT SERVICES

No. of Licensed Counselors on staff: Two part-time. **Counselor/ student ratio:** N/P. **Learning specialists on staff:** One. **Learning differences/disabilities support:** "Students identified in G1-5 with IEP receive services of the learning specialist." **High school placement support:** N/P.

STUDENT CONDUCT AND HEALTH

Code of conduct: "We expect students to act in a way becoming a Christian student. A primary consideration in all disciplinary decisions is the obligation of the school to maintain a safe place for students and an acceptable learning atmosphere." **Prevention education and awareness addressed in:** Talk About Touching program (K-3), Kid Safety (G4-8) conflict resolution program (K-8), drug program (G4-8), Take A Stand program (G5-6), and Second Step program (G7-8).

ATHLETICS
Sports offered: N/P. **Team play begins in:** G3-8 through CYO.

CAMPUS/CAMPUS LIFE
Campus description: Two classrooms of each grade K-8. **Library:** "Fiction and non-fiction, computer." **Sports facilities:** Gymnasium. **Theater/Arts facilities:** Auditorium with stage. **Computer lab:** Yes. **Science lab:** No. **Lunch program:** Two days per week. **Bus service:** No. **Uniforms/dress code:** Uniforms. **Opportunities for community service:** Yes.

EXTENDED DAY
Morning care: Begins at 7:10 a.m. **After-school care:** Until 6 p.m. **Grade levels:** K-8. **Cost:** N/P. **Drop-in care available:** No. **Coverage over major holidays:** No. **Homework help:** Yes. **Snacks:** Provided. **Staff/student ratio:** 1:10. **After-school classes:** N/P.

SUMMER PROGRAMS: N/P.

PARENT INVOLVEMENT
Parent/teacher communication: Conferences, website, e-mail, newsletter. **Participation requirements:** None. **Parent education programs offered?** Yes.

WHAT SETS THE SCHOOL APART FROM OTHERS
"A strong academic program within a Christian environment. We engender a family spirit within our school community."

HOW FAMILIES CHARACTERIZE SCHOOL: N/P.

St. Gabriel School

2550 – 41st Ave. (between Ulloa and Vicente) (Parkside/Sunset)
San Francisco, CA   94116
(415) 566-0314 *fax (415) 566-3223*
www.stgabrielsf.com

Sister Mary Pauline Borghello R.S.M., Principal, office@stgabrielsf.com

General

Coed K-8 parochial day school. Founded in 1948. Catholic. Nonprofit. **Member:** N/P. **Enrollment:** Approx. 510. **Average class size:** 28. **Accreditation:** WASC/WCEA (term: N/P). **Endowment:** N/A. **School year:** Aug.-June. **School day:** 8 a.m. to 2:45 p.m. for G1-3; 8 a.m. to 3 p.m. for G4-8.

Student Body Ethnicity

41% Caucasian (non-Latino), 33% Asian, 21% other, 5% Latino.

Admission

Applications due: Dec. (call for date). **Application fee:** $50. **Application process:** Kindergarten open house is held during business hours mid-Nov. Parents may visit in the morning on designated tour days twice monthly. **No. of applications:** Approx. 120 for K. **No. of K spaces:** 60. **Percentage of K class made up of school's preschool class:** N/A. **Admission evaluation requirements for K:** Applicants but be 4 years, nine months by Sept. 1; Preschool experience for development of social and group learning skills; age appropriate language and readiness for reading and math learning; "independence." A short standardized screening is administered to entering K students. **Other grades:** Applicants to G1-7 take an entrance test in the spring. **Preferences:** Catholics who are members of the parish, Catholics from other parishes and then siblings. **What sort of student do you best serve?** N/P.

Costs

Latest tuition: $6,595. **Sibling discount:** For families who complete parent participation and participate in the parish. **Tuition includes:** Lunch: No; Transportation: No; Laptop computer: No; Other: N/A. **Tuition increases:** Approx. 5% annually. **Other costs:** N/P. **Percentage of students receiving financial aid:** 11%. Financial aid is based on need. **Financial aid deadline:** N/P. **Average grant:** N/P. **Percentage of grants of half-tuition or more:** N/P. **Donations:** None required.

School's Mission Statement

"Our mission is to provide excellent Catholic elementary education that is true to our philosophy and responsive to the needs of the families we serve."

Academic Program

Philosophy: "Our philosophy is grounded in the belief that each student should cultivate a lifestyle based on the teachings of the Catholic faith, the experience of a Christian community, and the striving for truth." **Foreign languages:** Cantonese and Spanish after-school program. **Computer training:** A full computer lab with computer specialist teachers. Networked classrooms, and library with Internet access. **No. of computers available for students:** N/P. **No. of hours weekly of:** Art- N/P ("integrated in classroom"); Drama- N/P ("integrated into classroom"); Music- 1; Computers- 1; Foreign language- N/A; PE- 1. **Outdoor education:** "Yes." **Grading:** Letter grades in G3-5; Percentages in G6-8. **Average nightly homework:** N/P. Posted on the Internet: G7-8. **Percentage of students participating in Johns Hopkins Center for Talented Youth Program:** N/P. **Other indicators of academic success:** "St. Gabriel School has placed first in the San Francisco Archdiocesan Academic Decathlon ten out of thirteen years." **High schools attended by latest graduating class:** SI, SHCP, Riordan, Mercy-SF, Mercy-Burlingame, ICA, Convent, Lowell, Lincoln, Lick.

Faculty

Ethnicity: N/P. **Percentage of teachers with graduate degrees:** 40%. **Percentage with current California credential:** 100%. **Faculty selection/training:** N/P. **Teacher/student ratio:** 1:15 in K, 1:28 in G1-8 with teacher aides available part of the day. **Special subject teachers:** Art, music, PE, library, computers, science. **Average teacher tenure:** 22 years.

Middle School

Description: G7-8, departmentalized. **Teacher/student ratio:** Approx. 1:28. **Elective courses offered:** N/P. **Achievement tracking in:** Based on the Iowa Test of Basic Skills. **Student social events:** N/P.

Student Support Services

No. of Licensed Counselors: Two part-time 4 days/week. **Counselor/student ratio:** N/P. **Learning specialists on staff:** Two. **Learning differences/disabilities support:** Accommodations and/or modifications for qualified students. **High school placement support:** N/P.

STUDENT CONDUCT AND HEALTH
Code of conduct: "Based on Christian values." **Prevention education and awareness addressed in:** Drug and family life education.

ATHLETICS
Sports offered: Basketball, baseball, volleyball, soccer. **Team play begins in:** G3-8 through CYO.

CAMPUS/CAMPUS LIFE
Campus description: N/P. **Library:** 8,000 volumes, 4 computers. **Sports facilities:** Gymnasium and paved playground. **Theater/Arts facilities:** Gymnasium. **Computer lab:** Yes. **Science lab:** Yes. **Lunch program:** Twice weekly. **Bus service:** No. **Uniforms/dress code:** Uniforms. **Opportunities for community service:** Yes.

EXTENDED DAY
Morning care: Begins at 7 a.m. **After-school care:** Until 6 p.m. **Grade levels:** K-8. **Cost:** $2.50/hour. **Drop-in care available:** No. **Coverage over major holidays:** No. **Homework help:** Supervision. **Snacks:** Provided. **Staff/student ratio:** N/P. **After-school classes:** Cantonese, Spanish, chess, art, piano. **Cost:** N/P.

SUMMER PROGRAMS
St. Gabriel School offers a 5-week academic summer school program from mid-June through mid-July. Classes in language arts, reading, and math are held from 8:30 a.m. to 11:15 a.m. No extended care is offered. **Cost:** G1-6, $230; G7-8, $120/class for science and/or math.

PARENT INVOLVEMENT
Parent/teacher communication: Conferences, website, e-mail, newsletter. **Participation requirements:** 40 hours per year per family, 20 hours for single parent families. **Parent education programs offered?** A parent support group for parents of students with learning differences.

WHAT SETS THE SCHOOL APART FROM OTHERS:
"St. Gabriel School is accredited by the Western Catholic Educational Association and the Western Association of Schools and Colleges and is served by a fully credentialed staff. We offer a comprehensive Kindergarten through eighth grade curriculum and a wide variety of enrichment and support services which include a computer specialist teacher, a Science Discovery Center and a science specialist teacher, individual and family counseling, and learning specialist instruction. Our

curriculum reflects the St. Gabriel philosophy of developing the total child through a variety of educational activities. By acknowledging the uniqueness of each child, the staff helps students to develop a positive self image and a sense of self-discipline. A challenging yet supportive environment fosters moral, intellectual, physical, emotional, and aesthetic growth. Favorable teacher to student ratios ensure academic progress. Children learn to recognize and appreciate the many unique ethnic and cultural contributions of their classmates. Community service opportunities contribute to the growth of positive social values and willingness to accept responsibility."

How Families Characterize School: N/P.

Saint Hilary School
765 Hilary Drive
Tiburon, CA 94920
(415) 435-2224 *fax (415) 435-5895*
www.sainthilary-school.org

Bryan Clement, Principal
Melissa Addleman, Director of Admission, admissions@sainthilary-school.org

General
Coed PK-8 parochial day school. Founded in 1963 staffed by the Sisters of the Holy Faith. Roman Catholic. Nonprofit. **Member:** NCEA. **Enrollment:** 268. **Average class size:** 30. **Accreditation:** WASC/ WCEA (6-year term: 2008-14). **Endowment:** N/P. **School year:** Aug.-June. **School day:** 8 a.m. to 12:30 p.m. for PK; 8 a.m. to 2 p.m. for K; 8 a.m. to 3 p.m. for G1-8.

Student Body Ethnicity
85% Caucasian (non-Latino), 5% Asian, 4% Hispanic, 3% Pacific Islander, 1% African-American, 2% other.

Admission
Applications due: Jan. 15. PK-K; G1-8 open. **Application fee:** $50. **Application process:** Grade level assessment, current teacher recommendation, transcripts, interview with principal. **No. of applications:** N/P. **No. of K spaces:** 33. **Percentage of K class made up of school's preschool class:** N/P. **Admission evaluation requirements for K:** Screening, school visit and tour, preschool recommendations. **Other

grades: Entrance test, transcript, current teacher recommendations and interview with principal. **Preferences:** Parishioners, siblings, Primary Kindergarten students currently enrolled, Roman Catholics. **What sort of student do you best serve?** N/P.

Costs

Latest tuition: $8,852. **Sibling discount:** No. **Tuition includes:** Lunch: No; Transportation: No; Laptop computer: No; Other: Field trips. **Tuition increases:** Approx. 3% annually. **Other costs:** $300 registration fee; $50 supplies; $150 uniforms. **Percentage of students receiving financial aid:** 15%. **Financial aid application deadline:** Jan. (call for date). Financial aid is based on need. **Average grant:** N/P. **Percentage of grants of half-tuition or more:** N/P. **Donations:** Voluntary.

School's Mission Statement

"Saint Hilary School is a faith-filled community where children receive a strong religious and academic foundation empowering them to become intelligent, contributing members of society."

Academic Program

Philosophy: "Led by a team of professional and dedicated teachers, our academic program is challenging and engaging. From our school-wide Step Up To Writing program to our Everyday Math curriculum, we endeavour to present our students with the best possible academic opportunities. The excellence of our academic program is enhanced by the active participation of our families—our partners in education. This is an active and supportive community, expressed in our motto, 'We take families, not students.' As a Catholic school, we believe that the religious and spiritual development of the child is indispensable in attaining a genuine whole-child education. By teaching about the Catholic Faith, both Catholics and non-Catholics learn a common set of values, beliefs, and expectations. It allows us to offer more than just intellectual engagement." **Foreign languages:** Spanish K-8. **Computer training:** PK- 8. **No. of computers available for students:** Approx. 120 laptops and 25 desktops. **No. of hours weekly of:** Art- N/P; Drama-N/P; Music- 1-1.5; Computers- N/P; Foreign language- 1-1.5; PE- 1-1.5. **Outdoor education:** For G6, 4-night trip to Walker Creek Ranch. **Grading:** A-F, beginning in G3-8. **Average nightly homework:** 10-20 min. in G1-2; 30-50 min. in G3-4; 50-70 min. in G5-6; 70-90 min. in G7-8. **Percentage of students participating in Johns Hopkins Center for Talented Youth Program:** N/P. **Other indicators of academic success:** "Saint Hilary's reputation of graduating students with high test scores and strong moral character results in high rates of acceptance to many top college preparatory schools." **High schools attended by latest graduating class:** MC, SI, College Prep, Convent, Stuart Hall, San Domenico, Branson, MA, University, Redwood, Tamalpais.

FACULTY
Ethnicity: 99% Caucasian (non-Latino), 1% Hispanic. **Percentage of teachers with graduate degrees:** 30%. **Percentage with current California credential:** 100%. **Faculty selection/training:** "Successful elementary school experience, degree, compatibility with mission of school, preferably a practicing Roman Catholic." **Teacher/student ratio:** 1:9. **Special subject teachers:** Math, science, music, PE, technology. **Average teacher tenure:** 10 years.

MIDDLE SCHOOL
Description: "The Middle School setting encourages interpersonal experience and wide access to a range of teachers, yet one that provides a supportive environment where teachers know their students well. Small class size (between 24 and 32 students per grade) is enhanced by one-on-one and small group instruction. G6-8 Literature is taught in small groups. Three math classes in G8—General Math, Algebra, and Advanced Algebra—ensure individual attention in this critical subject area. This balance of scale ensures our students face their social, personal and academic challenges with a team of supportive and caring adults. In addition to math and language arts, the Middle School's comprehensive curriculum includes science, history, social studies, Spanish, fine arts, music, public speaking, and religion. Critical thinking role-playing, and hands on, in-depth projects lead students beyond rote learning into true understanding in all of their classes." **Teacher/student ratio:** 1:15. **Elective courses offered:** "After school." **Achievement tracking in:** Math, science, English/literature, social studies, religion. **Student social events:** "Grade appropriate field trips, CYO sports, SF Giants baseball games for Altar Servers, annual family picnic, field-day, monthly Family Mass, retreats, family dinner/dance, Christmas and Spring Concert, Father & Daughter and Mother & Son Dances.

STUDENT SUPPORT SERVICES
No. of Licensed Counselors on staff: One part-time. **Counselor/student ratio:** 1:268. **Learning specialists on staff:** Full-time reading specialist and resource teacher. **Learning differences/disabilities support:** N/P. **High school placement support:** "8th grade high school application process and numerous high school speakers. The principal has an open door policy."

Student Conduct and Health

Code of conduct: "Since no list of norms can cover every situation, the Principal presumes that common sense, mature judgment, and Christian charity are the guides by which every Saint Hilary School student should measure his/her actions." **Prevention education and awareness addressed in:** Family Life Education, Health Education.

Athletics

Sports offered: Basketball, volleyball, golf, track and soccer. **Team play begins in:** N/P.

Campus/Campus Life

Campus description: N/P. **Library:** Yes. **Sports facilities:** Gym. **Theater/Arts facilities:** None. **Computer lab:** None **Science lab:** Yes. **Lunch program:** Optional outside vendor. **Bus service:** Golden Gate Transit School bus service. **Uniforms/dress code:** Uniforms. **Opportunities for community service:** Middle School students are required to complete 20 hours of community service before graduation.

Extended Day

Morning care: No. **After-school care:** Until 6 p.m. **Grade levels:** PK-8. **Cost:** $7.50/hour. **Drop-in care available:** Yes. **Coverage over major holidays:** No. **Homework help:** Time set aside for studying; no instruction. **Snacks:** Provided. **Staff/student ratio:** 1:6. **After-school classes:** G5-8 math and computer club, electives. **Cost:** "Varies."

Summer Programs: None.

Parent Involvement

Parent/teacher communication: School website, weekly newsletter, classroom teacher newsletters, e-mails, parent-teacher conferences. **Participation requirements:** 40 hours per year for 2-parent families and 20 hours for single families. **Parent education programs offered?** Yes.

What Sets the School Apart From Others

"As a Parish School, our Spirituality makes us unique. The moral and character development of our students is an integral part of our education. Beyond being strong academically, we pride ourselves on the types of young people that Saint Hilary students become. Over the course of the decade that a child attends Saint Hilary, we help to establish a solid foundation built on compassion, love, and justice that will guide them for the rest of their lives. It would be impossible to call an education 'whole-child' without addressing the spiritual needs of a student. Where other schools look to bring in an external character development program to address student needs, Saint Hilary was built to help guide young people on their spiritual journey. Working in conjunction with parents as the primary educators, our teachers and staff are proud to help students learn and grow in all aspects of life. It is the spiritual, emotional, and social growth, however, that ultimately helps the students to become the moral and just young adults of the future."

How Families Characterize School

Parent comment(s): "Saint Hilary is an exceptional school. In particular, we feel that the academic rigor of the school is in line with our wishes. As well, the commitment to 'moral integrity' maps with what we strive for at home. More than anything, we feel that Saint Hilary School works as an extension of the very lessons we try to impart."

Student comment(s): "Saint Hilary School provided me with a supportive and structured environment in which I learned the critical thinking skills necessary for a productive life, as a scholar, as well as an individual. The qualities and habits acquired during these years continue to impact me on an everyday basis."

Saint Mark's School

39 Trellis Drive
San Rafael, CA 94903
(415) 472-8007 *fax (415) 472-0722*
www.saintmarksschool.org

Damon Kerby, Head of School, dkerby@saintmarksschool.org
Wendy Broderick, admissions@saintmarksschool.org

General

Coed non-religious K-8 day school. Founded in 1980. Independent. Nonprofit. **Member:** NAIS, CAIS, BADA. **Enrollment:** Approx. 380. **Average class size:** 20 in K-3, 22 in G4-8. **Accreditation:** CAIS (6-year term: 2002-08). **Endowment:** $9.5 million. **School year:** Aug.-June. **School day:** 8:30 a.m. to 3:15 p.m.

Student Body Ethnicity

70% Caucasian (non-Latino), 14% multi-racial, 9% Latino, 5% Asian, 1% other, 1% African-American.

ADMISSION

Applications due: Early Jan. (call for date). **Application fee:** $100 ($25 for financial aid candidates). **Application process:** Parent Information Nights and Observation Mornings/Campus are held Oct.-Jan. for interested parents. Individual tours are provided upon request. Upon submission of the application and fee, a parent interview will be scheduled. Students applying to K-1 will be screened; those entering G2-8 will have a student visit and testing. All applicants G1-8 submit prior years' transcripts. All applicants submit teacher recommendations. **No. of applications:** 75-100 for K. **No of K spaces:** 40. **Percentage of K class made up of school's preschool class:** N/A. **Admission evaluation requirements for K:** Developmental readiness (average to above average), no behavioral problems, good teacher recommendation, parents who work in partnership with the school. **Other grades:** "We seek to admit students of average to above average ability who demonstrate developmental readiness, who have a successful class visit and strong school recommendations, and who score commensurately with current Saint Mark's students." **Preferences:** Siblings. **What sort of student do you best serve?** "We enroll students who will benefit from strong academic and creative challenges designed to help them meet their potential."

COSTS

Latest tuition: $21,760. **Sibling discount:** None. **Tuition includes:** Lunch: No; Transportation: No; Laptop computer: No; Other: N/A. **Tuition increases:** Approx. 5-7% annually. **Other costs:** Approx. $300-400 for books, $250-$1,500 for outdoor education G3-8, $700 for laptop G6-8. **Percentage of students receiving financial aid:** 24%. **Financial aid application deadline:** Early Jan. (call for date). Financial aid is based on need. **Average grant:** $13,670. **Percentage of grants of half-tuition or more:** 67%. **Donations:** "Parents are encouraged to participate in the annual fund which raises money to fill the gap between tuition and the actual cost of educating each child."

SCHOOL'S MISSION STATEMENT

"Saint Mark's School discovers and nurtures what is finest in each child in a vibrant, inclusive, non-sectarian learning community. Innovative and full of heart, Saint Mark's strives to develop well-rounded critical thinkers in a challenging program that fosters academic excellence and responsible world citizenship."

ACADEMIC PROGRAM

Philosophy: "At Saint Mark's we: offer a strong, dynamic academic curriculum, enriched by programs in the arts, physical education, service learning, and outdoor education, with an emphasis on social-emotional development; honor and are guided by the Seven Pillars of Character: caring, courage, citizenship, respect, responsibility, honesty, and fairness; embrace diversity in preparing students for a global future; combine thoughtful innovation with enduring best practices; provide a hands-on program that encourages curiosity, develops independence, and addresses different learning styles; strive to teach, learn, and live in a sustainable way; integrate technology for learning at age-appropriate levels; foster a partnership between our school and parents, which is vital to the success of each child; understand that each member of our community blossoms in an atmosphere of safety, encouragement, support, and collaboration; believe that school should be challenging, fun, engaging, and joyful."
Foreign languages: French (G5-8 in 2010-11, G6-8 in 2011-12, and so on), Mandarin (K-4 in 2010-11, K-5 in 2011-12, and so on), Spanish K-8. **Computer training:** "The use of technology is integrated into the daily life of the classroom in G4-8. The formal computer curriculum begins in G3. **No. of computers available for students:** For K-5 100 computers total (computer lab, mobile laptop carts, classroom computer clusters/mounted LCD projectors); for G6-8 a 1-1 laptop program (each student has his/her own individual laptop); for K-8 a smart board in each classroom, and a media center. **No. of hours weekly of:** Art- 1-2; Drama- .6; Music- 1-1.5; Computers (beginning G3)- .6-1.4; Foreign language- 1.5-3.5; PE- 2.5-3.5; Other: The school also has a nationally ranked chess team, open to K-8. **Outdoor education:** G3-8 includes Yosemite, Big Basin, and Pinnacles. G8 students visit Washington, DC. **Grading:** Comprehensive comments K-8; letter grades beginning in G5. **Average nightly homework:** Approx. 15 min. for G1; 30 min. for G2-3; 45-60 min. for G4-6; 2 hours for G7-8. Posted on the Internet: G7-8. **Percentage of students participating in Johns Hopkins Center for Talented Youth Program:** "66% of G4-8 invited to participate." **Other indicators of academic success:** "Our students are accepted by the finest private high schools and continue at wonderful colleges. High schools report back on how well our students do and how well prepared they are. Students demonstrate respect, responsibility, caring, trust, community, involvement, honesty, fairness, courage, and citizenship." **High schools attended by latest graduating class:** Branson, MA, MC, University, SI, Bay, Sonoma Academy, Redwood, Tamalpais, Drake, Novato, San Marin, George.

FACULTY

Ethnicity: 81% Caucasian (non-Latino), 11% Asian, 5% Latino, 3% African-American. **Percentage of teachers with graduate degrees:** 39%. **Percentage with current California credential:** 68%. **Faculty selection/training:** "Interested teaching candidates undergo a rigorous selection process, which includes teaching and interviewing with faculty, administration, and students." **Teacher/student ratio:** 1:10 in K-3, 1:11 in G4-8. **Special subject teachers:** Art, music, drama, technology, media studies, PE. **Average teacher tenure:** 12 years.

MIDDLE SCHOOL

Description: The school's middle division consists of G4-6; upper division is G7-8. "In middle and upper divisions, the methodology becomes more sophisticated, moving students from the concrete to the conceptual. There is also a focus on organizational and study skills, problem solving, and critical thinking. The skills are hierarchically arranged. Note that a block schedule is used as the overarching structure for the curriculum." **Teacher/student ratio:** 1:11. **Elective courses offered:** "Electives are offered in G7-8 with an emphasis on the arts. Further programs are offered through classes in rhetoric, media studies, and social-emotional learning (SEL)/life issues. Media Literacy is taught in G5-8 with intensive studies on the subject in G7-8." **Achievement tracking in:** None. G7-8 has 2 differentiated math groupings/classes. **Student social events:** Dances for G7-8. Sixth graders may attend the last dance. Students may bring guests.

STUDENT SUPPORT SERVICES

No. of Licensed Counselors on staff: One part-time. **Counselor/ student ratio:** 1:380. **Learning specialists on staff:** One; as well as on-campus Bay Area Speech and Learning specialists. **Learning differences/disabilities support:** G1-5 families independently contract with Bay Area Speech and Learning for support during the school day; for G6-8, a classroom support class (about 6 students) is offered. This is a graded course which students take in lieu of a world language. **High school placement support:** "The 7th grade English teacher/high school counselor works closely with students and families throughout the 8th grade year to assist them with high school placement. Graduates attending local private and public schools return to speak to 8th graders about their experience."

Student Conduct and Health

Code of conduct: Zero tolerance for drug and alcohol use. Vulgar language is handled on an individual basis. Sexual harassment is governed by a written policy forbidding sexual harassment by any student, parent or teacher. **Prevention education and awareness programs:** Drug/alcohol education is taught through a social-emotional learning (SEL)/life issues program. Outside experts are involved. Sex education starts with a short unit in G3-6 and a fall half-year course in G7. Annual diversity workshops are offered for G3, G5, and G7-8. Diversity is also addressed in the curriculum. A parent education program is included, as well.

Athletics

Sports offered: Basketball, volleyball, flag football, cross-country, track and field, golf. **Team play begins in:** G6.

Campus/Campus Life

Campus description: The school is located on 10 acres in the residential neighborhood of Terra Linda. Buildings include a new gymnasium, media center, and arts and science center. **Library:** Together with the Media Center, over 10,000 volumes. The library also contracts for online access to informational databases, reference materials, and services that provide streaming video and other media resources. Collection also includes some reference material in e-book format. **Sports facilities:** A new state-of-the-art gymnasium and recently enhanced athletic field. **Theater/Arts facilities:** Drama room, with stage and professional lighting. Two major annual productions are performed at the Marin Civic Center. **Computer lab:** Yes. **Science lab:** Yes, used primarily by G7-8. **Lunch program:** Optional organic hot lunch program. **Bus service:** Yes (pick up locations in Mill Valley and Larkspur); extensive carpool network. **Uniforms/dress code:** Dress code for daily wear and uniform (a Saint Mark's white collared shirt) for special events. **Opportunities for community service:** Community service is a part of the Saint Mark's curriculum. In addition to several all-school programs throughout the year, each grade organizes its own outreach. Recent service opportunities include visits to senior and daycare centers, environmental clean-up, and serving meals to the homeless.

Extended Day

Morning care: Begins at 7:30 a.m. **After-school care:** Until 6:30 p.m. **Grade levels:** K-8. **Cost:** $6.50/hour (discount for students receiving financial aid). **Drop-in care available:** Yes, $9/hour. **Coverage over major holidays: No. **Homework help:** Yes. **Snacks:** Provided. **Staff/ student ratio:** 1:8. **After-school classes:** The offerings of the school's After School Adventures program change each trimester. Recent classes include: band, ceramics, hip hop dance, computer game creation, golf. **Cost:** "Varies."

SUMMER PROGRAMS
"The Early Learners Program is offered for incoming Kindergartners to assist them in getting to know the school and each other better. The program is offered in 2- or 4-week sessions. Arts in Action is a camp especially designed for incoming students to G1-4 to explore art to the fullest. Performing and visual arts programs focus on encouraging each child's creativity and imagination. Super Tech camp invites incoming students to G5-7 to experience technology first hand. Students work with clay animation, flash animation, robotics and rocketry in our state-of-the-art computer lab, science/art building and media center." **Cost:** "Varies."

PARENT INVOLVEMENT
Parent/teacher communication: Weekly newsletter, updated website, frequent letters from faculty and administration, parent conferences in fall and spring. **Participation requirements:** "No parent participation required, but it is strongly encouraged." **Parent education programs offered?** Yes.

WHAT SETS THE SCHOOL APART FROM OTHERS
"Saint Mark's challenges students in a nurturing environment, where their love of learning is celebrated. The community lives out our 'Seven Pillars of Character'—honesty, caring, fairness, responsibility, courage, respect, and citizenship—on a daily basis."

HOW FAMILIES CHARACTERIZE SCHOOL
Parent comment(s): "The level of commitment, the caring, and the sense of community at Saint Mark's are all amazing. The staff is dedicated, the kids are happy, and the parents are involved."
Student comment(s): "I think the teachers are great. All of the faculty cares for each student in a different way. Classes are small enough that teachers can spend one-on-one time." • "You can be the best of whatever you want to be at Saint Mark's." • "At Saint Mark's, it's cool to be smart."

Saint Monica School

5950 Geary (at 24th Avenue) (Richmond District)
San Francisco, CA 94121-2007
(415) 751-9564 *fax (415) 751-0781*
www.stmonicasf.org

Mr. Vincent M. Sweeters, Principal and Director of Admissions,
sweeters@stmonicasf.org

General
Coed K-8 parochial day school. Founded in 1919 by the Sisters of the Holy Names of Jesus and Mary. Catholic. Nonprofit. **Member:** NCEA. **Enrollment:** Approx. 160. **Average class size:** 22-25. **Accreditation:** WASC/WCEA (6-year term: 2008-14). **Endowment:** $1.3 million. **School year:** Aug.-June. **School day:** 8 a.m. to 3 p.m.

Student Body Ethnicity
42% Chinese and other Asian, 24% Caucasian (non-Latino), 23% multi-racial, 5% Latino, 4% Filipino, 2% African-American.

Admission
Applications due: Jan.-April. **Application fee:** $50. **Application process:** Submit application, make readiness assessment or shadow day appointment. **No. of applications:** 50. **No. of K spaces:** 25-28. **Percentage of K class made up of school's preschool class:** N/A. **Admission evaluation requirements for K:** School tour/Open House for parents (optional), K readiness assessment, recommendation from preschool. **Other grades:** School tour/Open House for parents (optional), classroom visitation (shadow) day for student, admission test, submission of report cards from last 2 years from previous school. **Preferences:** Siblings from current families, new parish families, Catholics from other parishes, non-Catholic families. **What sort of student do you best serve?** "Respectful, highly motivated, well-rounded students with strong parental support."

Costs
Latest tuition: $5,830-$6,590. **Sibling discount:** 50%-70%. **Tuition includes:** Lunch: No; Transportation: No; Laptop computer: No; Other: N/A. **Tuition increases:** Approx. 3-6% annually. **Other costs:** Approx. $300-400 registration fees; $50 Parent Club fee. **Percentage of students receiving financial aid:** 15-20%. **Financial aid application deadline:**

April 15 (external sources), May (internal sources). Financial aid is based on need. **Average grant:** $1,200. **Percentage of grants of half-tuition or more:** 5%. **Donations:** Parents are required give $250 annually toward the School Maintenance Fund, and participate in 2 mandatory fundraisers.

SCHOOL'S MISSION STATEMENT

"The Mission of Saint Monica School is to provide a supportive, Christ-Centered environment and a vigorous, comprehensive academic curriculum, which both engage the full range of a student's development."

ACADEMIC PROGRAM

Philosophy: "In the tradition of the Sisters of the Holy Names of Jesus and Mary, the Saint Monica School Community strives to live Jesus' message of respect, love, and concern for one another in our contemporary and multicultural world. In cooperation with our parents, the faculty and staff build a community that fosters the religious, intellectual, moral, social, cultural, and physical growth of each student." **Foreign languages:** Mandarin and Spanish after school program. **Computer training:** Yes. **No. of computers available for students:** 50. **No. of hours weekly of:** Art- 1.5; Drama- 2 after school; Music- .5- 1.0; Computers- 1; Foreign language- up to 4 after school; PE- 1.5. **Outdoor education:** N/A. **Grading:** A-F, beginning in G3. **Average nightly homework:** 15-120 min. based on grade level. Posted on the Internet: No. **Percentage of students participating in Johns Hopkins Center for Talented Youth Program:** N/A. **Other indicators of academic success:** "All students G2-8 score above the 70th percentile on the Iowa Test of Basic Skills (ITBS) test and 85+% of students are at grade level or above in math, reading and language arts. Saint Monica School ranks as one of the highest scoring academic schools in the Archdiocese of San Francisco on the ITBS nationally-normed test taken each Sept." **High schools attended by latest graduating class:** SI, SHCP, Mercy-SF, Mercy-Burlingame, Riordan, Lowell.

FACULTY

Ethnicity: 82% Caucasian, 12% Hispanic/Latina. **Percentage of teachers with graduate degrees:** 30%. **Percentage with current California credential:** 100%. **Faculty selection/training:** "Experience, degree, and credential." **Teacher/student ratio:** 1:12.5 in K-1, 1:20-25 in G2-8. **Special subject teachers:** Art, music, PE, K-4 reading. **Average teacher tenure:** 14 years.

MIDDLE SCHOOL

Description: "G5-8 are departmentalized with teachers instructing their homeroom in language arts. Science, social science and math/algebra are taught by specialized teachers to the entire junior high level. Students also have art, music, and PE and computer skills are integrated throughout." **Teacher/student ratio:** 1:25. Elective courses: Co-curricular programs in Chinese language, drama, student choir, yearbook, creative writing. **Achievement tracking in:** N/A. **Student social events:** On-going sports program, quarterly school community fun social events, Christmas Program, Spring Talent Show, Altar Service, Book Club, Drama Club, Ecology Club, Jr. High Service Club, Student Choir, Student Council, Yearbook.

STUDENT SUPPORT SERVICES

No. of Licensed Counselors on staff: One part-time. **Counselor/ student ratio:** N/A. **Learning specialists on staff:** Reading specialist for K-4. **Learning differences/disabilities support:** Yes. **High school placement support:** The junior high school team assists students with the high school application/entrance process, including entrance test preparation and parent meetings.

STUDENT CONDUCT AND HEALTH

Code of conduct: "The San Francisco Archdiocese Code of Christian Conduct as outlined in our parent/student handbook. Also, discipline in the school is to be considered as an aspect of moral guidance and not a form of punishment. It is a means of training the child to assume more and more the control of her/his own behavior, whether this conduct has physical, mental, or moral aspects, so that she/he can progressively grow in self-competency and maturity." **Prevention education and awareness addressed in:** Taught in conjunction with science and religious education classes.

ATHLETICS

Sports offered: Soccer, basketball, girls volleyball and boys baseball. **Team play begins in:** G3. Students in K-2 are encouraged to participate in parent administered micro leagues.

CAMPUS/CAMPUS LIFE

Campus description: The campus contains a large building which houses all classrooms. There are 2 paved play areas comprising approx. 1 quarter acre and a full gymnasium. **Library:** "The library has hundreds of volumes. Students may check out books for 2-week periods." **Sports**

facilities: Gymnasium and outdoor sports courts. **Theater/Arts facilities:** Parish hall stage and church facilities. **Computer lab:** Yes. **Science lab:** Yes. **Lunch program:** Yes. **Bus service:** No. **Uniforms/dress code:** Uniforms. **Opportunities for community service:** "Children in each grade participate in age-appropriate service in community outreach programs to the elderly, veterans, and the homeless. G8 students participate in a mandatory service program as part of their curriculum."

EXTENDED DAY
Morning care: Free, beginning 7:15 a.m. **After-school care:** Until 6 p.m. **Grade levels:** K-8. **Cost:** $2,394/year for 1 child, full-time; $1,436 for each additional child. **Drop-in care available:** Yes, $6/hour. **Coverage over major holidays:** No. **Homework help:** Yes. **Snacks:** Provided on Fridays. **Staff/student ratio:** 1:12. **After-school classes:** Middle School Study Hall is offered 3 times a week and peer tutoring is offered 2 times per week for students of G1-5, both free of charge. For a fee, Mandarin is offered 4 days a week (writing, reading, speaking, history and culture); Spanish, Science Adventures afterschool club, group guitar and piano lessons offered once a week. **Cost:** "Varies."

SUMMER PROGRAMS: None.

PARENT INVOLVEMENT
Parent/teacher communication: End of 1st Quarter Parent Teacher Conferences, website, e-mail, and telephone calls; a weekly communication envelope goes home to each family from the school administration. **Participation requirements:** Parents are required to complete 28 hours of service to the school per year (25 hours of general service and 3 hours of service toward the Annual Auction Dinner in March). Parents are also required to give $250 annually toward our School Maintenance Fund and participate in 2 mandatory fundraisers. **Parent education programs offered?** No.

WHAT SETS THE SCHOOL APART FROM OTHERS
"Saint Monica School provides a nurturing environment and rigorous academic program which gives all students the opportunity to achieve and thrive. We pride ourselves upon guiding students to become spiritually centered people, academically empowered learners, effective communicators, globally conscious citizens, and well-rounded individuals. The students of Saint Monica School earn some of the highest averages in the S. F. Archdiocese on the annual standardized testing scoring and our graduates are well prepared to excel in the high school of their choice."

How Families Characterize School

Parent comment(s): "Saint Monica School has an excellent academic program, and strong, dedicated teachers who care about children. The environment emphasizes Christian moral values and prepares students for success in life."

Student comment(s): "Saint Monica is a school that makes learning fun, challenging and exciting."

St. Paul's Elementary School

1690 Church Street (at 29th Street) (Mission/Noe Valley)
San Francisco, CA 94131
(415) 648-2055 *fax (415) 648-1920*
www.stpaulsf.net

Arleen Guaraglia, Principal, aguaraglia@stpaulsf.net

General

Coed PK-8 parochial day school. Founded in 1916 by BVM Sisters. Roman Catholic. Nonprofit. **Member:** NCEA. **Enrollment:** Approx. 235. **Average class size:** 25. **Accreditation:** WASC/WCEA (6-year term: 2010-16). **Endowment:** N/P. **School year:** Aug.-June. **School day:** 8 a.m. to 3:15 p.m.

Student Body Ethnicity

48% Latino, 36% Caucasian (non-Latino), 12.5% Asian, 1.5% multi-racial, 1.5% African-American.

Admission

Applications due: Jan. 31st for K; open for G1-8. **Application fee:** $75. **Application process:** Grade level assessment, previous school questionnaire, transcripts, interview with principal. **No. of applications:** N/P. **No. of K spaces:** 35. **Percentage of K class made up of school's preschool class:** 10%. **Admission evaluation requirements for K:** Screening, school visit and tour, preschool recommendations. **Other grades:** Entrance test, transcript, previous school teacher questionnaire and interview with principal. **Preferences:** Siblings, preschool applicants from St. Paul Parish program, St. Paul Parish members, Roman Catholics. **What sort of student do you best serve?** "We serve urban and suburban families interested in a faith-based curriculum in the Roman Catholic tradition within a family atmosphere that is gifted in cultural diversity. We strive to educate the whole child preparing him/her for the competitive secondary schools to which they apply and to which they are accepted—in most cases, to their first choice school."

Costs

Latest tuition: $5,724. **Sibling discount:** Yes, 5%. **Tuition includes:** Lunch: No; Transportation: No; Laptop computer: No; Other: N/A. **Tuition increases:** Approx. 6% annually. **Other costs:** $340 registration fee. **Percentage of students receiving financial aid:** 30%. **Financial aid application deadline:** Call for date. Financial aid is based on need. **Average grant:** $500. **Percentage of grants of half-tuition or more:** N/P. **Donations:** A financial agreement stipulates that families will raise $450 in school sponsored fundraisers such as the walkathon, candy sale, e-script, holiday gift sale.

School's Mission Statement

"We are called as a Catholic School to teach as Jesus taught. In partnership with parents, St. Paul's School attempts to educate students for what they can be spiritually, intellectually, psychologically, socially and aesthetically. We encourage and support the role of parents as primary educators by helping students to live as responsible Christians in the St. Paul parish and school community and the larger community of San Francisco. We hope as adults they will continue to grow in Christian development."

Academic Program

Philosophy: "It is the goal of St. Paul's School to provide for the development of each child to his or her fullest potential as an integrated individual: spiritually, socially, emotionally, aesthetically and physically. We offer a solid curriculum in religion, reading/literature, English, mathematics, science, Spanish, and social studies. We supplement that core curriculum with art, music, PE and computer classes." **Foreign languages:** Spanish. **Computer training:** Yes. **No. of computers available for students:** 18 in lab, 2-3 in classrooms. **No. of hours weekly of:** Art- .75; Drama- N/P; Music- .5; Computers- .5; Foreign language- 1; PE- 1. **Outdoor education:** G6 overnight at the Marin Headlands. **Grading:** A-F, beginning in G3. **Average nightly homework:** 20-30 min. in G1; 20-40 min. in G2-3; 35-55 min. in G4; 45-60 min. in G5; 60-90 min. in G6; 60-110 min. in G7-8. Posted on the Internet: Yes. **Percentage of students participating in Johns Hopkins Center for Talented Youth Program:** N/P. **Other indicators of academic success:** "St. Paul graduates are accepted at the private and public academic high schools of their first choice." **High schools attended by latest graduating class:** Riordan, SHCP, Lick, SI, ICA, Mercy-SF, Lowell.

Faculty
Ethnicity: 100% Caucasian. **Percentage of teachers with graduate degrees:** 30%. **Percentage with current California credential:** 100%. **Faculty selection/training:** "Successful elementary school experience, degree, compatibility with mission of school, preferably a practicing Roman Catholic." **Teacher/student ratio:** 1:25. **Special subject teachers:** Science, music, PE, computers. **Average teacher tenure:** 12 years.

Middle School
Description: In G6-8 science is departmentalized and in G7-8, math and English. **Teacher/student ratio:** 1:30. **Elective courses offered:** None. **Achievement tracking in:** N/P. **Student social events:** Grade appropriate field trips, CYO sports, annual family picnic, field-day, music program at Davies Symphony Hall, Labs, Family Bingo Night, Christmas and Spring Concerts.

Student Support Services
No. of Licensed Counselors on staff: None. **Counselor/student ratio:** N/A. **Learning specialists on staff:** N/P. **Learning differences/ disabilities support:** N/P. **High school placement support:** N/P.

Student Conduct and Health
Code of conduct: "Discipline within St. Paul's is considered an aspect of moral guidance and not a form of punishment. It is a means of training the students to take control of their own choices and to assume responsibility for their own actions. Our main purpose at St. Paul's School is to learn and to grow both individually and also as a Catholic Christian Community. At St. Paul's School the expectation is that relationships are based on mutual respect, patience, and kindness." **Prevention education and awareness addressed in:** Family Life Education, Health Education.

Athletics
Sports offered: Basketball, baseball, volleyball, boys soccer. **Team play begins in:** G3.

Campus/Campus Life
Campus description: "St. Paul's Elementary School's new school building opened in 1999. The preschool program is located on campus

in a separate building. **Library:** Yes. **Sports facilities:** Gym. **Theater/Arts facilities:** None. **Computer lab:** Yes, 18 computers. **Science lab:** Yes. **Lunch program:** Daily. **Bus service:** None. The school is located on the J MUNI line. **Uniforms/dress code:** Uniforms. **Opportunities for community service:** Students in G8 are required to complete 20 hours of community service before graduation. The school community sponsors toy drives, food drives, special fundraising for international emergencies and an annual coat drive for the homeless.

EXTENDED DAY
Morning care: Begins at 7 a.m. **After-school care:** Until 6 p.m. **Grade levels:** K-8. **Cost:** $240/mo. **Drop-in care available:** Yes. **Coverage over major holidays:** No. **Homework help:** Yes. **Snacks:** Provided. **Staff/student ratio:** 1:5. **After-school classes:** Art, drama, piano. **Cost:** "Varies."

SUMMER PROGRAMS: None.

PARENT INVOLVEMENT
Parent/teacherm communication: Through parent-teacher conferences, school website, e-mail, weekly newsletter, voicemail. **Participation requirements:** 40 hours per year for 2-parent families and 20 hours for single families. **Parent education programs offered?** Yes.

WHAT SETS THE SCHOOL APART FROM OTHERS
"The administration, faculty and staff of St. Paul's give attentiveness to each student to help them succeed academically and assist them in developing a personal moral value system and service-orientated attitude that will become the basis for civic responsibility. Secondly, we value the partnership developed within our parent community to help both our students and families develop a strong sense of faith and family centered well-being."

HOW FAMILIES CHARACTERIZE SCHOOL
Parent comment(s): "In a recent WASC survey, when asked to comment on the strengths of St. Paul's School, parents indicated the top five areas in order of priority as: a dedicated and caring staff, the Catholic values of the school, a sense of community, excellent instruction and a safe environment. Other areas listed as the strengths of the school included: the parents, the pastor, the principal, the clean environment, the athletic program, and the extended care program."
Student comment(s): "St. Paul's school is a clean, safe, friendly, and

nurturing environment for learning … the curriculum is challenging and well-rounded." • "I relate well to my teachers and the school staff. I think my teachers are fair, helpful, caring and the staff listen and respond to our needs." • "At St. Paul's, we have a real sense of community—all of us feel respected by teachers and staff. We think it is a fun, safe place to learn."

St. Philip School

665 Elizabeth Street (at Diamond Street) (Noe Valley)
San Francisco, CA 94114
(415) 824-8467 *fax (415) 282-0121*
www.saintphilipschool.com

Ms. Remy Everett, Head of School and Director of Admission, reverett@saintphilipschool.com

General
Coed PS-8 parochial day school. Founded in 1938. Roman Catholic. Nonprofit. **Member:** NCEA. **Enrollment:** Approx. 214. **Average class size:** 24. **Accreditation:** WASC (6-year term: 2010-16). **Endowment:** N/P. **School year:** Aug-June. **School day:** 7:50 a.m. to 3 p.m.

Student Body Ethnicity
56.2% Caucasian (non-Latino), 21% Hispanic, 12.3% multi-racial, 7.8% Asian, 1.8% African American.

Admission
Applications due: Open enrollment. **Application fee:** $50. **Application process:** Call for appointment. **No. of applications:** N/P. **No. of K spaces:** 35. **Percentage of K class made up of school's preschool class:** 40%. **Admission evaluation requirements for K:** School visit, screening, recommendations. **Other grades:** Test scores and report card from previous school. **Preferences:** Siblings, parishioners. **What sort of student do you best serve?** N/P.

Costs
Latest tuition: $5,738. **Sibling discount:** Yes. **Tuition includes:** Lunch: No; Transportation: No; Laptop computer: No; Other: N/A. **Tuition increases:** Approx. 5% annually. **Other costs:** Approx. $150 for uniforms. **Percentage of students receiving financial aid:** 11%. **Financial aid application deadline:** March (call for date). Financial aid

is based on need. **Average grant:** $1,500. **Percentage of grants of half-tuition or more:** 3%. **Donations:** N/P.

School's Mission Statement

"St. Philip the Apostle School is a community of faith whose mission to educate the whole child is based upon the Gospel Values and the teachings of the Catholic Church. As a Catholic and parish school, we believe that the Gospel Values provide students a framework for responsible decision making. We are committed to preparing our students for a life as an active Christian and responsible citizen."

Academic Program

Philosophy: "St. Philip the Apostle School is a Catholic elementary school that offers a rigorous education that is comprehensive and in accordance with Archdiocesan guidelines. We strive to meet the needs of each student and provide opportunities for all students to achieve; develop their skills and talents; and grow spiritually, intellectually, physically, socially and emotionally. We believe that parents are the primary educators of their children and teachers the facilitators of learning. We affirm that through a partnership between the school and family, all students can learn and be successful. We challenge our students to live a life of integrity, inquiry and purpose that is larger than the self. We strive to develop in our students a respect for diversity, pride in their cultural heritage and as members of a larger community." **Foreign languages:** Spanish K-8. **Computer training:** Yes. **No. of computers available for students:** 40. **No. of hours weekly of:** Art- .5; Drama- N/P; Music- .5; Computers- 1; Foreign language- 1; PE- 1. **Outdoor education:** G6 Science Camp Week. **Grading:** A-F, beginning in G3. **Average nightly homework:** 1 hour. Posted on the Internet: No. **Percentage of students participating in Johns Hopkins Center for Talented Youth Program:** N/A. **Other indicators of academic success:** "Strong test scores." **High schools attended by latest graduating class:** SI, Riordan, Mercy-SF, SHCP, ICA, Lowell, SOTA, Bay, Stuart Hall.

Faculty

Ethnicity: 87% Caucasian (non Latino), 23% Asian. **Percentage of teachers with graduate degrees:** 100%. **Percentage with current California credential:** 100%. **Faculty selection/training:** Education and experience. **Teacher/student ratio:** 1:15 GK-2; 1:24 G3-8. **Special subject teachers:** Music, PE, technology, Spanish. **Average teacher tenure:** 6 years.

MIDDLE SCHOOL
Description: G6-8; departmentalization for literature, mathematics, history/social studies, science. **Teacher/student ratio:** 1:24. **Elective courses offered:** N/A. **Achievement tracking in:** Language arts, mathematics, history/social studies, science. **Student social events:** N/P.

STUDENT SUPPORT SERVICES
No. of Licensed Counselors on staff: One part-time. **Counselor/student ratio:** 1:210. **Learning specialists on staff:** One. **Learning differences/disabilities support:** Reading Specialist/Archdiocesan Special Needs Representative on site. **High school placement support:** G8 teacher, principal and pastor.

STUDENT CONDUCT AND HEALTH
Code of conduct: "Discipline in a Catholic School is to be considered an aspect of moral guidance. The purpose of discipline is to promote student development, increase respect for authority and provide a classroom situation conducive to learning. All concerns should first be addressed to the classroom teacher and then to the principal." **Prevention education and awareness addressed in:** The school brings speakers to campus to discuss drug abuse, harassment, etc.

ATHLETICS
Sports offered: T-ball, soccer, football, basketball, volleyball and baseball. **Team play begins in:** K through Park & Recreation, CYO Firemen's League and SF Park and Recreation.

CAMPUS/CAMPUS LIFE
Campus description: Located in the heart of San Francisco's Noe Valley. **Library:** Newly renovated. **Sports facilities:** Limited, use gyms and parks. **Theater/Arts facilities:** Parish Hall. **Computer lab:** "Mobile laptops." **Science lab:** Yes. **Lunch program:** Yes. **Bus service:** No. **Uniforms/dress code:** Uniforms. **Opportunities for community service:** "This is encouraged at all grades, but is expected from the middle school grades."

EXTENDED DAY
Morning care: Begins at 6:30 a.m. **After-school care:** Until 6 p.m. **Grade levels:** K-8. **Cost:** $4/hour. **Drop-in care available:** Yes. **Coverage over major holidays:** No. **Homework help:** Yes. **Snacks:** Yes. **Staff/student ratio:** 1:17. **After-school classes:** Spanish, guitar, keyboard, academic chess, science adventures, art, cooking. **Cost:** "Varies."

SUMMER PROGRAMS: None.

PARENT INVOLVEMENT
Parent/teacher communication: E-mail, telephone, in person communications, newsletters, meetings. **Participation requirements:** Auction and festival plus 20 hours of service. **Parent education programs offered?** Yes, through the PTA.

WHAT SETS THE SCHOOL APART FROM OTHERS
"St. Philip the Apostle School has a long tradition of academic excellence. Students come to our school from all neighborhoods of San Francisco. Today, we serve a student body population of 214 children in grades K-8. We strive to develop respect for diversity and pride in the cultural heritage of our children. Our goal is to instruct our students in a program that establishes and builds upon basic skills, which will provide them with a strong foundation in the areas of language arts, mathematics, social studies and science. Teachers employ a wide variety of techniques and activities to meet the differing needs of children."

HOW FAMILIES CHARACTERIZE SCHOOL
Parent comment(s): "St. Philip School was a great experience for our daughter. She loved it and the teachers thoroughly prepared her for high school."
Student comment(s): "Our teachers are nice and take good care of us. They work hard to make learning a good experience."

ST. STEPHEN ELEMENTARY SCHOOL
401 Eucalyptus Drive (at 22nd Avenue) (Lakeshore)
San Francisco, CA 94132
(415) 664-8331
www.ststephenschoolsf.org

Sharon McCarthy Allen, Principal, ststephensf@yahoo.com

GENERAL
Coed K-8 parochial day school. Founded in 1952 by the Sisters of Mercy. Roman Catholic. Nonprofit. **Member:** NCEA. **Enrollment:** Approx. 323. **Average class size:** 35. **Accreditation:** WASC/WCEA (6-year term: 2005-11). **Endowment:** N/P. **School year:** Aug.-June. **School day:** 8 a.m. to 2:50 p.m.

STUDENT BODY ETHNICITY
66% Caucasian, 9% Asian, 10% multi-racial, 8% Hispanic, 6% Filipino, 1% Pacific Islander.

ADMISSION
Applications due: Jan. for K; call for G1-7. **Application fee:** $50. **Application process:** N/P. **Number of applications:** N/P. **No. of K spaces:** N/P. **Percentage of K class made up of school's preschool class:** N/A. **Admission evaluation requirements for K:** Screening, school visit and tour. **Other grades:** Teacher screening test and transcript. **Preferences:** Siblings, St. Stephen Parish members, Roman Catholics. **What sort of student do you best serve?** N/P.

COSTS
Latest tuition: $5,800 (for parishioners) - $6,410 (for non-parishioners). **Sibling discount:** "Yes." (amount N/P) **Tuition includes:** Lunch: No; Transportation: No; Laptop computer: No; Other: N/A. **Tuition increases:** Approx. 5% annually. **Other costs:** $300 registration fee, $200 gym fee, $70 parent organization fee, $150 uniforms. **Percentage of students receiving financial aid:** 7% . **Financial aid application deadline:** Jan. (call for date). Financial aid is based on need. **Average grant:** N/P. **Percentage of grants of half-tuition or more:** N/P. **Donations:** Families also must participate in the school scrip fund raising program.

SCHOOL'S MISSION STATEMENT
"It is the mission of St. Stephen School community to educate children in a nurturing faith-filled environment that addresses the whole child, spiritually and intellectually. Parents are recognized as the primary educators of their children and we collaborate with them in our role as their children's teachers."

ACADEMIC PROGRAM
Philosophy: "It is our philosophy to provide students with an opportunity to grow in their relationship with God as they pursue academic excellence. Students in this community are encouraged to be mindful of the dignity of all people, and to actively work for peace and justice in the world. Instructional programs designed to reflect the Gospel teachings of Jesus Christ prepare students to become empathetic, responsible members of society, who are committed to working within their diverse community and the global society." **Foreign languages:** Spanish. **Computer Training:** In-class and after-school instruction. **No. of computers**

available for students: 35 in lab, 1 per classroom. Number of hours weekly of: Art- .5; Drama- N/P; Music- .75; Computers- .75; Foreign language- .5; PE- N/P. **Outdoor Education:** G4 overnight to Coloma; G7 overnight to CYO Outdoor Environmental Education Camp. **Grading:** Letter grades beginning in G3. **Average nightly homework:** 15-30 min. in G1-2; 30-45 min. in G3-4; 45-60 min. in G5-6; 60-90 min. in G7-8. **Percentage of students participating in Johns Hopkins Center for Talented Youth Program:** N/P. **Other indicators of academic success:** "St. Stephen School students' results from the IOWA Test of Basic Skills consistently rank among the top 10 percent of schools in the San Francisco Archdiocese." **High Schools attended by latest graduating class:** SI, SHCP, Mercy-SF, Mercy-Burlingame, Riordan, Convent, Stuart Hall, Lowell, Serra, Notre Dame, ICA, Drew, Gateway, SOTA.

FACULTY
Ethnicity: N/P. **Percentage of teachers with graduate degrees:** N/P. **Percentage with current California credential:** 100%. **Faculty selection and training:** N/P. **Teacher/student ratio:** 1:35. **Special subject teachers:** Math, science, language arts, PE, music, computers, Spanish. **Average teacher tenure:** N/P.

MIDDLE SCHOOL
Description: Departmentalized G6-8. **Teacher/student ratio:** 1:35. **Elective courses offered:** None. **Achievement tracking in:** Math, science, English/literature, social studies, religion. **Student social events:** Field trips, CYO athletics, Family Bingo Night, Pancake Breakfast, St. Patrick's Day Dinner, Easter Egg Hunt, altar server, safety patrol picnics.

STUDENT SUPPORT SERVICES
No. of Licensed Counselors on staff: One part-time. **Counselor/student ratio:** 1:323. **Learning Specialists on staff:** One learning specialist and one resource teacher, 3 days per week. **Learning differences/ disabilities support:** "Standardized tests provide a foundation for our student assessments. Classroom interventions and other strategies are instrumental in helping to ensure high achievement. As individual student needs are identified, teachers revise academic expectations and instructional methods accordingly, and provide a modified curriculum if necessary, in conjunction with our learning resource specialist." **High school placement support:** N/P.

STUDENT CONDUCT AND HEALTH

Code of conduct: "Discipline at St. Stephen is considered an aspect of moral guidance and not simply a form of punishment. The purpose of discipline is to help the students assume responsibility for their own actions. Responsible freedom is compatible with the development of self-discipline, effective study habits and respect and understanding of others. **Prevention education and awareness programs:** N/P.

ATHLETICS

Sports offered: Soccer, basketball, boys baseball, girls volleyball. **Team play begins in:** G3.

CAMPUS/CAMPUS LIFE

Campus Description: St. Stephen was built in 1952. A new school wing was added in 1999, which includes a school library, computer lab, science lab, kindergarten, learning resource classroom, principal and administrative offices. In 2009, St. Stephen Church opened a new, 2-story 20,000-square foot Parish Center, which features a regulation gymnasium on the top floor and a large reception hall on the lower floor with numerous amenities. St. Stephen School uses the Parish Center almost daily for athletic practices and games, weekly hot lunch, bi-weekly P.E. classes, art instruction and assemblies. **Library:** Yes. **Sports Facilities:** Gym. **Theater/Arts facilities:** Performance stage and art classroom. **Computer lab:** Yes. **Science lab:** Yes. **Lunch program:** Once per week. **Bus service:** No. **Uniforms/dress code:** Uniforms. **Opportunities for community service:** "Monthly Student Council-sponsored charity events raise money for organizations such as UNICEF, the Make-A-Wish Foundation, St. Jude's Hospital and Habitat for Humanity. Since 2003, St. Stephen School has made the St. Vincent de Paul Society a major focus of our community outreach with our students. We conduct sock drives, sundry collections, fundraisers and an annual Christmas food drive for the St. Vincent de Paul food pantry, helping to feed hundreds of homeless families."

EXTENDED DAY

Morning Care: No. **After-School Care:** Until 5:50 p.m. **Grade levels:** K-8. **Cost:** $4/hour or $1,800/year. **Drop-in care available:** Yes. **Coverage over major holidays:** No. **Homework help:** Yes. **Snacks:** No. **Staff/student ratio:** 1:10. **After-School Classes:** Computer, piano, math, technology labs. Costs: N/P.

SUMMER PROGRAMS: None.

Parent Involvement
Parent/teacher communication: Monthly parent meetings, weekly family newsletter, weekly student work folders, mid-quarter progress reports and school website. **Participation requirements:** 40 hours per year for 2-parent families and 20 hours for single families. **Parent education programs offered?** N/P.

What Sets the School Apart from Others
"St. Stephen School maintains a strong commitment to Catholic Identity and educating students in a faith-filled environment. Our school is inclusive at every level and enjoys tremendous support from our parent group and the parish-at-large who form the backbone of our St. Stephen community. Approximately 10 percent of our students are children of St. Stephen School alumni, a testament to the school's enduring legacy over several generations of families."

How Parents Characterize School: N/P.

Saint Vincent de Paul School
2350 Green Street (at Pierce) (Pacific Heights/Cow Hollow)
San Francisco, CA 94123
(415) 346-5505 *fax (415) 346-0970*
www.svdpsf.com

Mrs. Barbara Harvey, Head of School, Bharv1@aol.com
Mrs. Maria Balestrieri, Director of Admission, mbalestrieri@svdpsf.com

General
Coed K-8 parochial day school. Founded in 1924. Catholic. Nonprofit. **Member:** N/P. **Enrollment:** Approx. 250. **Average class size:** 30. **Accreditation:** WASC/WCEA (term: N/P). **Endowment:** N/P. **School year:** Aug.-June. **School day:** 8:10 a.m. to 3:20 p.m.

Student Body Ethnicity
"74% Caucasian (non-Latino)."

Admission
Applications due: Approx. Dec. 1 (call for date). **Application fee:** $100. **Application process:** Application and fee, parent interview, kindergarten screening or standardized test, recommendation(s); class visit and report

cards for children entering G1-8. **No. of applications:** N/P. **No. of K spaces:** 32. **Percentage of K class made up of school's preschool class:** N/A. **Admission evaluation requirements for K:** A preschool recommendation and a K readiness screening will be administered in Jan. on an individual basis which will last about 15 minutes. A K applicant must be 5 years old by Sept. 1 of the admission year. **Other grades:** Class visit, recommendation, previous report cards and standardized tests. **Preferences:** Parish Catholics, siblings, non-parish Catholics then non-Catholics. **What sort of student do you best serve?** "Each student is unique and valuable because his or her life comes from God. We believe the purpose of Catholic education is to assist each student to become a life-long learner, to identify and communicate his or her personal worth and message, to be aware of the same dignity in others, and to acquire a sense of responsibility to society."

COSTS
Latest tuition: $7,700 (parish Catholics with service hours) - $11,500 (non-Catholics with no service hours). **Sibling discount:** No. **Tuition includes:** Lunch: No; Transportation: No; Laptop computer: No; Other: Books. **Tuition increases:** Approx. 8% annually. **Other costs:** $200 uniforms, $500 other fees. **Percentage of students receiving financial aid:** 10%. **Financial aid application deadline:** April (call for date). Financial aid is based on need. **Average grant:** N/P. **Percentage of grants of half-tuition or more:** 1%. **Donations:** $500 or more requested per family.

SCHOOL'S MISSION STATEMENT
"The mission of Saint Vincent de Paul School is to educate our students in the Catholic tradition. We aspire to teach as Jesus did, with a focus on Gospel values. As facilitators of learning, we recognize parents as the primary educators of their children. We strive to acknowledge and celebrate the cultural differences in each individual student. We encourage our students to be responsible and sensitive to Church, school, and neighboring communities. We challenge our students to be self-motivated, life-long learners who will share their God-given gifts and talents with the global community."

ACADEMIC PROGRAM
Philosophy: "It is the goal of St. Vincent de Paul School to provide for the development of each child to his or her fullest potential as a whole person: spiritually, morally, socially, physically, intellectually, and emotionally. We strive to do this by offering an excellent curriculum

in religion, mathematics, reading, science, English, social studies and Spanish. To assist each child in further development, we also include art, library skills, drama, music and PE. Computer skills are integrated throughout the curriculum. Sacramental programs for Catholic students are also offered in G2 (Reconciliation and First Eucharist) and G7-8 (Confirmation)." **Foreign languages:** Spanish. **Computer training:** Yes. **No. of computers available for students:** 85. **No. of hours weekly of:** Art- 1; Drama- 1; Music- 1; Computers- 1; Foreign language- N/P; PE- 2. **Outdoor education:** "Yes." **Grading:** Letter grades beginning in G3. **Average nightly homework:** N/P. Posted on the Internet: No. **Percentage of students participating in Johns Hopkins Center for Talented Youth Program:** N/A. **Other indicators of academic success:** N/P. **High schools attended by latest graduating class:** SI, Stuart Hall, Convent, Lowell, Riordan, Santa Catalina, Mercy, Lincoln, SHCP.

FACULTY
Ethnicity: N/P. **Percentage of teachers with graduate degrees:** 75%. **Percentage with current California credential:** 95%. **Faculty selection/training:** N/P. **Teacher/student ratio:** 1:15. **Special subject teachers:** 9. **Average teacher tenure:** N/P.

MIDDLE SCHOOL
Description: G7-8. **Teacher/student ratio:** 1:15. **Elective courses offered:** N/P. **Achievement tracking in:** N/P. **Student social events:** N/P.

STUDENT SUPPORT SERVICES
No. of Licensed Counselors on staff: One. **Counselor/student ratio:** N/P. **Learning specialists on staff:** Two. **Learning differences/ disabilities support:** Yes. **High school placement support:** Yes.

STUDENT CONDUCT AND HEALTH: N/P.

ATHLETICS
Sports offered: Basketball, soccer, girls volleyball, boys baseball. **Team play begins in:** G3 (intramural). Students in G3-8 may participate in the De Paul Youth Club, which offers sports and participation in city-wide sports competition.

CAMPUS/CAMPUS LIFE
Campus description: "We have the distinct advantage of being located next door to our parish church. We have a main building, built

in 1924, which houses our administrative offices, K-5, our library, faculty lounge, cafeteria and full operating kitchen. We also have an annex which contains our gym, junior high, computer lab, special needs classroom, music room, art room, Spanish, and learning specialist room. **Library:** Yes. **Sports facilities:** Gymnasium and auditorium. **Theater/ Arts facilities:** Theatrical stage. **Computer lab:** Yes. **Science lab:** Yes. **Lunch program:** Yes. **Bus service:** No. **Uniforms/dress code:** Uniforms. **Opportunities for community service:** Yes.

EXTENDED DAY
Morning care: N/P. **After-school care:** Until 6 p.m. **Grade levels:** K-8. **Cost:** $2,750/year full-time. **Drop-in care available:** Yes. **Coverage over major holidays:** No. **Homework help:** For 1 hour. **Snacks:** Provided. **Staff/student ratio:** 1:10. **After-school classes:** Chess, boys chorus, girls chorus. **Cost:** "Varies."

SUMMER PROGRAMS
Legarza Basketball Camp.

PARENT INVOLVEMENT
Parent/teacher communication: Yes. **Participation requirements:** Yes, 30 hours per family. **Parent education programs offered?** Yes.

WHAT SETS THE SCHOOL APART FROM OTHERS
"Serving generations of families, the mission of Saint Vincent de Paul School is to educate students in the Catholic tradition and to provide for the development of the whole person. With a science center, music department, Spanish department, drama program and state of the art computer lab, it is the school's philosophy to provide a variety of activities to stimulate intellectual curiosity and to build an individual's sense of personal worth. Saint Vincent de Paul is proud of its many achievements as a school family, and as a community we are dedicated to realizing every student's potential."

HOW FAMILIES CHARACTERIZE SCHOOL: N/P.

STS. PETER AND PAUL SALESIAN SCHOOL

660 Filbert Street (between Stockton and Powell)
San Francisco, CA 94133
(415) 421-5219 *fax (415) 421-1831*
www.sspeterpaulsf.org

Dr. Lisa Harris, Principal, lharris@sspeterpaulsf.org

GENERAL

Coed PK-8 parochial day school. Founded in 1925 by the Salesian order. Catholic. Nonprofit. **Member:** NCEA. **Enrollment:** Approx. 250. **Average class size:** 25. **Accreditation:** WCEA/WASC (N/P term). **Endowment:** N/A. **School year:** Aug.-June. **School day:** 8:10 a.m. to 3:15 p.m. Mon.-Thurs.; 8:10 a.m. to 1:15 p.m. on Fri.

STUDENT BODY ETHNICITY

52.4% Caucasian (non Latino), 23.2% Asian, 13.6% multi-racial, 3.6% Hispanic, 3% Filipino, 1% African American.

ADMISSION

Applications due: N/P. **Application Fee:** $25. **Application process:** Grade level assessment, previous school assessment, transcripts, interview with principal. **No. of applications:** N/P. **No. of K spaces:** N/P. **Percentage of K class made up of school's preschool class:** N/A. **Admission evaluation requirements for K:** Screening, school visit, tours and preschool recommendation. **Other grades:** Transcripts, shadowing, school tours, previous school teacher questionnaire and interview with principal. **Preferences:** N/P. **What sort of student do you best serve?** N/P.

COSTS

Latest tuition: From $6,300 (participating) to $8,350 (non-participating). **Sibling discount:** N/P. **Tuition includes:** Lunch: N/P; Transportation: No; Laptop computer: No; Other: N/A. **Tuition increases:** N/P. **Other costs:** Registration fees: $1,060 K-5; $1,260 G6-8. **Percentage of students receiving financial aid:** N/P. **Financial aid application deadline:** Call for date. Financial aid is based on need. **Average grant:** N/P. **Percentage of grants of half-tuition or more:** N/P. **Donations:** Participating families are required to participate in school sponsored fundraisers such as the walkathon, candy sale, e-script, Columbus Day Bazaar, spring fundraiser, faculty sponsored fashion show.

School's Mission Statement

"Saints Peter and Paul Salesian School follows the educational method of St. John Bosco providing students a well-rounded academic experience and a strong spiritual formation based on reason, religion and loving kindness. We believe in the uniqueness of each individual child and strive to provide an environment that allows each child to utilize his or her talents to become good citizens of this world and the next."

Academic Program

Philosophy: N/P. **Foreign language:** Spanish. **Computer training:** N/P. **No. of computers available for students:** N/P. **No. of hours weekly of:** Art- N/P; Drama- N/P; Music- N/P; Computers- N/P; Foreign Language- N/P; PE- N/P. **Outdoor education:** N/P. **Grading:** N/P. **Average nightly homework:** 20 min. in K-2; 45 min. in G3-4; 60 min. in G5; 90 min. in G6-8. **Percentage of students participating in Johns Hopkins Center for Talented Youth Program:** N/P. **Other indicators of academic success:** N/P. **High schools attended by latest graduating class:** Riordan, SHCP, SI, Mercy-SF, Mercy-Burlingame, Convent, Bay, Lowell, Washington, Galileo.

Faculty

Ethnicity: N/P. **Percentage of teachers with graduate degrees:** N/P. **Percentage with current California credential:** N/P. **Faculty selection/training:** N/P. **Teacher/student ratio:** N/P. **Special subject teachers:** N/P. **Average teacher tenure:** 15 years.

Middle School

Description: G6-8, departmentalized. **Teacher/student ratio:** 12:1 in G6 language arts; 14:1 in G7-8 math, science, and language arts. **Elective courses offered:** N/P. **Achievement tracking in:** N/P. **Student social events:** N/P.

Student Support Services

Number of Licensed Counselors on staff: One part-time. **Counselor/ student ratio:** N/P. **Learning specialists on staff:** One reading specialist. **Learning differences/disabilities support:** N/P. **High school placement support:** Yes.

Student Conduct and Health: N/P.

Athletics: N/P.

Campus/Campus Life

Campus description: N/P. **Library:** Yes. **Sports facility:** N/P. **Computer lab:** Yes. **Theater/Arts facilities:** Yes. **Science Lab:** Yes. **Lunch program:** Daily. **Bus service:** N/P. **Uniform/dress code:** Uniform. **Opportunities for community service:** Students are encouraged to join the Salesian Service Learning committee which addresses the needs of those less fortunate by spearheading food, clothing and toy drives.

Extended Day

Morning care: Begins at 7:30 a.m. (no charge). **After-school care:** Until 5:30 p.m. **Grade levels:** PK-8. **Cost:** $200/month, drop in $13/hour for PK-2; Salesian Boys' and Girls' Club for G3-8 for $10/year. **Drop-in care available:** Yes. **Coverage over major holidays:** N/P. **Homework help:** N/P. **Snacks:** N/P. **Staff/student ratio:** N/P. **After-school classes:** Contemporary/Jazz dance, academic chess, Mandarin. **Cost:** N/P.

Summer Programs: N/P.

Parent Involvement

Parent/teacher communication: Parent-teacher conferences, progress reports, report cards, website, e-mail/voice mail, weekly principal letter. **Participation requirements:** 30 hours/year for 2 parent families and 15 for single parent families. **Parent education programs offered?** N/P.

What Sets the School Apart From Others

"The administration, faculty and staff of Saints Peter and Paul Salesian School take a holistic approach in developing future citizens in mind, body and spirit. The preventive system of St. John Bosco uses reason, religion and loving kindness to guide our students to become responsible citizens of heaven and earth."

How Families Characterize School

Parent comment(s): "Saints Peter and Paul Salesian School has a strong parent community and an exceptional faculty; service learning activities allow students to reach out to the community and those in need; wonderful communication with parents, teachers and students; structured learning environment where the children know what to expect each day; low turnover of staff."
Student comment(s): "Saints Peter and Paul Salesian School provides a safe environment; it's a place where I feel welcome and am encouraged to do my best; helps me open doors to new opportunities; teachers use every day examples in class to help us understand the topic they are

teaching; I like that we are one big family and that everyone helps and cares about each other."

SAN DOMENICO SCHOOL
1500 Butterfield Road
San Anselmo, CA 94960
(415) 258-1905 *fax (415) 258-1906*
www.sandomenico.org

Dr. David Behrs, Head of School

GENERAL
Coed PK-8 day school, girls day and boarding G9-12. Founded in 1850. Independent. Catholic, "Welcoming students of all faiths." (35% Catholic). **Member:** CAIS, NAIS, NCGS, TABS, CBSA, BADA, BAAD. **Enrollment:** Approx. 525, with 400 in PK-8. **Average class size:** N/P. **Accreditation:** WASC/CAIS (6-year term: 2007-13). **Endowment:** $5.5 million. **School year:** Aug.-June. **School day:** Approx. 8:15 a.m. to 3:10 p.m. (varies by grade).

STUDENT BODY ETHNICITY
82% Caucasian (non-Latino), 12% Asian, 3% multi-racial, 2% African-American, 1% Latino.

ADMISSION
Applications due: Jan. (call for date). **Application fee:** $100. **Application process:** Call to request a tour and application packet. **No. of applications:** N/P. **No. of K spaces:** 44. **Percentage of K class made up of school's preschool class:** 75%. **Admission evaluation requirements for K:** Parent tour and meeting, student screening and school visit, PK teacher's recommendation. **Other grades:** Parent tour and meeting, student screening and campus visit, transcripts, teacher recommendations, standardized test scores (ISEE for G6-8). **Preferences:** N/P. **What sort of student do you best serve?** "Engaged students and creative thinkers."

COSTS
Latest tuition: $9,975 for PK, $18,600 for K, $21,000 for G1-3, $21,750 for G4-5, $22,500 for G6-8. **Sibling discount:** None. **Tuition includes:** Lunch: Yes; Transportation: Yes; Laptop computer: No; Other: N/A. **Tuition increases:** N/P. **Other costs:** Approx. $395-$600 for Science

Camp in G4-7. **Percentage of students receiving financial aid:** N/P. **Financial aid application deadline:** Jan. (call for date). Financial aid is based on need. **Average grant:** N/P. **Percentage of grants of half-tuition or more:** N/P. **Donations:** Voluntary donations for the annual fund, auctions, and endowment.

School's Mission Statement

"We celebrate diversity recognizing God's presence in ourselves and in all of creation. We explore and develop the unique gifts of each individual in mind, heart, body and spirit. We inspire inquiry and provide a strong academic foundation for lifelong intellectual growth. We recognize what it means to be human in a global community and respond with integrity to the needs and challenges of our time."

Academic Program

Philosophy: "The overall philosophy of San Domenico's curriculum, PK through 12, is to ensure a dynamic, relevant educational program by using a model of connected learning that is based upon integrated, inter-disciplinary and thematic learning." **Foreign languages:** Spanish K-5, Spanish and French G6-8. **Computer training:** "Primary School- computer labs; Middle School-classrooms." **No. of computers available for students:** 350. **No. of hours weekly of:** Art- 2-3; Drama-N/P; Music- 2; Computers- 2; Foreign language- 2-6; PE- 2-3. **Outdoor education:** N/P. **Grading:** A-F, beginning in G3. **Average nightly homework:** 20 min. to 2 hours. Posted on the Internet: Yes. **Percentage of students participating in Johns Hopkins Center for Talented Youth Program:** N/A. 10% of students participate in the Stanford EPGY program. **Other indicators of academic success:** "Standardized tests, academic performance, school median profile on ERB/CTP scores is above independent school median profile and high school placement." **High schools attended by latest graduating class:** San Domenico, Bay, Branson, Drew, MA, MC, SI, Stuart Hall, University, Urban, Drake, Redwood, Tamalpais.

Faculty

Ethnicity: 97% Caucasian (non-Latino), 3% African-American. **Percentage of teachers with graduate degrees:** 82%. **Percentage with current California credential:** N/P. **Faculty selection/training:** N/P. **Teacher/student ratio:** 1:12. **Special subject teachers:** Art, vocal music, music conservatory, computers, science, PE, religious studies, sustainability, Spanish, and French (G6-8). **Average teacher tenure:** 13 years.

MIDDLE SCHOOL
Description: Departmentalized G6-8. **Teacher/student ratio:** 1:12. **Elective courses offered:** Yes. **Achievement tracking in:** Math. **Student social events:** Daily morning meeting, quarterly Pizza & Movie Nights, 1-2 day retreats, Spirit Week, excursions and parties.

STUDENT SUPPORT SERVICES
No. of Licensed Counselors on staff: Two full-time. **Counselor/student ratio:** 1:200. **Learning specialists on staff:** One. **Learning differences/ disabilities support:** "We can work successfully with students with mild to moderate learning differences and assist parents in locating support services; after-school support available in Middle School." **High school placement support:** Counseling by Division Head and High School Advisement Counselor; 7th grade Parent Night, High School Packet, weekly 8th grade advisory dedicated to high school advisement.

STUDENT CONDUCT AND HEALTH
Code of conduct: "San Domenico is a community dedicated to learning. The primary focus of discipline is directed towards helping students become responsible and mature, to accept the consequences of their actions, and to become persons of integrity and self-discipline." **Prevention education/awareness addressed in:** Integrated into the curriculum, including Life Skills workshops and counselor support. Full-time nurse on campus.

ATHLETICS
Sports offered: Cross-country (G3-5), girls volleyball (G5-8), basketball, track and field, boys flag football (G6-8). **Team play begins in:** G5.

CAMPUS/CAMPUS LIFE
Campus description: "515 spectacular acres of hills and fields, creek and one acre organic garden with outdoor kitchen." **Library:** Three separate areas for Primary, Middle and Upper School students with 23,000 volumes and 20 computers. **Sports facilities:** "State-of-the-art Athletic Center, dance and yoga studio, sports fields, pool, and tennis courts." **Theater/Arts facilities:** Primary School and Middle School Art Studios, new Performing Arts center, 2 auditoriums for smaller performances. **Computer labs:** 'Yes." **Science lab:** Yes. **Lunch program:** Cafeteria with choice of hot entrees including vegetarian. **Bus service:** Yes, 9 routes including Marin, San Francisco and the East Bay. **Uniforms/dress code:** Uniforms. **Opportunities for community service:** "San Domenico is dedicated to service learning in our community and globally."

Extended Day
Morning care: None. **After-school care:** Until 2:50 p.m. for PK and 4:30 p.m. for K-5. **Grade levels:** PK-5. **Cost:** $30/day (2 day minimum) for PK, drop in PK is $35, $15 flat fee for K-5. **Drop-in care available:** No. **Coverage over major holidays:** Yes. **Homework help:** Yes. **Snacks:** Provided. **Staff/student ratio:** 1:15. **After-school classes:** In addition to sports, the school offers drama for school musicals; private music lessons for piano, violin, cello, flute, saxophone, clarinet, voice, recorder, guitar, viola, oboe, harp. **Cost:** "Varies."

Summer Programs
The school offers a variety of summer programs, most recently, SportsKids for G2-7 ($250/week or $425/2 weeks); Volleyball for G4-8 ($250/week); Northern CA Elite Basketball Camp for G3-7 ($195/4-day week); Tennis Camp for ages 6-15 yrs. ($300/week, half days a.m. or p.m./ $450/week full days); Horseback Riding (Beginner $400/week, half day, Intermediate $400/week half day or $700/week full day, Advanced $300/week half day); Secret Garden for GK-2 ($220/week); Explorers for GK-5 ($175/week, half day or $350/week, full day); Lego Free Play for GK-5 ($150/week half day or $250/week full day); Lego Mindstorm NXT 2.0 Robotics for G4-5 ($250/week); Summer Arts Intensive for G2-6 ($425/week) and G6-12 ($425/week); Summer Music Lessons at our Conservatory for children and adults.

Parent Involvement
Parent/teacher communication: Conferences, meetings with Division Head and Head of School, website, e-mail, newsletter. **Participation requirements:** "Parent participation is welcomed and encouraged, and is coordinated by the Parent Service Association." Parent education programs? Yes, meetings, lectures and workshops.

What Sets the School Apart From Others
"San Domenico is an innovative and challenging school in a spectacular setting with a state-of-the-art Music Conservatory, and arts and athletic facilities. Our talented faculty helps students develop qualities of leadership, independent thinking and spiritual development. We are known for our commitment to sustainability, service learning and joyful celebrations."

How Families Characterize School
Parent comment(s): "A San Domenico education encompasses the whole child: academically, athletically and spiritually." • "I am amazed at

how much the teachers know about my kids, how they learn and think."
"San Domenico has given our entire family a sense of community and
friendship." • "The teachers at San Domenico are dedicated to their
trade and to their students, are very responsive and hardworking, and are
inspirational in getting the kids to think in different ways. I can see the
difference they've made in my child."
Student comment(s): "At San Domenico, there is something for
everyone." • "We are so lucky to go to San Domenico with all the
opportunities we have here." • "I love having really fun teachers!"
"Adults here are supportive and nurturing. They care about our academics
and do all they can to help us succeed."

SAN FRANCISCO DAY SCHOOL
350 Masonic Ave. (at Golden Gate) (Western Edition/Inner Richmond)
San Francisco, CA 94118
(415) 931-2422 *fax (415) 931-1753*
www.sfds.net

David E. Jackson, Head of School
Homa Hanjani Tabatabai, Director of Admission, htabatabai@sfds.net

GENERAL
Coed K-8 day school. Founded in 1981. Independent. Nonprofit.
Member: CAIS, NAIS, POCIS, BADA. **Enrollment:** Approx. 400.
Average class size: 22-23. **Accreditation:** CAIS (6-year term: 2006-
12). **Endowment:** Approx. $11 million. **School year:** Sept.-June. **School
day:** 8:15 a.m. to 2:15 p.m. for K; 8:15 a.m. to 3 p.m. for G1-2; 8:15 a.m.
to 3:30 p.m. for G3-4; 8 a.m. to 3:30 p.m. for G5-8. (G2-8 have 3 p.m.
dismissal Mon. and Fri.).

STUDENT BODY ETHNICITY
63% Caucasian (non-Latino), 20% multi-racial, 8% Asian, 3% Latino,
3% African-American, 2% other.

ADMISSION
Applications due: Early Jan. (call for date). **Application fee:** $90.
Application process: Starts with an evening open house where
prospective families meet the Head of School, tour the school, and
talk to teachers. If interested, families submit an application, and then
schedule a 20-minute parent interview (Oct.-early Jan.) and a student
visit (K visits take place in Jan.; G1-8 visits typically take place in
Feb.). Optional daytime tours are also available to families that have

submitted an application. **No. of applications:** N/P. **No. of K spaces:** N/P. **Percentage of K class made up of school's preschool class:** N/A. **Admission evaluation requirements for K:** Age 5 by Aug. 1st of K year, screening, school visit, parent interview, and recommendations. **Other grades:** Screening, school visit, grades, test scores, parent interview, recommendations, and the ERB. **Preferences:** Siblings. **What sort of student do you best serve?** "Children with intellectual curiosity and social skillfulness who come from families committed to supporting the school and their child's school experience."

Costs

Latest tuition: $24,720. **Sibling discount:** No. **Tuition includes:** Lunch: No; Transportation: No; Laptop computer: No; Other: N/A. **Tuition increases:** Approx. 6% annually. **Other costs:** None. **Percentage of students receiving financial aid:** Approx. 24%. **Financial aid application deadline:** Jan. (call for date). Financial aid is based on need. **Average grant:** $16,200. **Percentage of grants of half-tuition or more:** 71%. **Donations:** "All families are asked to support the growth of the school's programs and facilities by making the school a top priority for their annual giving. In the past 2 years, the school has celebrated 100% participation from the parents, faculty, and staff. San Francisco Day School also hosts an annual auction to fundraise for tuition assistance, as well as other smaller fundraisers throughout the year. There is a gap of about $1,800 between the tuition fee and the cost of education per child."

School's Mission Statement

"San Francisco Day School educates, nurtures, and inspires girls and boys of diverse backgrounds to achieve their highest academic and creative potential, to embrace ethical values, and to become active contributors to their communities. The cornerstones of San Francisco Day School are: academic excellence; diversity and inclusiveness in our community, strong partnership between family and school; shared values of compassion, integrity, and responsibility; active involvement in the city."

Academic Program

Philosophy: "Students acquire the skills of lifelong learners, well equipped for the world beyond the Day School. They have command of the essential skills of reading, writing, speaking, computing, and problem solving. They are expected to master technology to access and exchange information, to solve problems, and to assist in individual research. They learn to value and appreciate their creative potential in the arts and master a wide range of physical skills. They are aware of their gifts and challenges as learners and come to understand their own and other learning styles. The curriculum developed at San Francisco Day School relies significantly on students thinking critically and working collaboratively." **Foreign languages:** Spanish G4-6; Spanish or Latin G7-8. **Computer training:** "Integrated into the classroom curriculum for all students. Up-to-date iMac lab as well as roving carts of wireless laptops for class and individual use." **No. of computers available for students:** Approx. 100. **No. of hours weekly of:** Art- 1.5; Music- 1-1.5; Computer- N/P; Foreign language- 1.5 in G4, 2.5 in G5, 3.75 in G6-8; PE- 1.5; Library- 1. **Outdoor education:** N/P. **Grading:** Twice yearly progress reports consisting of narrative and progress grid. Letter grades begin in G5. **Average nightly homework:** 20 min. in G2; 30 min. in G3; 1 hr. in G4; 1.5 hrs. in G5-6; 2 hrs. in G7; 2.5 hrs. in G8. Posted on the Internet: Yes. **Percentage of students participating in Johns Hopkins Center for Talented Youth Program:** N/P. **Other indicators of academic success:** N/P. **High schools attended by latest graduating class:** N/P.

FACULTY
Ethnicity: 79% Caucasian (non-Latino), 4% Asian, 5% Multi-racial, 5% other, 4% African-American, 3% Latino. **Percentage of teachers with graduate degrees:** Approx. 50%. **Percentage with current California credential:** Approx. 75%. **Faculty selection/training:** "BA/BS and relevant teaching experience." **Teacher/student ratio:** 1:10-11 in K-5, 1:22-23 in G6-8. **Special subject teachers:** Art, music, PE, technology. **Average teacher tenure:** Approx. 14 years.

MIDDLE SCHOOL
Description: "The Upper School (middle school) at SFDS is G5-8. In G5 the students are in homeroom-based settings for core subjects and morning meeting. In G6-8 the students transition to an advisory program and different teachers for all core and extracurricular subjects. In the second semester of G5, the students begin to receive letter grades as well as narrative comments and a rubric based assessment. Students in G6-8 participate in small advisory groups each school day. Faculty advisors facilitate a program to develop character values, build peer relationships, improve student performance, and work on service learning projects together. Service learning is a teaching and learning strategy that combines principles of experiential learning with service to the community. Each grade level has a theme to guide students' study and work in service learning. The SFDS Student Congress is made up

of 22 girls and boys. There are four elected representatives for each grade, one boy and one girl per class. In addition to the reps, there are 2 treasurers, 2 secretaries, and 2 presidents. Student Council is in charge of planning fundraisers, food days, spirit weeks, dances, and parties. Students Striving for Diversity is a self-selected group that meets once a week during lunch to discuss issues of diversity and multiculturalism. They make presentations during school assemblies. Some of the topics they have covered are self-identity, homophobia, and human rights activists." **Teacher/student ratio:** 1:10-11 in G5, 1:22-23 in G6-8. Each class is supported by Learning Resource Teachers, and Associate, or Co-Teachers. **Elective courses offered:** N/P. **Achievement tracking in:** Algebra. **Student social events:** School picnics, performances, Concert for Community, Copa Soccer Tournament, Sally's Day Out, 8th Grade Graduation, dances.

STUDENT SUPPORT SERVICES
No. of Licensed Counselors on staff: Two part-time. **Counselor/ student ratio:** N/P. **Learning specialists on staff:** Eight full-time, 1 part-time. **Learning differences/disabilities support:** "The learning resource center is a 3-person department providing assessment, direct instruction, and consultation with faculty, administrators, and parents to help students reach their full academic potential. The services include the following: early screening in K and G1; educational screening for learning strengths and weaknesses in G2-8 as needed; referrals for outside in-depth testing and/or remediation; remedial instruction in language arts skills for students in G1-3 needing additional support; weekly support in G4 with language arts curriculum; assistance to teachers regarding strategies and accommodations for students with learning differences; learning specialists who attend weekly grade level meetings; office hours for upper school students requesting additional support; assistance with interpretation and analysis of ERB testing in G3-8. The school holds the same expectations and course requirements for all students, but will make reasonable efforts to provide accommodations for students with learning differences." **High school placement support:** "The high school counseling program is for 8th graders and their families. The Secondary School Placement Counselor works closely with students/ parents to gather information about high schools, assess students' strengths, and make sound choices for continuing their education."

STUDENT CONDUCT AND HEALTH
Code of conduct: "When the school's behavioral expectations are not met, classroom teachers will intervene and communicate with the

parents. A teacher may issue a discipline slip to document the event. If the inappropriate behavior is particularly harmful or is a repeated infraction, the Division Head will contact the parents to discuss ways to resolve the situation and help the student meet community standards. Students who demonstrate a pattern of repeated occurrences may be placed on probation while the administration considers whether continued enrollment at SFDS is appropriate. In instances of extremely inappropriate, persistent, or disruptive behavior, the administration may take more severe measures, including suspension or expulsion from school." **Prevention education and awareness addressed in:** "The school recognizes the primary role of the family in educating children about sexuality and drugs. Classes are prepared with the age level of students in mind and with the expectation that students and parents will discuss these topics at home. The presentation of these subjects at school is matter-of-fact, with a focus on the natural development of the human body and the effects harmful agents can produce. Teachers and the school counselor create a safe and comfortable forum in which students discuss situations they are likely to encounter while growing up in today's society. The G5 curriculum covers biology of reproduction and puberty, and sexual choice. The G6 curriculum covers drugs and alcohol. The G7 curriculum covers sexuality/intimacy. The G8 curriculum covers HIV/AIDS, review of substance use, sexuality and social pressures."

ATHLETICS
Sports offered: Soccer, cross-country, volleyball, and basketball. **Team play begins in:** G5.

CAMPUS/CAMPUS LIFE
Campus description: The school has a California mission-style campus with several courtyards on the corner of Masonic and Golden Gate Ave. The campus includes a library, classrooms, computer lab, science labs, cafeteria, gym, 2 music rooms, and 2 art studios. **Library:** Large 2-floor library with 20,000 volumes; 90 computers for student use, all with internet access; 20 subscription databases; and remote access for all catalogs and databases. **Sports facilities:** Gym, rooftop and ground level play areas. The school uses the USF field across the street for sports and physical education. **Theater/Arts facilities:** Gym/performing arts center. **Computer lab:** One lab, 2 traveling carts with enough laptops for class use, and a computer area in the library. **Science lab:** Two labs. **Lunch program:** Lunches may be purchased daily for approx. $5.50. **Bus service:** No. **Uniforms/dress code:** All students are expected to

wear clean and neat clothing. **Opportunities for community service:** Available for all grades and families.

Extended Day
Morning care: 7:30 a.m. teacher supervision until school begins. **After-school care:** Until 6 p.m. **Grade levels:** K-8. K-3 have outdoor play, games, sports, cooking, art, music, science, and drama; G4-8 have after school enrichment classes, sports, study hall, or Homework Café. **Cost:** $8.50/hour with prepaid blocks of 25 hours or more. **Drop-in care available:** Yes. All children not picked up at 3:30 p.m. are automatically sent to the extended care program as "drop-ins" at the cost of $12/hour. Any parent may arrange for drop-in care on the same day of use. **Coverage over major holidays:** No. **Homework help:** Yes. **Snacks:** Provided. **Staff/student ratio:** Approx. 1:10. **After-school classes:** Art, computer, film making, theater, karate, supervised study, gymnastics, jewelry making, Spanish and Mandarin language have been offered. Classes change each quarter and are available to all students. **Cost:** $20/class. Musical instrument lessons are available for $38 a lesson (30 min. lessons).

Summer Programs: N/P.

Parent Involvement
Parent/teacher communication: Weekly all-school updates via e-mail, monthly electronic newsletter, e-mail/voice-mail available for all faculty and staff, and weekly classroom newsletters. Twice yearly parent/teacher conferences. **Participation requirements:** "Parents are not required, but are encouraged to give time to the school. Opportunities include fundraising, mailings, art studio volunteers, tour guides, room parents, library assistants, gardening, and bringing any special talents or knowledge they have to the classroom and the community." **Parent education programs offered?** The parent-led and run Parent Education Committee meets several times a year to discuss current topics in education that reflect the SFDS mission. The committee also sponsors events like movie nights and lectures.

What Sets the School Apart From Others
"Exceptional faculty, well-equipped facility, strong commitment to best educational practices in each discipline, supportive families, thoughtful approach to benefits of coeducation, student leadership opportunities, active use of cultural and artistic resources of the city, and a diverse and multicultural community."

How Families Characterize School
Parent comment(s): "The community is truly warm and welcoming and the education program is outstanding."
Student comment(s): "Teachers really know and care about us."

San Francisco Friends School
250 Valencia Street (between 14th St. and Duboce)(Mission District)
San Francisco, CA 94103
(415) 565-0400 *fax (415) 565-0401*
www.sffriendsschool.org

Cathy Hunter, Head of School, chunter@sffriendsschool.org
Yvette Bonaparte, Director of Admission, ybonaparte@sffriendsschool.org

General
Coed K-8 day school. Founded in 2002. Independent. Nonprofit. **Member:** CAIS, CASE, BADA, BAISHA, ISBOA, POCIS. **Enrollment:** Approx. 420. **Average class size:** 22 for K-4, 18 for G5-8. **Accreditation:** NAIS, CAIS, Friends Council of Education (FCE) (term N/P). **Endowment:** N/A. **School year:** Sept.-June. **School day:** 8:30 a.m. to 2:30 p.m. for K-3; 8:20 a.m.-3:15 p.m. for G4-8.

Student Body Ethnicity
66% Caucasian (non-Latino), 19% multi-racial, 6% Asian, 4% Latino, 4% African-American, 1% Middle-Eastern.

Admission
Applications due: Dec. (call for date). **Application fee:** $75. **Application process:** School tours including evening and Saturday open houses, application, teacher recommendation, parent interview, student visit. School tours begin mid-Oct. **No. of applications:** Approx. 300. **No. of K spaces:** 44. **Percentage of K class made up of school's preschool class:** N/A. **Admission evaluation requirements for K:** Age 5 by Aug. 1 of K year; screening/playdate, school visit, recommendations, parent interview. **Other grades:** All of the above, transcripts and standardized test scores from previous school. **Preferences:** Siblings, faculty children, Quaker affiliation. **What sort of student do you best serve?** "We seek students and families who value the school's Quaker mission and philosophy."

COSTS

Latest tuition: $23,345. **Sibling discount:** None. **Tuition includes:** Lunch: No; Transportation: No; Laptop computer: Yes; Other: N/A. **Tuition increases:** Approx. 2%-5% annually. **Other costs:** N/P. **Percentage of students receiving financial aid:** 25%. **Financial aid application deadline:** Feb. (call for date). Based on need. **Average grant:** $15,900. **Percentage of grants of half-tuition or more:** 77%. **Donations:** Voluntary for annual fund, capital campaign, auction.

SCHOOL'S MISSION STATEMENT

"San Francisco Friends School is dedicated to educating, inspiring, and nurturing girls and boys in the tradition of Quaker learning. The daily life of our school is rooted in the Quaker values of simplicity, integrity, mutual respect, peaceful problem-solving, and service to others. We strive to develop in each child intellectual curiosity and passion for learning. We challenge students with academic rigor, while honoring individual strengths and abilities. We seek to create a community that embraces children and families of all backgrounds, recognizing that diversity is essential to the vitality of our school. We engage with the larger world around us, working toward the Quaker ideal of a caring and just society."

ACADEMIC PROGRAM

Philosophy: "SFFS provides a nurturing and stimulating environment in which we encourage each child's natural love of learning; a focus on simplicity and clarity; a respectful, kind, and inclusive community; cooperative and collaborative learning; the development of independence, resourcefulness, and responsibility; an appropriate balance of challenges and successes." **Foreign languages:** Spanish. **Computer training:** Computer curriculum begins in G3. **No. of computers available for students:** 190. **No. of hours weekly of:** Art- 1-2; Drama- 1-2; Music- 1-2; Computers- N/P ("integrated into the curriculum in G3-8"); Foreign language- 1-3, PE- 1.5-2. **Outdoor education:** "Built into science curriculum starting in K." **Grading:** Progress reports with progress grid and narrative comments each semester. **Average nightly homework:** Beginning in 20 min. in G2; 30 min. in G3; 40 min. in G4; 50 min. in G5; 1-2 hrs. in G6-8. Posted on the Internet: No. **Percentage of students participating in Johns Hopkins Center for Talented Youth Program:** N/A. **Other indicators of academic success:** N/P. **High schools attended by latest graduating class:** The school's first eighth grade class will graduate in June 2011.

FACULTY

Ethnicity: "29% faculty of color." **Percentage of teachers with graduate degrees:** 51%. **Percentage with current California credential:** 33%. **Faculty selection/training:** Several years of experience, degree, Quaker affiliation. **Teacher/student ratio:** 1:11. **Special subject teachers:** Art, music, drama, Spanish, PE, library. **Average teacher tenure:** 5 years.

MIDDLE SCHOOL

Description: "The San Francisco Friends School middle school comprises G5-8 and is another entry point because we accept 10-12 new students to our middle school. There are three sections at each grade level, with 15-18 students in each section. Teachers embed service learning, outdoor and environmental education, study skills, and character education into the main strands of the curriculum—language, history, math, and science—and constantly strive to bring the values of our Quaker mission to life. Our advisory program is of central importance to our students' development. Advisors work with groups of 10-12 students to coach and support their academic, social, and emotional growth. Students meet in mixed 5th/6th and 7th/8th homerooms, with the possibility of 'looping' with the same advisor for 2 years. Advising groups cover topics related to physical and emotional health, communication and self-advocacy skills, the overall social climate, and the skills that support academic success. Advisors help middle school students develop a reliable moral compass, and understand the difference between internal and external motivation. Our middle school students take 4 significant trips during the 5th through 8th grade years. Each of these trips is integrated thoroughly with curriculum and include camping in Mendocino, cultural immersion trips to Nicaragua and the Supai region of Arizona, and the 8th grade trip to Washington DC and Gettysburg." **Teacher/student ratio:** 1:15 **Elective courses offered:** Yes. **Achievement tracking in:** N/A. **Student social events:** N/P.

STUDENT SUPPORT SERVICES

No. of Licensed Counselors on staff: None. **Counselor/student ratio:** N/A. **Learning specialists on staff:** Three. **Learning differences/ disabilities support:** "Our Developmental Support Services Department provides early identification and early intervention. We provide flexible services available at school and recommendations for outside resources." **High school placement support:** "The High School Transition Team consists of our Head of Middle School, Head of School, Assistant Head of School, and Academic Dean. They provide support and guidance to students and parents throughout the application and transition process, helping with everything from identifying schools to considering how to complete applications in a timely and thorough fashion. Starting in the spring of their 7th grade year, each student meets with his or her parents and members of the team to begin the discussion about available options. Concurrently, students work on interviewing skills, test-taking strategies, essay-writing, application timelines and how to make informed decisions. As the process unfolds, we advocate for students to high schools where they have applied and provide information as requested by high school admissions committees."

STUDENT CONDUCT AND HEALTH

Code of conduct: "School-based behavioral program-responsive classroom. Honor each community member." **Prevention education and awareness addressed in:** Included in health curriculum which starts in K.

ATHLETICS

Sports offered: Cross-country, volleyball, basketball, and futsal, rock-climbing, ultimate Frisbee, flag football, dance, circus arts. **Team play begins in:** G5.

CAMPUS/CAMPUS LIFE

Campus description: "We moved into our permanent home in the refurbished Levi Strauss building in Sept. 2008. Our architect designed the school to retain the open, light feeling of the historic space, and honored the school's mission with close attention to sustainability and simplicity. The 80,000 square foot building consists of 3 floors which include classrooms, music studios, science labs, visual art studios, a spacious library and a Quaker meeting room. The designated spaces are supplemented with commons areas, offices, a dining hall and galleries. In the front of the building, a 10,000 square foot playground and garden provides ample space for recess, lunch and outdoor play. When construction of the third floor is complete, we will add additional classrooms, nature and outdoor education facilities and a 'black box' theatre." **Library:** "Our collection includes over 6,000 books. We also have a growing collection of periodicals, audio books, DVDs, digital and online collections of encyclopedias; computerized and online catalog." **Sports facilities:** Gymnasium and outdoor yard. **Theater/Arts facilities:** Two art studios, and a large multi-purpose room. **Computer lab:** Mobile laptop carts. All access is wireless and networked. **Science lab:** Two labs. **Lunch program:** Bag and hot lunches are delivered daily through outside vendor at an additional charge. **Bus service:** No. **Uniforms/**

dress code: No. **Opportunities for community service:** Yes, built into the curriculum for students, also available for parents who serve on our parent Community Involvement Committee.

EXTENDED DAY

Morning care: Begins at 7:45 a.m. **After-school care:** Until 6 p.m. **Grade levels:** K-8. **Cost:** Approx. $7/hour. Support is available for students with tuition assistance. **Drop-in care available:** Yes. **Coverage over major holidays:** Yes. **Homework help:** Yes. **Snacks:** Provided. **Staff/student ratio:** 1:10. **After-school classes:** Enrichment classes such as yoga, Mandarin, chess, woodworking, crafts, Spanish. **Cost:** Approx. $10/hour. Music lessons are available through the music department. Tuition assistance is available.

SUMMER PROGRAMS

Five week-long summer sessions are offered and open to any K-8 student. Children may enroll for single or multiple weeks. Offerings include Mural Painting, Cooking, Sewing, Photography, Web Design, High School Prep, Science, Basketball. Extended care is available until 6 p.m. **Cost:** $425/week; $7/hour for extended care.

PARENT INVOLVEMENT

Parent/teacher communication: Two conferences annually. Written progress reports twice a year; special link for parents to website, e-mail communication with parents, weekly newsletter. **Participation requirements:** Voluntary. **Parent education programs offered?** Yes. Topics include Quaker values, child development, parenting workshops.

WHAT SETS THE SCHOOL APART FROM OTHERS

"We are the only Quaker-based program in the Bay Area. SFFS is dedicated to educating, inspiring and nurturing girls and boys in the tradition of Quaker learning. Friends Schools have a 300-year tradition of academic excellence and thoughtful concern for the emotional and spiritual growth of children. Friends schools are much admired for their outstanding academic programs, grounded by strongly-held values and focus on social responsibility. There are a few significant aspects of our curriculum: learning through inquiry, reflection and service, along with a continual striving for academic vigor. Friends educators attend to the growth and development of each child's capacity for independent thought, creativity, and reflection."

How Families Characterize School

Parent comment(s): "The San Francisco Friends School curriculum is 'narrow and deep—the Quaker values of service, silent reflection, peaceful problem-solving and simplicity infuse the curriculum, and all of the programs and activities at the school."

Student comment(s): "All my friends are at Friends. My favorite subjects are science and chess—we do experiments in science, and then we write about what we learned. Sometimes when we go for a hike in Muir Woods, we sit and have quiet time so we can write about what we see in our journals."

The San Francisco School

300 Gaven Street (at Boylston) (Excelsior/Portola District)
San Francisco, CA 94134
(415) 239-5065 *fax (415) 239-4833*
www.sfschool.org

Steve Morris, Head of School, smorris@sfschool.org
Nina Wang, Director of Admission, nwang@sfschool.org

General

Coed PS-8 day school. Founded in 1966. Independent. Nonprofit. **Member:** CAIS, BADA, POCIS. **Enrollment:** Approx. 200 K-8. **Average class size:** 22. **Accreditation:** WASC/CAIS (term: 6 years, N/P dates). **Endowment:** Approx. $2 million. **School year:** Aug.-June. **School day:** 8:30 a.m. to 3 p.m.

Student Body Ethnicity

45% Caucasian (non-Latino), 25% Asian, 14% African-American, 13% Latino.

Admission

Applications due: Jan. (call for date). **Application fee:** $75. **Application process:** Kindergarten applicants must attend an open house prior to signing up for a tour. All other applicants may choose to attend an evening open house or daytime tour. They then submit records and recommendations. Interviews are scheduled after the Jan. application due date. **No. of applications:** 150 (50 for K, 100 for G1-8). **No. of K spaces:** Approx. 5. Key point of entry is 3-year old class. **Percentage of K class made up of school's preschool class:** Approx. 90%. **Admission**

evaluation requirements for K: In-class interview and assessment, recommendation. **Other grades:** Assessment, school visit, grades, recommendations. **Preferences:** Siblings. **What sort of student do you best serve?** "Academically prepared, inquisitive, compassionate and eager for the challenges ahead."

Costs

Latest tuition: $20,510 for PS-5; $22,120 for G6-8. **Sibling discount:** None. **Tuition includes:** Lunch: Yes; Transportation: No; Laptop computer: No; Other: Camping trips and 8th grade trip. **Tuition increases:** Approx. 3-5% annually. **Other costs:** Approx. $25 for other fees. **Percentage of students receiving financial aid:** 35%. **Financial aid application deadline:** Feb. (call for date). Financial aid is based on need. **Average grant:** N/P. **Percentage of grants of half-tuition or more:** 65%. **Donations:** Voluntary.

School's Mission Statement

"The San Francisco School cultivates and celebrates the intellectual, imaginative and humanitarian promise of each student in a community that practices mutual respect, embraces diversity and inspires a passion for learning."

Academic Program

Philosophy: See Mission Statement. **Foreign languages:** Spanish PS-8. **Computer training:** begins in G4. **No. of computers available for students:** Laptop carts for G4-8. **No. of hours weekly of:** Art-N/P; Drama- N/P; Music- N/P; Computers- N/P; Foreign language- N/P; PE- N/P. **Outdoor education:** Camping trips. **Grading:** A-F, beginning in G6. **Average nightly homework:** N/P. Posted on the Internet: N/P. **Percentage of students participating in Johns Hopkins Center for Talented Youth Program:** N/P. **Other indicators of academic success:** Awards at local and regional science fairs. **High schools attended by latest graduating class:** Bay, Crystal, Drew, Gateway, IHS, Leadership, Lick, Lincoln, Lowell, Midland, Riordan, SHCP, SOTA, Stevenson, Stuart Hall, SI, Thacher, University, Urban, Waldorf, Washington.

Faculty

Ethnicity: 65% Caucasian (non-Latino), "35% faculty/staff of color." **Percentage of teachers with graduate degrees:** 29%. **Percentage with current California credential:** 70%. **Faculty selection/training:** Experience, degree and teaching philosophy. **Teacher/student ratio:** Approx. 1:10. **Special subject teachers:** Art, music, Spanish, PE and technology. **Average teacher tenure:** 9 years.

MIDDLE SCHOOL

Description: "Commences in Grade 6. SFS middle school students learn accountability in an atmosphere that continually asks them to make decisions and to reflect on the wisdom of their choices. There is a strong emphasis on critical thinking, social justice and equity, environmental sustainability and stewardship." **Teacher/student ratio:** 1:15. **Elective courses offered:** Varies from year to year. **Achievement tracking in:** N/A. **Student social events:** Dances.

STUDENT SUPPORT SERVICES

No. of Licensed Counselors on staff: One part-time. **Counselor/student ratio:** 1:275. **Learning specialists on staff:** Three part-time. **Learning differences/disabilities support:** "The school works with student, teachers and family to identify strengths, learning styles and sources of learning difficulties, and to recommend in-class, at-home, and outside services and interventions as necessary. The school also has an on-campus tutorial program as part of its extended care program." **High school placement support:** "At SFS, our high school placement counselor, faculty and administrators are well-versed in guiding families through the application process and helping them select the schools that best fit the strengths of each student. In any given year, our graduating class of 32 students goes to 15-16 different high schools, most of which are their top choice schools."

STUDENT CONDUCT AND HEALTH

Code of conduct: "The middle school program is specifically designed to nurture and guide students on their journey to becoming responsible, thoughtful and actively engaged adults." **Prevention education and awareness programs:** Programs cover drugs, sex, health and harassment.

ATHLETICS

Sports offered: Volleyball, basketball, futsal, cross-country. **Team play begins in:** G6 (intramural). School sports teams organized by parents begin in K.

CAMPUS/CAMPUS LIFE

Campus description: "The school resembles a quiet village tucked in a corner of a bustling metropolis. We have managed to retain an amazing outdoor space which we call our adventure playground. Many parents are amazed to find such a lush and green campus within the confines of the city." **Library:** Yes. **Sports facilities:** Outdoor basketball courts, use of nearby fields and gymnasium. **Theater/Arts facilities:** Multi-purpose room, large music room and art studio with kilns. The school rents nearby theaters for performances. **Computer lab:** No. Wireless laptop carts. **Science lab:** Yes, for middle school. **Lunch program:** Yes, for PS-G5. **Bus service:** No. **Uniforms/dress code:** "Respectful." **Opportunities for community service:** Yes.

Extended Day
Morning care: Begins at 7:30 a.m. **After-school care:** Until 6 p.m. **Grade levels:** All. **Cost:** Approx. $8-10/hour. **Drop-in care available:** Yes. **Coverage over major holidays:** No. **Homework help:** Yes. **Snacks:** Provided. **Staff/student ratio:** 1:10. **After-school classes:** Elementary students sign up for specialty classes, which can include classes such as edible art, fencing, academic chess, instrumental music classes, hip hop dancing, yoga, cooking, art, academic enrichment and team sports. Middle school students can choose student government, supervised homework or other specialty clubs and classes such as amnesty international. **Cost:** "Varies."

Summer Programs
"SFS offers a variety of day camps at the school, including one for preschool students, ages 4 to 6. Elementary and middle school students can choose from a variety of academic and athletic programs and a Shakespeare camp. Current offerings can be referenced online." **Cost:** "Varies."

Parent Involvement
Parent/teacher communication: Conferences, website, e-mail, newsletters. **Participation requirements:** "Expected but not required." **Parent education programs offered?** Yes.

What Sets the School Apart From Others
"The School embraces San Francisco's ethnic, cultural, and economic diversity. Our progressive approach to education encourages children to develop self-reliance, solid academic skills, integrity, and a sense of social values. • The school is respected for a strong sense of community, personal attention to students, and a dynamic arts program. Our students graduate academically prepared, inquisitive, compassionate, and eager for the challenges ahead. • The San Francisco School program is designed by the faculty to stimulate conceptual understanding, critical thinking, and creative expression. Teachers encourage students to approach learning in a variety of ways and through various disciplines, and subject matter from a given discipline is often interwoven throughout

the program. Overarching themes such as 'When are we learning?' in Kindergarten, and 'How does education transform society?' in the Eighth Grade provide the student perspective that binds all facets of the school experience. • The San Francisco School is committed to ethnic and cultural diversity, with over 50% students of color and an inclusive ethos. Family economic diversity, also an important goal, is achieved through a moderate tuition, the school's location in a modest neighborhood, and a strong indexed tuition program which supports more than 30% of students on reduced tuition. • Parents, staff, and faculty form a collaborative atmosphere, where there is a clear sense of adults working together in a vibrant learning community. Both teachers and parents serve on the Board of Trustees. The administrative model recognizes the value of strong faculty leadership and serious professional development. All are committed to creating a school where students can live and learn with confidence and joy."

How Parents/Students Characterize School
Parent comment(s): "Like a village in an urban atmosphere."
Student comment(s): N/P.

San Francisco Waldorf School
2938 Washington Street (at Divisadero) (Pacific Heights)
San Francisco, CA 94115
(415) 931-2750 *fax (415) 931-0590*
www.sfwaldorf.org

Erin Kemp, Grade School Chair ekemp@sfwaldorf.org
Dan Ingoglia, Head of Administration dingoglia@sfwaldorf.org
Lori Grey, Enrollment Director lgrey@sfwaldorf.org

General
Coed PS-12 day school. High school is on a separate campus. Founded in 1979. Independent. Nonprofit. **Member:** NAIS, AWSNA. **Enrollment:** 426. **Average class size:** 25. **Accreditation:** WASC (7-year term: 2009-26), AWSNA. **Endowment:** N/P. **School year:** Sept.-June. **School day:** 8:30 a.m. to 1 p.m. for K; 8:30 a.m. to 2:30 p.m. for G1-3; 8:30 a.m. to 3:20 p.m. G4-8.

Student Body Ethnicity
70% Caucasian (non-Latino), 13% multi-racial, 8% Asian, 6% Latino, 3% African-American.

ADMISSION
Applications due: Jan. (call for date). **Application fee:** $50-$75. **Application process:** Tour/Open House, playdate or interview. **No. of applications:** 150. **No. of K spaces:** 30. **Percentage of K class made up of school's preschool class:** 65%. **Admission evaluation requirements for K:** Interview, student evaluation form. **Other grades:** Interview, transcripts, class visit. **Preferences:** Siblings. **What sort of student do you best serve?** "Waldorf education meets the needs of the developing human being, and therefore serves a very wide range of students."

COSTS
Latest tuition: $17,700-$18,800. **Sibling discount:** 10% for the first sibling, 20% for the second, 30% for the third. **Tuition includes:** Lunch: No; Transportation: No; Laptop computer: No; Other: Snack and lunch in the preschool, snack in the K. **Tuition increases:** Approx. 2-4% annually. **Other costs:** Approx. $200-$650 which include tuition insurance, sports program fees (G6-8), field trip fees (G3-8). **Percentage of students receiving financial aid:** 35%. **Financial aid application deadline:** Jan. (call for date). Financial aid is based on need and available pool of money. **Average grant:** N/P. **Percentage of grants of half-tuition or more:** N/P. **Donations:** Voluntary.

SCHOOL'S MISSION STATEMENT
"Our purpose is to provide a Waldorf education in San Francisco for children from early childhood through high school. Academic excellence, social responsibility, and the recognition of each individual's gifts are the guiding educational ideals. The curriculum integrates the student's developmental needs with intellectual and artistic skills. Our deeply committed faculty works together to foster each student's sense of self-reliance, concern for community, and moral purpose. The student's educated, disciplined imagination will be the foundation for leadership into the future."

ACADEMIC PROGRAM
Philosophy: "Each child is viewed as a growing human being of body, soul and spirit, all of which must be nurtured by education. The school places human development and art at the center of its work and curriculum. It prepares young people to meet the world with inner confidence, to trust in the value of each human being, and to think and work with initiative in their lives." **Foreign languages:** Spanish and German G1-6, Spanish or German G7-8. **Computer training:** G8. **No. of computers available for students:** N/A. **No. of hours weekly of:**

Art- N/P; Drama- N/P; Music- N/P; Computers- N/P; Foreign language- N/P; PE- N/P. **Outdoor education:** Weekly hikes (K), Biodynamic gardening program (K-3), weeklong field trips to Point Reyes, Big Sur, Covelo, Yosemite, Catalina Island. **Grading:** Narrative evaluations, percentages. **Average nightly homework:** .5-2 hours in G4-8. Posted on the Internet: No. **Percentage of students participating in Johns Hopkins Center for Talented Youth Program:** N/A. **Other indicators of academic success:** "Happy, healthy, self-confident children." **High schools attended by latest graduating class:** SF Waldorf, Urban, Drew, SHCP, JCHS, SOTA.

FACULTY

Ethnicity: 87% Caucasian (non-Latino), 10% Latino, 3% Asian. **Percentage of teachers with graduate degrees:** 50%. **Percentage with current California credential:** N/P. **Faculty selection/training:** Experience, bachelor's degree or more, Waldorf teacher training graduate. **Teacher/student ratio:** 1:25. **Special subject teachers:** Music, upper grades math, languages, handwork, woodwork, Eurythmy, PE. **Average teacher tenure:** 12 years.

MIDDLE SCHOOL

Description: Students in G1-8 have a class teacher with them throughout the entire 8 years providing continuity. Special subject teachers work with students and additional resource teachers work with G6-8 in specialized academic areas. **Teacher/student ratio:** 1:20. **Elective courses offered:** Spanish or German G7-8. **Achievement tracking in:** G8 Algebra. **Student social events:** Field Day, May Faire, Beach Day, Harvest Dinner, Winter Fair, Middle School dances.

STUDENT SUPPORT SERVICES

No. of Licensed Counselors on staff: N/P. **Counselor/student ratio:** N/P. **Learning specialists on staff:** Educational Support Coordinator and Outside Learning Specialist. **Learning differences/disabilities support:** Faculty Care Group. **High school placement support:** "The Waldorf High School Admissions Director meets with parents and students to give information about our high school and gives general information about other high schools."

STUDENT CONDUCT AND HEALTH

Code of conduct: Stated in Parent Handbook. In addition, G6-8 have a Student Handbook that they read and sign. **Prevention education and awareness addressed in:** G7-8.

ATHLETICS
Sports offered: Basketball, volleyball, track and field. **Team play begins in:** G6.

CAMPUS/CAMPUS LIFE
Campus description: "A small oasis in an urban setting." **Library:** Yes. **Sports facilities:** Multi-purpose hall, nearby park and additional basketball practice space. **Theater/Arts facilities:** Multi-purpose hall. **Computer lab:** N/A. **Science lab:** No. **Lunch program:** No. **Bus service:** No. **Uniforms/dress code:** Warm, neat and clean, modest, functional. **Opportunities for community service:** G7-8.

EXTENDED DAY
Morning care: None. **After-school care:** Until 5:30 p.m. **Grade levels:** K-5. **Cost:** $7-$9/hour sliding scale. **Drop-in care available:** Yes. **Coverage over major holidays:** Feb. and Spring Break. **Homework help:** Study Hall. **Snacks:** Provided. **Staff/student ratio:** 1:10 for K, 1:16 for G1-5. **After-school classes:** Weekly craft day, baking day and local park trips included. **Cost:** None.

SUMMER PROGRAMS
Two 4-week programs for nursery and K. **Cost:** Approx. $400 for 2 weeks.

PARENT INVOLVEMENT
Parent/teacher communication: Parent evenings by class approx. every 2 months, individual conferences twice a year. **Participation requirements:** Voluntary participation in field trips, special projects, library and festival celebrations. **Parent education programs offered?** Yes.

WHAT SETS THE SCHOOL APART FROM OTHERS
"The sense of aesthetics and the full integration of the arts into the academics are quite unique and palpable. This wholeness allows students to absorb material through all their senses and develop a full range of capacities for expressing themselves and their knowledge of material presented."

HOW FAMILIES CHARACTERIZE SCHOOL
Parent comment(s): "SFWS not only opens doors for my child, but more to the point, doesn't close them. Each year, as she grows and develops, I am thrilled that she has not been pigeon-holed and can discover new

and unexpected abilities." • "In an urban setting, it is wonderful to have a school that is so beautiful to walk into and that sees and welcomes nature everywhere."

Student comment(s): "Our class teacher sees us grow both as opinionated individuals and as a whole. The teacher becomes somewhat of a co-parent and a major authority figure in the student's life."

STUART HALL FOR BOYS

2222 Broadway (between Webster and Fillmore) (Pacific Heights)
San Francisco, CA 94115
(415) 563-2900 *fax (415) 929-6928* (Admissions)
www.sacredsf.org

Jaime Dominguez, Head of School, dominguez@sacredsf.org
Pamela Thorp, Director of Admission, thorp@sacredsf.org

GENERAL

Boys K-8 day school. Founded in 1887. Independent, Catholic. Stuart Hall for Boys along with Convent of the Sacred Heart Elementary School, Convent of the Sacred Heart High School and Stuart Hall High School, is one of the four Schools of the Sacred Heart in San Francisco. Nonprofit. **Member:** CAIS, Network of Sacred Heart Schools, NAIS, IBSC, NCEA, ERB, CASE, BADA. **Enrollment:** 324. **Average class size:** 15-20. **Accreditation:** CAIS/WASC (6-year term: 2005-11), Network of Sacred Heart Schools. **Endowment:** $12 million. **School year:** Sept.-June. **School day:** 8:15 a.m. to 2:45 p.m. Mon.-Thurs. for K. Dismissal for G1-8 is staggered between 3 p.m. and 3:30 p.m. Friday dismissal for K is 2 p.m. and for G1-8 is staggered between 2:15 p.m. and 2:45 p.m.

STUDENT BODY ETHNICITY

"24% students of color."

ADMISSION

Applications due: Mid-Dec. for K, for G1-8, early Jan. (call for dates). **Application fee:** $100. **Application process:** Parent tours are held 2 hours on weekday morning beginning in late Sept. The Head of School meets with parents for a question and answer period during the tour. Parents are also invited to meet with the Head of School when their child attends the playgroup activity. **No. of applications:** N/P. **No. of K spaces:** 40. **Percentage of K class made up of school's preschool**

class: N/A. **Admission evaluation requirements for K:** Applicants must be 5 years old by the fifteenth of July. Assessment for readiness to begin the full day program offered by the school includes both individual screening and a playgroup date. Preschool evaluations are also part of each child's application. **Other grades:** Includes a parent tour, teacher recommendation, previous grades and testing. **Preferences:** Siblings receive priority consideration. **What sort of student do you best serve?** "Students and families who will support the school's Mission Statement."

Costs

Latest tuition: $23,750. **Sibling discount:** None. **Tuition includes:** Lunch: No; Transportation: No; Laptop computer: No; Other: N/P. **Tuition increases:** Approx. 6% annually. **Other costs:** Approx. $200 for K uniform including shoes. Uniforms are also available through school's thrift shop, Seconds-To-Go. **Percentage of students receiving financial aid:** 15%. **Financial aid application deadline:** Jan. (call for date). Financial aid is based on need. **Average grant:** N/P. **Percentage of grants of half-tuition or more:** N/P. **Donations:** Parents are solicited to participate in annual giving; participation is voluntary.

School's Mission Statement

"Founded in 1887 as an independent Catholic school, Schools of the Sacred Heart, San Francisco, carry on the educational mission of the Religious of the Sacred Heart. We share with the other members of the nationwide Network of Sacred Heart Schools five common goals and the commitment to educate to: A personal and active faith in God; A deep respect for intellectual values; A social awareness which impels to action; The building of community as a Christian value; Personal growth in an atmosphere of wise freedom. A K-12, four-school complex, Schools of the Sacred Heart, San Francisco offer the unique experience of single-sex education within a coed community. Students are expected to achieve their highest level of scholarship while learning to assume leadership roles as responsible, compassionate and contributing members of society."

Academic Program

Philosophy: "Stuart Hall's academic program provides a balance between the best of traditional (concepts, skills, facts, disciplines) and progressive (experiential learning, projects, cross-curriculum) methodologies and pedagogy. The spirit of the Program of Studies provides an environment that is a center of sound learning, new discovery, and the pursuit of wisdom. Instruction is tailored around the ways boys learn best. Stuart Hall boys are encouraged to participate in all activities - academics, athletics, arts and community service. The emphasis is always on the student as a whole child." **Foreign languages:** French, Spanish beginning in G3. Latin is mandatory in G6. **Computer training:** Yes, K-8. **No. of computers available for students:** Approx. 175 "state-of-the art computers." Computers are located in the Unkefer Computer Lab, the elementary school library and laptop carts outside the classrooms. **No. of hours weekly of:** Art- N/P; Drama- N/P; Music- N/P; Computers- N/P; Foreign language- N/P; PE- N/P. **Outdoor education:** "Yes." **Grading:** Narrative reports in K-4; letter grades beginning in G5. **Average nightly homework:** "Varies by grade." Posted on the Internet: For G5-8. **Percentage of students participating in Johns Hopkins Center for Talented Youth Program:** N/P. **Other indicators of academic success:** "Stuart Hall for Boys graduates are well prepared for their high school experience. They maintain high academic standards and participate in the full life of high school including sports, clubs and leadership roles in student government." **High schools attended by latest graduating class:** Stuart Hall, Lick, University, SI, Lowell, Bay, Exeter, Hotchkiss, Marin Academy, Thacher, Trinity-Pawling, Tamalpais, Sacred Heart, Loyola Academy, Drew, Urban.

FACULTY

Ethnicity: N/P. **Percentage of teachers with graduate degrees:** 65%. **Percentage with current California credential:** N/P. **Faculty selection/training:** "Experience, college degree and/or credential. Professional teacher development is an integral part of the school's program." **Teacher/student ratio:** 1:10 in the Lower Form; 1:15-20 in the Middle Form. **Special subject teachers:** Art, music, computers, religion, foreign language, music, PE, media literacy, contemporary issues, and the after-school program, which includes private instrumental music lessons in piano, violin and guitar. **Average teacher tenure:** 9 years.

MIDDLE SCHOOL

Description: "The core curriculum builds on knowledge gained in the Lower Form, moving students into increasingly comprehensive and rigorous academic study. Writing, both creative and expository, is emphasized in all subject areas. Stuart Hall students build upon their experience in a science lab and the scientific method of discovery. All students complete Algebra 1 in G8. Collaboration between the departments enhances in-depth studies. The values of citizenship continue to be stressed through the Goals and Criteria of Sacred Heart Education. A strong esprit de corps defines the atmosphere for students and faculty within each classroom and across the school. Departmentalization begins in G5." **Teacher/student ratio:** 1:15-20. **Elective courses offered:** No. **Achievement tracking in:** None. **Student social events:** With Convent Elementary School: Dances, drama club and the after-school program including orchestra.

STUDENT SUPPORT SERVICES

No. of Licensed Counselors on staff: One full-time. **Counselor/student ratio:** N/P. **Learning specialists on staff:** Three. **Learning differences/disabilities support:** "Educational resources as needed." **High school placement support:** A High School Counselor counsels students and their families.

STUDENT CONDUCT AND HEALTH

Code of conduct: "As articulated in the Goals and Criteria of Sacred Heart Schools." **Prevention education and awareness addressed in:** Health classes mandatory in K-8.

ATHLETICS

Sports offered: Soccer, cross-country, basketball, baseball, lacrosse, volleyball and golf. **Team play begins in:** G5 (intermural). Stuart Hall for Boys belongs to the Bay Area Interscholastic Athletic League (BAIAL) and Catholic Youth Organization (CYO).

CAMPUS/CAMPUS LIFE

Campus description: Stuart Hall for Boys occupies the former Hammond House and is located on the same campus as Convent Elementary School and Convent High School. Stuart Hall High School is located several blocks away at Pine and Octavia. **Library:** Houses 27,600 volumes including fiction, non-fiction and reference books, periodicals, audiobooks, videos, DVDs and computers. **Sports facilities:** Gymnasium with a basketball court and running track. Theater/Art facilities: Two theaters. The Syufy Theater is used for school presentations including plays, musical presentations and guest lectures. The Siboni Arts and Science Center houses all the art, music and science classrooms for Stuart Hall, Convent Elementary School and Convent High School. **Computer lab:** Yes. **Science lab:** Yes. **Lunch program:** Hot lunch daily. **Bus service:** No. **Uniforms/dress code:** Uniforms. **Opportunities for community service:** "From its inception, Sacred Heart education has had a deep and abiding commitment to social service. Stuart Hall students involve themselves in community service through classroom projects, fundraisers and active on-site work.

The development of social awareness and the expectation to become involved in responsible social action is an integral part of the Sacred Heart program for all students. Community service cultivates a spirit of cooperation and collaboration and fosters a comprehension of leadership today and tomorrow."

EXTENDED DAY
Morning care: Begins at 7:30 a.m. **After-school care:** Until 6 p.m. (coed). **Grade levels:** K-4. **Cost:** No charge for a.m. care. For a 5 p.m. pick up, $3,400/year; for a 6 p.m. pick up, $4,400/year. **Drop-in care available:** Yes. **Coverage over major holidays:** No. **Homework help:** Yes. **Snacks:** Provided. **Staff/student ratio:** Average 1:10. **After-school classes:** Coed for students in K-8, these have included Italian, robotics, fencing, art, sports, chess, gymnastics, cooking, creative writing, SSAT preparation and debate club. The after-school program for middle school students is available on a drop-in basis at no charge until 6 p.m. Music lessons are also available. **Cost:** "Varies."

SUMMER PROGRAMS
Classes are coeducational and include sports camp for G3-8 and academic and enrichment classes for G7-8. **Cost:** "Varies."

PARENT INVOLVEMENT
Parent/teacher communication: Conferences are scheduled twice yearly and as needed. Parents also utilize e-mail, the Schools' website, eThursday Notes and Lower Form monthly grade newsletters. **Participation requirements:** Parents are encouraged to volunteer for activities assisting with the Schools' annual fundraising activity auction/ dinner and Saturday family-fest, creating gift items for the boutique and as well as assisting with phoning and mailings. Parents also volunteer to help on class field trips and in the school library. **Parent education programs offered?** Yes.

WHAT SETS THE SCHOOL APART FROM OTHERS
"Among the oldest independent schools in California, Schools of the Sacred Heart are a part of a worldwide network of Sacred Heart Schools having their beginnings in the Society of the Sacred Heart founded in Paris in 1800. Our independent Catholic school draws on the rich tradition of Sacred Heart education worldwide, including strong intellectual challenge, faith development, social awareness and growth of the individual as a community member. Stuart Hall for Boys offers the benefits of single sex education in a coed environment and prepares

boys to assume leadership responsibilities as intelligent, compassionate, self-confident and contributing members of society."

How Families Characterize School
Parent comment (s): "This education focuses on an approach to the whole child which is unique. The program emphasizes not only academics but equally the emotional, social, and spiritual development of my sons. "
Student comment(s): "My school is well-rounded with something for everyone. We have strong academics and strong athletics. It's good to have Convent Elementary School next door. Social activities are great."

Synergy School
1387 Valencia Street (at 25th St.) (Mission District)
San Francisco, CA 94110
(415) 567-6177 *fax (415) 567-0607*
www.synergyschool.org

Tanya Baker, Director-Administration, tanya@synergyschool.org
Rita Franklin, Director-Admissions, rita@synergyschool.org
Joan Pettijohn, Director-Finance, joan@synergyschool.org

General
Coed K-8 day school. Founded in 1973. Independent. Nonprofit. **Member:** Progressive Educators Network. **Enrollment:** Approx. 185. **Average class size:** In K-3, 24 to 27 with 2 teachers in each class; in G4-5, 21 with 1 teacher and 1 aide; in middle school, 23 with 1 teacher and 1 aide. **Accreditation:** N/P. **Endowment:** $2,000,000. **School year:** Sept.-June. **School day:** 8:30 a.m. to 3 p.m.

Student Body Ethnicity
"55% students of color, 45% Caucasian (non-Latino), 14% in BLGT families."

Admission
Applications due: Jan. (call for date). **Application fee:** $50. **Application process:** Schedule a tour by going to the website or calling the school office. Applications are given out on the tour. **No. of applications:** Approx. 180. **No. of K spaces:** For young K (2-year K), 6; for regular K, 18. **Percentage of K class made up of school's preschool class:** N/A. **Admission evaluation requirements for K:** Playdate, teacher

recommendation, conversation with preschools. **Other grades:** School visit, grades, recommendations. **Preferences:** Siblings. **What sort of student do you best serve?** "We have an inclusive community with many types of students."

Costs

Latest tuition: $14,100. **Sibling discount:** None. **Tuition includes:** Lunch: No; Transportation: No; Laptop computer: No; Other: Farm school trip and most field trips. **Tuition increases:** Approx. 5%. **Other costs:** Approx. $60 for middle school books, $160 for snow trip (financial aid available), $20 for a yearbook. **Percentage of students receiving financial aid:** 33%. **Financial aid application deadline:** Jan. (call for date). Financial aid is based on need. **Average grant:** $6,629. **Percentage of grants of half-tuition or more:** 62%. **Donations:** Auction, Annual Fund, Endowment Campaign.

School's Mission Statement

"The mission of Synergy School is to provide a quality education by empowering children to flourish academically, to blossom as individuals, and to become self-confident, creative learners. The Synergy educational journey takes place in an environment based on encouragement, cooperation, mutual respect, and responsibility. Our approach inspires confidence and allows each child to work and develop at her/his own pace. An excellent teacher-student ratio helps each child feel known and valued and able to take personal risks. Education at Synergy is both challenging and joyful. Active, hands-on learning fosters each child's curiosity, critical thinking skills, and love of discovery. Strong conceptual foundations are built through challenging explorations in all academic subjects. A rich and varied curriculum is taught with the expectation that each child will strive for personal and academic excellence. At Synergy there is a commitment to developing global awareness and to learning to appreciate and honor differences both inside and outside the school community. We affirm the necessity of creating and sustaining a socially just, equitable environment which actively works against racism and all forms of bias. We accomplish these goals through ongoing curriculum development, teacher selection and training, and by actively recruiting a diverse student population. Synergy's approach to children's behavior is based on cooperation, logical and natural consequences, and the belief that we all have the ability to look at ourselves honestly, to change and to grow. The Agreement System is a vehicle through which our philosophy is expressed. It is a unifying force in the school and involves parents, staff, and children in a common goal: the creation of a supportive educational environment where children's enthusiasm for learning is fostered."

ACADEMIC PROGRAM

Philosophy: "Synergy is a progressive school, providing numerous opportunities for hands-on, project-based learning. We provide the skills and encouragement for students to become competent, independent, and enthusiastic learners throughout their lives. Academic skills are achieved in a non-competitive and cooperative atmosphere. Children work at their individual ability levels and pace, participating in whole class activities, small groups, and individual learning centers." **Foreign languages:** Spanish K-8. **Computer training:** Keyboarding, word processing, file sharing, Powerpoint, Excel spreadsheets in G4-5. Middle school adds web design, yearbook design and production, more advanced research, multi-media, publishing software. **No. of computers available for students:** In G4-5, 4 to 6 per classroom plus periodic use of middle school laptops. In G6-8, 1 laptop per every 3 students. **No. of hours weekly of:** Art- 1.5; Drama- N/P ("each class works intensively on 1 play per year"); Music- 1.5; Computers- N/P ("varies"); Foreign language- .75 (K) to 2 (G6-8); PE- 1.5. **Outdoor education:** In G4-8, 1-2 weeks per year; students in K-5 have 1 overnight trip per year ranging from 1-3 nights. **Grading:** Non-graded skills checklist in K-5. Letter grades begin in G6. **Average nightly homework:** For G1, 30 min., increasing every year up to 2 hours in middle school. Posted on the Internet: G4-8. **Percentage of students participating in Johns Hopkins Center for Talented Youth Program:** N/A. **Other indicators of academic success:** "The enthusiasm for learning demonstrated in so many ways by our students. Our students are welcomed enthusiastically by diverse high schools." **High schools attended by latest graduating class:** Lick, Urban, Drew, Dunn, ICA, IHS, Riordan, SHCP, SI, Mercy, Shawnigan Lake, Bay, Leadership, Lowell, Gateway, SOTA, Balboa.

FACULTY

Ethnicity: 53% Caucasian (non-Latino), 32% African-American, 11% Latino, 5% Asian. **Percentage of teachers with graduate degrees:** 16%. **Percentage with current California credential:** N/P. **Faculty selection/training:** Extensive interview process, experience in grade level and subject matter, philosophical match with the school, degree. **Teacher/student ratio:** 1:12 in K, 1:13 in G1-3, 1:15 in G4-5, 1:23 in G6-8. **Special subject teachers:** Art, music, PE, drama, Spanish, computers in middle school. **Average teacher tenure:** 12.6 years.

MIDDLE SCHOOL

Description: "Our middle school program (G6-8) remains committed to the goals set forth in our Mission Statement with particular emphasis on providing an optimum environment to meet the specific needs of younger adolescents within a supportive K-8 community of learners. Synergy's program development and implementation recognizes that young adolescents require the following: a rigorous, challenging and engaging academic program; continued opportunities for concrete, experiential learning along with bridging to their growing capacity for more abstract thinking; a safe community in which to explore their growing sense of self; emphasis on problem solving and critical thinking skills; on-going education in and understanding of diversity and equity issues; service learning connected to real life issues and problems; leadership opportunities within the school community and beyond; regular physical fitness and health activities; an environment that encourages a lifelong love of learning and strong sense of community. Departmentalization commences in G6." **Teacher/student ratio:** 1:23 not including specialists. **Elective courses offered:** "Students take 7 elective courses per year. Four or 5 electives are offered each session. Examples are: web design, yearbook, pod-casting, basketball, cross-country, martial arts, fine arts, cartooning, print-making, surrealism. **Achievement tracking in:** All subject areas. **Student social events:** Dances, parties.

STUDENT SUPPORT SERVICES
No. of Licensed Counselors on staff: None. **Counselor/student ratio:** N/A. **Learning specialists on staff:** One half-time. **Learning differences/disabilities support:** "Many Synergy teachers are trained in Schools Attuned. On site and off site workshops and training provided as needed. Synergy works closely with outside learning specialists. We have an active parent/teacher Unique Learners Committee which provides support to parents and educational events." **High school placement support:** Regular meetings for parents and students with the High School Placement Counselor, high school blog for G8 with key dates and critical information to help parents stay organized through the process, application essay writing feedback, and practice interviews. SSAT and CAT6 preparation are offered on site.

STUDENT CONDUCT AND HEALTH
Code of conduct: "The Agreement System is based on agreements that the students and teachers make with the school and must keep to be a part of the school." **Prevention education/awareness programs:** "Programs on drug awareness and human sexuality are offered through the regular classrooms at age appropriate levels. In middle school the advisory program brings in outside facilitators in addition to middle school teacher-advisors. We explicitly teach anti-bullying and anti-bias curricula."

ATHLETICS
Sports offered: Cross-country, basketball. **Team play begins in:** G5. There are teams organized by parents for K-5 students in soccer, basketball and softball.

CAMPUS/CAMPUS LIFE
Campus description: "Bright airy building in the heart of the Mission." **Library:** On-site library with 5,000 volumes plus periodicals. The collection provides curriculum support and reading enhancement. K-5 classes visit the library weekly. **Sports facilities:** Outdoor basketball and volleyball courts on campus. The school also utilizes sports facilities in the neighborhood including Garfield Pool and Dolores Park. **Theater/ Arts facilities:** A multipurpose room provides space for the whole school for class performances. Larger theatrical and musical productions are performed at other sites in the city. The school has a dedicated art room with kiln. **Computer lab:** Computers are in the classrooms and there is a mobile laptop cart for middle school. **Science lab:** Yes. **Lunch program:** No. **Bus service:** No. **Uniforms/dress code:** Dress code. **Opportunities for community service:** "The Middle School Student Council and POCIS (People of Color in Independent Schools) organize fundraisers and support for various organizations, including On Lok Senior Center and the SF Food Bank, where they also volunteer. The choir performs for the senior center at a local church during the winter holidays and meets with the seniors."

EXTENDED DAY
Morning care: Begins at 7:15 a.m. **After-school care:** Until 6 p.m. **Grade levels:** K-8. **Cost:** $240/month; $9/hour for drop in. **Drop-in care available:** Yes. **Coverage over major holidays:** Varies. **Homework help:** Yes. **Snacks:** Provided. **Staff/student ratio:** 1:12 **After-school classes:** Yoga, art, ceramics, cooking, dance. **Cost:** "Varies."

SUMMER PROGRAMS
The school offers two 4-week summer sessions from 9 a.m.-3 p.m., with extended care available at no additional cost. Students entering K-6 have a range of classes in poetry, art, dance, science and sports coupled with regularly scheduled "Out and About" field trips. **Cost:** $750/session for 5 days/week; $585 for 3 days/week.

PARENT INVOLVEMENT
Parent/teacher communication: Scheduled twice per year; teachers are available by phone, e-mail or for additional conferences as

needed. Regular weekly newsletter, website, and class blogs for G4-8. **Participation requirements:** Each family is asked to serve on a fundraising event committee (the school has 2 per year) or a committee that provides a service to the school such as library, yard, technology, etc. Families are asked to support both fundraising events and an all-school clean up day. **Parent education programs offered?** Yes, based on parent interest.

WHAT SETS THE SCHOOL APART FROM OTHERS

"Our teacher cooperative structure gives teachers a strong voice in what happens in their classroom and in the school as a whole. They are, therefore, very committed to and empowered within the school. This contributes to our low teacher turnover. The second factor is our approach to working with students around behavior. The Agreement System is based on logical and natural consequences for behavior and is used consistently throughout all classes in the school. A third factor is our combination classrooms which permit students and teachers to work together for two years and which create strong teaching teams. Finally, Synergy has an ongoing commitment to maintaining a diverse community which reflects the racial, economic and family structure diversity in San Francisco. This affects all aspects of our growth and development, from curriculum to admissions to hiring. We work hard to keep our tuition in the lowest 5% of Bay Area Independent Schools."

HOW FAMILIES CHARACTERIZE SCHOOL

Parent comment(s): "Synergy is more like a community than just a school—whole families are often present and involved, in various ways, from the infant siblings being passed around in the hallways to the grandparents showing up at the school plays. For a private school, the families at Synergy are pretty diverse—in family structure and class as well as ethnic background." • "I truly appreciate the teachers' commitment to the student as a whole person—not just as an academic learner but a member of our society to whom they mentor, influence and share ideas." • "Synergy's academic program encourages creativity and critical thinking." • "Synergy teachers excel at what they do because they are encouraged to be innovative in the classroom."

Student comment(s): "Synergy has built my confidence academically and socially." • "At my old school the students weren't as enthusiastic about their work as they are here at Synergy. At my old school we had more homework, but I learn so much more here. We have more intellectual work instead of stressful and time-consuming work that we didn't get anything out of." • "I'm in 8th grade and I've been here since kindergarten. Instead of being sick of the school, I'm sad to leave."

TOWN SCHOOL FOR BOYS

2750 Jackson Street (at Scott) (Pacific Heights)
San Francisco, CA 94115
(415) 921-3747 *fax (415) 921-2968*
www.townschool.com

W. Brewster Ely IV, Head of School, ely@townschool.com
Lynn McKannay, Director of Admission, mckannay@townschool.com

GENERAL
Boys K-8 day school. Founded in 1939. Independent. Nonprofit. **Member:** NAIS, IBSC, CASE, CAIS, WASC, ERB, ISAL, POCIS, BADA. **Enrollment:** Approx. 400. **Average class size:** 22. **Accreditation:** WASC (term N/P). **Endowment:** $19,350,000. **School year:** Sept.-June. **School day:** Begins at 8:30 a.m. for K-4 and 8:10 a.m. for G5-8. Dismissal times are staggered from 2 p.m. to 3:20 p.m.

STUDENT BODY ETHNICITY: N/P.

ADMISSION
Applications due: Jan. (call for date). **Application fee:** $100. **Application process:** Families tour the school, meet the Headmaster and have an interview with the Director of Admission. **No. of applications:** N/P. **No. of K spaces:** 44. **Percentage of K class made up of school's preschool class:** N/A. **Admission evaluation requirements for K:** Playdate at the school and recommendations from preschool. **Other grades:** Full-day visit, recommendation and records from current school and testing, if appropriate. **Preferences:** N/P. **What sort of student do you best serve?** N/P.

COSTS
Latest tuition: $24,430 for K-5, $25,370 for G6-8. **Sibling discount:** None. **Tuition includes:** Lunch: Yes; Transportation: No; Laptop computer: No; Other: N/A. **Tuition increases:** N/P. **Other costs:** Families purchase laptop computers in G5. **Percentage of students receiving financial aid:** N/P. **Financial aid application deadline:** Feb. (call for date). Financial aid is based on need. **Average grant:** N/P. **Percentage of grants of half-tuition or more:** N/P. **Donations:** Voluntary.

SCHOOL'S MISSION STATEMENT
"At Town School, learning is prized, love of school is essential, and boyhood is celebrated."

ACADEMIC PROGRAM

Philosophy: N/P. **Foreign languages:** Spanish, Latin. **Computer training:** Training in Lower School and families purchase laptop computers in G5. **No. of computers available for students:** N/P. **No. of hours weekly of:** Art- N/P; Drama- N/P; Music- N/P; Computers-N/P; Foreign language- N/P. **Outdoor education:** N/P. **Grading:** A-F, beginning in G5. **Average nightly homework:** N/P. Posted on the Internet: Yes. **Percentage of students participating in Johns Hopkins Center for Talented Youth Program:** N/P. **Other indicators of academic success:** N/P. **High schools attended by latest graduating class:** Bay, Branson, College Prep, Drew, IHS, Lick, Lowell, MA, SI, University, Urban, Deerfield, Groton, Hotchkiss, Lawrenceville, Middlesex, St. Paul's, Thacher.

FACULTY

Ethnicity: N/P. **Percentage of teachers with graduate degrees:** N/P. **Percentage with current California credential:** N/P. **Faculty selection/training:** N/P. **Teacher/student ratio:** 1:11. **Special subject teachers:** Art, music, drama, science, digital photography, woodworking. **Average teacher tenure:** N/P.

MIDDLE SCHOOL

Description: "The goals of the Upper School are designed to provide a challenging, enriching, and effective education for the fifth through eighth grader. Building on the skills taught in the K-4 division of the school, the curriculum is designed to develop competency while emphasizing the academic and character developmental needs of the students. In order to develop independence and responsibility, students are no longer taught in self-contained classrooms." **Teacher/student ratio:** 1:11 and some classes smaller. **Elective courses offered:** Drama, woodshop, bells, introduction to digital design, Lego Robotics, digital design. **Achievement tracking in:** N/P. **Student social events:** N/P.

STUDENT SUPPORT SERVICES

No. of Licensed Counselors on staff: One full-time. **Counselor/student ratio:** N/P. **Learning specialists on staff:** Two. **Learning differences/disabilities support:** N/P. **High school placement support:** Yes.

STUDENT CONDUCT AND HEALTH

Code of conduct: "Students in the Town School for Boys community are expected to show respect, courtesy, kindness, and consideration for others. Each individual is expected to act with regard for the safety and welfare of others." **Prevention education and awareness addressed in:** Curriculum.

ATHLETICS
Sports offered: Cross-country, soccer, basketball, and lacrosse. **Team play begins in:** Intermural play begins in K and intramural play begins in G5.

CAMPUS/CAMPUS LIFE
Campus description: The school has a 60,000 sq. ft. building with classrooms and offices, gym, library and media center, computer lab, science lab, art studio, music rooms, dining room, performing arts theater, and a woodworking shop. **Library:** "18,000 print volumes." **Sports facilities:** The school currently leases Morton Field in the Presidio. **Theater/Arts facilities:** Yes. **Computer lab:** Yes. **Science lab:** Yes. **Lunch program:** Yes. **Bus service:** No. **Uniforms/dress code:** Dress code. **Opportunities for community service:** Yes, opportunities are available at each grade level.

EXTENDED DAY
Morning care: N/P. **After-school care:** Until 6 p.m. **Grade levels:** K-8. **Cost:** "Varies." **Drop-in care available:** Available with sufficient notice. **Coverage over major holidays:** Yes. **Homework help:** Yes. **Snacks:** Provided. **Staff/student ratio:** N/P. **After-school classes:** Lego engineering, language, video, cartooning, cooking, chess, roller hockey, lacrosse, Tree Frog Treks Science, fencing. **Cost:** "Varies."

SUMMER PROGRAMS
The school offers two 2-week sessions of Town Tiger Camp, a camp offering a variety of courses and activities for boys entering the school's K program. Athletic camps are also available. **Cost:** N/P.

PARENT INVOLVEMENT
Parent/teacher communication: Conferences, website, Wednesday newsletter, e-mail, and any other communication upon request. **Participation requirements:** No required hours. **Parent education programs offered?** Yes.

WHAT SETS THE SCHOOL APART FROM OTHERS
"See Mission Statement."

How Families Characterize School

Parent comment(s): "I love shaking the Headmaster's hand each day, walking through the halls, seeing the smiles, the engagement and hearing the laughter."
Student comment(s): "Town's awesome!"

West Portal Lutheran School

Kindergarten - G3
3101 Moraga Street (at 37th Avenue) (Sunset)
San Francisco, CA 94122

G4 - 8
200 Sloat Boulevard (at 19th Avenue) (Lakeshore/Lakeside)
San Francisco, CA 94132
(415) 665-6330 *fax (415) 242-8876*
www.westportallutheran.org

Gary Beyer, Head of School
Christy Wood, Director of Admission, Christy.Wood@lsportal.net

General

Coed K-8 day school. Founded in 1951. Lutheran. Nonprofit. **Member:** N/P. **Enrollment:** Approx. 505. **Average class size:** 30. **Accreditation:** WASC/NLSA (6 year term: 2010-16). **Endowment:** N/P. **School year:** Sept.-June. **School day:** 8:30 a.m. to 2:45 p.m. for K; 8:30 a.m. to 3 p.m. for G1-3; 8:30 a.m. to 3:15 p.m. for G4-8.

Student Body Ethnicity: N/P.

Admission

Applications due: Due in Jan. for K (call for date), open for G1-8. **Application fee:** $150. **Application process:** Parents attend an open house; application packets are provided at the open house. **No. of applications:** N/P. **No. of K spaces:** 60. **Percentage of K class made up of school's preschool class:** N/A. **Admission evaluation requirements for K:** Preschool recommendation. **Other grades:** School visit, grades, test scores. **Preferences:** West Portal Lutheran Church members; siblings. **What sort of student do you best serve?** "Those who desire a Christian environment of nurturing and are motivated to learn and value an education highly."

Costs

Latest tuition: $6,156 for K, $5,859 for G1-8. **Sibling discount:** Yes. **Tuition includes:** Lunch: No; Transportation: No; Laptop computer: No; Other: N/A. **Tuition increases:** Approx. 3.5-4% annually. **Other costs:** N/P. **Percentage of students receiving financial aid:** N/P. **Financial aid application deadline:** N/P. Financial aid is based on need. **Average grant:** N/P. **Percentage of grants of half tuition or more:** N/P. **Donations:** N/P.

School's Mission Statement

"By the grace of God, West Portal Lutheran Church operates a Christian Day School in our Evangelical Lutheran tradition. Our goals: to offer a high-quality academic experience; to nurture and help each child grow as a whole, happy, and healthy person; to minister to the spiritual, moral, educational, interpersonal, cultural, and physical needs of each child; to strive to touch the hearts and lives of the families of the children in a caring, Gospel context."

Academic Program

Philosophy: N/P. **Foreign languages:** Spanish or German G7-8. **Computer training:** GK-8. **No. of computers available for students:** In the computer lab at primary campus, 15; in the computer lab at main campus, 33. **No. of hours weekly of:** Art- 1; Drama- N/P; Music- .75; Computers- .75; Foreign language- 4 (G7-8); PE- 1.5. **Outdoor education:** Coloma in G4; Washington, DC in G7-8 every other year. **Grading:** A-F, beginning in G3. **Average nightly homework:** 15-30 min. in K; 30 min. in G1; 45 min. in G2; less than 60 min. in G3; up to 60 min. in G4-5; 2 hrs. in G6-8. Posted on the Internet: Yes. **Percentage of students participating in Johns Hopkins Center for Talented Youth Program:** N/P. **Other indicators of academic success:** N/P. **High schools attended by latest graduating class:** Lowell, Mercy-SF, SI, SHCP, Riordan, Convent, Lick, Stuart Hall, SOTA.

Faculty

Ethnicity: N/P. **Percentage of teachers with graduate degrees:** N/P. **Percentage with current California credential:** N/P. **Faculty selection/training:** N/P. **Teacher/student ratio:** N/P. **Special subject teachers:** N/P. **Average teacher tenure:** N/P.

Middle School

Description: G7-8, departmentalized. **Teacher/student ratio:** 1:30. **Elective courses offered:** Foreign language in G7-8; art, humanities, and public speaking in G8. **Achievement tracking in:** N/P. **Student social events:** N/P.

STUDENT SUPPORT SERVICES
No. of Licensed Counselors on staff: N/P. **Counselor/student ratio:** N/P. **Learning specialists on staff:** N/P. **Learning differences/ disabilities support:** N/P. **High school placement support:** A meeting is held for parents in G6-7 in the spring, G8 in the fall. Private meetings are held with the principal.

STUDENT CONDUCT AND HEALTH
Code of conduct: "Very strict, but loving and nurturing in a Christian environment." **Prevention education and awareness addressed in:** "Internet safety and conduct, as well as drug prevention is addressed. In G6-8, awareness of the body from a Christian perspective is also addressed."

ATHLETICS
Sports offered: Soccer, basketball, boys baseball, girls volleyball. **Team play begins in:** Soccer in G3; basketball and volleyball in G4.

CAMPUS/CAMPUS LIFE
Campus description: "A safe and secure environment." **Library:** "One on each campus. A librarian is on campus weekly." **Sports facilities:** Each campus site has a gym. **Theater/Arts facilities:** N/P. **Computer lab:** Yes. **Science lab:** Yes. **Lunch program:** Yes, provided by an outside company **Bus service:** No. **Uniforms/dress code:** Uniforms. **Opportunities for community service:** Yes.

EXTENDED DAY
Morning care: Begins at 7 a.m. **After-school care:** Until 6 p.m. **Grade levels:** K-8. **Cost:** Approx. $4/hr. **Drop-in care available:** Yes. **Coverage over major holidays:** No. **Homework help:** Yes. **Snacks:** Provided. **Staff/student ratio:** 1:20. **After-school classes:** Art, music (orchestra, choral, hand bells, instrumental), Mandarin. **Cost:** "Varies."

SUMMER PROGRAMS
The school offers a 4-week summer school. The morning academic program (8:30 a.m.-12:15 p.m.) includes 1 hour of reading, 1 hour of mathematics, and 1 hour of language arts. The afternoon recreation program (1-4 p.m.) includes age-appropriate field trips, movies, playground activities, on/off campus activities, music, and arts and

crafts. Before school care is available starting at 7 a.m. After-school care is available until 6 p.m. **Cost:** N/P.

Parent Involvement
Parent/teacher communication: The main line of communication is via the internet through Fast Direct Communications. Parent/teacher conferences are held twice a year; mid-quarter (G6-8) and quarterly grades (K-8) are given; newsletters, Principal's Notes, and notices are distributed. The school participates in a parent notification system as well. **Participation requirements:** 20 hours of volunteer work for families with 1 student; 30 hours for families with more than 2 students. **Parent education programs offered?** Yes, at some Parent Teacher League meetings.

What Sets the School Apart From Others
"West Portal Lutheran School has been in existence since 1951. We are a multi-cultural, Christian, highly academic, traditional school. We value the partnership that has developed between the church, home, and school and strive to maintain open lines of communication. In developing our curriculum, we strive to educate the spiritual, academic and physical aspects of our students. Our students, upon graduation, are accepted into the most desired high schools in San Francisco and the Upper Peninsula. We treasure each student for his/her abilities and work with our families to provide the best education possible so that each child may reach his/her potential and become a productive member of society. Respect for individual differences and tolerance for all cultures are important aspects in the curriculum."

How Families Characterize School: N/P.

Zion Lutheran School
495 Ninth Avenue (between Anza and Geary) (Inner Richmond)
San Francisco, CA 94118
(415) 221-7500 *fax (415) 221-7141*
www.zionsfschool.org

Donna Laughlin, Principal, dlaughlin@zionsf.org, (415) 221-7500 ext. 202

General
Coed K-8 day school. Founded in 1946. Lutheran. Nonprofit. **Member:** Lutheran Church, Missouri Synod. **Enrollment:** 140. **Average class size:**

25. **Accreditation:** WASC/NLSA (6-year term: 2006-12). **Endowment:** N/A. **School year:** Mid Aug.-early June. **School day:** 8:30 a.m. to 3 p.m.

STUDENT BODY ETHNICITY
66% Asian, 22% Caucasian (non-Latino), 7% African-American 2% Latino, 2% other.

ADMISSION
Applications due: The priority deadline is Dec. 30; thereafter, rolling admissions. **Application fee:** $50. **Application process:** Personal school tour, application, and assessment and parent interview. **No. of applications:** N/P. **No. of K spaces:** 25. **Percentage of K class made up of school's preschool class:** N/A. **Admission evaluation requirements for K:** Must be 5 years old before Dec. 2, K readiness assessment, a recommendation from the preschool. **Other grades:** Provide a copy of most recent report card, achievement testing scores, and a 1-day visit to the school. **Preferences:** Siblings and church members. **What sort of student do you best serve?** "Given the small class sizes that Zion offers, we best serve students who benefit from individual attention, a caring environment, and a challenging curriculum with support through a partnership between parents, faculty, and staff."

COSTS
Latest tuition: $7,020. **Sibling discount:** $200 for the second child, $1,000 for the third child. **Tuition includes:** Lunch: No; Transportation: No; Laptop computer; No; Other: N/A. **Tuition increases:** Approx. 4% annually. **Other costs:** Approx. $150-$250 uniforms, $200-$600 for Outdoor Education in G5-8. **Percentage of students receiving financial aid:** N/P. **Financial aid application deadline:** Contact the Principal with any financial aid questions. **Average grant:** N/P. **Percentage of grants of half-tuition or more:** N/P. **Donations:** N/P.

SCHOOL'S MISSION STATEMENT
"Zion Lutheran School serves each individual child in a caring, yet challenging, environment to help them grow as an active Christian, an academically proficient learner, a globally conscious individual, and a healthy (socially, emotionally, and physically) individual."

ACADEMIC PROGRAM
Philosophy: "In addition to following the California state educational standards, our school utilizes the Core Knowledge Sequence, which is a research-based curriculum that answers the call for academic excellence

and higher literacy with its solid, specific, integrated core curriculum that establishes a strong educational foundation for our students." **Foreign languages:** Spanish G6-8. **Computer training:** Weekly 45 min. classes begin in K. **No. of computers available for students:** In the computer lab, 1 laptop per student; in addition, each classroom has computers. **No. of hours weekly of:** Art- 1; Music (K-5)- 1; Choir (K-6)- .5; Computers- .75; Foreign language (G6-8)- 3; PE- 1.5. **Outdoor education:** "G5-8." **Grading:** A-F, beginning G3. Posted on the Internet: Yes. **Average nightly homework:** .5 to 1 hr. in K-2; 1-2.5 hrs. in G3-5; 2.5-4 hrs. in G6-8. **Percentage of students participating in Johns Hopkins Center for Talented Youth Program:** N/A. **Other indicators of academic success:** "Students take an active role in their education and enthusiastically participate in all forms of learning. Zion graduates are accepted at the most competitive high schools in the Bay Area and have continued success in their academic endeavors." **High schools attended by latest graduating class:** Lowell, SHCP, Lick, Riordan, Gateway.

FACULTY

Ethnicity: 67% Caucasian (non-Latino), 33% Asian. **Percentage of teachers with graduate degrees:** 30%. **Percentage with current California credential:** 100%. **Faculty selection/training:** BA and MA. **Teacher/student ratio:** 1:25 in G1-8, 1:12.5 in K. **Special subject teachers:** Spanish, computer, PE, algebra. **Average teacher tenure:** 9 years.

MIDDLE SCHOOL

Description: G6-8, departmentalized. **Teacher/student ratio:** 1:25. **Elective courses offered:** Student council, hand bells, yearbook. **Achievement tracking in:** All subject areas. A high school level algebra class is also offered to eighth graders who display readiness. **Student social events:** Youth group events, dances, community service involvement.

STUDENT SUPPORT SERVICES

No. of Licensed Counselors on staff: N/P. **Counselor/student ratio:** N/A. **Learning specialists on staff:** N/P. **Learning differences/ disabilities support:** Private tutoring is available after school and an after-school study hall is offered 4 times a week (both for an additional fee). If necessary, recommendations are made to obtain outside evaluations and support. **High school placement support:** The Principal hosts a high school information night each fall with a local admissions consultant.

Student Conduct and Health

Code of conduct: "Students will show respect toward all staff members and each other." **Prevention education and awareness addressed in:** Family Life Planning, which includes nutrition, personal health, alcohol and tobacco awareness, mental health, family health, and sex education.

Athletics

Sports offered: Basketball in G5-8; volleyball in G7-8; all-school track meet in the spring. **Team play begins in:** N/P.

Campus/Campus Life

Campus description: The school has 2 buildings. The main building houses the church, Parish Hall, K-6 classrooms, offices, and a gym. The Middle School Building includes G7-8 classrooms and a computer lab. The school has a fenced yard with a play structure. **Library:** Each classroom has its own library. **Sports facilities:** Gym and outdoor basketball court. **Theater/Arts facilities:** Full-size stage is constructed each year for the Spring Musical in our gym. **Computer lab:** 20 laptops for student use and a Smart Board. **Science lab:** No. **Lunch program:** Hot lunches may be purchased in advance each month ($4.50 daily). **Bus service:** No. **Uniforms/dress code:** Uniforms. **Opportunities for community service:** Quarterly chapel projects and classroom community service projects.

Extended Day

Morning care: Begins at 7 a.m. **After-school care:** Until 6 p.m. **Grade level:** K-8. **Cost:** $2/day for morning; $12/day for after-school. **Drop-in care available:** As needed. **Coverage over major holidays:** No. **Homework help:** "Quiet time." **Snacks:** Provided. **Staff/student ratio:** N/P. **After-school classes:** G3-8 study hall, academic chess, art, cooking, piano, violin, GK-4 basketball workshop, Lego engineering, Mandarin. **Cost:** "Varies."

Summer Programs

The school offers a 6-week Summer Enrichment Program with academics in the morning and recreation in the afternoon. A week-long Vacation Bible School is also offered. The programs are open to all. **Cost:** "Varies."

Parent Involvement

Parent/teacher communication: Two mandatory conferences during the first 2 quarters, voluntary after that. **Participation requirements:**

Yes, 25 hours of volunteer time (field trip chaperones, room parents, spring musical helpers, etc.) to receive a $200 reimbursement on the Parent Volunteer fee of $300. **Parent education programs offered?** Yes, Parent Teacher League (PTL) sponsors guest speakers for discussions.

What Sets the School Apart From Others

"We are a challenging academic school that supports each child with an individual education."

How Families Characterize School

Parent comment(s): "I love Zion Lutheran School because it is a school that truly cares about its students and their families. Zion supports its students spiritually, academically, and emotionally, and they know they are loved. Zion instills a passion for life-long learning, which is essential for academic success in the students' futures. The principal and staff work tirelessly to provide the best well-rounded education possible. Their dedication is very inspiring. They have the students' and their families' best interests at heart."

Student comment(s): "Zion itself is a family. I think back about my years at Zion and know for a fact that those were the best nine years of my life."

ADDITIONAL SCHOOLS IN SAN FRANCISCO

HILLWOOD ACADEMIC DAY SCHOOL
2521 Scott Street (at Broadway) (Pacific Heights/Cow Hollow)
San Francisco, CA 94115
(415) 931-0400
www.hillwoodschool.com

Mr. Eric Grantz, Head of School, ericgrantz@yahoo.com
Coed K-8 day school. Founded in 1949. Proprietary. **School year:** Sept.-June. **School day:** 9 a.m. to 3 p.m. **Latest tuition:** $7,000. Uniforms.

ST. ANTHONY IMMACULATE CONCEPTION
200 Precita Avenue (at Shotwell) (Bernal Heights/Mission)
Francisco, CA 94110
(415) 648-2008 *fax (415) 648-1825*
www.saicsf.org

Dennis Ruggiero, Principal, druggiero@saicsf.org
Coed K-8 parochial day school. Catholic. Nonprofit.

ST. BRENDAN SCHOOL
940 Laguna Honda Boulevard. (at Portola)(Twin Peaks)
San Francisco, CA 94127
(415) 731-2665 *fax (415) 731-7207*
www.stbrendansf.com

Carol Grewal, Principal, cgrewal@stbrendansf.com
Coed K-8 parochial day school. Founded in 1947. Catholic. Nonprofit.
Enrollment: Approx. 327. **Accreditation:** WASC/WCEA. **School year:** Aug.-June. **School day:** 8 a.m. to 3 p.m. **Applications due:** Jan. (call for date). **Application process:** Call to request an application and arrange a tour (weekly from mid-Sept.-Nov.) **Latest tuition:** $5,490 (participating)-$5,890 (non-participating). **Sibling discount:** "Yes." **Foreign languages:** Spanish. **Special subject teachers:** Art, PE, motor skills, dance, technology, librarian, science, math, language arts. **Campus description:** Main school building, Learning Center, gymnasium, science lab, library, computer lab. **After-school care:** Until 6 p.m.

Saint Charles Borromeo School

3250 18th Street (btwn. Shotwell and South Van Ness)(Mission Dist.)
San Francisco, CA 94110
(415) 861-7652 *fax (415) 861-0221*
www.sfstcharlesschool.org

Daniel Dean, Principal, ddean@sfstcharlesschool.org
Coed K-8 parochial day school. Founded in 1894. Catholic. Nonprofit.
Latest tuition: $4,300. **Other costs:** $375 registration fee. Financial aid is based on need. Faculty includes Dominican Sisters. **Learning differences/disabilities support:** Remedial math and reading instructors. Title 1 funding for special needs students. **Team sports:** Basketball beginning in G4. Computer lab. Lunch program. Uniforms. **Parent Participation:** 40 parent volunteer hours required for 2 parent families and $350 of fundraising profits. **What sets school apart from others:** "We provide a safe, caring and family-oriented environment."

St. Finn Barr School

419 Hearst Avenue (near Monterey Blvd.)(Outer Mission District)
San Francisco, CA 94112
(415) 333-1800
www.stfinnbarr.org

Thomas Dooher, Principal, tdooher@stfinnbarr.org
Coed K-8 parochial day school. Founded in 1962. Catholic. Nonprofit.
Accreditation: WASC/WCEA (N/P term). **School day:** 7:55 a.m. to 3 p.m. **Applications due:** Rolling. **Latest tuition:** N/P. **Mission Statement:** "We are dedicated to meeting the needs of the whole child, embracing his or her potential to become an independent thinker and productive member of society in accordance with gospel values and Catholic tradition." **Academic program:** "Integrated music, drama, art, and choir program." Uniforms. Extended day until 6 p.m.

St. James School

321 Fair Oaks St. (between 24th & 25th Street) (Noe Valley/Mission)
San Francisco, CA 94110
(415) 647-8972 *fax (415) 647-0166*
www.saintjamessf.org

Sister Mary Susanna Vasquez, O.P., Head of School, sms@saintjamessf.org
Mrs. Lucia Vazquez Harp, Director of Admissions, office@saintjamessf.org

Coed K-8 parochial day school. Founded in 1924. Catholic. Nonprofit. **Member:** NCEA.

ST. JOHN'S SCHOOL
925 Chenery Street (at Diamond) (Glen Park)
San Francisco, CA 94131
(415) 584-8383 *fax (415) 584-8359*
www.stjohnseagles.com

Kenneth Willers, Head of School and Director of Admission, principal@ stjohnseagles.com
Coed K-8 parochial day school. Catholic. Nonprofit. **Accreditation:** WASC (6-year term: 2005-11). **Applications due:** Open. **Application fee:** $30. **Application process:** Individual assessment.

ST. MARY'S CHINESE DAY SCHOOL
910 Broadway (at Mason) (Chinatown)
San Francisco, CA 94133
(415) 929-4690 *fax (415) 929-4699*
www.stmaryschinese.org

Nancy Fiebelkorn, Principal, nfiebelkorn@stmaryschinese.org
Coed K-8 parochial day school. Founded in 1921. Catholic. Nonprofit. **Member:** NCEA, WASC, WCEA. **Enrollment:** Approx. 200. **Admission evaluation requirements for K:** Must be 5 years old by Dec. 1. **Latest tuition:** $6,313. **Sibling discount:** Yes. **Mission Statement:** "St. Mary's Chinese Day School is a Catholic School whose existence is an integral part of the mission of the Church. Our core values of Catholic identity, dignity, excellence and justice are included in all our curriculum and in all our programs." **Philosophy:** "We recognize the uniqueness of each person and maintain an academic program which enables all students to fully cultivate their abilities." **Summer programs:** English, reading, math, fine arts.

ST. PETER'S SCHOOL
1266 Florida Street (at 25th Street) (Mission District)
San Francisco, CA 94110
(415) 647-8662 *fax (415) 647-4618*
www.sanpedro.org

Victoria Butler, Principal and Director of Admission, vbutler@sanpedro.org

Coed K-8 parochial day school. Founded in 1878. Catholic. Nonprofit. **Member:** N/P. **Enrollment:** Approx. 500. **Average class size:** 30.

St. Thomas More School

St. Thomas More Way (at Brotherhood Way) (Lakeshore)
San Francisco, CA 94132
(415) 337-0100 *fax (415) 452-9653*
www.stthomasmoreschool.org

Marie Fitzpatrick, Principal, marifitz@stthomasmoreschool.org
Coed K-8 Archdiocesan day school. Catholic. **Average class size:** 36.
Applications due: Approx. Feb 1. **Latest tuition:** $4,800. **Philosophy:** "Catholic education is intended to make one's faith become living, conscious and active through the light of instruction. It is the unique setting within which this ideal can be realized in the lives of Catholic children and young people. ... As Catholic educators, we at St. Thomas More School hold as primary: belief in God, Christ, Church, the value of the human person and commitment to a mission of service, that every person as a child of God has equal dignity and an inalienable right to an education. ...That parents have the primary responsibility for the education of their children. Therefore ... we support, enhance and complement this role." Uniforms. Extended day until 6 p.m.

St. Thomas the Apostle School

3801 Balboa Street (at 39th Avenue) (Outer Richmond)
San Francisco, CA 94121
(415) 221-2711 *fax (415) 221-8611*
www.sfsta.org

Judith Borelli, Principal
Coed K-8 parochial day school. Catholic. **Latest Tuition:** $4,658 (Catholic) - $5,170 (non-Catholic). Mission Statement: "St. Thomas the Apostle School is dedicated to making Christ a vital part of the lives of its students by providing a strong Catholic/Christian community, a solid doctrinal foundation in the Catholic tradition, academic excellence, and an environment in which each child, respected and valued as a unique individual, is encouraged to achieve his/her full potential. In community with the parents, the primary educators, all school personnel respond to this challenge by providing a Christ-centered atmosphere and opportunities in which the dignity and worth of each child is valued and respected by all." Uniforms. Extended day: Until 6 p.m.

SAN FRANCISCO ADVENTIST SCHOOL

66 Geneva Avenue (at Mission) (Outer Mission)
San Francisco, CA 94112
(415) 585-5550 *fax (415) 585-4155*
www.sfsaonline.org

Beverly Church, Principal
Coed K-8 day school. Founded in 1912. Seventh Day Adventist.
Nonprofit. **School year:** Aug.-June. **School day:** 8 a.m. to 2:15 p.m.
for K; 8 a.m. to 3:30 p.m. for G7-8. Applications accepted year-round.
Application process: The family interviews with the principal and
presents achievement/grade report info. The child is interviewed and has
basic testing with the classroom teacher. **Latest tuition:** $3,990-$6,520.
Financial aid and scholarships are available. **Mission statement:** "The
mission of San Francisco Adventist School is to provide a learning
environment that fosters a growing Christian experience in each child
and also nurtures and encourages optimum cognitive, physical, social,
emotional, spiritual, and creative development in each child, that will
result in increased personal self-esteem needed for a happy, productive
life."

SCHOOL OF THE EPIPHANY

600 Italy Street (near Geneva) (Excelsior)
San Francisco, CA 94112
(415) 337-4030 *fax (415) 337-8583*
www.sfepiphany.org

Diane Elkins, Principal
Coed K-8 parochial day school. Catholic. Founded in 1938. **Enrollment:**
Approx. 590. **Average class size:** Approx. 33. **Accreditation:** WASC/
WCEA. **Latest tuition:** $5,604. **Mission Statement:** "The School of the
Epiphany is a Catholic, Parochial school serving the youth of Epiphany
Parish and its surrounding areas. We challenge students to achieve
educational excellence within a Catholic tradition. The School of the
Epiphany operates in service to Epiphany Parish and in the spirit of
the Presentation Sisters." **Academic program:** "Various in-curriculum
programs are offered in Spanish, computer, music and PE. The middle
school's exploratory program includes classes in advanced computers,
card making, wood working, cooking, Tagalog, music, library, tutoring."
Uniforms. Extended day until 6 p.m.

STAR OF THE SEA SCHOOL
360 9th Avenue (at Geary) (Inner Richmond)
San Francisco, CA 94118
(415) 221-8558 *fax (415) 221-7118*
www.staroftheseasf.com

Terrence Hanley, Principal
Coed K-8 parochial day school. Founded in 1909. Catholic.
Accreditation: WASC/WCEA. **Enrollment:** Approx. 230. **Average class size:** 15-20 in lower school, approx. 32 in middle school. **School year:** Aug.-June. **Ethnicity:** 32% Asian, 32% Caucasian (non-Latino), 23% multi-racial, 8% Latino, 4% African-American. **Applications due:** Rolling. **What sort of student do you best serve?** "Families who value a solid, basic education and want Christian values for their children." **Latest tuition:** $5,800. **Sibling discount:** "Yes." **Mission Statement:** "Star of the Sea School is a unique, loving Christian community of caring persons who enthusiastically strive to instill Christ-like values and academic excellence in a way that challenges us, our students and our parents. Our school is about people, with the rich ethnic backgrounds of those entrusted in our care, we strive to bring out the uniqueness and potential of each child. We see the parents as the primary educators. As parents work to develop their child holistically (spiritually, academically, psychologically, physically and culturally) we, as educators, are here to reinforce what has begun in the home. We are dedicated to guiding our students to form a thinking conscience, and to learn to make sound decisions, so that they may be responsible adults of tomorrow. Star of the Sea Catholic School exists for people; it is our desire to lead each other, and our students and parents to real love and respect for each individual. Each person has been gifted by God with life, and in turn shares personal gifts with others." **Philosophy:** "Star of the Sea exists as part of a thriving faith community over 100 years old. Under the advocacy of Mary, our patroness, we guide families who trust their children's education to our care. Inspired by the educational tradition of the Sisters of St. Joseph of Carondelet, we meet students where they are, in order to lead them on the path toward Christ. As dedicated educators we realize that parents are the primary educators of their children. In choosing Star of the Sea they show us the commitment they have. In turn we pledge ourselves to work with parents to prepare children to become responsible, contributing member of the community. We see effective education as stewardship. As gifted individuals we share knowledge and resources available in order to make the world a better place through our academic curriculum we

strive to call forth the very best each student has to offer. Our students' gifts find affirmation through our holistic educational program that addresses religious, intellectual, social aesthetic, emotional and physical needs. ... We are rich in ethnic diversity and consider this to be one of our great strengths. We strive to educate so that real love and respect for the uniqueness and potential of each individual will be evident in our school community." **Academic program:** "Star of the Sea is known for its strong academic curriculum. Students receive daily instruction in religion, English, social studies, math, science, and reading. Art, music, computer training, and PE are also part of our well-rounded curriculum. Spanish and Chinese language classes are available on the premises after school hours." **Athletics:** In GK-8, soccer, basketball, volleyball, baseball, track and cross-country. Teams play in the CYO. **Middle School:** "G6-8 are departmentalized. The Student Council is an active and productive group of students meeting on a weekly basis with a faculty moderator. Students can be involved in the production of the school newspaper under the guidance of a faculty advisor. Students in G4-8 have the opportunity to become Altar Servers." **Campus description:** The campus consists of a school building, library and extended care building, and a gymnasium. **Parent/teacher communication:** "Star of the Sea promotes open and active communication between school and home. A weekly e-mail (or envelope) is sent home with a letter from the Principal and notification of upcoming events. A yearly calendar is provided, as well as updated monthly calendars. Student work packets are sent home on a regular basis to keep parents abreast of their child's work, and report cards are sent home 4 times a year. In addition to regular scheduled parent/teacher conferences in Nov., the faculty is available for consultation whenever necessary."

VOICE OF PENTECOST ACADEMY
1970 Ocean Avenue (West of Twin Peaks)
San Francisco, CA 94127
(415) 334-0105 *fax (415) 586-3990*

R. Sherwood Jansen, Principal
Coed PK-12 day school. Pentecostal. Founded in 1974. **Enrollment:** Approx. 150.

Additional Marin Schools

Good Shepherd Lutheran School
1180 Lynwood Drive
Novato, CA 94947
(415) 897-2510
www.goodshepherdlutheran.org

Carol Wise, Administrator
Coed PS-8 day school. Lutheran. **Applications due:** Nov. 15. **Application fee:** $50. **Application process:** Schedule a tour, submit an application, teacher recommendation. **Latest tuition:** $5,778-$7,146. **Foreign language:** Spanish. Uniforms.

North Bay Christian Academy
6965 Redwood Boulevard.
Novato, CA 94945
(415) 892-8921 *fax (415) 893-1750*
www.nbcs.com

Pam Carraher, Principal
Coed K-12 day school. Christian. **School day:** 8 a.m. to 4 p.m. **Latest tuition:** $4,100 for K-1; $4,700 for G2-6; $5,300 for G7-8. **Sibling discount:** Yes (N/P amount). Mission Statement: "NBCA is a caring community of Christians committed to: Serving God's purposes in our generation; Imparting a Christian Worldview; Nurturing the intellectual, emotional, spiritual, social and physical development of students; Equipping students, in partnership with the home and the church, to become transforming influences in the world." **What sets the school apart from others:** "A unique feature of our school is the range of ages that learn and play together. While the elementary program is housed in one wing and the middle school and high school in another, between classes students of all grades interact. This atmosphere fosters valuable interpersonal skills across generational lines."

Our Lady of Loretto School
1811 Virginia Avenue
Novato, CA 94945
(415) 892-8621 *fax (415) 892-9631*
www.ollnovato.org

Annette Bonanno, Principal, principal@ollnovato.org
Coed K-8 day school. Founded in 1959 by the Ursuline Sisters. Catholic. **Enrollment:** Approx. 235. **Average class size:** 28. **Accreditation:** WASC/WCEA (N/P term). **School Year:** Aug. – June. **School Day:** 8 a.m. to 3 p.m. **Latest Tuition:** For participating families (doing service hours) $6,950; for non-participating, $7,750. Financial aid is based on need; call for deadline. **Mission Statement:** "Our Lady of Loretto School is dedicated to excellence in education that is Christ centered and rich in Catholic tradition. With Christ as the model and teacher, we foster the development of students who are: Compassionate, Humble, Responsible, Involved, Spiritual, Thinkers." Uniforms. Extended Day.

ST. ANSELM SCHOOL
40 Belle Avenue
San Anselmo, CA 94906
(415) 454-8667 *fax (415) 454-4730*
www.stanselmschool.com

Odile Steel, Principal, stanselmsschool@comcast.net
Coed K-8 parochial day school. Founded in 1924. Catholic. Nonprofit. **Accreditation:** WASC, WCEA. **School year:** Aug.-June. **School day:** 8:15 a.m. to 3:15 p.m. (2 p.m. dismissal for K). **Applications due:** Mid-Feb. **Application fee:** $25. **Application process:** Submit application fee, schedule interview and tour. **Admission evaluation requirements for K:** Student must be 5 years old by Sept. 1, assessments, teacher recommendations, immunization records. **Other grades:** Half or full day visit, teacher recommendations, test scores, grades. **Preferences:** Siblings, participating parish members, non-participating parish members, then members of other Catholic churches. **What sort of student do you best serve?** "We offer a strong academic curriculum with several co-curricular programs geared to the average and above-average student." **Latest tuition:** $7,000-$7,350 (scrip-no scrip). **Sibling discount:** Yes (amount N/P). **Mission Statement:** "St. Anselm School is a community of faith in the Catholic tradition. Through a collaborative partnership with our parent and parish community, we are committed to the growth and development of the whole child. We provide an engaging, challenging, and comprehensive academic program." **Academic philosophy:** "St. Anselm School is an educational community that emphasizes the spiritual, intellectual, and personal development of students. We complement the home in developing the whole child, instilling in each student a love for God and His Church. We foster an enthusiasm for lifelong learning and an aspiration to academic

excellence. St. Anselm School encourages appreciation for the intrinsic value of life, a respect for the dignity of others, and a commitment to social justice. We promote in each of our students a positive self-image while inspiring them to work collaboratively and be responsible citizens." **Foreign languages:** Spanish. **Special subject teachers:** Science, technology, PE, music, Spanish. Uniforms. **Extended day:** From 7:15 a.m.; after school care until 6 p.m. **Grade levels:** K-8. **Cost:** $3.70/hour. **Snacks:** Provided. **Parent Participation requirements:** 40 volunteer hours for 2 parent families, 20 hours for single parent families. **Student comment(s):** "I have benefited in my experience at St. Anselm School in many ways. I have great friends, great memories, and a great education. I have faith in God and love for everyone. St. Anselm was the perfect choice for me and my family."

St. Isabella School
1 Trinity Way
San Rafael, CA 94903
(415) 479-3727 *fax (415) 479-9961*
www.stisbellaschool.org

Coed K-8 parochial day school. Founded in 1962. Catholic. Nonprofit. **Enrollment:** Approx. 250. **Mission Statement:** "St. Isabella Parish school is committed to providing an education that challenges students to live out the Catholic faith in service to God, family and society responsibly. We provide a solid foundation for the spiritual, psychological, and academic development of our students. St. Isabella educates tomorrow's leaders." Uniforms.

St. Patrick School
120 King Street
Larkspur, CA 94939
(415) 924-0501 *fax (415) 924-3544*
www.stpatricksmarin.org

Linda Kinkaid, Principal, l_kinkaide@stpatricksmarin.org
Coed K-8 parochial day school. Catholic. **Enrollment:** Approx. 230. **Average class size:** Approx. 29. **Accreditation:** WASC/WCEA. **Application fee:** $75. **Latest tuition:** $7,200 (participating) - $7,700 (non-participating). **Mission Statement:** "To instill in our students a love and respect for our Catholic tradition, a strong academic foundation, and a reverence for themselves, others and the world around them." Uniforms. **Extended day:** From 7:15 a.m. until 8 a.m. and from dismissal to 6 p.m.

ST. RAPHAEL SCHOOL

1100 Fifth Avenue
San Rafael, CA 94901
(415) 454-4455 *fax (415) 454-5927*
www.saintraphael.com

Maureen Albritton, Principal
Coed PK-8 parochial day school. Founded in 1889. Catholic.
Enrollment: Approx. 161. **Average class size:** 19. **Accreditation:**
WASC/WCEA (6-year term: 2009-15). **Ethnicity:** 39% Caucasian,
41% Hispanic. **Latest tuition:** $6,672 (parishioners) - $7,240 (non-parishioners). **Mission Statement:** "Saint Raphael's School, rooted in
the Dominican tradition, is dedicated to living out Catholic values in a
richly diverse population while providing a strong academic education
for all students." **Foreign language:** Spanish. Uniforms. Extended care
until 6 p.m.

ST. RITA SCHOOL

102 Marinda Drive
Fairfax, CA 94930
(415) 456-1003 *fax (415) 456-7946*
www.strita.edu

Carol Arritola, Principal
Maria Kimball, Director of Admissions, mkimball@strita.edu

Coed PS-8 parochial day school. Catholic. Founded in 1957.
Enrollment: Approx. 170.

APPENDIX

At parents' request in response to the prior editions of this book, certain statistics from the schools' profiles are compiled below.

SCHOOL SIZE

The New Village School	40
Marin Preparatory School	52
Cascade Canyon	66
Kittredge School	85
The Laurel School	85
The Discovery Center School	90
Lisa Kampner Hebrew Academy	100
Megan Furth Catholic Academy	110
Krouzian-Zekarian-Vasbouragan Armenian School	120
Ring Mountain Day School	120
Montessori de Terra Linda	130
Zion Lutheran School	140
Greenwood School	150
Voice of Pentecost Academy	150
Saint Monica School	160
St. Raphael School	161
Adda Clevenger Junior Preparatory and Theater School	170
St. Rita School	170
Synergy School	185
Presidio Hill School	197
Brandeis Hillel Day School – Marin	200
Corpus Christi	200
Marin Christian Academy	200
Mission Dolores Catholic School	200
St. Mary's Chinese Day School	200
The San Francisco School	200
St. Philip School	214
Marin Montessori School	230
Marin Waldorf School	230
St. Patrick School	230
Star of the Sea School	230
Our Lady of Loretto School	235
St. Paul's Elementary School	235
Our Lady of the Visitacion School	241
Saint Vincent de Paul School	250
Sts. Peter and Paul Salesian School	250

Live Oak School	260
Cathedral School for Boys	268
Saint Hilary School	268
Saint Brigid School	270
Mount Tamalpais School	272
Ecôle Notre Dame Des Victoires	280
Marin Horizon School	285
St. Stephen School	323
Convent of the Sacred Heart Elementary School	324
Stuart Hall for Boys	324
St. Brendan School	327
Children's Day School	335
Holy Name of Jesus	360
Marin Primary & Middle School	370
Saint Mark's School	380
Brandeis Hillel Day School-San Francisco	400
The Hamlin School	400
Katherine Delmar Burke School	400
San Domenico School	400
San Francisco Day School	400
Town School for Boys	400
San Francisco Friends School	420
San Francisco Waldorf School	426
Chinese American International School	460
St. Anne School	500
St. Peter's School	500
West Portal Lutheran School	505
St. Gabriel School	510
Marin Country Day School	560
School of the Epiphany	590
St. Cecilia School	600
French-American International School	650
Lycée Français La Perouse, The French School (SF & Marin)	900

N/P: Good Shepherd Lutheran School, Hillwood Academic Day School, North Bay Christian Academy, Our Lady of Loretto School, St. Anselm School, St. Anthony Immaculate Conception, Saint Charles Borromeo School, St. Finn Barr School, St. Isabella School, St. James School, St. John's School, St. Thomas More School, St. Thomas the Apostle School, San Francisco Adventist School

AVERAGE CLASS SIZE

The New Village School	8
The Laurel School	9
The Hamlin School	10-22
The Discovery Center School	12
Krouzian-Zekarian-Vasbouragan Armenian School	12
Lisa Kampner Hebrew Academy	12
Ring Mountain Day School	12
Presidio Hill School	12-14
Synergy School	12-23
Cascade Canyon	14
Kittredge School	14
Megan Furth Catholic Academy	14
Marin Preparatory	14-16
Adda Clevenger Junior Preparatory and Theater School	15
Marin Christian Academy	15
Convent of the Sacred Heart Elementary School	15-20
Lycée Français La Pérouse, The French School	15-20
Star of the Sea School	15-32
Stuart Hall for Boys	15-20
French-American International School	16
Mount Tamalpais School	16
Cathedral School for Boys	16-24
Greenwood School	17
Live Oak School	17-22
Marin Country Day School	18
Chinese American International School	18-20
San Francisco Friends School	18-22
St. Raphael School	19
Brandeis Hillel Day School-Marin	20
Saint Mark's School	20-22
Marin Montessori School	20-30
Brandeis Hillel Day School-San Francisco	22
Children's Day School	22
Marin Waldorf School	22
The San Francisco School	22
Town School for Boys	22
San Francisco Day School	22-23
Corpus Christi School	22-25
Saint Monica School	22-25
Marin Horizon School	24

Marin Primary & Middle School	24
Montessori de Terra Linda	24
St. Philip School	24
Holy Name of Jesus School	25
Mission Dolores Catholic School	25
St. Paul's Elementary School	25
Sts. Peter and Paul Salesian School	25
San Francisco Waldorf School	25
Zion Lutheran School	25
Our Lady of the Visitacion School	27
Our Lady of Loretto School	28
St. Gabriel School	28
St. Patrick School	29
Saint Brigid School	30
St. Cecilia School	30
Saint Hilary School	30
St. Peter's School	30
Saint Vincent de Paul School	30
West Portal Lutheran School	30
Ecôle Notre Dame Des Victoires	32
St. Anne School	32
School of the Epiphany	33
St. Stephen School	35
St. Thomas More School	36

N/P: Good Shepherd Lutheran School, Hillwood Academic Day School, Katherine Delmar Burke School, North Bay Christian Academy, St. Anselm School, St. Anthony Immaculate Conception, St. Brendan School, Saint Charles Borromeo School, St. Finn Barr School, St. Isabella School, St. James School, St. John's School, St. Mary's Chinese Day School, St. Rita School, St. Thomas the Apostle School, San Domenico School, San Francisco Adventist School, Voice of Pentecost Academy

LATEST TUITION OR TUITION RANGE BEGINNING WITH KINDERGARTEN

The Hamlin School	$24,775
San Francisco Day School	$24,720
Town School for Boys	$24,430-$25,370
Katherine Delmar Burke School	$24,200-$25,000
Marin Country Day School	$23,775-$26,715

Convent of the Sacred Heart	$23,750
Stuart Hall for Boys	$23,750
Cathedral School for Boy	$23,375
San Francisco Friends School	$23,345
The Laurel School	$22,500
Mount Tamalpais School	$22,350
Children's Day School	$22,250
The Laurel School	$22,250
Live Oak School	$22,200
Marin Horizon School	$21,790-$24,190
Saint Mark's School	$21,760
Brandeis Hillel Day School-Marin	$21,735-$23,000
Brandeis Hillel Day School-SF	$21,735-$23,000
Chinese American International School	$21,010
Presidio Hill School	$20,975-$22,250
Marin Primary & Middle School	$20,900-$23,050
French-American International School	$20,810-$22,500
Ring Mountain Day School	$20,800-$21,700
The San Francisco School	$20,510-$22,120
Marin Montessori School	$20,090-$21,420
Adda Clevenger Junior Preparatory	$20,000
Marin Preparatory School	$18,700-$20,000
San Domenico School	$18,600-$22,500
San Francisco Waldorf School	$17,700-$18,800
Lycée Français La Pérouse, The French School	$17,400-$18,450
Greenwood School	$14,995-$17,395
The New Village School	$14,995
Kittredge School	$14,500-$15,300
Cascade Canyon	$14,238
Synergy School	$14,100
Marin Waldorf School	$14,000-$16,600
Montessori de Terra Linda	$13,375
The Discovery Center School	$9,000
Saint Hilary School	$8,852
Ecôle Notre Dame Des Victoires	$7,793-$8,193
Saint Vincent de Paul School	$7,700-$11,500
St. Patrick School	$7,200-$7,700
Zion Lutheran School	$7,020
Hillwood Academic Day School	$7,000
North Bay Christian Academy	$7,000
St. Anselm School	$7,000-$7,350
Our Lady of Loretto School	$6,950-$7,750

St. Raphael School	$6,672-$7,240
Marin Christian Academy	$6.633
Krouzian-Zekarian-Vasbouragan Armenian School	$6,615
St. Gabriel School	$6,595
St. Mary's Chinese Day School	$6,313
Sts. Peter and Paul Salesian School	$6,300-$8,350
Saint Brigid School	$5,900
West Portal Lutheran School	$5,859-$6,156
Saint Monica School	$5,830-$6,590
St. Stephen School	$5,800-$6,410
Star of the Sea School	$5,800
Good Shepherd Lutheran School	$5,778-$7,146
St. Philip School	$5,738
St. Paul's Elementary School	$5,724
School of the Epiphany	$5,604
Holy Name of Jesus School	$5,500-$6,600
Marin Christian Academy	$5,500-$12,000
St. Brendan School	$5,490-$5,890
St. Anne School	$5,400-$6,800
Mission Dolores Catholic School	$5,100-$6,500
St. Cecilia School	$4,975-$5,880
St. Thomas More School	$4,800
Corpus Christi School	$4,700
St. Thomas the Apostle School	$4,658-$5,170
Saint Charles Borromeo School	$4,300
Our Lady of the Visitacion School	$4,100
San Francisco Adventist School	$3,900-$6,520
Megan Furth Catholic Academy	$3,000

N/P: Lisa Kampner Hebrew Academy, St. Anthony Immaculate Conception, St. Finn Barr School, St. Isabella School, St. James School, St. John's School, St. Peter's School, St. Rita School, Voice of Pentecost Academy

PERCENTAGE OF STUDENTS RECEIVING FINANCIAL AID

Lisa Kampner Hebrew Academy	88%
Megan Furth Catholic Academy	85%
The New Village School	70%
Mission Dolores Catholic School	67%
Corpus Christi School	48%
Children's Day School	39%
The San Francisco School	35%

San Francisco Waldorf School	35%
Marin Waldorf School	34%
Greenwood School	33%
Synergy School	33%
Brandeis Hillel Day School-Marin	30%
Brandeis Hillel Day School-San Francisco	30%
French-American International School	30%
Krouzian-Zekarian-Vasbouragan Armenian School	30%
The Laurel School	30%
St. Paul's Elementary School	30%
Live Oak School	29%
Chinese American International School	25%
Lycée Français La Pérouse, The French School	25%
Marin Country Day School	25%
Marin Montessori School	25%
San Francisco Friends School	25%
Saint Mark's School	24%
San Francisco Day School	24%
The Hamlin School	22%
Presidio Hill School	22%
Katherine Delmar Burke School	22%
Marin Primary & Middle School	22%
Mount Tamalpais School	20%+
Cathedral School for Boys	20%
The Discovery Center School	20%
Marin Horizon School	20%
Saint Brigid School	20%
Montessori de Terra Linda	18%
Saint Monica School	15%-20%
Ring Mountain Day School	15%
Saint Hilary School	15%
Stuart Hall for Boys	15%
Convent of the Sacred Heart Elementary School	11%
St. Gabriel School	11%
St. Philip School	11%
Marin Christian Academy	10%
Marin Preparatory School	10%
St. Cecilia School	10%
Saint Vincent de Paul School	10%
Cascade Canyon	9%
Holy Name of Jesus School	8%
St. Stephen School	7%

| Kittredge School | 5% |
| St. Anne School | 5% |

None: Adda Clevenger Junior Preparatory and Theater School

N/P: Ecôle Notre Dame des Victoires, Good Shepherd Lutheran School, Hillwood Academic Day School, North Bay Christian Academy, Our Lady of Loretto School, Our Lady of the Visitacion School, St. Anselm School, St. Anthony Immaculate Conception, St. Brendan School, Saint Charles Borromeo School, St. Finn Barr School, St. Isabella School, St. James School, St. John's School, St. Mary's Chinese Day School, St. Peter's School, St. Rita School, St. Patrick School, St. Raphael School, St. Thomas More School, St. Thomas the Apostle School, Sts. Peter and Paul Salesian School, San Domenico School, San Francisco Adventist School, School of the Epiphany, Star of the Sea School, Town School for Boys, Voice of Pentecost Academy, West Portal Lutheran School, Zion Lutheran School

PERCENTAGE OF FINANCIAL AID AWARDS OF ½+ TUITION

Marin Christian Academy	90%
Montessori de Terra Linda	90%
Mount Tamalpais School	85%
San Francisco Friends School	77%
Presidio Hill School	75%
Marin Country Day School	72%
San Francisco Day School	71%
Marin Primary & Middle School	70%
Children's Day School	67%
Saint Mark's School	67%
Marin Horizon School	65%
The San Francisco School	65%
Marin Montessori School	64%
Synergy School	62%
Cathedral School for Boys	60%
The Hamlin School	60%
Lycée Français La Pérouse, The French School	60%
Katherine Delmar Burke School	51%
Children's Day School	50%
Corpus Christi School	50%
Megan Furth Catholic Academy	50%
Mission Dolores Catholic School	50%

Ring Mountain Day School	50%
San Francisco Waldorf School	40%
The Discovery Center School	25%
The New Village School	18%
Saint Brigid School	6%
Saint Monica School	5%
St. Philip School	3%
Saint Vincent de Paul School	1%

None: Adda Clevenger Junior Preparatory and Theater School, Cascade Canyon School, Krouzian-Zekarian-Vasbouragan Armenian School, Marin Waldorf School

N/P: Brandeis Hillel Day School-Marin, Brandeis Hillel Day School -SF, Chinese American International School, Convent of the Sacred Heart Elementary School, Ecôle Notre Dame des Victoires, French-American International School, Good Shepherd Lutheran School, Greenwood School, Hillwood Academic Day School, Holy Name of Jesus School, Kittredge School, The Laurel School, Lisa Kampner Hebrew Academy, Live Oak School, Marin Preparatory School, North Bay Christian Academy, Our Lady of Loretto School, Our Lady of the Visitacion School, St. Anne School, St. Anselm School, St. Anthony Immaculate Conception, St. Brendan School, St. Cecilia School, Saint Charles Borromeo School, St. Finn Barr School, St. Gabriel School, Saint Hilary School, St. Isabella School, St. James School, St. John's School, St. Mary's Chinese Day School, St. Paul's Elementary School, St. Patrick School, St. Peter's School, St. Raphael School, St. Rita School, St. Stephen School, St. Thomas More School, St. Thomas the Apostle School, Sts. Peter and Paul Salesian School, San Domenico School, San Francisco Adventist School, San Francisco Waldorf School, School of the Epiphany, Star of the Sea School, Stuart Hall for Boys, Town School for Boys, Voice of Pentecost Academy, West Portal Lutheran School, Zion Lutheran School

FOREIGN LANGUAGES OFFERED IN THE CURRICULUM
ARABIC
Greenwood School
The New Village School

ARMENIAN
Krouzian-Zekarian-Vasbouragan Armenian School

FRENCH

Convent of the Sacred Heart Elementary School
The Discovery Center School
Ecôle Notre Dame des Victoires
French-American International School
The Hamlin School
Katherine Delmar Burke School
Lycée Français La Pérouse, The French School
Mission Dolores School
Mount Tamalpais School
Saint Mark's School (phasing out)
San Domenico School
Stuart Hall for Boys

GERMAN

French-American International School
Lycée Français La Pérouse, The French School
Marin Waldorf School
San Francisco Waldorf School
West Portal Lutheran School

HEBREW

Brandeis Hillel Day School-Marin
Brandeis Hillel Day School-San Francisco
Lisa Kampner Hebrew Academy

ITALIAN

French-American International School

JAPANESE

Mount Tamalpais School

LATIN

Cathedral School for Boys
Convent of the Sacred Heart Elementary School
French-American International School
Mount Tamalpais School
San Francisco Day School
Stuart Hall for Boys
Town School for Boys

MANDARIN
Cathedral School for Boys
Chinese American International School
French-American International School
Greenwood School
Katherine Delmar Burke School
Lycée Français La Pérouse, The French School
Marin Country Day School
Mount Tamalpais School
The New Village School
Saint Mark's School (phasing in)

SIGN LANGUAGE
*Cascade Canyon

SPANISH
*Brandeis Hillel Day School-Marin
*Brandeis Hillel Day School-San Francisco
Cascade Canyon School
Cathedral School for Boys
Children's Day School
Convent of the Sacred Heart Elementary School
The Discovery Center School
French-American International School
Good Shepherd Lutheran School
Greenwood School
The Hamlin School
Katherine Delmar Burke School
Kittredge School
Live Oak School
Lycée Français La Pérouse, The French School
Marin Christian Academy
Marin Country Day School
Marin Horizon School
Marin Montessori School
Marin Preparatory School
Marin Primary & Middle School
Marin Waldorf School
Megan Furth Catholic Academy
Mission Dolores School
Montessori de Terra Linda

Mount Tamalpais School
The New Village School
Presidio Hill School
Ring Mountain Day School
St. Anselm School
St. Brendan School
Saint Brigid School
Saint Hilary School
Saint Mark's School
St. Paul's Elementary School
St. Philip School
St. Raphael School
St. Stephen School
Saint Vincent de Paul School
Sts. Peter and Paul Salesian School
San Domenico School
San Francisco Day School
San Francisco Friends School
The San Francisco School
San Francisco Waldorf School
School of the Epiphany
Stuart Hall for Boys
Synergy School
Town School for Boys
West Portal Lutheran School
Zion Lutheran Day School
* Elective

FOREIGN LANGUAGE AFTER SCHOOL

CANTONESE
Holy Name of Jesus School
St. Anne School
St. Gabriel School

ITALIAN
Live Oak School
Convent of the Sacred Heart Elementary School

JAPANESE
Saint Brigid

MANDARIN
Greenwood School
Holy Name of Jesus School
Live Oak School
St. Anne School
Saint Brigid
Saint Monica School
Sts. Peter and Paul Salesian School
San Francisco Day School
San Francisco Friends School
Star of the Sea
Mount Zion Lutheran School

RUSSIAN
Adda Clevenger Junior Preparatory and Theater School

SPANISH
Adda Clevenger Junior Preparatory and Theater School
Holy Name of Jesus School
St. Finn Barr School
St. Gabriel School
Saint Monica School
St. Philip School
San Francisco Day School
San Francisco Friends School
Star of the Sea

None: The Laurel School
N/P: Corpus Christi School, Hillwood Academic Day School, North
Bay Christian Academy, Our Lady of Loretto School, Our Lady of the
Visitacion, St. Anthony Immaculate Conception, St. Cecilia School,
Saint Charles Borromeo School, St. Isabella School, St. James School,
St. John's School, St. Mary's Chinese Day School, St. Patrick School,
St. Peter's School, St. Rita School, St. Thomas More School, St.
Thomas the Apostle School, San Francisco Adventist School, School
of the Epiphany, Voice of Pentecost Academy

Schools with Learning Specialists on Staff

Brandeis Hillel Day School-Marin
Brandeis Hillel Day School-San Francisco
Cathedral School for Boys
Children's Day School
Chinese American International School
Convent of the Sacred Heart Elementary School
Ecôle Notre Dame des Victoires
French-American International School
Greenwood School
The Hamlin School
Holy Name of Jesus School
Katherine Delmar Burke School
Live Oak School
Lycée Français La Pérouse, The French School
Marin Christian Academy
Marin Country Day School
Marin Horizon School
Marin Montessori School
Marin Primary & Middle School
Marin Waldorf School
Megan Furth Catholic Academy
Mount Tamalpais School
Our Lady of the Visitacion
Presidio Hill School
Ring Mountain Day School
St. Anne School
Saint Brigid School
St. Cecilia School
Saint Charles Borromeo School
St. Gabriel School
Saint Hilary
Saint Mark's School
Saint Monica School
St. Philip School
St. Stephen School
Saint Vincent de Paul School
Sts. Peter and Paul Salesian School
San Domenico School
San Francisco Day School
San Francisco Friends School

The San Francisco School
San Francisco Waldorf School
Stuart Hall for Boys
Synergy School
Town School for Boys

None: Cascade Canyon School, The Discovery Center School,
Kittredge School, Krouzian-Zakarian-Vabouragan Armenian School,
The Laurel School (majority of teachers have special ed training), Lisa
Kampner Hebrew Academy, Marin Preparatory School, Montessori de
Terra Linda, The New Village School

N/P: Adda Clevenger Junior Preparatory and Theater School, Good
Shepherd Lutheran School, Hillwood Academic Day School, Mission
Dolores Catholic School, North Bay Christian Academy, Our Lady
of Loretto School, St. Anselm School, St. Anthony Immaculate
Conception, St. Brendan School, St. Finn Barr School, St. Isabella
School, St. James School, St. John's School, St. Mary's Chinese Day
School, St. Patrick School, St. Paul's School, St. Peter's School, St.
Raphael School, St. Rita School, St. Thomas More School, St. Thomas
the Apostle, San Francisco Adventist School, School of the Epiphany,
Star of the Sea School, Voice of Pentecost Academy, West Portal
Lutheran School, Zion Lutheran School

EXTENDED DAY PROGRAMS
Adda Clevenger Junior Preparatory and Theater School
Brandeis Hillel Day School-Marin
Brandeis Hillel Day School-San Francisco
Cathedral School for Boys
Children's Day School
Chinese American International School
Convent of the Sacred Heart Elementary School
Corpus Christi School
The Discovery Center School
Ecôle Notre Dame des Victoires
French-American International School
Greenwood School
The Hamlin School
Holy Name of Jesus School
Katherine Delmar Burke School
Kittredge School
Krouzian-Zakarian-Vasbouragan Armenian School

The Laurel School
Lisa Kampner Hebrew Academy
Live Oak School
Lycée Français La Pérouse, The French School
Marin Christian Academy
Marin Country Day School
Marin Horizon School
Marin Montessori School
Marin Preparatory School
Marin Primary & Middle School
Mission Dolores Catholic School
Montessori de Terra Linda
Mount Tamalpais School
New Village School
Our Lady of Loretto School
Our Lady of the Visitacion School
Presidio Hill School
Ring Mountain Day School
St. Anne School
St. Anselm School
St. Brendan School
Saint Brigid School
St. Cecilia School
St. Gabriel School
Saint Hilary School
Saint Mark's School
Saint Monica School
St. Patrick School
St. Paul's Elementary School
St. Philip School
St. Raphael School
St. Stephen School
St. Thomas More School
St. Thomas the Apostle School
Saint Vincent de Paul School
Sts. Peter and Paul Salesian School
San Domenico School
San Francisco Day School
San Francisco Friends School
The San Francisco School
San Francisco Waldorf School
School of the Epiphany

Stuart Hall for Boys
Synergy School
Town School for Boys
West Portal Lutheran School
Zion Lutheran Day School

None: Cascade Canyon School
N/P: Good Shepherd Lutheran School, Hillwood Academic Day
School, North Bay Christian Academy, St. Anthony Immaculate
Conception, Saint Charles Borromeo School, St. Finn Barr School,
St. Isabella School, St. James School, St. John's School, St. Mary's
Chinese Day School, St. Peter's School, St. Rita School, San Francisco
Adventist School, Star of the Sea School, Voice of Pentecost Academy

SUMMER PROGRAMS (MAY NOT BE OFFERED FOR ALL GRADES)

Adda Clevenger Junior Preparatory and Theater School
Brandeis Hillel Day School-San Francisco
Cathedral School for Boys
Children's Day School
Chinese American International School
Convent of the Sacred Heart Elementary School
Corpus Christi School
The Discovery Center School
French-American International School
The Hamlin School
Hillwood Academic Day School
Holy Name of Jesus School
Katherine Delmar Burke School
Kittredge School
Krouzian-Zekarian-Vasbouragan Armenian School
The Laurel School
Live Oak School
Lycée Français La Pérouse, The French School
Marin Christian Academy
Marin Country Day School
Marin Horizon School
Marin Montessori School
Marin Primary & Middle School
Marin Waldorf School
Montessori de Terra Linda
Mount Tamalpais School
Presidio Hill School

Ring Mountain Day School
St. Gabriel School
Saint Mark's School
St. Mary's Chinese Day School
Saint Monica School
St. Peter's School
Saint Vincent de Paul School
San Domenico School
San Francisco Friends School
The San Francisco School
San Francisco Waldorf School
Stuart Hall for Boys
Synergy School
Town School for Boys
West Portal Lutheran School
Zion Lutheran School

None: Cascade Canyon, Lisa Kampner Hebrew Academy,
Marin Waldorf School, Megan Furth Catholic Academy, Saint
Brigid School, Saint Hilary School, Saint Monica School, St. Paul's
Elementary, St. Philip School, St. Stephen School

N/P: Brandeis Hillel Day School-Marin, Good Shepherd Lutheran
School, Hillwood Academic Day School, North Bay Christian
Academy, Our Lady of Loretto School, Our Lady of the Visitacion
School, Presidio Hill School, St. Anne School, St. Anselm School,
St. Anthony Immaculate Conception, St. Brendan School, St. Cecilia
School, Saint Charles Borromeo School, St. Finn Barr School, St.
Isabella School, St. James School, St. John's School, St. Patrick
School, St. Peter's School, St. Raphael School, St. Rita School, St.
Thomas More School, St. Thomas the Apostle School, Sts. Peter and
Paul Salesian School, San Francisco Adventist School, San Francisco
Day School, School of the Epiphany, Star of the Sea School, Voice of
Pentecost Academy

--

ABOUT THE AUTHORS

Betsy Little and Paula Molligan provide public and private school consulting for preschool through high school in the San Francisco Bay Area and for boarding schools for families, relocation firms, and corporate offices. They have offices in Marin and San Francisco. e-mail: betsy@littleandmolligan.com or paula@littleandmolligan.com.

Little and Molligan, Inc.
4040 Civic Center Drive, Suite 200
San Rafael, CA 94903
(415) 492-2877

www.littleandmolligan.com

OTHER BOOKS

BY BETSY LITTLE AND PAULA MOLLIGAN

PRIVATE HIGH SCHOOLS OF THE SAN FRANCISCO BAY AREA (5TH ED.)
60+ schools from Sonoma to San Jose and the East Bay and expert
advice about the high school admission process.
ISBN: 978-1-930074-20-0, $29.95

These books as well as other works of fiction, nonfiction, poetry, and
humor, are available on our website at www.pince-nez.com as well as
in bookstores. To order directly from the publisher, please call 415-267-
5978 or e-mail susan@pince-nez.com.